To David

Joseph: A Story of Divine Providence

A Text Theoretical and Textlinguistic Analysis of Genesis 37 and 39–48

Robert E. Longacre
University of Texas at Arlington
Summer Institute of Linguistics

Eisenbrauns
Winona Lake
1989

Library of Congress Cataloging-in-Publication Data

Longacre, Robert E.
    Joseph: a story of divine providence : a text theoretical and text-linguistic analysis of Genesis 37 and 39–48 / Robert E. Longacre.
        p.   cm.
    Bibliography: p.
    ISBN 0-931464-42-0
    1. Bible. O.T. Genesis XXXVII, XXXIX-XLVIII—Criticism, interpretation, etc. 2. Joseph (Son of Jacob) I. Title.
BS1235.2.L65 1988
222'.11066—dc19   88-19754
                                                  CIP

Contents

ACKNOWLEDGMENTS

I gratefully acknowledge here the help of many people in assembling this volume. Especially I thank Rhoda Houge, JoNell Smith, Denise Bailey, Merieta Johnson, and various people from the Translation Department of the Wycliffe Bible Translators for secretarial and word-processing services. I also thank Robert Bergen, Matthew Carlton, Randall Buth, Don Slager, Doris Myers, and Nicolai Winther-Nielsen for their thoughtful and constructive criticism of this work, as well as the students who have suffered through these materials in graduate linguistic seminars. Nicolas Bailey spent many hours criticizing and correcting the transliteration of the Hebrew text in Part 4; I gratefully acknowledge his contribution. I thank my home university, the University of Texas at Arlington, for a summer stipend (1980) that facilitated some of the initial research that has culminated in this volume.

ABBREVIATIONS

In this list no attempt is made to reproduce the various type fonts used in Part 4.

A	answer
Add	addressee
Ampl	amplification
Anti	antithesis *or* antithetical
AwQ	awareness quotation
AwQF	awareness quotation formula
BU	build-up of a sequence paragraph (numbered from BU_1 to BU_n)
CU	continuing utterance
DISC	discourse
E	expository
Ep	episode
Eval	evaluation
Exec	execution
H	hortatory
IQ	indirect quotation
IQF	indirect quotation formula
IU	initiating utterance
N	narrative *or* noun
P	predictive
Para	paraphrase
Pr	pronoun
Prop	proposal
Q	quotation *or* question
QF	quotation formula
Rem	remark
Res	response
RU	resolving utterance
S	sentence

Sp   speaker
¶   paragraph
Ø   nul (where no verb 'be' occurs, but where such a verb
            would be grammatically possible; or no noun or pronoun
            present)
:   (colon) "expounded by" (the relation between a grammati-
            cal "slot" and its "filler")

PREFACE

How does one approach an ancient text, such as that here considered? What does one hope to gain from its study? Granted that the Judeo-Christian tradition recognizes that the story comes from what has been regarded as *Scripture*—that is, written materials in which, however strictly or broadly defined, the voice of God is heard—how do we orient ourselves in regard to this story? Is such an assumption, in fact, an asset or a liability in approaching the "Joseph" story,* that is, does it provide a key to our understanding of the story or does it simply hinder our approaching the story in an unbiased and objective manner?

Several specific problems emerge: (1) What is our primary concern, listening to the text as it now stands, or attempting to learn about the text by breaking it into putative sources? (2) If, as many on the contemporary scene, we decide to *listen* to the text rather than to continue to occupy ourselves with source criticism, then how do we delineate the story from its near and far context and at the same time relate it to that context? (3) What tools have we available to aid us in our *listening* to the text? (4) If we approach the text as linguists, or rather *textlinguists*, and thereby inevitably tread some of the terrain of traditional literary criticism, then we may well ask certain questions that are typical of the latter: "Do ancient and modern readers differ appreciably in their appreciation of the story?" "What are its timeless values?" (5) Granted the speech act theory distinction between illocutionary speech acts (what a text does) and perlocutionary speech acts (the carry through or *effect* of a speech act on the hearer/reader), can we really understand such a discourse as *Joseph* without being willing to let the text have its intended perlocutionary effects on *us*, that is, must *we* in some sense get emotionally and volitionally involved with the text if we are to understand it?

* *Joseph* (italicized) will be used in parts 1-3 of this work to indicate "the Joseph story," "the Joseph account," etc.; Joseph (roman type) will indicate the individual; 'Joseph' (in single quotation marks) refers to the Hebrew word *yōsêp*.

While the above is written to alert the reader to the possible significance of this work to the student of the Hebrew Scriptures, at the same
time this work is intended to embody and exemplify the author's own
textlinguistic methodology and the theory that underlies it. In this preface I am therefore making a bid for the interest of two sorts of readers:
the Old Testament scholar and biblical critic, and the contemporary
textlinguist (that is, the student of discourse). Admittedly, such a study
as this can easily fall into a crack between the two disciplines and attract
readers from neither. I dare to believe, however, that the time is ripe for
such an interdisciplinary study as this. Interest in linguistics is awakening within biblical scholarship in general; there is increasing desire that
the contemporary linguist have a voice in the understanding of the Bible.
On the other hand, classical Hebrew literature, as found in the Bible,
provides an extensive and varied corpus in a language whose grammar
has been worked on for many years in a tradition far older than that of
any European language. In a sense, classical Hebrew is ripe for textlinguistic analysis. Furthermore, as a basically verb-subject-object language, it is not without a certain intrinsic typological interest: How does
such a VSO language elaborate its discourse structure?

Part 1 is of more interest to the general biblical scholar. Its introduction treats source critical and text theoretical questions as they relate
to this ancient story from the Hebrew scriptures. Chapter 1, "Overview,"
considers the immediate contextual relations of *Joseph* and the gross
anatomical features of the story. The *tōlĕdôt yaᶜăqōb*, the 'life and times
of Jacob', of which *Joseph* is part, takes its place among the other
tōlĕdôt sections of Genesis. In turn, however, *Joseph* must be distinguished as a separate strand within the larger unity of its section. Next,
the gross anatomical features of the Joseph story are considered in
respect to the articulation of the parts, and in respect to the peak and
closure features that characterize the whole and the parts.

Chapter 2, "Macrostructures," tries to relate certain details of the
story to its germinal ideas. This I consider to be a basic ingredient of
text analysis of any text in any language. Here, as well as in chapter 1,
certain putative tell-tale vestiges of separate documentary sources are
seen to be analyzable within the normal range of effective story-telling
by a single author.

While the matters discussed in Part 1 are probably of more immediate concern to the Old Testament scholar, I nevertheless want to
emphasize vigorously here that they are integrally related to the two
following parts of the volume, which are more technical and analytical.
A piece of text, especially a literary text such as concerns us here, cannot
be understood by myopically inspecting it verse-by-verse without the
study of the whole informing the study of the parts. The linguistically-

oriented reader needs the materials that are covered in Part 1 to guide his understanding of Parts 2 and 3.

Part 2, while of special interest to the more linguistically-oriented reader, also has something to say to the general student of the Hebrew Scriptures as well. The broader appeal of this part of the work lies in its treatment of the various tense/aspects and moods of the Hebrew verb. Here a "divide-and-conquer" technique analyzes what the various forms of the Hebrew verb do in particular discourse types, as a guide to the semantics of the verb.

Chapter 3, "Verb Rank in the Story," embodies some of my more original work on the discourse structure of Biblical Hebrew; it spring-boards from a distinction that I made in the Flood Narrative (Longacre 1979a) between the preterite (*waw*-consecutive with the imperfect) and all other tense-aspect forms used in Biblical Hebrew narrative. I continue to believe that this distinction is basic to understanding the structure of the biblical narrative and that the perfect, for example, is only weakly sequential (in expressing temporal succession) in narration and typically reports past actions that are in some way backgrounded to those reported in the chains of preterites. An attempt is made in this chapter to understand the various Hebrew verb forms that function together in the framework of narrative discourse and determine their varying (and graded) relevance to the storyline. A ranking scheme for verbs (and the clauses that they characterize) is posited at the end of this chapter.

Chapter 4, "Verb Rank and Constituent Structure," applies the verb ranking scheme for narrative discourse to Biblical Hebrew paragraphs within *Joseph* and introduces the various paragraph types that figure in the narration. Predictive discourse and predictive variants of the paragraph types are then considered. A new verb rank scheme is posited for predictive discourse—since the mainline tense/aspect form of the latter is *waw*-consecutive + perfect, which is possibly an analogical creation modeled after the preterite (*waw*-consecutive + imperfect). Several such predictive discourses are found in *Joseph* and afford enough data for such initial hypotheses. Finally, a consideration of expository discourse and expository variants of the paragraph types closes the chapter. Expository discourses are even scarcer and briefer in *Joseph* than predictive discourses. Much more work is needed to explore, confirm, and modify the tentative conclusions of this section.

Chapter 5, "Sociolinguistic Dynamics of Hortatory Discourse," is devoted entirely to interpersonal hortatory discourses, of which *Joseph* contains a sizeable number. The presence of mitigation (making a command more mollified and socially acceptable) and deference (e.g., of commoner to monarch) make the analysis of hortatory discourse the more difficult. Fortunately, since these discourses are embedded in the longer framework of *Joseph*, the social situation in which each discourse is spoken is preserved for us. Hortatory variants of paragraph types come in incidentally to the broader sociolinguistic development. The command forms of Hebrew—imperative, cohortative, and jussive—figure prominently in this chapter along with the modal imperfect.

Part 2 of the work thus features the differing forms of the Hebrew verb and the clause types that are determined by those different forms in relation to narrative, predictive, expository, and hortatory discourse. At the same time, it embodies via the intermeshing of verb function and paragraph structure an approach to the exegesis of the text—a concern that is, after all, focal to the biblical scholar.

Part 3 has to do with participants, speech acts, and dialogue in *Joseph*. The actions and events of a story (as reported in the verbs) relate to participants. Participants are, in turn, involved not only in actions and events in general but in speech acts in particular. Speech acts are found not only as occasional isolated bits of reported speech but, more typically, as dialogue. Therefore participant reference in general is treated in chapter 6, participant reference in speech acts (variations in formulas of quotation) in chapter seven, and dialogue—as a means of advancing the story—in chapter 8.

Chapter 6, "Participant Reference," concerns itself with the use of noun, pronoun, verb affix, and nul in regard to participants and props found within the story. Matters are complicated by the fact that participants vary in their status (importance) in different parts of the story, and by the fact that reference to participants is put to work to accomplish different ends, for example, not only routine participant tracking but further special operations as well.

Chapter 7, "Variations in Formulas of Quotation," is possibly the most novel and controversial of any material in the volume. *Joseph* exhibits considerable variation in the formulas of quotation—as do the rest of the Hebrew Scriptures. As noticed below, it is part of the credo of a textlinguist that such variation is not random—it is not, for example, "free" or "stylistic" (whatever that means!), but is motivated. Little work has been done on such questions, but a beginning has been made in a few other languages (Koontz 1977 on Teribe of Panama; Reid 1979, Totonac of Mexico; Forster 1983, Dibabawon of the Philippines; and Wendell 1986, Kagan-Kalangan, also of the Philippines). I have done what I could within the limited corpus of *Joseph* and have cross-checked the results in some other portions of the Hebrew Bible. The initial observations and the wider generalizations are as broad as I have been able to make them to date. I believe that the resultant claims as they stand now are fundamentally correct but that certain of them are still not formulated with sufficient generality. All this must await further research.

Chapter 8, "The Role of Dialogue in *Joseph*," attempts to put together insights found in chapters 6 and 7 with a theory of dialogue that I formulated sometime ago but still find quite usable (Longacre 1968, 1976, 1983). The hope is that by putting together these various insights and systems, understanding can be gained of the dialogue structures of *Joseph*. For, indeed, a great deal of this story turns on dialogue and if we are to understand the story we must understand the dialogues. What is the general tone and thrust of a dialogue? Who dominates it? Is there a struggle for the control of the dialogue? What parts of the dialogue are mere pleasantries (social ritual)? Where is there sharp clash of opinion? Where does a dialogue reach a stalemate? How and by whom is it redirected? Above all, who is talking to whom and how does that color the whole? These are some of the questions that chapter 8 attempts to raise and answer regarding the dialogues of *Joseph*. Here, as throughout the volume, the intent is not simply to vindicate the unity of the story but to develop new tools for understanding it better.

Part 4 is a *constituent structure analysis*, displaying the function of each individual sentence in the paragraphs and embedded discourses of *Joseph* in its entirety. Such a display is ultimately needed for the serious student of the text. One does not, on the other hand, *read* such a display but must work through it.

Perhaps the deepest and most pervasive assumption of this volume is the assumption that *variation in a text is not random but motivated*. In brief, where the author has a choice in regard to a lexical item or a grammatical construction, his particular choice is motivated by pragmatic concerns of discourse structure. Of course, if a text reflects a dialect mixture (which can be partly caused by inconsistent editorial emendations) variations of this sort must be taken into account. This is quite plausible, for example, in regard to certain ancient poems versus their surrounding contexts (e.g., the Testimony of Jacob, the Song of Miriam, the Song of Deborah). A later editor has presumably not wanted to risk the integrity of the poems by updating their diction and grammar, although he apparently has uniformly updated the surrounding narrative framework. But aside from variation of this sort, it need not be assumed that a writer simply varied his style to avoid monotony or repetition, unless this can be clearly demonstrated to be a motivating factor within a given language and culture. Rather, a good working hypothesis is the axiom that variation can be explained in terms of the pragmatics of author choices within discourse structure (including the structure of part of a discourse). If we initially assume random variation we give up the work of discourse analysis before it is fairly started.

Notice here that no claim is offered that the author's choices are consciously made. More likely than not, they are unconscious adjustments to the conventions of discourse structure in a given type of discourse, in a given language, at a given period.

Finally, a word of candor and caution: this volume embodies an interpretation of the *Joseph* story—and no interpretation can make claims to finality however much it is based on the morphosyntactic texture of the text. The text itself remains a greater reality than any interpretation of it. If this volume stimulates at least a few to interact more vigorously with this particular text, I will feel gratified in having written it.

Transliteration of Hebrew follows the style used in *Journal of Biblical Literature*. In regard to the vocalization of *šĕwa*, I have chosen the methodology set forth in Thomas O. Lambdin's *Introduction to Biblical Hebrew* (New York: Charles Scribner's Sons, 1971). Thus, I have transliterated the frequent introductory word 'and it happened' as *wayhî* (with *y* as a semiconsonant in syllable final position), not as *wayĕhî* (with consonantal *y* and vocal *šĕwa*).

PART 1

INTRODUCTION TO *JOSEPH*

INTRODUCTION

Before plunging into the two following substantive chapters, I discuss here in order the following matters that relate to holistic concerns in this study: (1) interpretation versus source criticism; (2) the *broader* contextual relations of *Joseph* (cf. the more immediate contextual relations as traced in chap. 1); (3) how the design of the whole—in particular, the macrostructure—must be taken to be crucial to any methodology of text theory. The reader who is frankly uninterested in source criticism, can proceed immediately to the reading of the substantive chapters 1 and 2—although he will probably find it helpful to at least read §3 of this introduction.

1. *Interpretation versus source criticism*

1.1. The source criticism of the Old Testament, especially of the Pentateuch, has had a long and complicated history, which I briefly summarize here at the risk of gross over-simplification. Jean Astruc, a French physician and university professor, in a work published in 1753 observed variations in names for deity in Genesis and suggested that they are traces of two sources. With his (posthumous) work the literary partitioning of the Pentateuch according to variations in vocabulary and style got underway and continued throughout the rest of the eighteenth and nineteenth centuries. At first it did not seem necessary to challenge the traditional Mosaic authorship of the Pentateuch, but under the influence of the Enlightenment, the challenging of that tradition came more to the fore. The work of J. G. Eichhorn (1780–83) and W. M. L. de Wette (1806–07) are typical of this later emphasis.

The publication of C. Darwin's *The Origin of Species* in 1859, which had a spreading influence in many fields beyond biology, brought in a new era of biblical criticism. Biblical scholars began to interest themselves more in the evolution of Israel's religion and religious institutions. The stage was set for an integration of the literary partitioning of the Pentateuch with such a theory of development. All of this culminated in the work of K. H. Graf (1865) and J. Wellhausen (1883 and 1894).

Here the traditional view of the Old Testament and of the Pentateuch was set on end; contending that "the law is later than the prophets," developmental criticism took the legal portions of the Pentateuch (especially portions of Exodus, Leviticus, and Numbers) to be more recent than the narrative portions, while Deuteronomy came somewhere in between as a seventh century B.C. work (contemporary with Josiah and Jeremiah).

The main sources posited were: (1) J, the Jahwist, which among other stylistic features used the divine name Yahweh (*yhwh*), was assumed to be a distillation of tradition from South Israel (Judah) harking back to the eighth or ninth centuries B.C. (2) E, the Elohist, used the divine name Elohim (*ʾĕlōhîm*) and was assumed to be a distillation of tradition from North Israel (Ephraim and other clans), going back to approximately the same time horizon. (3) P, the Priestly writer, is very late (exilic or post-exilic) and had a twofold contribution: the law codes, and interpolation of passages especially concerned with dates and genealogies. (4) D, the Deuteronomist, is a seventh-century work, the brilliant pseudoepigraphic work that Josiah's priests "discovered" in the temple and used as a lever to bring about the religious revival of Josiah's time.

On these premises, the Pentateuch is a slow accretion. D and P not only made their own contributions but edited and modified former work. Taking the sources chronologically we can trace the development of monotheism, the sacrificial system, an emphasis on a central sanctuary, and other such features. As we might expect, every generation since Graf and Wellhausen has seen endless modification and development of the original critical framework. Nevertheless, the Graf-Wellhausen hypothesis gained wide acceptance in a comparatively short time as it spread through Europe, England, and United States. In many quarters it came to be confidently accepted as the assured results of modern criticism.

1.2. There is, however, no doubt that the hold of the traditional source criticism (JEPD) on Old Testament scholarship is currently weakening. A good cross-section of opinion regarding this discussion is found in the July 1977 issue of *JSOT*, in which an article by R. Rendtorff (building somewhat on G. von Rad 1966) is found, accompanied by varying reactions, and followed by a rebuttal by Rendtorff. Rendtorff clearly seems to be opting for redaction criticism (i.e., careful attention to editing on various horizons) over traditional source criticism: "Anyone who wants to grasp the theological intentions which stand behind the collection and editing of the material of the Pentateuch must rather examine these editorial traces in very exact detail. In this way one will come across various important theological statements, but he will not meet the authors of the 'sources' as understood in the classical documentary hypothesis" (1977a: 10).

Rendtorff's argument is variously evaluated in the same volume. G. E. Coats is content to observe that Rendtorff does not altogether dismiss source criticism but shifts his emphasis to "the context of redaction criticism" (1977: 29). R. E. Clements in his review (1977) of a larger work of Rendtorff's (1977c) is also reluctant to loosen his hold on the traditional sources; he interprets Rendtorff's work as largely rearrangement and redating of them (to a still later period). The crucial question seems to be whether there was an overall framework for the Pentateuch in monarchical times (by J, or JE, or R^{JE}) or whether, in effect, J was merged with D in giving shape to the whole at a considerably later date.

Other who react to Rendtorff's article show more impatience with the traditional sources. Thus R. N. Whybray comments regarding the nagging suspicion that many scholars have had concerning the works of von Rad and Noth, that is, "there is a hidden flaw somewhere in the masterly and impressive marshalling of hypotheses." He goes on to say "Rendtorff has confirmed these suspicions and put the situation plainly: much recent study of the Pentateuch, including that of von Rad and Noth, has been continuing—at least to some extent—to use the tools of the Documentary Hypothesis to perform tasks for which they are quite unsuitable" (1977: 11).

N. E. Wagner goes so far as to say "If anything, Rendtorff has understated the significance of the major shifts which have occurred during the past century in the very foundations of pentateuchal criticism" (1977: 20). After sketching J, E, P, D as they were at the close of the nineteenth century, and describing the "modifications" and "subtle moves" by which critics have departed from the classical documentary hypothesis, he states, "The scholars today who focus on the theology tend to view only the overall picture, assuming, apparently, that the literary question is solved, irrelevant or simply too complex to consider" (1977.21).

H. H. Schmid understands the thrust of Rendtorff's work to be a call for a new approach in pentateuchal studies. He observes: "But the time has passed for disputations upon the usual basis of the differentiation of sources. Such debates could only be rear-guard actions, which have become irrelevant in view of the way the question of fundamentals has become urgent" (1977: 33).

1.3. Along, however, with declining interest in traditional source criticism is the coming to the fore of a kind of neo-Wellhausen position, which is partly a reaction against the Albright-Wright-Bright school (which affirmed, for example, the general historicity of the patriarchal narratives, and found "Mosaic material" even in the late sources). Again, the dictum of Wellhausen, 'the law is later than the prophets', comes to the fore so that the whole idea of the covenant is considered to be a late (seventh century B.C.) development. Again, the patriarchal narratives are considered to be late developments without much factual base (contrast Albright 1961). The "big chunks" (e.g., Primal History, Patriarchal History—with Abraham, Jacob, and Joseph as smaller chunks—the Exodus, Sinai, etc.) are the *new sources*. Like the older classical sources, the newer sources are also considered to be only loosely bound together with each other—but, at least, the internal unity fares somewhat better at the hands of contemporary critics. In all this, however, the essential position of Wellhausen in regard to the historical development of Israel's religious institutions is maintained. The old sources—which represent an extreme of fragmentation—are given up or quietly laid aside and newer sources are posited. In the process, however, the main pieces are later than ever (no more are J and E considered to be from monarchical times) and the patriarchal narratives are less factual than ever.

The emergence of this newer position is specifically noted by G. J. Wenham in his review of H. H. Schmid's *Der sogennante Jahwist*: "He [Schmid] believes that a late dating of J gives a clearer and simpler picture of the evolution of Israel's religion than an earlier date. Fundamental to his view is the work of Perlitt [*Bundestheologie im Alten Testament* (1969)] and others who have revived Wellhausen's theory that the covenant was an innovation of the deuteronomic school unknown before the 7th century." Note here that late dating of J (and, in effect, the merging of J with D) is tantamount to giving up the traditional J and E, which were considered to be from the monarchic period. Since the patriarchal narratives also feature the idea of the covenant in various forms, the patriarchal narratives—minus the factual basis that Albright and others claimed for them—must also be dated late. This position is exemplified by T. L. Thompson (1974) and J. van Seters (1975).

As for the newly posited "big chunk" sources, these are assumed in Rendtorff's own work, according to Schmid and Wagner, who in this respect agree with him. Thus Wagner: "It seems only sensible to regard Genesis as being composed of at least four major blocks of material: the primeval stories, Abraham, Jacob, and Joseph. Each block must be studied in and of itself. Only at a later stage can we begin to discuss the eventual joining of blocks to form the present book. This procedure can then be extended to the entire Pentateuch" (1977: 22).

Clements, while clinging to the traditional sources, nevertheless mentions that the patriarchal stories as a block do "not properly anticipate the subsequent stories of the oppression in Egypt, the exodus event, nor the revelation on Mount Sinai, or wandering in the wilderness" (1977: 47). His position is typical of the "loose connection" stance of advocates of the big blocks as sources. Typically, the fore-references inherent in our present text of the patriarchal narratives are attributed to late redactors; such absence of connections cannot be maintained if we take the present texts as given. In this response advocates of the big blocks do not entirely respect the integrity of the blocks—but this is getting a bit ahead of our argument.

At any rate, as Wenham observes, "Fashions in OT scholarship change more slowly than in Paris salons, and are therefore more difficult to spot. But with D. B. Redford's work on the Joseph story, and J. van Seters on the Abraham traditions, and now H. H. Schmid on *Der sogennante Jahwist*, a new trend is unmistakable: *the late dating of the patriarchal traditions, particularly those associated with the sources J and E*" (1977: 57, emphasis added).

1.4. The newer position has, however, its own critics who in some sense continue to argue for and develop the Albright-Wright-Bright position. Representative of this position is the volume *Essays on the Patriarchal Narratives,* edited by A. R. Millard and D. J. Wiseman (1983). In general, writers in this volume do not consent to the old and new Wellhausen position that "the law is later than the prophets"— although this is not a focal issue in the volume except insofar as they argue that the covenant idea is early. The patriarchal narratives are regarded as having a factual base. And one writer (J. Goldingay) eloquently ties the patriarchal narratives, as they stand in our present text, into their broader biblical context as constituting along with that context one consistent coherent account extending from Genesis to the end of 2 Kings. While the latter concern is covered in the next section, I want to comment briefly here on the matter of the *factuality* of the patriarchal narrative as conceived in this volume.

While Goldingay admits that in the patriarchal narratives bare history is reworked into story (event plus interpretation of the event), he strongly argues for a factual base. In this respect he contrasts his position with that of T. L. Thompson who argued that the story need not be historical in order to be "true" in a broader sense: "Israel's faith is rather a response of hope in God in some present situation, which expresses itself by drawing an imaginative picture of the past to embody its present hope" (1983: 28). Thus, according to Goldingay's interpretation of Thompson, the patriarchal accounts are *retrospective* constructions that arose out of the needs of God's people at a time considerably later than their putative horizon. Goldingay, in taking issue with this point of view, insists that "the way in which the biblical testimonies to faith refer us to past historical events for their explanation and justification makes it difficult to believe that they imply no claim for their story's factuality" (28–29). He goes on to say: "If the patriarchal narrative is pure fiction (which Thompson suggests it may as well be), is anything lost? Surely much is, because the exodus-conquest narrative grounds its statements of faith in these events" (29). In commenting on the reference to Abraham and Sarah in Isa 51:1–2, Goldingay comments that the prophet's attitude doesn't seem to be "that faith creates Abraham, but that Abraham creates faith" (30).

Goldingay also comments on the positions of von Rad and K. Barth, who referred to the patriarchal stories as *saga*. While admitting that neither really denies a factual basis for the narratives, Goldingay nevertheless goes on to caution: "To describe these stories as saga testifies to their background in some historical event, but if in the stories there is really more of the faith of the tellers than there is of actual events, we still seem to have faith creating Abraham rather than vice versa" (32).

A. R. Millard, in the same volume, wants "to scrutinize the patriarchal narratives in the context of the ancient Near East" (1983: 38). Arguing that classical Old Testament criticism and its modern variants have increasingly isolated themselves from the accruing knowledge of the ancient Near East as brought to light by archaeology, Millard wants again to attempt to bring the patriarchal stories into proper cultural context. He starts with the position that the patriarchal stories are, as purported, a piece of Israelite "family history" constituting a witness in and of itself—a witness that is innocent until proven guilty. He argues that the so-called anachronisms (e.g., references to camels and to the Philistines) in the stories are illusory and are no witness against the veracity of the stories. He then goes on to examine other purported accounts of individuals in Near Eastern sources: (Gilgamesh, Sargon of Akkad, Naram-Sin) and affirms that later traditions about these individuals seem increasingly to be verified as factual (in terms of fragmentary discoveries from early times): "The contribution of such discoveries is to give greater plausibility to the ancient traditional accounts, on occasion also refuting the charge of anachronism. Where there is no other evidence, where a literary text alone exists, we should be no less ready to treat it as a valuable and reliable record, unless it can be conclusively shown to be false in many matters" (48). He concludes his article with these words: "Let all who read remember that the patriarchal narratives are our only source for knowledge of the earliest traditions of Israel, that traditions can be correct reflections of ancient events, and that they do not pretend to be textbooks of ancient near-eastern history or archaeology" (51).

I note here briefly two other contributions in the same volume, those by J. J. Bimson and M. J. Selman. Bimson, who argues for an early fifteenth-century date for the Exodus, posits that the patriarchal period spans from 2092 (call of Abraham) to 1877 (the descent of Jacob into Egypt) and that with a minimum of problems this span of time squares quite well with the archaeological picture, which has the Negev populated in Abraham's time (Middle Bronze I), but relatively unpopulated in Jacob's time (Middle Bronze II). He even suggests: "It is tempting to speculate that the famine which drove Isaac from the southern Negeb to Gerar was part of the change in conditions which led to the depopulation of the Negeb as a whole of the end of MB I" (1983: 86).

Selman sifts through the evidence of alleged cultural parallels between the patriarchal accounts and the surviving material from Nuzi, Alalaḫ, Ugarit, and a few other places, insisting on careful control of both biblical and non-biblical materials. Nevertheless, he insists that there remain thirteen valid parallels between the patriarchal stories and non-biblical materials (1983: 134–38).

Thus, from various points of view the factuality of the patriarchal accounts is argued and this, in turn, argues that the stories, in some form not too substantially different from that in which we find them today, are relatively early.

1.5. Along with all the milieu pictured above comes the demand, arising from various quarters, that we *listen* to the text. Thus, J. P. Fokkelman calls for giving priority to exegesis over the study of the process of text creation. He further insists that interpretation/exegesis of the text should be undertaken as an end in itself rather than simply as a means to various ends, "such as increased knowledge of the period in which a work was written, or greater insight into the author's psyche, his system of metaphysical values or that of his time, etc." (1975: 4). He concludes his introduction with a word of advice about how to enter "the hermeneutic circle": "Go into the text carefully, in an attitude of confidence, thus hoping to find an entrance to the work, those keys to its understanding, which the stylistic means of the text offer to us" (8). Thus, while Fokkelman does not ignore the process of the creation of text, his interest here is in the *recreation* by reading and interpretation.

N. R. Petersen (1980), following P. Ricoeur, pleads for a "second naïveté" to which we can return from the "desert of criticism"—although Petersen himself feels that the latter phrase may be excessively drastic. We have, in effect, been shorn of our primitive naïveté by the epoch of criticism, but this, he argues, need not keep us from cultivating a post-critical naïveté in which we listen again to the voice of the text itself—however it may have originated. His whole stance is that we should pay attention to the textually integrative, rather than to the textually dis-integrative, factors.

E. V. McKnight pleads for a genuine literary criticism of the Bible. He concludes: "Biblical critics are discovering that it is possible to make sense out of literary criticism, to <u>develop literary approaches</u> to biblical <u>texts</u> which, while not completely objective and scientific, are <u>orderly</u> and <u>rational</u>" (1980: 66).

R. M. Polzin, while insisting on the relevance of both historical and literary analysis of the Bible, gives methodological priority to the latter: "To know one's object intimately (the literary work), we <u>ought to make</u> it <u>the starting point of our efforts</u>" (1980: 105). He follows R. Alter (1975) in lamenting the almost total absence of serious literary analysis of the Hebrew Bible (103–4).

To the above can be added the approach of I. Kikawada (1974, 1977) and M. Kessler (1974), which they call *rhetorical criticism*. This method, which is entirely synchronic, attempts to recover the meaning (or author intent) by intensively studying the recorded text as we have it today. They approach the text of the Bible as we might approach a text in any language, by paying attention to the grammatical signals, pros-odies, and rhetorical devices used. Kikawada comments: "The Masoretic text is the only primary, empirical evidence for rhetorical criticism of the Hebrew Bible. I consider it to be the only logical starting point of my study, since I do not wish to base my research on a phantom text of any sort" (1977: 69).

It is instructive in this regard to examine two recent attempts to "listen to the text." W. M. W. Roth, still heavily influenced by tradi-tional source criticism, studies the Jacob story (Genesis 25–36) by sep-arating out a P story, a J story, and an E story (the latter is very fragmentary): "P is a time-table compiler, J an architect, and E a case history writer" (1979: 112). Using a methodology suggested by Ricoeur, Roth attempts to approach each story according to structural linguistics, phenomenological analysis, and ontological analysis (103). He then at-tempts to consider the whole story as we now have it by exploring the mutual relations of the P, J, and E stories as successive contextualiza-tions in our present text. The analysis is excellent—considering its faulty empirical basis. After all, the three stories as Roth views them continue to be putative at best, and imaginary and shop-worn at worst. Very little is specifically given of the structure of the *whole*, and in fact it is difficult to see how much could be given, granted the initial disruption of the data by resort to source criticism.

J. G. Gammie also offers an analysis of the Jacob story. In applying a three-pronged literary analysis (motif analysis, analysis of composition and stylistic analysis) he simply takes the text as we find it: "These all deal with the text as it stands in its present context in the Hebrew Bible and treat it synchronically" (1979: 117). He briefly notes that source criticism considers the story to be J and E plus a bit of P, but dismisses these considerations: "In the main, source criticism will not command attention in this essay" (118). Having thus recognized and dismissed source criticism, Gammie proceeds to give a quite delightful and insightful analysis of the material at hand. He includes a section on "Analysis of the History of Traditions," in which he suggests that there are three layers in the story, so that Jacob and Esau are successively presented as ecological types, that is, hunter versus settler, rival twin brothers, and prototypes of two warring nations (126–27). But Gammie does not try to isolate out portions of the text that represent each layer; to do so would have fragmented the text and made it recalcitrant to his analysis. Additionally, I would suggest that Levi-Strauss style structural oppositions would be as fully satisfactory here as the putative "layers of tradition."

1.6. Confronted with all the above my own position is (a) complete skepticism toward the classical sources (JEPD) and their contemporary derivatives, (b) opposition to neo-Wellhausen positions, such as T. L. Thompson, and (c) eagerness to *listen* to the text.

As I have attempted to show in an earlier study (1979a), careful textlinguistic or "discourse" analysis of the text can account for almost all the "internal tensions," "contradictions," and "duplications" on which source criticism was originally based. Divergences of style, names, and vocabulary are appropriate to differing parts of a well-told narrative. For example, the grammar and style of parts of the story that propel the narrative forward are different from the grammar and style of various sorts of backgrounded material, explanation, evaluation, etc. Dissimilar to both is material found in quoted speech (e.g., the speeches of God to Noah). Furthermore, the style of routine narration is modified at a high moment of a story (Gen 7:17–24) to an especially elevated style appropriate to that place in the story. Duplications are often cohesive back-references (to a previous part of the story) or, again, have to do with the peculiar style of a Peak (i.e., a high moment of a story).

In the Flood Narrative, where most of the story is considered to be J with an interwoven P story, source criticism plays havoc with the structure of the text. It fragments beyond recognition the structure of the Peak (Gen 7:17–24), impairs the structure of many of the story's constituent Hebrew paragraphs (by assigning chronological notes that begin and/or end a paragraph to P, but the body of the paragraph to J),

and utterly misconstrues the palindromic (chiastic) structure pointed out
by Wenham (1977), by pitting J's chronology against P's. One gets the
impression that one can do source criticism *or* discourse analysis of a
story such as the Flood Narrative—but hardly both. (See the attempt of
Roth, noted above, to try to combine source criticism and discourse
analysis in approaching the Jacob story.)

I find the work of Goldingay, Millard, Bimson, Selman, and others
very refreshing, especially since I want to take the patriarchal narratives
seriously and not simply as retrojective creations of a later age. I appreciate their emphasis on the antiquity of the covenant idea, the authentic-
ity of the patriarchal story as family history, and the contextual cohesion
between these narratives and the rest of the Pentateuch (more of this
below).

Above all, I stand on the side of those who want to *listen* to the
text. Like many contemporaries, much of my coolness towards source
criticism is that it hinders us from listening to the text; it muffles the
voice which we want to hear.

2. *Broader contextual connections of the story*

In the first chapter of this book, the *tōlĕdôt* divisions of Genesis
are taken as the basic framework, and the context of *Joseph* within
the *tōlĕdôt yaʿăqōb*, 'generations of Jacob', is noted. Here I want to
range over broader questions. Goldingay—to whom I am considerably
indebted—takes as the key to the patriarchal stories the twin ideas of
promise and obstacles to the fulfillment. The promise, within the context
of the Abraham story, is formalized in the covenant of chapters 15 and
17. Obstacles to fulfillment of the promise are found to crop up almost
immediately on the heels of the original giving of the promise (Gen 12:1–
9). One set of obstacles is in the circumstances of Abraham's day: 'The
Canaanites were then in the land' (12:6b). Another set of obstacles lies in
the character of Abraham himself as seen in his behavior in Egypt
(12:10–20) and later with Abimelech, king of Gerar (chap. 21), as well as
in the taking of Hagar and the birth of Ishmael. Here, Goldingay emphasizes, we often find a kind of "antifulfillment."

Taking these central ideas—blessing and obstacles to fulfillment—
we find the promise renewed to Isaac and Jacob, with abundant exem-
plifications of obstacles and antifulfillments. But, taken thus, is this not
the theme of the whole narrative (Genesis–2 Kings) that climaxes in the
Exile, and for that matter extends through to the Restoration? Looked
at this way, in our attempts to "contextualize" the patriarchal stories, we
see that they were relevant to a long and varied historical context,
provided one lets the promise (the covenant idea) be sufficiently early.

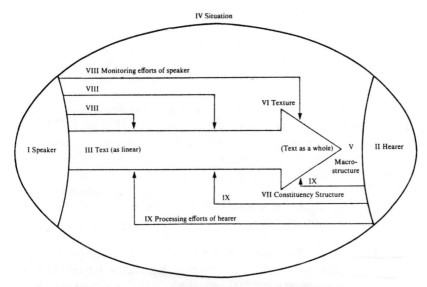

DIAGRAM 1. Some Aspects of Text Analysis in their Broader Setting

Goldingay specifically examines the patriarchal narratives in the contexts of the Exodus and Conquest, the Monarchy, and the Exile.

Noticeably, in a rear-guard exercise of source criticism, those who want to emphasize the "loose" contextual association of the patriarchal stories with the rest of the Pentateuch have to excise from the stories as we now have them passages such as Gen 15:12–16 (enslavement in Egypt and the Exodus), Gen 46:3–4 (the descent into Egypt and the return to Canaan), as well as Gen 50:24–25. A passage such as Genesis 14—while highly cohesive with the later importance of Jerusalem/Salem under the Davidic line—again, can on these very grounds be excised as P (or some other obscure source). What then? One who believes in the general coherence of the patriarchal narratives with the rest of the Pentateuch (and, indeed, with the whole Hebrew Bible) has no problem demonstrating its coherence. Those, on the other hand, who seek for evidence of textual disintegration, pare away from the stories as we find them the available evidence of coherence with the rest of Scripture, considering such coherence to be *prima facie* evidence that they are late additions by P, D, or some other redactor. But this argumentation is circular.

3. *The methodology of this work*

3.1. To begin with, note the accompanying Diagram 1, which summarizes elements important to the analysis of a contemporary oral text.

The most obvious thing about a text is that *Speaker* (I) is transmitting to *Hearer* (II) a *message* (III)—which necessarily proceeds linearly word-for-word. Quite important to the whole process of message transmission and reception is a common *situation* (IV), which like a cartouche encompasses the whole process; no communication can take place without at least a minimum of commonality. The message, although linearly (and hence dynamically) transmitted and received, constitutes a unified whole that can be statically conceived (V, VI and VII) as well. Approaching such a message we note that it has an overall meaning and thrust—a *macrostructure* (V), which in turn controls its *texture* (VI) and its *constituent structure* (VII), that is, the nature of its breakdown into mutually related parts such as embedded discourses, paragraphs, sentences, clauses, phrases, and words. VIII and IX represent the *monitoring efforts of the speaker* and the *processing (interpreting) efforts of the hearer*.

In applying this model to recorded texts in contemporary languages, it is reasonable to require of a field worker that she/he be able to state the conditions under which a text was given, that is, salient facts about the narrator (if it be a story), the audience (whether peers in the same culture, superiors or inferiors in that culture, or an audience composed wholly or in part of outsiders to that culture), and the way the text was obtained (elicited in response to a request or a question, volunteered, or given as a matter of course in a certain sociological situation). All these analytical requirements are for the sake of aiding the analyst in respect to factors I–IV.

In applying this model to a written text where the text transmitter and receiver are not in a face-to-face relationship when the text is given, our scheme is necessarily fissioned into two halves (cf. Ricoeur 1976: 25–44). The writer is presumably writing for a given audience but the audience is not immediately present. A written work may even prove to be of not great interest to the audience to which the (hopeful) writer addressed it and may prove instead to be of interest to a rather different sort of audience (especially when a work is ahead of its time). The reader likewise has no immediate access to the writer, whose intentions he must judge wholly from the written work itself. Indeed, as so eloquently put by Ricoeur, the text is alienated from its author and must be appropriated by its reader in spite of distanciation.

In applying the model to a literary text that has existed for several millenia, we necessarily shift ground even more in regard to such matters. With a contemporary or recent work where the author and time of a composition are known, we require some idea of the milieu in which the composition was penned (circumstances, issues currently under debate, interests, values, fears, probable audience, particular stimulus for writing, and other works of the same sort by the same and different authors), although we indeed recognize in a literary work that, once released from the author's hand, a composition has a life of its own. With a truly ancient text, however, most of the above information is either nonexistent or highly speculative—the text is "on its own." But, precisely because the text has stood the test of time it is a literary work that has something to say to another time, place, and set of circumstances other than that in which it was originally composed. It *is* a literary work because it has something to say to us, as well as to its original audience (even though here and there a word, an expression, a turn of argumentation is somewhat opaque to us as contemporary readers until it is clarified by reference to the original milieu of the composition).

With the patriarchal narratives, of which *Joseph* is our special focus here, we are locked in to the study of a literary composition concerning which it is difficult to frame questions regarding the original narrator, audience, and circumstances of composition. In fact, raising of questions of this sort has resulted in countless scholarly battles, in which no matter how long one hypothesis stands up it is fated in the end to be knocked down by its successor. Thus for many years the authoritative scholarly view of *Joseph* has been that it is largely a weaving together of separate J and E stories that arose during the early monarchical period. The more recent view, impatient with this, dates a common JE account from the deuteronomic period (late pre-exilic and exilic). The traditional belief has been that the patriarchal accounts are family history committed to writing by Moses, who gave us essentially the core of our present Pentateuch, plus some subsequent additions. Obviously, the three contextualizations that I have indicated imply diverse audiences.

But is there not a common core even in all the above contextualizations? For example, apparently Israel's hold on the land was always precarious and unsure. Even the most cursory reading of the book of Judges yields the view that the hold of Israel on the land in the face of other population elements in Canaan was very precarious. Similarly, after a brief period of glory under David and Solomon, monarchical Israel is again on the defensive and trying to hold its own against foreign incursions and encroachments. In the period of the Exile, Israel finally succumbs—although there is a partial restoration to the land. At the opposite extreme is the time of the Conquest, when—as represented in the book of Joshua—Israel was fighting for her initial control of the land. Would not, therefore, a common theme of promise and obstacles (such as suggested by Goldingay, see above), or even conditional occupation of the land, be appropriate to these several contexts?

Certainly then, the speaker of our story is an Israelite who is writing to other Israelites. His common assumption with them could plausibly be expressed in the words of Heb 11:6b, "Anyone who comes to God must believe that he exists and that he rewards those who earnestly see him." The author was a theist and a believer in a god who is providentially active in the affairs of men, specifically in regard to Israel and her occupancy of the land; the traditional view of the origin of *Joseph* is quite in keeping with these observations.

A literary work, however (as noted above), speaks to others than those for whom it was originally composed. In this respect our diagram of the oral transmission of a text proves partially relevant in understanding the impact of an ancient text on a modern reader. If we are to understand the text at all we must enter into the communicative cartouche, whose outer skin (feature IV) consists of common speaker/hearer assumptions, and become the new II (hearer) at whom the text is now beamed. McKnight puts it quite well: "The literary approaches dissolve the distance between the ancient texts and the modern reader-critic and allow consideration of the multiplicity of meanings and meaning-effects which impinge upon the modern reader" (1980: 66). Notice that while I here approvingly quote McKnight, I still insist upon the commonality factor (IV), which unless present makes a story such as *Joseph* have little relevance to us.

In regard to this commonality factor, Polzin has a further word that is quite relevant at this juncture. He insists that the Scriptures (I would add, like *any* text) have built-in specifications as to the proper attitude in which we are to make our approach as hearer/reader. What Polzin says is that the Scriptures ask of us an involvement and commitment that is at odds with approaching the text in an uninvolved, uncommitted, "scholarly" stance (assuming that such scholarship is defined on an analogy with the reputedly uninvolved, objective stand of the natural sciences). But here I would hasten to point out that Polzin's model of objective modern science is itself at fault, for Toulmin (1981: 92–96) has pointed out that "post-modern science" emphasizes the *involvement* of the observer with the object of his investigation.

In brief, if we approach *Joseph* as theists and as believers in divine providence we get ourselves inside the hermeneutic cartouche along with the writer and message that we are studying. Otherwise the story reduces to a pleasant pabulum, or a music-hall farce such as Andrew Lloyd Webber and Timothy Rice's (brilliant) production *Joseph and the Amazing Technicolor Dreamcoat*—a work that renders faithfully and provocatively many scenes of the story but utterly misses its overall thrust, its macrostructure.

3.2.   Leaving aside these matters of the hermeneutic cartouche (the interrelationship of factors I–IV in Diagram 1), I address now the matter of the macrostructure (factor V) and, in passing, factor VI—although this more properly figures in Part 2 of this volume.

3.2.1. Text theory (as an interdisciplinary endeavor) and textlinguistics (a more specifically linguistic approach to text) both recognize the importance of the *macrostructure* to discourse analysis. Every text, if it is truly a text, has a germinal idea (or closely related complex of germinal ideas) that acts as an overall plan in the development of the discourse. T. A. van Dijk (1972) suggested rules whereby a text can be generated from its abstract. Following him, I attempted to develop a set of such generative rules relative to a text by James Thurber (Longacre 1976). Meanwhile, since clearly a text cannot be generated from its abstract until the abstract itself is crystallized out from the text, van Dijk (1977) shifted his attention to the elaboration of reduction rules for deducing a macrostructure from a text. While one skilled at writing an abstract or precis performs this operation intuitively, nevertheless such rules as van Dijk suggests (1977: 143–48) are useful in explaining how such highly skilled abstracters operate: (1) The less predictable material in a discourse is more essential to its abstract than the predictable, for example, necessary presuppositions, results, or steps in a process. (2) Specific detail can be generically summarized in the abstract. (3) An assortment of somewhat disparate material can be brought together in a construction that captures their underlying unity. The process of abstracting can proceed in cycles in which the steps performed on the original text are performed again on its abstract. A skillfully constructed macrostructure can typically be captured in a line or two but the macrostructure can be shown, in turn, to have a governing effect on the relative inclusion, balance, and elaboration of detail throughout the text.

Thus, in relation to the Genesis Flood Narrative (Longacre 1979a), I have shown that the macrostructure is triple: (1) a highly destructive flood, (2) safety through embarkation within an ark, and (3) God's covenant with Noah and the others involved. Resort to this macrostructure was seen to explain many unique and sometimes puzzling features of the stories: (1) The slow-moving, repetitious, suspense-building pace of the pre-peak episodes, (2) the multiple references to embarkation in planes of overlay (repetitions), (3) the unique structure of Gen 7:17–24 where paraphrase and paraphrase-within-paraphrase picture the mounting catastrophe, (4) the long didactic portion in chapter 9, in which the covenant is elaborated—and several further details besides. My experience in doing this analysis has led me to posit a practical rule-of-thumb for the discourse analyst: Whenever one is bogged down in the analysis of the details of a text she/he needs to back off from it and remind herself/himself of the main thrust and intent of the text.

3.2.2. The texture of a discourse (factor VI) refers especially to cohesion and coherence in its linear development. This development is responsive to the macrostructure but without cohesion and coherence the macrostructure could never be realized in the linear development. By "cohesion" I refer especially to surface structure devices such as grammatical forms and conjunctions, while "coherence" is reserved for lexical and referential continuity. Somewhat intermediate between the two is the realm of logical relations, which can be marked or unmarked.

The cohesion and coherence of a discourse is not simply a matter of successive binary ties (Halliday and Hasan 1976) that unite one point in the discourse to another. Rather the texture is largely dependent on cohesive *strands* that run vertically down the discourse. Since two such vertical strands are especially important, a discourse tends to shape up as a sort of double helix, analogous to the DNA and protein molecules. One strand of the helix has to do with the mainline of development of a text—whether the storyline of a narrative, the line of exhortation in a hortatory text, or the line of exposition in an expository discourse. To this main helical strand relate other strands of structurally less important information (chapter 3). The second main helical strand is that of participant/thematic reference. This strand also is complex in that line of reference to various participants or themes must be kept distinct while indication is included as to major versus minor participants/themes (chapter 6).

Texts of any sort typically have a cumulative development. The plot of a story moves towards climax and resolution. A hortatory text typically has a culminating exhortation near its end. An expository discourse can have culminating explanation that replaces or rounds out the partial (or even erroneous) explanations given earlier in the discourse.

It has been my contention for several years now that the cumulative development(s) of a discourse usually manifests itself in certain grammatico-lexical characteristics. I have therefore referred to *peak-marking features* (carefully described and illustrated elsewhere: Longacre 1976, 1981, 1983 and 1985a). Essentially, *peak* is a kind of zone of turbulence (Longacre 1985a) in which predictable discourse features are skewed so that certain typical features are removed or partially suppressed, while other features are introduced. It represents a kind of a gear shift in the dynamic flow of discourse. Only rarely does a language have special peak-marking features that are used only at peak; rather it is the *shift* from one set of features to another that marks the onset of a peak in a given discourse. Thus a story may have reported dialogue occurring only at its peak or may have the longest stretch of dialogue involving the longest speech at that point; it may shift from dialogue to drama (no formulas of quotation) at peak; or it may phase out dialogue completely in favor of a quick moving sequence of action at the peak of the story. Shifts in tense/aspect and person, use or disuse of discourse particles, introduction of onomatopoeia or oaths or obscenity, variation in sentence length and complexity of constructions, incidence of repetition and paraphrase—these are some other typical ways of indicating to the reader that the rhythm of the text is picking up (or, alternatively, that the camera is slowing down and picking up more detail).

In describing a text we can draw its profile once we identify its peak(s). The profile attempts to represent diagrammatically the rising and falling tension of text with the beginning, peak, and end as reference points. This gives us an overall morphology of the discourse. Furthermore, peak constitutes a reference point—a quite significant one—in reference to which other parts of the discourse can be plotted.

CHAPTER ONE
OVERVIEW

In this initial chapter an attempt is made to fit the *Joseph* story into its immediate far and near context in Genesis, and to trace some of the gross anatomical features of the story and its various parts. This, in turn, is balanced against a study of the macrostructures in the following chapter.

1. *Contextual relations of* Joseph

The *Joseph* story occurs within the last *tōlĕdôt* ('generations of', 'life and times of') section of Genesis, that is, under the caption *ʾelleh tōlĕdôt yaʿăqōb*, 'these [are] the generations of Jacob' (37:2). Ten previous such sections occur in the book. Of these the first is unmarked and consists of the account of the creation of the heavens and the earth (1:1–2:3). The second section (2:4–4:26), *tôlĕdôt haššāmayim wĕhāʾāreṣ*, 'generations of the heavens and the earth', is a less cosmic and more personalized section that deals with Adam, Eve, their fall, and their immediate descendants, who are presented as immediate heirs of creation. The third section (5:1–6:8), *sēper tôlĕdôt ʾādām*, 'book of generations of Adam', deals with the descendants of Adam, and ends with a preview of oncoming judgment (the flood). The fourth section (6:9–9:29), *tôlĕdōt nōaḥ*, 'generations of Noah', contains the flood story and Noah's interaction with his sons after the flood. The fifth section (10:1–11:9), *tôlĕdōt bĕnê-nōaḥ*, 'generations of sons of Noah', treats of the descendants of the sons of Noah (the "table of nations") and ends with an account of rebellion and punishment (Babel). The sixth section (11:10–26), *tôlĕdōt šēm*, 'generations of Shem', is brief and purely genealogical. The seventh section (11:27–25:11) is entitled *tôlĕdōt teraḥ*, 'generations of Terah'. Terah himself receives but brief treatment (11:27–32) and the remainder of the section has to do with Terah's son, Abram. At the close of this section Abraham dies and is buried by his two sons Ishmael and Isaac (25:7–11). Ishmael's descendants are listed in section eight (25:12–18), *tôlĕdōt yišmāʿēʾl*, 'generations of Ishmael', which is very brief and almost entirely genealogical. Isaac, in whom the line of promise continues, gives his name to section nine (25:19–35:29), *tôlĕdōt yiṣḥāq ben-ʾabrāhām*, 'generations of Isaac, son of Abraham'. Isaac himself, however, figures prominently only in chap. 26; for the balance of this section the story is about his son Jacob. Isaac dies and is buried by his sons Esau and Jacob at the end of this section (35:28–29). Section ten (36:1–37:1) is the double-titled (36:1, 9) *tōlĕdōt ʿēśāw*, 'generations of Esau', which is composed of several distinct lists, including the descendants of 'Seir the Horite' with whom, presumably, the Edomites amalgamated to form a nation.

It is evident from the above outline that (1) a *tôlĕdôt* in minimal form is a genealogical table, (2) the bare genealogical facts may be accompanied by almost any amount of anecdote and story, and (3) an established head of the clan (already born and introduced in the previous section) gives his name to a section that may be largely about his son (e.g., the *tôlĕdōt teraḥ* is concerned with Abraham; the *tôlĕdōt yiṣḥāq* is concerned with Jacob). From this point of view, Genesis is primarily an annotated genealogical record (cf. the Anglo-Saxon Chronicle, which is an annotated list of successive reigns).

Typically, the end of one *tôlĕdôt* section anticipates the next one, and/or the beginning of a *tôlĕdôt* section makes back reference to the previous section. Thus, section three, with its preview of the flood narrative anticipates section four; and section four, with Noah's blessing and curses on his sons, anticipates section five (the "table of nations").

In the light of the above considerations, we can now look at the beginning of the *tōlĕdôt yaʿăqōb*, 'generations of Jacob'. To begin with, note the ending of the previous section in 36:43b–37:1: 'This is Esau, the father of the Edomites. And Jacob dwelt in the land of the sojourning of his fathers, in the land of Canaan.' The first sentence is a summary of most of chap. 36. The next sentence (which opens chap. 37 but concludes the previous *tôlĕdôt*) implicitly contrasts Esau and Jacob, while the use of the *waw*-consecutive on the verb in 37:1 is almost like 'Now let's get back to the story. . . .' Here the penchant for anticipating in one section the subject of the following section leads to a link that is created almost by tour de force.

Gen 37:2, the opening of the new section, has a striking juxtaposition of proper names: *ʾēlleh tōlĕdōt yaʿăqōb yôsēp*, 'These [are] generations of Jacob, Joseph. . . .' Here the proper names 'Jacob' and 'Joseph' are juxtaposed across sentence boundary. The sentence beginning with 'Joseph' is initial in a paragraph that uses several grammatical devices to present Joseph as the central participant of the following narrative. This is not strange per se, in that (as we have seen) even though a *tôlĕdôt* section is named for X, it is typically concerned with the doings of the

DIAGRAM 2. Interrelations of the Joseph Story and
tōlĕdôt yaʿĕqōb (Jacob and his family)

	1	2	3	4	5	6	7
	37	*38*	*39:1–6*	*39:7–23*	*40*	*41*	*42*
	Episode₁		*Episode₂*	*Episode₃*	*Episode₄*	*Peak*	*Interpe*
	Joseph / Jacob and his family						
Contents	Joseph sold into Egypt	Judah and Tamar	Joseph in Potiphar's house	Joseph's ruin	Prisoners' dreams	Pharaoh's dreams, Joseph's rise to power	The brothers first trip Egypt
Peaks						Climax of *Joseph*	

son(s) of X. In some *tōlĕdôt* sections the individual for whom a section
is named is, however, more prominent in that section. Thus section
four begins *ʾelleh tōlĕdōt nōaḥ nōaḥ*, 'These are generations of Noah,
Noah . . . .' Here the concerns of Noah, the ark, and the flood hold the
spotlight until 9:18ff. when the sons of Noah come to the fore. In still
other sections, even where 'these are the generations of X' is followed by
a sentence beginning with X, the content of the section concerns itself
with the sons of X rather than with X himself (cf. 11:10 and 11:27).

2. *The* Joseph *story within the* tōlĕdôt *of Jacob*

A principal consideration here is the placement of the *Joseph* story
in its own *tōlĕdôt* section, that is, in its immediate context. Obviously,
even though Joseph is marked as central participant in many parts of
chaps. 37–50, there are parts where he is not mentioned at all, or if he is
mentioned, he is offstage. Thus we have chap. 38 (Judah and Tamar),
which tends to impress the person reading this part of the Bible for the

DIAGRAM 2. *(Continued)*

8	9	10	11	12	13	14
43–45	46:1–47:12	47:13–31	48	49:1–28	49:29–50:21	50:22–26
Peak'	Post Peak$_1$	Post Peak$_2$	Post Peak$_3$			
…ne …cond …p, …seph …veals …mself	Jacob goes to Egypt	Last years of Joseph's famine administra-tion	Joseph and the dying Jacob, Blessing of Manasseh and Ephraim	Blessing on the Twelve Tribes	Death and burial of Jacob	Death of Joseph
…enou- …ent of …seph				Peak of *tōlĕdôt*		

first time as a rather outrageous interruption of the ongoing *Joseph* story. Then we have chap. 49 in which the dying Jacob is blessing his sons and predicting the future fortunes of their descendants. This chapter, in that it is poetry, seems intended to be a high point of the *tōlĕdôt yaʿăqōb*, if not of the whole book of Genesis. But how do such concerns relate to the dramatic high points of *Joseph*, his rise to power (chap. 41), and his revelation of himself to his brothers (chap. 45)? Clearly, as important as Joseph is, he is not the *whole* concern of 37–50.

Questions such as the above are best resolved by recognizing that the *tōlĕdôt yaʿăqōb* has essentially two interwoven strands: the *Joseph* story and the broader concerns of Jacob and his family. I therefore suggest in this section an outline for chaps. 37–50 in which certain passages will be seen to deal jointly with Joseph and the broader concerns, while others deal only with Joseph, and still another passage (chap. 38) only with other members of Jacob's family. In reading the following subsections, the reader may wish to refer to Diagram 2 where I divide 37–50 into fourteen discrete sections.

1. Joseph sold into Egypt (chap. 37). Here we have concerns that are common to all of Jacob's family. Joseph, however, as the central participant, is introduced in the first paragraph (37:2-4) which serves as Stage for the entire *Joseph* story insofar as it is a separate but interwoven strand in the broader fabric. The action of this section serves as the inciting incident in the development of the plot of *Joseph*.

2. Judah and Tamar (38). Here we depart from *Joseph* and are given some background on Judah, who comes to play a crucial role in the denouement of the entire story and who counts high in the scale of honor and blessing in Jacob's prophecies (49).

3. Joseph in Potiphar's house (39:1-6). This briefly presented episode in *Joseph* is clearly set off from what follows by the transition in 39:7. This is a "success" story before Joseph's fortunes take another downward turn.

4. Joseph's ruin (39:7-23). This episode in Joseph's life brings him to the prison where the King's prisoners are kept—and this puts him in line, ultimately, for his fateful interview with Pharaoh.

5. Joseph interprets the dreams of two courtiers of Pharaoh (40). This chapter constitutes an embedded narrative in which two courtiers of Pharaoh are imprisoned with, and entrusted to, Joseph. Joseph interprets their dreams, and in accordance with his interpretation one is restored to power and the other executed. Joseph's plea for help on the part of the one restored is apparently forgotten.

6. Pharaoh's dreams and Joseph's rise to power (41). This is the first Peak (climax) of *Joseph*. In an atmosphere of rising excitement, Pharaoh's dreams are described, along with the inability of the Egyptian soothsayers to interpret them. Then the forgetful (and somewhat disdainful) courtier remembers Joseph, who is called from prison to interpret Pharaoh's dreams. Joseph interprets Pharaoh's dreams, predicts a famine, and counsels Pharaoh to create an emergency grain storage program. Pharaoh makes Joseph his economic vizier in a quick-moving installation passage, which is itself an internal climax in this subsection.

7. The brothers' first trip to Egypt to buy grain (42). The previous section leaves us with a problem: Joseph is dictator of a pagan country and removed farther than ever from his family in Canaan. In this present section, however, Joseph (incognito) meets his brothers when they come to buy grain. He gives them a hard time and tells them not to come again unless they bring their younger brother Benjamin.

8. The second trip to buy grain; Joseph reveals himself (43-45). We have here a very long section that is the second Peak (denouement)

of the *Joseph* story. After long haggling with Jacob about taking along the youngest son Benjamin, the brothers come again to Joseph in Egypt. They have a prolonged and happy banquet with Egypt's ruler, but when they start out for home things go wrong. They are accused of stealing Joseph's silver cup, which (slyly planted) is found in Benjamin's bag. In an agony of guilt (over Joseph) and dread concerning Benjamin (Jacob's favorite since Joseph's disappearance), they go back to Joseph's house. There, in an impassioned plea Judah offers to stay as a slave in Egypt if only Benjamin can go free. Joseph, recognizing that his brother have had a change of heart, reveals his true identity to them. After the initial shock they agree to go home to Canaan and bring all their families and their father Jacob down to Egypt.

9. Jacob and all his clan go down to Egypt where Joseph and Jacob are reunited (46:1–47:12).
10. Last years of Joseph's famine relief administration (47:13–31). This is the only section after chap. 42 that deals with the affairs of Joseph (and Egypt) to the exclusion of the broader concerns of the *tōlĕdôt yaʿăqōb*.
11. Jacob blesses Ephraim and Manasseh (48).
12. Jacob blesses his sons (49:1–28). This is the didactic peak of the whole *tôlĕdôt*.
13. Jacob's death and burial (49:29–50:21). At the end of this section, there is a brief recurrence of the sold-into-Egypt theme that is so prominent in the *Joseph* story (50:14–21).
14. Death and burial of Joseph (50:22–26).

3. *Gross structural features of* Joseph

In this section I now propose to examine some features of sections 1 and 3–11, that is, the sections that pertain to the *Joseph* story as an entity within the broader framework. The two features that will be examined briefly here are the articulation of these sections (which prove to be episodes) and the marking of peak and closure within the episodes.

3.1. *The articulation of episodes of* Joseph *and linkage between episodes*

3.1.1. The inciting incident of the story—which poses a problem to be resolved through the coming years—is the plot against Joseph and his sale into Egypt. Here chap. 37 is somewhat self-contained. This first episode (= Ep) is bounded by the beginning of the *tôlĕdôt*, with Joseph established as central in the words that immediately follow, and is bounded at its far end by the intrusive material concerning Judah and Tamar in chap. 38. Granted that the author wanted to include the latter concerning Judah somewhere in the *tōlĕdôt yaʿăqōb*, why is it found precisely here? Perhaps there were chronological considerations of the sort mentioned in 38: *wayhî bāʿēt hahiwʾ*, 'And it happened about that time that. . . .' Obviously, the events recorded in chap. 38 need, however, a few years to work themselves out! Another distinct possibility is that with a true instinct for suspense in storytelling, the writer deliberately ran in this incident concerning Judah in order to leave his reader dangling for a while—even as the whole family was left in total ignorance of what had happened to Joseph for some thirteen years.[1]

3.1.2. Chapter 39 resumes the *Joseph* story after the intrusive material in chap. 38. Here the main device in the reintroduction of Joseph is *casus pendens* (*wĕyôsēp*, i.e., 'Now, as for Joseph') and extensive recapitulation in 39:1 of the material found in 37:36 (and in 28b). Indeed 37:36 is not related to the immediately preceding verses (29–35), and seems to be appended to Ep₁ of *Joseph* with the explicit purpose of providing a cataphoric link to Ep₂ (which does not immediately follow and therefore requires all the more explicit marking).

3.1.3. In 39:7 the onset of the a further episode (Ep₃ of *Joseph*) is marked by a strong episode marker: *wayhî ʾaḥar haddĕbārîm hāʾēlleh*, 'and it came to pass after these things' (cf. the use of this episode marker in Gen 22:1 and a similar but simpler formula in Gen 25:1). In general, *wayhî* + a temporal phrase marks an episode break in Hebrew narrative prose. For this reason, although the preceding episode (39:1–6) is short, I see no reason not to recognize it as a major episode of the story. Length as such is not decisive.

At the end of Ep₃ of *Joseph* (39:7–23), the new locality where Joseph finds himself is established with great care. Thus in 39:20 we are

---

[1] The story of Judah and Tamar is not, of course, without significance to the broader story. As I point out in chap. 1, §2, the whole *tōlĕdôt yaʿăqōb* is essentially the story of the three *Js*: Jacob, Joseph, and Judah. Furthermore, within the *Joseph* story itself, Judah's role in the resolution of the story is crucial. Additional biographical material concerning him is clearly, therefore, appropriate to this whole *tôlĕdôt* section (cf. 3.1). Doris Myers (private communication) further suggests that there is a general parallelism of the Tamar story to Joseph. (a) She suffers injustice from her brothers-in-law and father-in-law, even as Joseph suffered from his own family; (b) the problem is solved through her concealing her identity, degradation (and threatened death), and revelation; and (c) her sons cross-up at birth in a way reminiscent of Jacob and Esau, and Manasseh and Ephraim (Jacob's crossed hands).

told 'And he put him in the *guard house*, the *place* where the prisoners of the King are imprisoned. And he was *there in the guard house*.' The locality is crucial—it is here that Joseph's path crossed with that of the courtiers of Pharaoh—and the author spares no pains to mark the new locale as significant. Furthermore we are given a clue as to coming events in the clause 'the place where the prisoners of the King are imprisoned'.

Here at the end of Ep₃, there is a paragraph (39:21–23) that recounts Joseph's rise to position of chief trustee in the prison. This further prepares us to accept the events of the next chapter, which is a new episode of the story.

3.1.4. Ep₄ of Joseph (chap. 40) opens again with the episode marker that opened the previous episode: *wayhî ʾaḥar haddĕbārîm hāʾēlleh*. Furthermore (see below) this section, which is clearly an embedded narrative, takes new central participants: the chief cupbearer and the chief baker. The crossing of the destinies of these men with that of Joseph is, again, emphasized by pointing out the common locale: 'and he put them in the *prison* of the *house* of the captain of the *guard*, into *the guard house*, the *place* where Joseph was imprisoned *there*' (40:3). Furthermore, the author points out that Joseph, as chief trustee, was the one to whose personal care the two courtiers (no ordinary prisoners!) were commended. Here the attention to the locale in 40:3 correlates with the attention to the locale at the end of the preceding episode.

3.1.5. These episodes are followed by an episode whose special structural features entitle us to call it the Peak (see below). This peak episode (chap. 41) begins with an episode marker that indicates a considerable lapse of time: *wayhî miqqēṣ šĕnātayim yāmîm*, 'and it came to pass at the end of two full years'. There follows an unusual use of the *waw*-conjunctive with the noun Pharaoh: 'and Pharaoh was dreaming'. The thrust of this is probably: 'We've heard about Joseph's dreams and about the dreams of the two courtiers, but now it's Pharaoh's turn to dream.' Thus, the new embedded narrative establishes its new time horizon and its new central participant.

This episode, the narrative of Joseph's rise to power, ends again in a fashion that prepares the reader for the episode to follow. The passage in question is a paragraph that begins in the center of 41:54, 'and there was a famine in all lands, but in all the land of Egypt there was bread', and ends with the words of 41:57, 'and all countries came into Egypt to Joseph to buy bread, for strong was the famine in all the earth'. These words prepare us for the following episode in which the brothers come to Egypt to buy grain.

3.1.6. The following episode (chap. 42) lies in a valley between the Peak (climax) in chap. 41 and the Peak' (denouement) in chaps. 43–45. It is marked simply by a temporary shift of the locale to Canaan and a bringing of Jacob (absent since the end of 37) onto the stage again. Essentially here the episode division is marked lexically rather than grammatically. We find here the story of the first trip of the brothers to Egypt to buy grain.

The acrimonious debate (of Jacob's sons with Jacob) over the necessity of taking Benjamin on the second trip (42:36–38) closes this episode and prepares the way for the next episode in which, after a similar debate, Benjamin is finally sent along with his brothers.

3.1.7. The next episode, section 8 of our overall analysis of the *tōlĕdôt yaᶜăqōb*, is the longest in the story and probably the most dramatic (chaps. 43–45). It patterns as Peak' (denouement), in that it addresses itself to resolution of the question, "Has there been sufficient change in the attitude and conduct of his brothers for Joseph (wronged by them years ago and now holding the whip-hand of power) to attempt a reconciliation?"

This Peak' episode begins with a reiteration of the severity of the famine: 'and the famine was severe in the land'. This is followed by the familiar construction *wayhî* + a temporal phrase in backreference: 'and it came to pass that when they finished eating the grain that they had brought from Egypt' (43:2a). The lengthy dialogue that follows is initiated by Jacob's suggestion that they go again to buy food—which in turn elicits the objection that they can't go again without Benjamin. As we have seen, this continues an argument begun on the occasion of their return from Egypt a year before (in the previous episode). This time, however, Judah is able to persuade his father to let Benjamin go under Judah's personal protection and surety. This Peak' episode ends with the story of how the brothers broke the good news to Jacob on their return to Canaan. Jacob's words, 'Enough! My son Joseph is still alive; I will go down and see him before I die,' prepare us for the next episode in which the whole clan migrates to Egypt.

3.1.8. There are three post-peak Episodes of *Joseph*: 46–47:12, 47:13–31, and 48:1–22. The first of these episodes gets Jacob to Egypt where he is reunited with his son Joseph; the second episode closes out the record of Joseph's famine administration; and the third records the blessing of Jacob on Joseph's two sons (with a brief forecast of the future). No special markers set off the beginnings of the first two post-peak episodes; rather, radical shifts in the movement of participants and in shifts of subject matter seem to be decisive. Post-peak Ep$_3$ is, however, clearly marked.

3.1.9. To backtrack a bit, the episode that I consider to be Peak′ seems, rightly, to end with the second return of the brothers to Canaan and their conversation with (the incredulous) Jacob. In this respect 45:24–28 is parallel with 42:29–38 (the conversation after their first return from Egypt). Therefore, the descent of Jacob into Egypt seems plausibly to pattern as a new Episode (Post-peak Ep$_1$). Jacob and his family are thematic in the new episode: Jacob's clan moves down to Beersheba where he has a vision of God; the names and subgrouping of the clan are listed; Jacob meets Joseph in Goshen; and finally some of Joseph's brothers and Jacob himself are presented to Pharaoh.

3.1.10. Section 10 (47:13–27, Post-peak Episode$_2$) abruptly shifts the focus again to Joseph as economic czar of Egypt. This passage is in some ways similar to the paragraph found in 41:54b–57. The two passages, both of which portray Joseph's dealing with the famine-pressed populace of Egypt, bracket the episodes that treat Joseph's interactions with his brothers and with his father (42:1–47:12). While there is no explicit episode marker to correlate with the onset of the new episode in 47:13, there is the initiation of a new chain of *waw*-consecutives preceded by a nominal clause with a dependent stative perfect: 'And bread [was] none in all the land, for heavy the famine exceedingly. *And it languished* the land of Egypt and the land of Canaan because of the famine.' Not until the third clause does a chain of *waw*-consecutives get underway. However, while such a device is clearly paragraph-initial it is not necessarily indicative of a new episode. Rather, it is the lexical shift that marks the fresh beginning.

It is worth noting that the last passage of this episode (47:27–31) prepares us for the eventual transition back to the broader concerns of Jacob's family. Note especially v 27, 'And Israel dwelt in the land of Egypt in the land of Goshen, and they acquired possessions in it, and they were fruitful, and became very numerous.' This verse also anticipates Exod 1:7—the crisis that provoked the oppression—while further on, at the death of Joseph, there is a promise of the exodus and a command on the part of the dying Joseph that his bones be carried along to Canaan when Israel is brought out (Gen 50:25–26). Within the overall unity of the Pentateuch there is, therefore, evidence that the story begun in Genesis will be continued.

3.1.11. Nevertheless, there is one more episode, section 11 (Post-peak Episode$_3$), that probably should be considered to be part of *Joseph*.

Thus, chap. 48 begins with the strong episode marker *wayhî ʾaḥarê haddĕbārîm hāʾēlleh*.

3.2. *Marking of peak and closure*

Here I will discuss not only the features that mark sections 6 and 8 as peaks of *Joseph* but also the marking of Peak and Closure within the embedded narratives that expound certain episodes. The assumption here is that in most stories—except those that relatively short and uncomplex—it is routine to find that main episodes are themselves structured as (embedded) narratives.

3.2.1. The episodes of Ep₁ (chap. 37), an embedded narrative, are (1) Joseph's dreams (the Inciting Incident; 37:5–11), (2) Joseph's going to visit his brothers (37:12–17), (3) the plot (37:18–22), (4) the seizure and sale of Joseph (37:23–28; Peak), (5) the cover-up (37:29–35; post-peak), and (6) closure (cataphoric link; 37:36). (The Stage, 37:2–4, is discussed in chap. 6.) Each of these episodes has the structure of a Hebrew paragraph, but a detailed examination of this constituent structure is beyond the scope of this chapter.

Some of the features that mark 37:23–28 as Peak are: (1) *wayhî kaʾăšer-bāʾ yôsēp ʾel-ʾeḥāyw*, 'and it came to pass when Joseph arrived where his brothers were'. Such an introduction of an episode in this more explicit fashion may serve here to prepare the reader for a crescendo of activity. (2) The solemn threefold repetition of the name 'Joseph' in v 28, which records the sordid transaction: 'And they drew and lifted *Joseph* out of the pit. And they sold *Joseph* to the Ishmaelites for twenty pieces of silver. And they brought *Joseph* to Egypt.' Certainly three occurrences of the name are hardly needed for participant identification; the repetition has some further function. Here it marks an extremely important and providential event in the family of Jacob and the history of the embryonic nation. (3) The amount of descriptive detail—which is more appropriate to a great moment of a story than to routine narration. Note, for example, the second part of 37:24: 'The pit [was] empty. No water [was] in it.'

I also include under (3) above 37:25 as compared with 37:28a. In the latter we come to a disputed text, subject to varying interpretations and considered by most source critics to be a telltale trace of two original sources. The problem turns largely on the identification of the Midianites in 37:28, 36. On first reading, the phraseology of 37:28a implies to the reader who is a speaker of an Indo-European language that a new group of people is being introduced, distinct from the Ishmaelites which are referred to in 37:25. I suggest, however, that this is primarily a stylistic bias which reflects a difference in discourse structure between languages such as English, German, or French, and Semitic structures. I sketch this argument briefly here.

To begin with, as we will see in chap. 6, "Participant Reference," Biblical Hebrew is extremely circumspect in the identification of new participants (especially minor ones) who are brought into a narrative. Having specifically studied the device of participant introduction, I find it hard to believe that a new group of people (appearing startlingly and unexpectedly on the scene) would be introduced and named in v 28a ('and there passed by Midianites, merchantmen') and *not* be made subject of the next verb. We should expect, 'and they drew out the Midianites and lifted up Joseph out of the pit', or even, 'and the Midianites sold Joseph to the Ishmaelites'—in that the preceding context has led us to expect that the brothers were to sell him. I assume, therefore, that according to normal devices in Hebrew participant reference, the brothers remain the subject of the verbs 'draw out', 'lift', and 'sell' in v 28.

Taking a clue from Judg 8:24—where 'Midianite' invaders are described as 'Ishmaelites'—I consider these two names in 37:25, 28, 36 and 39:1 to refer to the same group of people. Perhaps 'Ishmaelites' was sometimes used as a more generic term (= Bedouin nomad), while 'Midianite' is more specific and ethnic. Note that in 37:36 we are specifically told that the Midianites sold Joseph to Potiphar, while in the recapitulation of this information in 39:1 we are told that the Ishmaelites performed the sale to the same person.

But the question still remains: Why, if the caravan is identified in 37:25, is it renamed and reidentified in 37:28? Here, I believe, we must tie this matter into the fact that 37:23–28 is the Peak of its episode. Suspense and elaboration are characteristic of Peak. Note, moreover, two parallel developments in chap. 37: Joseph is sighted afar off (v 18), becomes the subject of discussion (vv 19–22), and action erupts (vv 23, 24) when Joseph arrives on the scene. Similarly, a caravan of 'Ishmaelites' is sighted afar off (v 25), becomes the subject of discussion (vv 26–7), and action erupts (v 28) when the caravan arrives on the scene. Graphically, the text first applies the term 'Ishmaelites' to the caravan seen from afar, and then on closer view calls them 'Midianite merchants'. Suspense of this sort is appropriate to the high point of a story. I would, therefore, render v 28a as follows: 'And so they passed by, Midianite traders [as they proved to be]; and the brothers drew Joseph up out of the pit, and they sold Joseph to the "Ishmaelites" for 20 pieces of silver.'

The paragraph (at the close of chap. 37) that pictures Jacob's grief is chiastic in structure. In some places in *Joseph* such chiastic units are used to sign off (with a flourish) a major episode. I present this chiasmus in the following diagram:

A and *he tore* Jacob *his clothes*
and *he put sackcloth on* his loins
  B and *he mourned* for his son many days
    C and *they rose up* all his sons and daughters to *comfort* him
    C′ and *he refused* to be *comforted*
  B′ and *he said* 'I will go down to my son *mourning* to Sheol'
A′ and *he bewailed* him his father

3.2.2. Ep₂ (Gen 39:1–6) episode is brief and is structured simply as one Hebrew paragraph—aside from v 1, which *restages* the narrative after the intervening material in chap. 38. On the other hand, while there is a Peak of sorts in this paragraph, it is rather what we would expect in the climax of a discourse rather than of a paragraph. Perhaps since this paragraph is a main (albeit brief) episode of the overall narrative we can expect more elaboration here than is normal for a paragraph per se. Note, for example, the elaborate paragraph setting in v 2 where three clauses build on the verb *hāyâ*, 'to be' (a descriptive verb rather than an event verb). The climax of this paragraph is probably in vv 5 and 6a: (note the elaborate *wayhî* + temporal, which is verse initial): 'And it came to pass from the time that he conferred on him all his house and all his possessions.' It is indeed unusual to have such an elaborate recapitulation paragraph medial; presumably it indicates here that important material is to follow. The balance of the verse contains a paraphrase construction in which we are first told that 'the Lord blessed the Egyptian's house for Joseph's sake', then a paraphrase (with the verb 'bless' nominalized and introduction of *hāyâ*, 'be') goes over the same ground: 'And the blessing of the Lord was upon all that he had, both in the house and in the field.' For that matter, v 6a, 'and he abandoned all that he had to Joseph', etc., may itself be a paraphrase of v 4. Paraphrase and other types of rhetorical underlining are characteristic of discourse peak, both for language in general (Longacre 1983, 1985a) and for Hebrew in particular (Longacre 1979a). Here, paragraph climax in a one-paragraph major episode has features similar to a discourse peak.

    Closure in this episode (39:6b) is unrelated in content to the preceding material. Rather it serves as linkage to what follows (the story of Joseph's ruin): 'Now Joseph was handsome and well proportioned.' Here, as in other places (cf. the ending of a *tôlĕdôt* section by anticipating the content of the next) Hebrew has the structure of continuation, as, for example, a continued drama on radio or television: "Tune in tomorrow same time same station for another chapter in the life of X."

3.2.3. Ep₃ (39:7–23), Joseph's ruin, is not a digression from the main story (cf. Coates 1976). It is rather a complication that plays its part in the ultimate resolution: without the "frame-up" against Joseph and his being put into prison his path would not have crossed with that of the two courtiers—which in turn led to his standing before Pharaoh and his installation as Lord of Egypt. This story has four episodes: (1) Ep$_1$, inciting incident (39:7–10), (2) Ep$_2$, climax or Crisis (39:11–12), (3) Peak, Denouement (39:13–20), and (4) Post-Peak Episode with anticipation of next *main* episode (39:21–23)—all marked with initial *wayhî* constructions.

The Peak of this embedded discourse is marked by multiple retelling of the same (putative) series of events; the reader is kept in suspense until Potiphar's wife gets the ear of her husband. The *wayĕhî* setting (39:13) features the main factual bit that Potiphar's wife used to fabricate her accusation: 'And it came to pass that when she saw that he had left his garment in her hand and he had fled.' She then tells her story and makes her accusation before the men of the house (39:14–15), keeps Joseph's garment as evidence, then retells her story to Potiphar on the latter's arrival. In both cases the punch line is, 'And he left his garment by me and fled [and went] outside' (39:15b, 18b).

The interior climax of the paragraph itself is an embedded paragraph describing Potiphar's reaction. This embedded paragraph starts off with a very involved recapitulation introduced with *wayhî*: 'And it came to pass when heard his [Joseph's] Lord the words of his wife that she said to him saying, "According to these words he did."' Then follows Potiphar's angry and swift reaction: Joseph is degraded and clapped into prison. The detail with which the same ground is gone over repeatedly and summarized is appropriate to the high point of a story rather than to routine narration.

The final incident of this embedded discourse is concerned with how Yahweh caused the captain of the guard house to make Joseph chief trustee among the prisoners. It is a fitting wrap-up and anticipation of what is to follow. I have already commented on the care with which the writer identifies the new locale in which Joseph finds himself (§3.1.3.). There is also another chiastic structure here in this paragraph: It begins and ends with statements concerning Yahweh's help: 'And *Yahweh* was with Joseph. *He* gave him grace in the eyes of the captain of the guard house . . . because *Yahweh* [was] with him. And whatever he did *Yahweh* made [it] prosper.' It contains in its center a statement and paraphrase of that statement regarding delegation of authority to Joseph: '[Statement:] Then the captain of the guard house put Joseph in charge of all the prisoners that were there. [Paraphrase] And whatever was done there he was the doer of it. The captain of the guard house did not see to anything personally.' Ep$_1$ of the main story also terminates with a similar chiastic flourish. In both cases situations are depicted (Jacob's grief, Joseph's position in jail) rather than sequences of events.

3.2.4. Ep₄ (40:1–23) is a brief embedded narrative that perhaps belongs to a special genre, *dream interpretation.*[2] It consists of: Stage (40:1–4), Ep₁ the dreams (40:5), Ep₂ the interpretation (40:6–19), Ep₃ fulfillment (40:20–23). Most of the graphic detail belong to Ep₂. Ep₃ wraps up the embedded narrative, brings together the various strands of participant reference, and directs us back to the central participant, Joseph. At the same time it anticipates the crucial role that Pharaoh is to play in what follows. There is no obvious peak in such a structure, but clearly Ep₃ provides Closure.

3.2.5. Peak and closure also occur within the narrative that expounds peak of the larger structure (chap. 41). This embedded discourse structures as follows: Ep₁, Inciting incident: Pharaoh's dreams (41:1–7); Ep₂, rising tension: no interpreter until the chief cupbearer remembers Joseph (41:8–13); Peak: Joseph interprets Pharaoh's dreams and is installed as Lord of Egypt (41:14–45); Post-peak Ep₁: Joseph's initial policies in the years of plenty (41:46–49); Post-peak Ep₂: birth of Joseph's sons (41:50–54a); Post-peak Ep₃: initial famine relief (41:54b–57).

The Peak episode within this embedded narrative has a markedly sandwich structure whose upper and lower layers consist largely of storyline (i.e., *waw*-consecutive verbs where a wealth of detail is presented as successive actions) and whose middle section consists of the dialogue of Pharaoh and Joseph (in which occurs Joseph's long speech concerning Pharaoh's dream). The crowded action line is typical of peak in many languages. At the same time, the long dialogue culminating in the second longest speech of the entire story embodies features typical of peak in many languages and literatures. Here the framer of the narrative has combined both these features in a masterful synthesis.

Joseph's call to stand before Pharaoh 41:14 is a self-contained unit with six *waw*-consecutives bracketed by the occurrence of the name Pharaoh:

> and he sent *Pharaoh*
> > and he called Joseph
> > and they hurried him from prison
> > and he shaved
> > and he changed his clothing
> and he came in unto *Pharaoh*

[2] Cf. the dream interpretation passages of Daniel, especially chaps. 4 (where the articulation into dream, interpretation, and fulfillment is clear) and 5 (where the cryptic handwriting on the wall appears, is interpreted, and is fulfilled all in the same night). Further chapters of Daniel contain visions that are less specific as to fulfillment.

Likewise, beyond the intervening dialogue there is a similar rush of *waw*-consecutives as Joseph is installed as Lord of Egypt (41:37–45). This chain of *waw*-consecutives gets going with clauses that have to do with Pharaoh and his courtiers: '*And it was good* the word in the eyes of Pharaoh and in the eyes of his courtiers. *And he said* Pharaoh to his courtiers "Shall we find [another] man such as this which the spirit of God [is] in him?"' The onrush of the storyline verbs follow closely on each other as details of Joseph's installation are presented. The only main verb that is not a *waw*-consecutive is found at the end of v 43; it gives the *result* of assigning Joseph the second chariot (or the result of all *waw*-consecutives that precede in 41:41–43), '[thus] he installed him over the land of Egypt', and is not properly a detail of the process of installation. The string of storyline verbs culminates in the only one of which Joseph is the subject (Pharaoh is subject of all the preceding verbs); 'And he went out Joseph [as lord] over all the land of Egypt.' Here the writer has chosen to present the result of the installation as the final verb of the storyline.

The intervening dialogue cannot be treated in detail here. Notice, however, that Pharaoh's account of his dreams as given to Joseph contains a few graphic comments not found in the dreams as narrated at the beginning of the chapter. Thus in 41:19b Pharaoh comments concerning the skinny and emaciated cows, 'I have never seen their likes for ugliness in all the land of Egypt.' He also comments in 41:21 that after the good cattle have 'entered into' the bad cattle 'one wouldn't know that they had entered into their insides, for their appearance [was] as bad as before'.

Joseph's speech (second in length only to Judah's in chap. 44) essentially consists of three points that build progressively on each other: 'I'm explaining X [the dream] to you as a prediction of Y [the famine] that you may implement Z [food conservation measures].' The third point, which is the main thrust of Joseph's speech, is signaled by the use of *wĕ῾attâ*, 'and now'.

Of the three post-peak episodes, the final one (41:54b–57) is markedly chiastic in structure (see diagram on p. 36). Thus, again with a chiastic flourish, ends an exciting and crucial episode of *Joseph*.

3.2.6. The inter-peak episode (the first trip of the brothers to Egypt; chap. 42) does not have clear marking of any part as Peak. Chiasmus, which in preceding episodes has been a feature of closure, here occurs at two places, neither of which is at the end, but both of which report a crucial pronouncement of Joseph. In brief, this is an *episodic* narrative without as much evidence of peak and closure as we have found in preceding episodes. Perhaps, since this is a stretch that lies between two dramatic high points of the story (chaps. 41 and 43–45), we could

 A and there was famine in *all the lands*
  but in all the land of Egypt there was bread
   B and *hungered* all the *land of Egypt*
    C and they cried out the *people* to Pharaoh for *bread*
     D and he said Pharaoh to all Egypt
      go to *Joseph*, whatever he says to you, do it
       (A″ and the famine was on all the face of
       the land)
     D′ and he opened *Joseph* all the stores which were
     in them
    C′ and he sold *grain* to *Egyptians*
   B′ nevertheless, the *famine* was strong in the *land of Egypt*
  A′ and *all the earth* came to buy grain to Joseph for strong was the
  famine in *all the earth*

---

consider that the treatment at this point is intentionally less dramatic. On the other hand, we might better conceive of the dramatic suspense as being held here at a high level *throughout* the narrative instead of being clustered around a peak. In keeping with the latter we can speak metaphorically of chap. 42 as consisting of a high *plateau* between the two peaks. There certainly is no lack of drama in Joseph's recognizing his brothers but in their not recognizing him, in his rough accusation of their being spies, in his throwing them into jail for three days, in their guilty remarks to each other regarding having sold Joseph (all the while not understanding that the Lord of Egypt was Joseph and that he understood their Canaanite language), in Joseph's turning aside to weep, in the general consternation at the discovery of money in their bags, and finally in Jacob's despair and apprehension—which is little helped by Reuben's rather irrational outburst in 42:37.

 Both of Joseph's crucial pronouncements within this section are chiastic. Take, for example, Joseph's speech in 42:14–16 (the other chiasmus is in vv 18–20):

 A it's as I have said to you saying, "You [are] *spies*"
  B in this you will be *tested*: by the life of Pharaoh you
   won't get out of here unless your little brother comes here
    C send *from you* one and let him go get your brother
    C′ *as for* [the rest of] *you*, let you be imprisoned
   B′ and [thus] your words will be *tested*, if truth [be] with you
  A′ and if not, by the life of Pharaoh you [are] *spies*

These pronouncements of Joseph are the crucial information that the brothers carry back to Jacob in Canaan (their report of the second speech to Jacob does not reflect the chiastic structure of the speech as originally given). Chiasmus here in chap. 42 marks two crucial bits of information rather than closure. As can be seen, the inter-peak episode is markedly different in structure from any other previously examined episode in Joseph.

3.2.7. The Peak' episode (brothers' second trip, Joseph reveals himself; 43–45) has the following constituents: Ep$_1$, dialogue with Jacob about the second trip (43:1–14); Ep$_2$, 'the men' and Joseph's steward (43:15–25); Ep$_3$, dining with Joseph (43:26–34); Peak episode, events that lead to the discovery of Joseph's cup in Benjamin's sack and Judah's impassioned speech (44:1–34); Peak' episode, Joseph's self-revelation (45:1–15); Post-peak Ep$_1$, Pharaoh and Joseph send the brothers back to get Jacob and their families (45:16–24); Post-peak Ep$_2$, the brothers carry the good news to Jacob (45:25–28). Post-peak Ep$_2$ has both strophic and chiastic features and again marks closure of a main unit (43–45).

In the Peak episode of this embedded narrative (44:1–13) a crisis is precipitated when Joseph's cup is found in Benjamin's sack. The climax of confrontation is developed and underscored in Judah's speech. The planting of the cup in his sack is described in 44:1–3. The following verse (4) graphically portrays the scene in a depictive departure from the storyline in which *hēm*, 'they', is opposed to *wěyôsēp*, 'Joseph' (the verbs are perfects, not storyline *waw*-consecutives; cf. chap. 4): '*They* had left the city. They hadn't gone far. And *Joseph* said to the one over his house, "Go, pursue these men. Overtake them. And say to them, 'Why have you repaid evil for good.'"' Following this the steward proceeds to overtake the men and to accuse them of theft. The flow of *waw*-consecutives picks up, only to delay a bit before the clause that depicts the fatal discovery (44:11–15), then rushes on to the end of the passage:

> and they hastened
> and they lowered [each man] his sack
> and he searched [the steward]
>> with the oldest began he
>> with the youngest finished he
> and was found the cup in the sack of Benjamin
> and they rent their clothes
> and they loaded [each] man his donkey
> and they returned to the city

Note in the above the consistent use of the *waw*-consecutive in each clause with the exception of the two clauses (inset) that depict with appropriate suspense the course of the search.

The crisis thus depicted leaves us with the following problem that calls for resolution: Benjamin is found guilty of theft punishable by enslavement. Will the older brothers sacrifice him (as they once got rid of Joseph) to save themselves? This is the question to which Joseph felt he must have a negative answer before he can reveal his true identity.

Judah, coming to the fore again (cf. 43:8–10), makes the longest single speech in *Joseph*. The second and third points of this speech are set off by the incidence of *wĕ͑attâ*, 'and now'. Again the points build on each other in such a way that the whole speech can be summarized: 'The background X of this matter [Jacob's loss of Joseph and his extreme love for and anxiety concerning Benjamin] points out a problem Y [Jacob can't survive a second loss and the sons can't endure bringing a fatal grief upon him] that can be resolved only by Z [Judah's offer to remain a slave in Benjamin's place].' That Z (Judah's offer) is the main point (Peak) of his discourse is evidenced by (1) the phasing out of the reported dialogue that characterize points X and Y, (2) resort to a rhetorical question (v 34: 'How can I go up to my father without the lad with me?'), (3) resort to the jussive ('let your servant stay here instead of the lad' and 'let the lad go up to our father'), and (4) the partial forgetting of and phasing out of the honorifics that characterize X and Y (thus 'your servant' goes to 'I' and 'your servant my Father' to 'my Father').

The problem, thus pinpointed by Judah, is now resolved in Peak' of this embedded discourse (itself Peak' of the larger whole). The seesaw dialogue of proposal and counter proposal culminates in Judah's speech— and Joseph reveals his true identity. But the ground is properly laid with due suspense and build-up before the fateful and unbelievable words are uttered (45:1–3):

> and not able was Joseph to control himself anymore before his
>   attendants
> and he cried out, "Let everyone leave me"
> and not remained anyone with him in Joseph's making himself
>   known to his brothers
> and he lifted up his voice in his weeping
> and they heard the Egyptians
> and they heard the house of Pharaoh
> and he said, "I'm Joseph. Is my Father yet alive?"

The final episode of this embedded narrative—the breaking of the news to Jacob (45:25–28)—has a chiastic structure of the sort that characterizes closure of Ep$_1$, Ep$_3$, and Peak. The chiasmus gives closure to Peak' (43–45). The chiasmus coexists, however, with a strophic organization (based on speaker alternation).

SONS: A *and they went up* from Egypt

        and they entered the land of Canaan to Jacob their father

       B and they declared to him saying,

         "*Joseph is yet alive*

        and he is ruler in all the land of Egypt"

JACOB: C and *went numb his heart* for he didn't believe them

SONS: D and they spoke to him all the *words of Joseph* which he had spoken to them

JACOB: D' and he saw carts that *Joseph* had sent to carry

         C' and it *revived the spirit of Jacob their father*

       B' and he said, "Enough! *Joseph is still alive*

     A' *Let me go down.* And I will see before I die."

3.2.8. In Post-peak Ep_1 Jacob and his family move to Egypt, the move itself being found in Ep_1 (46:1–27) of this embedded narrative. Within this episode 46:8–27 seems essentially to be an expansion of 46:6–7: 'And they took their cattle, and all their goods that they had acquired in the land of Canaan. And they came into Egypt, Jacob and all his descendants.' Following this, v 8 initiates a lengthy catalogue: *wĕᵓelleh šĕmôt bĕnê-yiśrāᵓel habbāᵓîm miṣrayĕmâ*, 'And these [are] the names of the sons of Israel who went to Egypt.' The catalogue closes with a summary statement in 46:27b: 'All the people of the house of Jacob who came into Egypt [were] seventy.' Presumably such a catalogue as this constituted a vital piece of information that could scarcely be omitted from such a work as Genesis, which is essentially an annotated genealogy.

But, granted the importance of the passage, is there any special effect achieved by putting this lengthy catalogue at this particular place? Keeping in mind that Peak is marked essentially by a change in pace or character of a narrative, we may speculate that the catalogue of names is here partly by way of contrast with the high moment in the story that follows (Peak: 46:28–30). In this ensuing section Joseph meets his father who has not seen Joseph since he was seventeen:

and Judah [object] sent he on ahead to Joseph to direct [the way] before him to Goshen

   and they came to the land of Goshen

   and he hitched up Joseph his chariot

   and he went up to meet Israel his father to Goshen

   and he appeared to him

   and he fell upon his neck

   and he wept upon his neck for a long time

and he said Israel to Joseph, "Now let me die, now that I've seen you [and know] that you are yet alive!"

One of its most striking features of this graphic and moving passage is the verb *wayyērā*, 'and he appeared Joseph to him' (*r*'*h* is regularly used for the appearance of God. To Jacob, Joseph standing erect in all the splendor of his state chariot ('the second chariot' of 41:43) must indeed have been a wonderful and moving sight. Joseph dismounts and throws himself upon his father's neck and weeps for a long time. Then Jacob utters his *nunc dimittis*.

This Peak episode winds down with a speech of Joseph's instructing his brothers as to what they should say when he presents them to Pharaoh. Two post-peak episodes follow in which five of the brothers and then Jacob are presented to Pharaoh.

3.2.9. Post-peak Ep$_2$ (the last years of Joseph's famine administration; 47:13–27) shifts the interest again to the administrative program of Joseph, which we had briefly glimpsed in 41:54–57. Essentially, the story of the last famine years is depicted as (1) exhaustion of all monetary sources available to the people for buying grain (47:13–14), (2) the sale of all available livestock to purchase food (47:15–17), and (3) the final crunch, a year later (last year of the famine?), when the populace of Egypt have to sign over themselves and their lands in serfdom to Pharaoh as a last desperate measure to obtain grain to eat and seed to sow at the end of the bad time (47:18–26). Plainly, this passage is meant to depict the cumulative desperation of the Egyptian populace during the last two or three of the famine years. The selling of themselves and their lands for food and seed is presented with considerable resort to paraphrase and dialogue. Probably, therefore, 47:18–26 patterns as Peak of this short passage.

This episode concludes with a rather lengthy passage (vv 27–31) that shows by contrast the favored position of the Israelites as compared to the Egyptians, and anticipates the final episode of *Joseph*.

3.2.10. Post-peak Ep$_3$, the last episode of *Joseph* proper (if indeed this is the best way to look at it), is 48:1–22: the blessing of Ephraim and Manasseh, Joseph's sons. Verses 1 and 2 apparently constitute Stage of this embedded narrative, which is a fairly close string of *waw*-consecutives with no obvious breaks except in terms of participant structure and physical movements. Thus, we might distinguish vv 3–7 from vv 8–11, 12–16, and 17–20, with vv 21–22 serving as closure. Gen 48:12–16 is most graphic and detailed as to physical movement and is perhaps the Peak; it also contains the longest section of poetry in the chapter. Perhaps we could consider that 12–16 is Peak (climax) and 17–20 is Peak′ (denouement)—since the latter solves the problem stated in the former (Jacob's crossing his hands in blessing the sons of Joseph).

CHAPTER TWO

MACROSTRUCTURES

If the story of Joseph is to be considered a distinct entity within the overall unity of *tōlĕdôt ya'ăqob*, 'the life and times of Jacob'—as is assumed in this study—then it must be considered to have a macro-structure of its own, that is, an overall meaning and plan (van Dijk 1977: 130–63). This is indeed not hard to demonstrate and is the purpose of this chapter. The story itself contains its own interpretive summary as we shall see in a moment. The macrostructure, however, need to be considered on two levels. One is overtly *given* within the story itself, is perhaps the more didactic, and lends itself to personal applications, while the other must be *deduced* from the story and has to do with the national origins of Israel. In that the former is explicitly given, I shall refer to it as the foregrounded macrostructure while the broader concerns that can be deduced belong rather to what one might term the backgrounded macrostructure. Furthermore, the latter macrostructure, while pervading the *Joseph* story, probably belongs rather to the entire *tōlĕdôt ya'ăqōb* of which the *Joseph* is a part.

Stories cannot and should not give all possible incidents or all the possible actions encompassed in an incident, or all the component motions that constitute an action. To attempt to produce such a story would be to create a product whose excessive length would be more than equalized by its excessive dullness. A story must be selective as to what it includes and what it elaborates if it is to be effective. Macrostructure analysis attempts to make explicit how the overall plan and global purpose of a story exercise a selective control on the incidents that are included and the relative elaboration of detail that characterize the presentation of each incident. The goal of this chapter is to posit macro-structures that can serve as such an (explanatory) control and that can be presumed to have exercised such a control in the composition of the story. Here, as everywhere, discourse analysis insists that the whole legislates the parts, while, in turn, a study of the parts is necessary to the comprehension of the whole. Our argumentation is, therefore, *necessarily circular*. Nevertheless, if we construct our circle with sufficient care so that the overall design and the detail are brought into plausible harmony, our circle is not a vicious one.

1. *Foregrounded macrostructure*

1.1. We are told in the story itself and in an echo of the story in Gen 50:20 that this is a story of *divine providence*. Thus, when Joseph reveals himself to his brothers, he immediately adds (45:5, 7): 'And, now, don't be distressed and don't be angry with yourselves for selling me here, because it was to save lives that God sent me ahead of you. . . . But God sent me ahead of you to preserve for you a remnant on earth and to save your lives by a great deliverance.' Somewhat more succinct is the summary in 50:20: 'You intended to harm me, but God intended it for good to accomplish what is now being done, the saving of many lives.' Putting these together and adding some nouns to make the reference explicit we obtain the following statement of the macrostructure:

> Joseph's brothers, meaning to harm him, sold him into Egypt, but in reality God sent him there so that he could save Jacob's family and many others from death by starvation.

Several elements enter into this macrostructure: (1) the intent of Joseph's brothers to harm him, (2) the selling into Egypt, (3) the divine intent to make Joseph a savior from starvation (and, by implication, the providential measures taken to bring Joseph to power), (4) the salvation of Jacob's family and others, (5) the severity of the famine. Of these, (3) is the dominant element, so thus divine providence *uses* (1) and (2) to accomplish (4) in the face of (5). In the balance of this section, I will trace out the way in which various episodes of *Joseph* are responsive to the macrostructure of the whole.

1.1.1. Ep$_1$ (chap. 37) is the story of the selling of Joseph into Egypt, corresponding to points (1) and (2) of the macrostructure. In launching into the story no time is lost in laying the groundwork for the sordid transaction that eventually takes place. In the opening paragraph (Stage) even as Joseph is being introduced and integrated into the story as the central participant, it is made clear that his brothers hate him; the verb 'hate' is indeed the last storyline verb of the paragraph. The last sentence of the paragraph reports the result of that hatred: 'And they could not speak to him peaceably,' that is, 'They couldn't speak a decent word to him.' The causes of the hatred are presented earlier in the same paragraph: talebearing to his father concerning them, Jacob's obvious favoring of him, and the outrageous gift of a cloak such as only supervisors or men of leisure wear, not common laborers.

The dreams, however, provide the inciting incident for the action that eventually follows. The dreams are two—on successive occasions—and the meaning of the second is even more transparent than the first. Joseph was to say to Pharaoh several years later concerning Pharaoh's dreams (41:32): 'The reason the dream was given to Pharaoh in two forms is that the matter has been firmly decided by God, and God will do it.' Furthermore, Joseph told the dreams on two occasions, thus adding to the resentment on the part of his brothers, who, no doubt, believed that *telling* a dream increased its likelihood of fulfillment. The dreams passage concludes: 'His brothers were jealous of him, but his father kept the thing in mind.' The telling of these dreams sealed Joseph's fate. His brothers now set out (cf. Greek drama at this point) to keep a prophecy from coming true!

The rest of the chapter moves with the inevitableness of a Greek tragedy. The unsuspecting Jacob sends Joseph from the valley of Hebron to Shechem to visit his brothers. On not finding him there—but providentially meeting 'a man' who redirects him to Dothan—Joseph finally catches up with them. Seeing him coming, they have time to hatch up a plot against him before he arrives on the scene. On Reuben's advice, outright murder is discarded in favor of throwing him into a dry cistern to die. The express intention is to frustrate the prophecies given in the dreams: 'then we'll see what becomes of his dreams' (37:20).

Joseph, arriving on the scene, is stripped of his robe and thrown into the pit. The sighting of a caravan of 'Ishmaelites' in the distance leads to still another change of plan. This time, on Judah's suggestion (in the absence of Reuben), it is decided to sell Joseph as a slave into Egypt. The caravan draws up to where they are sitting and Joseph is hauled out of the pit and sold. As already mentioned in chapter 1 the threefold repetition of the name Joseph in v 28 is very striking (smoothed out to one in some English translations, e.g., the NIV). The bell solemnly tolls for Joseph, Jacob's favorite son.

The chapter closes with the cover-up of the crime. Reuben, who had planned to rescue Joseph later, is frantic at the discovery of the empty pit. The cover-up is successful as far as concealing the crime from their father, Jacob, but the excessive and prolonged grief of Jacob is clearly somewhat heavier than the brothers anticipated. On the most obvious level it records the "crime of the century" as far as scandals within the families of the patriarchs. No attempt is made to play down the crime or its disastrous results on Jacob (and on the men themselves?). On the other hand, Joseph's destiny is foreshadowed clearly in the dreams and in the desperate attempt of his brothers to frustrate prophecy. The chapter closes with Joseph sold as a slave into Egypt—which in retrospect proves to be the first stage of his coming to power in that land.

If, as we are explicitly told, this is a tale of divine providence, the overarching *purpose* is evident everywhere. In the providence of God, Joseph "happens" to be sent off alone and unprotected to visit his brothers. Similarly, in the providence of God, Reuben "happens" to be absent when the actual selling of Joseph takes place. And, of course, a caravan "happens" by at just the right time—and the spur-of-the-moment impulse to sell Joseph is carried out. In one devastating clap everything is changed—and, of course, the chief participant (Joseph) has no sure clue as to the end of the drama in which he is involved.

1.1.2. Ep₂ is a brief episode that treats Joseph's initial rise to a position of trust in the house of Potiphar, his Egyptian master. In spite of the brevity of this episode (39:1–6), it contains several unusual features: (1) the remarkable paragraph setting (39:2), which consists of three coordinated *wayhî*, 'and it was', sentences, (2) the occurrence of the divine name *yhwh* five times in this passage (39:2, twice in 39:2d, and twice in 39:5), (3) the unusual paraphrase in 39:5 (*waybārek yhwh*, 'and YHWH blessed', and *wayhî birkat yhwh*, 'and it was the blessing of YHWH') where first a verb is used, then its nominalized counterpart.

The paragraph setting in 39:2 is unusual in that there is no other example in *Joseph* of such a structure; at the most one such *wayhî* clause is found in settings. But here the writer is especially solicitous that we understand immediately the new circumstances in which Joseph finds himself. The first sentence is the key: *wayhî yhwh ʾet-yôsēp*, 'and he was YHWH with Joseph'. The second *wayhî* clause tells us that 'he was a prosperous man' and the third tells that 'he was in the house of his master, the Egyptian'. (He *could* have been just a field hand.)

Likewise, the occurrence five times of the divine name *yhwh* is very striking. This divine name occurs, in fact, at only one other place in the entire story (see next episode). Both places where *yhwh* occurs are at the darkest moments of Joseph's life. Here in this episode Joseph, rudely rejected by his brothers and callously sold by them, finds himself abandoned in Egypt. 'But YHWH was with him'—not just *God*, but God in his more involved, particularistic, and covenant-keeping aspects.

Finally, I have noted the unusual paraphrase consisting of a verb and its corresponding nominalized form: 'and YHWH blessed him' and 'the blessing of YHWH was upon him' (where 'him' refers to the Egyptian and all that he had). Such a paraphrase clearly indicates a point considered to be worthy of reinforcement and underlining. This is also indicated by the unusual backreference at the beginning of 39:5: 'And it happened that from the time that he appointed him over all his house and over all that he had'. This echoes v 4b and prepares us for the main clause, 'and YHWH blessed the house of the Egyptian on account

of Joseph'—which, in turn, is paraphrased as described in the next
sentence.

What then? All these features seem to be responsive to element (3)
of the macrostructure (God's providence). YHWH, the God of his people, is with Joseph at the darkest moment of his life: he causes Joseph to
prosper in the house of the Egyptian. He peculiarly blesses the Egyptian
master in proportion as he promotes and honors Joseph.

1.1.3. In Ep$_3$ (39:7–23), the account of Joseph's sexual harassment on
the job and ruin through false accusation, the relevant tie-in to the main
plot is not indicated until toward the end. Short of that, it "happened"
that the wife of Potiphar was sexually attracted to the young and hand-
some Hebrew slave (39:7). It also "happened" that the day came when he
was in the house alone with her and she could press her designs (39:11–
12). That such matters are embraced in an overall Providence seems
implicit in the account but is not explicitly pointed out. If the selling of
Joseph into Egypt was to be good-coming-out-of-intended-harm, so this
action on the part of Potiphar's wife can no doubt be so interpreted.

The action of the scene is portrayed quickly, then retold twice by
the woman as a 'he-tried-to-force-me' story. Joseph's initial reply to
her, 'How can I do this great evil and sin against God?' (by violating
Potiphar's confidence; 39:8–9), is in keeping with his all-pervading God
consciousness so clearly represented in the story. In the end, after the
scorned woman has vented her fury, the narrative points out that Joseph
is put into the guard house (*bêt hassōhar*), 'the place where the king's
prisoners were kept imprisoned' (39:20). This anticipates the following
episode where the significance of this locality will become evident.

This embedded narrative has a post-peak episode that again starts
off with the sentence: *wăhî yhwh ʾet-yôsēp*, 'and YHWH was with
Joseph'. YHWH is the unstated subject of the next two verbs as well:
'And he extended him grace/covenant-love. And he gave him favor in
the eyes of the warden.' The passage ends up: 'Inasmuch as YHWH
[was] with him. And whatsoever he did, YHWH made it prosper.' YHWH
is mentioned three times here—and never again in the balance of the
story. Once more, as in two other dark hours in Joseph's life, the covenant God of his father is represented as giving him special interest and
protection. The result is by now somewhat predictable. As he rose in
Potiphar's house so now he rises to the status of the foremost trustee
among the prisoners.[1] Again, the providential care of God is the con-
trolling motif.

---

[1] What is not immediately evident is that his old master Potiphar is still
in charge of things. In 40:3 the prison is called the 'house of the captain of the

1.1.4. In Ep₄ (chap.40) Joseph interprets the dreams of two imprisoned courtiers of Pharaoh, thereby opening for himself the pathway to the throne of Pharaoh (after due delay and frustration, 40:23). I comment elsewhere (chap. 6, §5.5) on the careful way in which the two courtiers, the chief cupbearer and the chief baker, are introduced. These men, who were responsible for putting wine and bread on the king's table, were no ordinary prisoners. The intersection of their fortunes with Joseph's is carefully portrayed: 'And he [Pharaoh] put them in prison, in the house of the captain of the guard, the "tower," the very place where Joseph was kept. And he, the captain of the guard, entrusted Joseph with them. And Joseph looked after their needs' (40:3–4).

The dreams of the courtiers provide the opening that Joseph needs. The introduction of the dreams into the story emphasizes that the dreams have meaning for the two men involved: 'And the two of them, the cupbearer and the baker of the king of Egypt who were imprisoned in the tower, both dreamed dreams in the same night: each according to the interpretation of his dream so dreamed him.' In undertaking to hear and interpret the dreams, Joseph ascribes the power to interpret dreams to God (40:8b) in keeping with his pervasive God consciousness. He then interprets their dreams to mean that the cupbearer will be restored to his position in three days but the baker will be beheaded and impaled. At the end of his interpretation of the cupbearer's dream he puts in a tactfully worded request: 'No, I don't want a reward. Rather, when all's well with you again, please do me a favor. Please remember me to Pharaoh and do something to get me out of this place. For I was kidnapped from the land of the Hebrews. And even here I've not done anything that they should put me in this hole.' Thus runs the plea of a man not "in the know" of what God is doing—however nicely the story reads in retrospect.

The ending of this embedded narrative describes the fulfillments of the dreams. Pharaoh, as part of his birthday celebration, brings the two courtiers out of prison and judges their cases—disposing of them precisely when and how Joseph had predicted. But, we are told, the cupbearer once restored to favor 'didn't remember Joseph, but rather forgot him' (40:23).

This episode rather exquisitely pinpoints the contrast between the above-the-story and within-the-story points of view. We stand with the

---

guard/Lord High Executioner' (*śar haṭṭabbāḥîm*), which is Potiphar's title in 37:36 and 39:1. Evidently 'the tower' where the king's prisoners were kept was on Potiphar's estate. Presumably, however, the warden (39:21–23) intervened between Potiphar and Joseph—who may or may not have ever seen Potiphar again after his degradation.

narrator above the story and realize that God is working things out for
Joseph, for his family, and for the preservation of everyone in that part
of the world from famine. On the other hand, the narrator portrays
Joseph as *within* the story suffering degradation, disgrace, imprisonment,
and callous indifference on the part of a man whom he had just helped
in an hour of need but who forgot his promise as soon as the crisis was
past.

1.1.5. The Peak (chap. 41) is the story of Joseph's ascension to
power—a meteoric rise from prisoner to grand vizier of Egypt. The
stage of the story describes Pharaoh's dreams beginning with *wayhî
miqqēṣ šěnātayim yāmîm ûparᶜōh ḥōlēm*, 'And it happened, that at the
end of two full years Pharaoh too had dreams!' This opening sentence
stresses that two full years went past during which Joseph felt abandoned and forgotten, then it was Pharaoh's turn (in the providence of
God) to have dreams! Finally, after all the soothsayers and wisemen of
Egypt had confessed their inability to interpret Pharaoh's dreams, the
cupbearer rather hesitantly and disdainfully mentions Joseph. Prefacing
his remarks with 'I do remember my sins this day' (i.e., my period of
disfavor with Pharaoh), he goes on to mention the dreams that he and
the chief baker had in prison. Then he adds: 'And there was with us there
a Hebrew lad, a slave to the captain of the guard. We told him our
dreams. And he interpreted them for us, each man's dream according to
its interpretation. And as he interpreted to us, so it happened. Me you
restored to my place and him you hanged' (41:9–13).

I have commented in chapter 1 concerning 41:14–45, which is one
of the most dramatic points of the story. There is no need to cover that
ground again. In summary, the cupbearer's account concerning 'the
Hebrew lad' was quite sufficient for Pharaoh to send in haste for Joseph.
Before Joseph has time to know what is transpiring he is washed up,
shaved, and dressed for his presentation to Pharaoh. Pharaoh in turn
wastes no words in getting to the point: 'I've dreamed a dream and there
is not one to interpret it. But I've heard of you that you listen to
accounts of dreams, and interpret them.' Joseph's answer is again a
disclaimer of personal prowess or wisdom: 'It's not in me to do it
[*bilᶜādāy*]. God will give Pharaoh the answer he craves [*ᵓělōhîm yaᶜăneh
ᵓet-šělôm parᶜōh*].' This disclaimer is in keeping with Joseph's words to
the courtiers in 40:8b and even somewhat similar to the remark at the
end of 39:9 ('How can I . . . sin against God?').

In the rest of this interchange, Pharaoh tells Joseph his (twofold)
dreams and Joseph interprets it. In interpreting the dreams Joseph considers himself to be a spokesman for God. Thus in 41:25b Joseph says:
'God has revealed to Pharaoh that which he is about to do.' Much same

words are given in 41:28: 'This is just what I've already said to Pharaoh: God has shown Pharaoh what he is about to do.' In 41:32 the interpretation proper ends with the words: 'The matter has been firmly decided by God and he will soon put it into operation.' This is followed by a preliminary sketch of a food conservation and famine relief program. On finishing, Pharaoh himself is convinced that a supernatural power has spoken through Joseph: 'Where can we find another such man as this in whom is the spirit of God (or 'of the gods')?'

All this is quite in keeping with the macrostructure constraint that Joseph is 'sent ahead' (45:5) of his brothers to provide for them in a special contingency. When Joseph finally sends word to Jacob his father in 45:9, he says, 'God has made me lord of all Egypt.' Consequently, the interpretation of the dreams of Pharaoh is represented as per divine inspiration (*rûaḥ ʾĕlōhîm*) not as a triumph of ratiocination on Joseph's part.

The installation of Joseph as grand vizier is summarized in a quickly moving passage 41:37-45 culminating in the words: 'And Joseph went out [as lord] over the land of Egypt.' This is followed by three episodes that deal with: (1) Joseph's grain collection and storage during the years of plenty (41:46-49), (2) the birth of Joseph's sons, Manasseh and Ephraim (41:50-54a), and (3) the first year or so of the famine (41:54b-57).

In all this, both here and in the previous main episodes (Ep_2–Ep_4), the story has dealt exclusively with Joseph and his varying fortunes in Egypt. The story must now proceed to develop point (4) of its macrostructure: the salvation of Jacob's family. In this respect there are items of interest in the last two episodes of the embedded narrative here under consideration. In 41:50-53, where Joseph's first son is born, he calls him Manasseh because of a phonological resemblance to the verb 'forget'; Joseph's comment is: 'God has made me forget all my toil and the house of my father.' He calls his second son Ephraim (resembling the word for 'fruitful') with the comment: 'God has made me fruitful in the land of my affliction.' Perhaps the names given to his sons indicate a certain disposition on Joseph's part to settle down in Egypt and forget all the unpleasant and painful past. But the third of these episodes (41:54b-57) sets the stage for the eventual reunion of the family. This is evident in v 57: 'And all the world came to Egypt to buy food from Joseph for the famine was very strong in all the lands.'

As we have commented before, Joseph is *in* the story while we along with the narrator are *above* the story. If I am correct in seeing in the names that Joseph gave his sons a certain disposition to settle down in Egypt and forget the painful past, then the next wave of divine providence will catch him somewhat by surprise, if not off-balance.

1.1.6. The interpeak episode (chap. 42) maintains itself at a consistently high level of dramatic tension (as suggested in chap. 1). It occurs between the climax of Joseph's rise to power and the denouement of Joseph's revelation of himself to his brothers. It is the story of the first descent of the brothers to Egypt. They get the food that they came to buy and return (minus Simeon) to Canaan. Already the providential goal of preservation of the family from starvation is being met, but the estrangement remains.

What does Joseph's harassment of his brothers have to do with the macrostructure of the story? We can, of course, have resort again to the argument that Joseph who is *in* the story cannot be expected to know the end from the beginning. His harassment of his brothers is for him a necessary expedient. He cannot trust himself to them until he knows that they are trustworthy. In his dreams the brothers had done obeisance to him (as he recalls in 42:9) but the sudden fulfillment of this (in his brothers' appearing and groveling before him as supplicants for grain) is not in itself reassuring. He must know, for example, how they would act towards the remaining younger brother Benjamin if a crisis arose. Hence the centrality of Joseph's demand that they bring along Benjamin on their next trip. Not only did Joseph long to see his only full brother but he felt he had to observe and know how the older brothers would treat him. At this point, Benjamin becomes, in fact, an *echo* or *reflection* of Joseph himself for the purposes of this part of the story.

But the tie-in to the macrostructure can be shown to be somewhat closer. While the first point of the macrostructure, the intent of Joseph's brothers to harm him, may be providentially reconcilable with (3) the divine providential intent to save the family and with (4) the actual salvation of the family, nevertheless the stubborn fact of (2) remains: The older brothers have callously sold their younger brother as a slave. The problem in human relations, *trauma* and resultant *rift*, must be somehow worked out. What chap. 42 (interpeak episode) and chaps. 43 and 44 (as part of 43–45, denouement) portray is the testing that must precede the reconciliation. Without some such process as Joseph put his brothers through could there have been a genuine reconciliation? And does not the macrostructure imply and require such a reconciliation? Would mere salvation from physical starvation (macrostructure points 4 and 5) have been sufficient if the family of Jacob had been left at odds with each other?

Note also the specific touch in the scene portrayed in 42:21–24. Here the guilt of the brothers comes to the surface and at least remorse (possibly repentance) is seen at work in them. As Joseph tightens the screw to the next twist—insisting on keeping Simeon imprisoned and on their bringing Benjamin on the next trip—the brothers blurt out to each other: 'Surely we are guilty concerning out brother. We saw the distress of his soul when he pleaded with us, and we wouldn't listen. Therefore this distress has come upon us' (42:41). Reuben puts in his I-told-you-so: 'Didn't I tell you not to sin against the lad, but you wouldn't listen to me. And now we're held responsible for his death' (42:22). The narrator goes on to add they didn't realize that Joseph understood Canaanite (since he always spoke through an interpreter), and that Joseph was compelled to find a place alone where he could weep (42:23-24). Here the narrator graphically portrays the process of reconciliation at its mid-phase. A final touch: Joseph restores to his brothers the money for their grain purchase; he really couldn't bring himself to accept the payment from them—although the finding of the money in the sacks only added to the brothers' confusion and insecurity.

1.1.7. In Peak' (denouement, chaps. 43-45), the final testing of the brothers results in Judah's impassioned plea that he be allowed to remain a slave in place of Benjamin and in Joseph's revealing himself to his brothers. The general reaction of the brothers to Joseph's planting the cup in Benjamin's sack and Judah's reaction in particular remove all doubts from Joseph's mind concerning the present integrity of his brothers. However they had acted in the past, they will never again abandon or betray a younger brother or even be jealous of the doting favors of an old man on his youngest son. All that remains is for Joseph to reveal himself to them and convince them of *his* forgiveness. This he proceeds to do with the bombshell words, 'I am Joseph. Is my father yet alive?' (45:3), which are in turn followed by, 'And now, don't be distressed and don't be angry with yourselves for selling me here, because it was to save lives that God sent me ahead of you' (45:5). Admittedly, the brothers were not entirely convinced of Joseph's forgiveness, for we read in 50:15-21 of their need for further reassurance in this regard after Jacob's death. Nevertheless, the initial reconciliation takes place here and most of the loose ends of the story are sewn up. Gen 45:14-15 continues the picture of the reconciliation scene: 'Then he fell upon his brother Benjamin's neck and wept. And Benjamin wept on his neck. Then he kissed all his brothers and wept upon them. And after that his brothers talked with him for a while.'

Joseph's remarks in 45:5-8 and 50:19-21 also reveal that the central participant of the story has now caught up with its unfolding macrostructure. Enough of the story has gone past that he now, like the narrator and us, can stand above the story and view it as a whole. So, as we have seen, it is from these remarks of Joseph that we obtain in semifinished form the statement of the macrostructure.

One important loose end of the story, however, is yet to be sewn up: Jacob does not know yet that Joseph is alive. Hence Joseph's concern, immediately evident in the words: 'I am Joseph. Is my father yet alive [or, have you been deceiving me with this talk of your father?]' (45:3). Likewise, as soon as he finished explaining the continuing famine and his own power as economic czar, he adds: 'Hurry now and go up to my father and tell him: "Thus says your son Joseph: God has made me Lord of all Egypt. Come down to me. Don't delay."' (45:9). This is carried out by the brothers in 45:25–28 where in a passage of rare beauty and power, Jacob's reception of the news is depicted.

But what of Gen 45:16–20, where Pharaoh intervenes to be sure that Joseph gives the proper red carpet treatment to the little band that is to emigrate to Egypt from Canaan? How does this fit into the whole? Perhaps, in terms of the strict macrostructure of the story the aim of this paragraph is to demonstrate the fulness to which the "salvation" of Jacob and his clan is brought: They are to be greatly favored of Pharaoh in keeping with his fondness for Joseph. But here, the strict concerns of the *Joseph* story fade into the broader concerns of the whole clan—as becomes evident in the ensuing three post-peak episodes that I have (perhaps somewhat arbitrarily) assigned to *Joseph* rather than simply to part of the surrounding *tôlĕdôt*.

1.1.8. In Postpeak Ep$_1$ (46:1–47:12) Jacob and his clan emigrate to Egypt. The devastating loss of Joseph and the emotional trauma suffered by Jacob as recorded at the end of chap. 37 are reversed and healed here. Jacob pronounces his *nunc dimittis* (46:30): 'Now let me die, since I've seen your face and know that you're still alive.' The presentation of the brothers (47:1–6) and Jacob to Pharaoh (47:7–10) is perhaps a continuation of the "salvation" theme, as is also the note of the settlement of Jacob's clan in one of the most fertile parts of the delta where they will live as pensioners of Joseph and Pharaoh. Undoubtedly here also broader concerns are coming to the fore. We can scarcely appreciate Exod 1:8 ('Now there arose a new king over Egypt, a king that didn't know [recognize, appreciate] Joseph') without this background concerning Israel's favored position under the Pharaoh of Joseph's time.

1.1.9. In Postpeak Ep$_2$ (47:13–31) another loose end of the Joseph story is sewn up: What about Joseph's continued famine relief during the last five years of the bad time? For one thing, this is the one place where point (5) of the macrostructure, the severity of the famine, is graphically portrayed. The picture here is of a Joseph who played Pharaoh's game to the hilt. Successively the Egyptians lose their money, their livestock, their lands, and their liberty in exchange for bread. Egypt is reduced to serfdom by the end of the famine. Only the priests of Egypt—and Jacob's little clan—are exempt from these pressures. Israel dwelt in Egypt and prospered as royal pensioners (as did also the priests to whom Joseph was personally related by marriage). In contrast to the Egyptians, who were reduced to serfdom, the descendants Israel 'gained possessions, and were fruitful and multiplied exceedingly'. Were the seeds of future ethnic jealously sown right here?

This episode loosely appends a section regarding Jacob's imminent death and his causing Joseph to swear that he will bury him in Canaan. This is largely transitional in respect to what follows.

1.1.10. In Postpeak Ep₃ (48:1–22) (if indeed I am right in considering it part of *Joseph*) Joseph's two sons are blessed by Jacob. The birth of the two sons is recorded in 41:50–52 in a peculiarly structured paragraph. There, while the birth of the first born, Manasseh, is presented as the major event of the paragraph, contrastive focus is thrown on Ephraim as the second son. And at the blessing of the two sons by their grandfather Jacob, the younger son Ephraim is singled out for preeminence. In a sense, then, chap. 48 is working out some vague implications given in 41:50–52.

Verses 13 and 14 of this chapter are very explicit in terms of the physical movements on the part of Joseph and Jacob: 'And Joseph took them both, Ephraim in his right hand toward Israel's left hand, and Manasseh in his left towards Israel's right hand. And he drew near to him. But Israel stretched out his right hand and laid it upon the head of Ephraim, the younger, and his left hand upon the head of Manasseh— and Manasseh was the older.' The blessing then immediately follows. Joseph, thinking his blind father to be confused, tries to change Jacob's hands but Jacob insists that the younger, Ephraim, was to be the greater. This deals plainly with concerns that outrun the Joseph story narrowly defined, although (as previously explained) all this helps to illuminate 41:50–52, which is assuredly part of that story. All of which brings us indeed to raise the problem of the place of these broader concerns in the structure of *Joseph*. Since *Joseph* is embedded within—or intertwined with—the *tōlĕdôt yaˤăqōb*, are the concerns of the broader picture properly relevant to the macrostructure of *Joseph* also? This brings us to the second major point of this chapter.

2. *Backgrounded macrostructure*

Within the *tōlĕdôt yaˤăqōb*, chap. 49 contains Jacob's blessings on the twelve tribes: vv 3–27, the blessing itself, constitute 25 verses, of which five refer to Judah and five to Joseph, that is, 40 percent of the total. By contrast the other sons of Jacob are typically passed over with one or two verses each. Judah as fourth in line is given preeminence in that the "blessings" on Reuben, Simeon, and Levi, the three older than he, are more negative than positive. All the other blessings (vv 13–21) are positive, but somewhat perfunctory, until we come in vv 22–26 to the blessing on Joseph.

In this chapter, which is probably the peak of the *tōlĕdôt yaʿăqōb* (which is in turn the high point of Genesis), we have a glimpse of the embryonic nation—with the Judah and Joseph tribes destined to have preeminence in the south and north respectively. It is, therefore, no accident that the three prominent participants in the *tōlĕdôt yaʿăqōb* are Jacob, Joseph, and Judah. Nor is it an accident that a chapter like 38 is included, where a vital piece of Judah's family history is told. Nor should it be surprising that *Joseph* itself has the same three central participants. In a very real sense, all this is the story of Joseph, Jacob, and Judah. Other participants clearly take the secondary place—although locally thematic at certain parts of the story.

I therefore raise the question: Is there in the background of Joseph a further macrostructure (probably shared with the *tōlĕdôt yaʿăqōb*) that treats clan origins and dominance? Conceivably this backgrounded macrostructure could co-exist with the foregrounded one just described. I think that this is precisely the case. The backgrounded macrostructure can be summarized as follows: *Among the descendants of Jacob, Joseph and Judah are to be preeminent both as individuals and as tribes.* I deal first with the preeminence of Judah, then with the preeminence of Joseph.

2.1. Reuben, as firstborn, should have had the natural preeminence among the sons of Jacob. The story represents him as gradually loosing ground before the superior capacity of Judah. Thus, in the selling of Joseph (chap. 37) Reuben has a plan to save Joseph by having him put in a pit from which Reuben can later rescue him. Reuben is initially successful in saving Joseph from outright murder. But—presumably while Reuben is away on an errand—Judah frustrates his plan by suggesting that they sell Joseph to the traders and by persuading the brothers to carry out the transaction. In all this Reuben acted responsibly as the eldest son—but not with sufficient vigor to save Joseph from slavery. He did not openly advocate returning Joseph to Jacob, but hoped to accomplish this end by stealth. Consequently, in this the supreme crisis in Jacob's family, the oldest son failed and in the end felt constrained to go along with the coverup suggested by the other brothers. His outburst of frustration and grief on finding Joseph gone is perhaps typical of the man and is at least partially selfish: 'The lad is gone. And as for me, where shall I go' (37:30).[2]

---

[2] It seems to me to be much more natural to see in this incident the working out of the above mentioned macrostructure than to believe that we have here a somewhat awkward joining of a "Reuben account" with a "Judah account."

Reuben, Judah, and all the other brothers of Joseph are off stage in Episodes $_{2-4}$ and in the Peak. In the interpeak episode (chap. 42) they are on stage once more, and Reuben is mentioned explicitly twice in the chapter: first, when in front of Joseph, he reminds his brothers how he had advocated not harming 'the lad' and, second, on return to Canaan when he ineffectually tries to persuade Jacob that Benjamin must go with them on their next trip to Egypt to buy grain. The latter contains another emotional outburst of Reuben (in speaking to Jacob): 'You may kill my two sons if I don't bring him [Benjamin] back to you.' As if a grandfather would be glad to see two of his grandchildren killed because he had lost a son! (In this same incident Simeon is singled out for detention in Egypt by Joseph. As next in order of primogeniture from Reuben, Simeon should have been a candidate for preeminence. Actually, however, he is entirely passive in the story and is on stage more as a prop than as a participant. It may also be that he was one of the ringleaders of the conspiracy to dispose of Joseph and was therefore a natural one for detention.) Perhaps all this is quite congruent with Jacob's description of Reuben as 'unstable as water, you will not have preeminence' (49:4) and of Simeon (and Levi) as men of violence 'weapons of violence are their swords' (49:5ff.). At any rate, in the episodes of the story so far considered, Reuben is not proving effectual as a leader, Simeon is not in the running, and Levi is not even mentioned. This leaves the way clear for Judah, the fourth in line, to come to the fore.

Judah comes to the fore in chaps. 43–45, the Peak (Denouement) of *Joseph*. To begin with, when the grain purchased in Egypt has run out, it is Judah who finally persuades Jacob that they must take Benjamin with them on the second trip (43:3–10). Judah accomplishes this by personally going surety for Benjamin: 'I will go surety for him, from my hand you shall require him. If I don't bring him back to you, if I don't set him before you, then I shall bear the guilt of it before you all my days' (43:9).

In chap. 44 after the debacle in which the (planted) cup is found in Benjamin's sack and the brothers return in desolation and despair to Joseph's house, they are referred to as 'Judah and his brothers' (44:14)— since Judah proves to be the spokesman in the crisis (vv 16 and 18ff.). This leads to Judah's impassioned plea in 44:18–34 (the longest speech in the story). A careful examination of this speech shows that Judah is not concerned for Benjamin merely on account of his having gone surety for him, but above all for the effect that this additional sorrow might have on the old man, already shattered by the loss of Joseph. The speech eloquently winds up with the words: 'For how can I go up to my father without the lad's accompanying me—lest I see the calamity that will come upon my father' (44:43). Judah is here represented as having arrived at a moral earnestness and sacrificial responsibility that qualifies him for preeminence. To offer to stay as a slave in place of Benjamin was an offer that for all he knew he would be called upon to implement!

A final detail is found in 46:28, the account of Jacob's descent into Egypt. Here Jacob sends Judah on ahead to Joseph to arrange for the details concerning the long-delayed reunion of Jacob and Joseph. Evidently the old man Jacob had come to rely on Judah for tasks of special importance.

2.2. As central participant in the story here under analysis, Joseph is obviously preeminent. He is represented as the divinely appointed instrument for the salvation of his people. The birth of his sons calls for very special comment in 41:50–52 (cf. the coverage given to Judah's family in chap. 38). Furthermore, in the end Jacob adopts them as his own, so that there is no tribe of Joseph as such but rather the tribes of Ephraim and Manasseh (chap. 48)—with the former the more populous and powerful. Curiously enough, however, after the blessing on Ephraim and Manasseh in 48, Joseph is himself singled out for the blessing in 49:22–26:

> Joseph is a fruitful vine,
>> a fruitful vine near a spring,
>> whose branches climb over a wall.
> With bitterness archers attacked him;
>> they shot at him with hostility.
> But his bow remained steady,
>> his strong arms stayed limber,
> because of the hand of the Mighty One of Jacob,
>> because of the Shepherd, the Rock of Israel,
>> because of your father's God, who helps you,
> because of the Almighty, who blesses you
> with blessings of the heavens above,
>> blessings of the deep that lies below,
>> blessings of the breast and womb.
> Your father's blessings are greater
>> than the blessings of the ancient mountains,
>> than the bounty of the age-old hills.
> Let all these rest on the head of Joseph,
>> on the brow of the prince among his brothers (NIV).

And so the Joseph tribes, Ephraim and Manasseh, came to be the core of the northern kingdom. Years afterwards a psalmist was to write (77:15):

> You did with you arm redeem your people,
> the sons of Jacob and Joseph (NIV).

TEXTLINGUISTIC AND SOCIOLINGUISTIC ANALYSIS

PART 2
INTRODUCTION

Traditionally, within a grammar of a given language all the uses of each tense/aspect or mode of a language are listed and described en bloque in the same section of the grammar. Thus, for Biblical Hebrew the Gesenius-Kautzsch-Cowley grammar (1910) devotes five pages to the use of the perfect, six pages to the use of the imperfect, a page or two each to the cohortative and jussive, then nine pages to the imperative, some four pages to the imperfect with the *waw*-consecutive, and finally further pages to the infinitives and participles.

Part 2 of this volume is, among other things, a challenge to this time-honored way of describing the functions of the verb forms of a verb system within a language. Rather, I posit here that (*a*) every language has a system of discourse types (e.g., narrative, predictive, hortatory, procedural, expository, and others); (*b*) each discourse type has its own characteristic constellation of verb forms that figure in that type; (*c*) the uses of given tense/aspect/mood form are most surely and concretely described in relation to a given discourse type. These assumptions inform chapters 3, 4, and 5 of this volume, where they are illustrated in regard to narrative, predictive, expository, and hortatory discourse.

The constellation of verb forms that figure in a given discourse type are structured so that one or more privileged forms constitute the mainline or backbone of each type, while other forms can be shown to encode progressive degrees of departure from the mainline. This is developed empirically in chapter 3 in regard to narrative discourse and the verb forms that characterize it. Here the *waw*-consecutive imperfect is seen to be mainline in that it is punctiliar and sequential in function; the perfect is found to be (as a whole) a non-punctiliar and non-sequential kind of past tense in narrative; the imperfect and the participles are, respectively, implicitly and explicitly durative in the framework of the story; *hāyâ* clauses and verbless clauses represent static elements toward the bottom of the scheme; and negated clauses rank lowest.

In regard to these various matters, Biblical Hebrew can be shown more and more to be a rather run-of-the-mill example of a language with a special narrative or "consecutive" tense—a statement that can be easily documented in regard to the narrative structures of a variety of African languages (cf. Longacre, in press). Some of the latter have consecutive forms that necessarily depend on a special initial form that must precede them; other such languages simply have a special consecutive form that need not have a special initial form to initiate the chain in narrative. Biblical Hebrew belongs to the latter type of language, but has traditionally been described as if it belongs to the former type. Thus the legend has grown up that a *waw*-consecutive imperfect simply continues on after a perfect that necessarily initiates the chain, while a *waw*-consecutive perfect must similarly follow an imperfect (or some other tense/aspect/mood form).

Some further assumptions characterize this part of the volume: (*d*) Once the verb forms that characterize a given discourse type are plotted according to the mainline of that type and progressive degrees of departure from the mainline, then local spans of text that are identifiable as that discourse type can be analyzed so that the relative structural importance of a given sentence is determined by the rank of its main verb (not verbs in relative or adverbial clauses). In brief, relative height in the rank scheme determines relative salience in the local span. (*e*) A structural unit, the paragraph (not necessarily coextensive with orthographic indentation-bounded paragraphs), is posited as intermediary between sentence and discourse, and a system of paragraph types (described elsewhere) is used to facilitate the description. (*f*) A system of logical relations or notional categories is assumed to underline the paragraph (as well as most non-simple sentences).

Applying (*a*), (*b*),and (*c*) above to Biblical Hebrew, one can construct the following argument: (1) For Biblical Hebrew we must (at least) distinguish narrative (N), predictive/procedural (P), hortatory (H), and expository (E) texts and paragraphs. (2) Within each of these types the verb forms/clauses used in that type can be arranged on a scale from the most relevant (mainline) in that discourse type, down to the type of verb/clause that is least relevant. In Hebrew narrative discourse the scale is one of most dynamic to most static—with the preterite (*waw*-consecutive with the imperfect) as the most dynamic and the nominal/verbless clause as the most static. (3) Once such a scale is posited, we then approach a paragraph as follows: Is it N, P, H, or E? Resorting to the correct verb ranking scheme, we ask of each sentence: What is the relative rank of its main verb? Then, in analyzing the internal structure of the paragraph, we give highest relative rank in the paragraph to the sentence(s) with the highest ranking verb according to (*d*) above.

Consider for example, the following illustrative English paragraph (sentences are numbered for convenience of reference):

(1) I was walking along the sidewalk down a few doors from my house yesterday. (2) I saw a dog coming along towards me. (3) Suddenly the dog put his teeth into my leg. (4) That dog, I learned later, had bitten three people previously the same day.

The simple past tense ranks highest in English narrative (unless a story is told in the historical present). Therefore, sentences (2) and (3) outrank (1), which has a past progressive verb, and (4) which has a pluperfect verb in its main clause. In addition (3) outranks (2) because in English action verbs terminating in an object outrank motion verbs. Therefore, the sentences in this paragraph rank (3)-(2)-(4)-(1) in order of dominance. A paragraph analysis must take this into account. Thus, (3) must be made the *Text* of the paragraph with (2) as *Introduction* of the dog relative to (3). In turn, (4) is a *Comment* on sentences (3) plus (2), while (1) functions as *Setting* to (2), (3), and (4).

As for (*e*) above, the concept of paragraph is focal in organizing the constituent structure of a discourse. To the notion of paragraph must be added, however, the notion of embedded discourse, since discourses are often, in effect, constituted by smaller discourses that develop episodes/ points of the main discourse. An embedded discourse often lacks the features of aperture and closure that are typical of unembedded discourse in that the structure of the embedded discourse is, in a sense, parasitic to that of the main discourse. Simple texts are straightforward sequences of component paragraphs—as are texts on the lowest layer of embedding in the nested arrangement of embedded discourses.

Paragraphs are also recursive units, so that one paragraph is found embedded in another, often down to multiple layers of embedding. In a language such as English (but not as markedly in Biblical Hebrew), the sentence is also a highly recursive unit in which one sentence type embeds in part of another sentence, down to several successive layers of embedding.

Once we allow for recursion in both discourse and paragraph there is no need to posit further units such as chapters and sections (between discourse and paragraph) or "sentence clusters" (within paragraphs). Some chapter divisions are orthographic and visual; others are structural, that is, they articulate episodes of a story or points of an argument. Likewise we need to distinguish orthographic and visual paragraphs (which break up the monotony of the solid page) from structural paragraphs. The viewpoint of this volume is: In any discourse, a group of paragraphs that hang together by virtue of cohesion and/or coherence can be shown to have the structure of an (embedded) discourse of a recognizable type. Likewise, within *any* paragraph, any group of sentences that go together by virtue of cohesion and/or coherence can be shown to have the structure of an (embedded) paragraph of a recognizable type. On these premises there are no tag ends. (At this point, I remind the reader again that an extensive constituent structure display of *Joseph* is available in Part 4.)

The paragraph types I use here are introduced gradually in the course of chapters 4 and 5, where they are illustrated specifically in regard to Biblical Hebrew and the text of *Joseph*. (For a more systemic and general discussion of paragraph types cf. Longacre 1979b; 1980).

As for (*f*), the notional categories I employ in my analysis of paragraph structure have a long and checkered history. My own most recent catalogue of such relations (1983: 77–149) is based on earlier work of myself and others (Ballard, Conrad, and Longacre 1971a; 1971b) with subsequent expansion (Longacre 1972; 1983). Larson (1984: 271–345) gives a somewhat similar catalogue, which is based on unpublished work of John Beekman and colleagues from 1976 onward; of the latter the most noteworthy is Beekman, Callow, and Kopesec (1981). All the latter to varying degrees are influenced by Fuller (1959), who elaborated these relations for the purpose of exegesis of Scripture. Grimes (1976: chap. 14) describes these relations as rhetorical predicates and presents his own particular formulation of them. Quite distinct from my own work and all the above is that of Halliday and Hasan (1976), which ties the analysis of interclausal relations in English to English conjunctions (while the rest of us have been trying to marshall catalogues of relations that are linguistically universal and notional, and that may or may not be marked in the surface structure). Van Dijk (1977) and de Beaugrande and Dressler (1981) present partial catalogues of such relations in their works as well. Still more recently, Mann and Thompson (1987) have come out with another partial catalogue; like Grimes they conceptualize these relations as predicates with their arguments.

What then? I have made extensive reference to those working in the area of interclausal relations simply to reinforce one point: *Every serious student of discourse ends up eventually positing such a catalogue of relations (however conceived).* Why? Because they are *required* by the data and reflect some basic facts about our cognitive apparatus as human beings. That one cannot put together a discourse without resort to such categories implies that we cannot really function as human beings without them. I must add here that such relations are neither specifically English nor even specifically characteristic of Indoeuropean languages; various of us have applied them to a considerable number of non-Indoeuropean languages.

If I have not sufficiently bared my analytical soul to the reader by confessing to all the above assumptions, I may add that a kind of dejargonized tagmemics pervades this volume and is especially noticeable in this section. Tagmemics, originated by K. L. Pike (for current presentations see Pike 1982 and Longacre 1985d), facilitates the analysis of discourse by assuming a function-set correlation. Thus, the sentence "The intrepid hunter shot the charging buffalo" has three main constituent parts: (1) the intrepid hunter, (2) shot, and (3) the charging buffalo. How can these constituents be described? We can say that the constituents are subject, predicate, object—but this misses the "stuff" of which the sentence is composed. We could say that the sentence is composed of noun phrase, verb phrase, and noun phrase—but this misses the function of the three parts. Tagmemics suggests: Why not refer to *both*; the former as *slots* or *functions* and the latter as *fillers* (representatives of a filler *set*). Hence the three parts of the sentence are: Subject filled by noun phrase, transitive predicate filled by (minimal) verb phrase, and object filled by noun phrase. This approach is useful, for example, in dealing with the topic sentence (so-called) of a paragraph. What do we do when the "topic sentence" is a complex of three sentences in a long and involved paragraph? Tagmemics says: Posit a topic (I prefer *Text*) slot, filled (in this instance), by an embedded paragraph. (For more on tagmemics see the Appendix on that subject.)

CHAPTER THREE

VERB RANK IN THE STORY

In several places, especially in chapter 1, there has been occasion to refer to chains of *waw*-consecutives, constructions that introduce a new episode, and "off-the-line" materials. These considerations have been held in abeyance throughout Part 1 while we gave initial priority to the overall view of the story and of its major segments and attempted to catch its overall thrust and plan (macrostructures) as related to the design of the parts. It is now necessary, however, to consider in detail the clause structure of the language of our text, especially in relation to the tense/aspect/mood of the verbs that are used in narrative discourse within Biblical Hebrew. The following chapter will in turn relate clause structure and verb structure to sentence and paragraph units, that is, to the constituent building blocks of the narrative. Attention will also have to be paid to instances of other discourse types as they are found embedded here and there within the narrative framework. Part of the justification of what we do here will necessarily wait until the following chapters, where we are able to demonstrate the usefulness of what we do in reference to broader considerations.

I go back here to two important clues in the Gesenius-Kautzsch-Cowley Hebrew grammar (GKC). This grammar recognizes in the 1910 English edition (and I do not know how early in the successive German editions since 1813) that the so-called *waw*-consecutive is a special narrative tense (326). If this sounded strange to me as a seminary student in 1944, it no longer sounds the least bit strange. Discourse grammarians are coming to recognize more and more that in the telling of a story in any language, one particular tense is favored as the carrier of the backbone or storyline of the story while other tenses serve to present the background, supportive, and depictive material in the story. Another important clue in GKC was its passing on to us a certain insistence of the Arab grammarians that any clause that starts with a noun should be regarded as a noun clause (whether or not it has a finite verb), while any clause that starts with a verb should be regarded as a verb clause (451). In effect, the claim here is that when a clause starts with a noun, it is talking about the participant or prop represented by the noun; but when it starts with a verb, it is talking about the action represented in the verb. It is these two clues from Gesenius that I would like to exploit and develop further in the light of contemporary discourse research in linguistics.

1. *On-the-line material*

I have assumed, then, that the storyline or the backbone of a discourse in Biblical Hebrew is conveyed by use of clauses that begin with a *waw*-consecutive verb—in the balance of this book simply called the *preterite*.

The addition of this fused form of 'and' takes an *a*- quality vowel (*pataḥ*) in place of the usual *ĕ* (*šĕwāʾ*) of the conjunctival *w*-. Consequently (GKC, 46), it regularly doubles whatever consonant immediately follows it. It also in some cases retracts the accent towards the fore of the word. To these formal peculiarities is added the fact that the meaning of the form is apparently reversed. Thus, while *yiqqaḥ* means 'he will take' or 'he takes', *wayyiqqaḥ* means 'and he took'. A further grammatical peculiarity of the preterite is that neither a noun phrase nor the negative *lōʾ*-, 'not', may precede it; the preposing of any such element requires resort to the corresponding form of the perfect, (i.e., the suffixal tense). Thus, *wayyiqqaḥ*, 'and he took', but *wĕlōʾ lāqaḥ*, 'and he didn't take', and *wĕyôsēp lāqaḥ*, 'and Joseph took'.

Comparative Semitic studies reveal, however, that the preterite is *not* a historical development from the imperfect, but is a separate tense form that has come by convergence to resemble the imperfect. For this reason it seems best to give the construction a name unrelated to the imperfect, hence, *preterite*. Formally, however, this aspect of the verb looks if it were an imperfect (or prefixal) tense preceded by a fused form of *w*-, 'and'.

A chain of (necessarily verb-initial) clauses that contain preterites is the backbone of any Old Testament story; all other clause types contribute various kinds of supportive, descriptive, and depictive materials. In the case of clauses that begin with a noun (and cannot therefore contain a verb in the preterite), such background material serves to introduce or highlight something about the noun in question, whether it refers to a participant or to a prop in the story. Clauses that begin with a non-preterite (perfect) verb portray secondary actions; for example, actions that are in some sense subsidiary to the main action, which is described by a following preterite. On occasion, a verb in the perfect (whether or not it begins with a noun) is repetition or paraphrase of some action already reported as a preterite on the storyline. In developing these notions in detail, we will use the phrase *on the storyline* or *on-the-line* versus *off the storyline* or *off-the-line* to indicate a basic dichotomy that divides these two sorts of materials used in building a story (Longacre 1978: 253–58; 1979a: 96–97).

1.1.   *The special status of* hāyâ, *'be'*

It is immediately necessary, however, to qualify the above hypothesis in one important particular. The verb *hāyâ*, 'be', even in its preterite form *wayhî*, 'and it happened', does not function on the storyline of a narrative. In this respect, the behavior of Hebrew is similar to that of a great many contemporary languages around the world. For example, English uses its past tense to encode the storyline of a story, but the verb *be* (and some other stative verbs)—even when in the past tense (for example, forms such as *was*, *were*)—is typically descriptive and depictive and does not figure on the backbone of a story. This is simple a peculiarity of the verb *be* in many languages past and present.

1.2.   *Material that precedes the initiation of a chain*

The material that precedes the initiation of a chain of preterites is a relevant and involved consideration. Admittedly, a chain of preterites may simply begin with the preterite without anything else preceding—this was a difficulty with the previous definition of the form as "*waw*-consecutive": it was not necessarily consecutive. For example, the books of Leviticus, Numbers, 2 Kings, and 2 Chronicles begin with a backbone preterite. One might argue, of course, that in a sense Leviticus and Numbers are consecutive within the ongoing structure of the Pentateuch and that 2 Kings and 2 Chronicles obviously continue books that precede them. Nevertheless, the fact remains that they articulate very important sections (even if in larger wholes) and represent fresh beginnings. We find also within the structure of Old Testament stories occasional instances of paragraphs that begin abruptly with a preterite. Nevertheless it is more usual to have at least a phrase or a clause or two precede the onset of a chain of preterites—sometimes a rather fantastically complex array of clauses, for example, Esth 1:1–11. I want to briefly summarize here some of the introductory combinations that occur (they will be evaluated functionally in §2). In rounding out the picture, I will occasionally have recourse to examples not found in *Joseph*, but most of my citations will be from that story. (Unmarked references such as 7:17 are to Genesis; references to other parts of the Hebrew Bible are indicated.)

1.2.1. A chain of preterites may be preceded by one or more *wayhî* clauses that are existential or equative in thrust (not *wayhî* in the function described under §1.2.2. below). In Gen 39:2, which introduces us to the fortunes of Joseph in Potiphar's house, there is a series of three such *wayhî* clauses, all of which form the setting of the paragraph and precede the onset of the chain of preterites. In the parallel 39:21, only one such clause occurs: *wayhî yhwh ʾet-yôsēp*, 'and YHWH was with Joseph'. Other similar examples are not hard to find in the rest of the Hebrew Bible. Thus, in 7:17 a *wayhî* clause, 'and there was a flood', serves to introduce the chain of preterites that encode the peak of the flood story. In 12:10, we have a similar clause: *wayhî rāʿāb bāʾāreṣ*, 'and there was a famine in the land', which is introductory to the storyline of Abraham's going to sojourn in Egypt.

1.2.2. A temporal expression may precede the verb of a preterite clause. This expression may be a phrase or an adverbial clause. In *Joseph* there are apparently no examples of this construction without *wayhî*, 'and it happened that . . .', preceding the temporal. Nevertheless, this construction occurs elsewhere, as in 22:4: *bayyôm haššělîsî wayy-* . . . , 'and on the third day, then. . . .'[1]

Much more frequently an introductory *wayhî* precedes the temporal expression before the preterite, which then functions as a complement of *wayhî*. Thus, in 40:20 we have *wayhî bayyôm haššělîsî*, 'and it happened on the third day', which makes a fruitful comparison with 22:4 referred to above (even though 40:20 has a further appositional noun phrase, *yôm hulledet ʾet-parʿōh*, 'the day that Pharaoh was born', before the *wayy-* form). Gen 41:8 has an introductory *wayhî babbōqer watt-*, 'and it happened in the morning that. . . .' While the introduction of any such temporal expression into a stream of preterites can indicate a paragraph or episode break, nevertheless as we have seen in chapter 1, such breaks are more regularly marked by an episode marker, such as *wayhî ʾaḥar haddĕbārîmhāl5ʾ ēlleh*, 'and it happened after these things/matters that. . . .'

The inseparable preposition and conjunction *kĕ-*, 'like, as, when', is very commonly used in the temporal expressions here described. Thus 39:11: *wayhî kĕhayyôm hazzeh*, 'and it happened on a certain day that. . . .' Even more frequently *kē-* is used with the infinitive construct: 39:15: *wayhî kĕšāmeʿô kî . . . wayy-*, 'and it happened in his hearing that . . . then he. . . .'; and 39:13: *wayhî kirʾôtāh kî . . . watt-*, 'and it happened in her seeing that . . . then she. . . .' With finite verbs in adverbial temporal clauses *kaʾašer* or *kî* is used: 37:23: *wayhî kaʾašer-bāʾ yôsēp ʾel-eḥāyw wayy-*, 'and it happened when Joseph came in to his brothers, then they. . . .'; and 43:21: *wayhî kî-bāʾnû ʾel-hammālôn wann-*, 'and it happened when we came to the inn, then. . . .' Other

---

[1] I follow the convention here of indicating a following preterite by *wayy-* (3 s.m.), *watt-* (3 s.f.), or *wann-* (1 pl.c).

conjunctions/propositions are also used with *wayhî* and the finite verb: *ûbĕṭerem*, 'before', in 37:18 and *mēʾāz*, 'from the time that', in 39:5.

1.2.3. Very commonly a clause with a perfect precedes a chain of preterites as in 39:1, 41:10, 41:50, 44:19, 45:1, and 45:16. Thus, in 39:1 *wĕyôsēp hûrad miṣrāyĕmâ*, 'and Joseph was brought down to Egypt', precedes the preterite clause 'Potiphar . . . bought him'. In 41:10 *parʿōh qāṣap ʿal-ʿăbādāyw*, 'Pharaoh got angry with his servant', precedes a chain of preterites in which the chief cupbearer tells of his being put in prison and how he fared there. Not too dissimilar from these examples are others in which a noun + a perfect precedes a chain of preterites: 4:1, 6:9, 11:27, 14:51f., 16:1ff., and 21:1 (suggestion of Nicholas Bailey). In 45:1 a negated perfect *wĕlōʾ-yākōl yôsēp lĕhitʾappēq*, 'and Joseph wasn't able to control himself', precedes a chain of preterites that build up to Joseph's self disclosure, 'I am Joseph', in v 3.

Of course a temporal expression can attach itself to the clause whose verb is in the perfect. Here, again, examples without a *wayhî* preceding the temporal are rare and I have to resort to an example not found in *Joseph*, namely Esth 6:1: *ballayĕlâ hahûʾ nādĕdâ šĕnat hammelek*, 'in that night the sleep of the king fled' (i.e., 'the king couldn't sleep'); the whole sentence precedes a chain of preterites that describe the king's discovery of a service for which Mordecai had not been rewarded.

More commonly, however, a *wayhî* precedes the temporal expression + a perfect, and the whole is preposed to one or more preterites; as in Gen 40:1: *wayhî ʾaḥar haddĕbārîm hāʾēlleh ḥāṭĕʾû mašqēh . . . wĕhāʾōpeh*, 'and it happened, after these matters [that] sinned the cupbearer . . . and the baker'. This precedes the chain of preterites that recounts Pharaoh's anger, the imprisonment of the two men, and their being committed to Joseph's keeping.

1.2.4. A participial clause may precede a chain of preterites—with *hinnēh*, 'behold', often initial in such clauses. Thus in 41:1–2 two such clauses (with somewhat different functions—see Part 4) precede the preterite clause 'and they fed among the reeds': *wĕhinnēh ʿōmēd ʿal-hayʾōr*, 'and behold he was standing above the river' (i.e., on the bank); and *wĕhinnēh min-hayʾōr ʿōlōt šebaʿ pārôt yĕpôt marʾeh*, 'and behold from the river were coming up seven cows beautiful of form'. In vv 3 and 4 a similar sequence occurs: *wĕhinnēh šebaʿ pārôt ʾăḥērôt ʿōlōt*, 'and behold seven other cows were coming up', then a chain of two preterites: 'And they took their stand. And they ate up [the good cows].'

A participial clause and a perfect clause may occur in sequence before a preterite. Such a sequence occurs at the end of 1 Samuel 9—

while the chain of preterites thus introduced is found at the beginning of chap. 10. Thus 1 Sam 9:27: *hēmmâ yôrĕdîm biqṣēh hāʿîr ûšĕmûʾēl ʾāmar ʾel-šāʾûl,* 'they going down towards the outskirts of the city and Samuel said to Saul' (the participial clause is probably temporal in thrust, i.e., 'as they were going down . . .').

A participial clause may be in the main slot in the *wayhî* + Temporal + Main clause construction, which has already been pointed out in preceding sections. Compare Gen 41:1: *wayhî miqqēṣ šĕnatayim yāmîm ûparʿōh ḥōlēm.* Here *ûparʿōh ḥōlēm,* 'and also Pharaoh was dreaming' is the main clause, which is preceded by the *wayhî* and the expression 'at the end of two full years'. This whole sentence is followed by two other participial constructions before the preterite occurs, as mentioned above.

Esth 2:21 contains an example of a temporal phrase followed by a participial clause, followed in turn by a perfect clause before the chain of preterites begins.

A participial clause in this function can also—under conditions not yet well understood—add the copula (some form of *hāyâ,* 'be'). Thus the aperture of the whole Joseph story: *yôsep ben-šĕbaʿ-ʿeśrēh šānâ hāyâ rōʿeh ʾet-ʾeḥāyw baṣṣōʾn,* 'Joseph, being 17 years old was [*hāyâ*] shepherding [*rōʿeh*] with his brothers among the flocks' (37:2).

1.2.5. A nominal clause may precede a preterite clause as in Gen 40:11 and 42:6. Thus in 40:11, *wĕkôs parʿōh bĕyādî,* 'and the cup of Pharaoh [was] in my hand', precedes a chain of three preterites in the cupbearer's recital of his dream. Gen 42:6 has a nominal followed by a participial clause, both of which precede a rather lengthy chain of preterites: *wĕ-yôsēp hûʾ haššallîṭ ʿal-hāʾāreṣ hûʾ hammašbîr lĕkol-ʿam hāʾāreṣ,* 'now, as for Joseph, he was the ruler, he was the one selling to all the people of the land'.

In 42:35 a chain of preterites is initiated by a *wayhî* + Temporal + Main clause construction in which the temporal expression is a participial clause and the main clause is nominal: *wayhî hēm mĕrîqîm śaqqêhem wĕhinnēh-ʾîš ṣĕrôr-kaspô bĕśaqqô.* Here the *hēm mĕrîqîm śaqqêhem,* 'they were opening their sacks', is clearly indicated to be temporal because of its position in the *wayhî* complement construction. The whole can be rendered: 'And it happened [that] when they were opening their sacks, behold for each man his bundle of silver [was] in his sack.'

Occasionally, under conditions not yet well understood, an overt copula *hāyâ,* 'be', may occur internally within a nominal clause, as in 41:56, where we have not *wĕhārāʿāb* [∅] *ʿal kol-pĕnê hāʾāreṣ,* 'the famine [was] on all the land', but rather *wĕhārāʿāb hāyâ ʿal kol-pĕnê hāʾāreṣ.* Is the thrust of the interposed copula to raise description of a background *situation* to something more on the order of a background *event*?[2]

Before going on to discuss a few other possible ways of initiating a chain of preterites, I pause here to summarize the *wayhî* + Temporal + Main Clause construction: (1) Its verb is impersonal, for example, a plural form such as *wayyihyû*, 'and they were', does not occur (cf. 11:32 where the occurrence of this 3 m. pl. form indicates clearly that the string is *not* a *wayhî* complement construction; compare 11:32 with Ruth 1:1). (2) The main clause can contain a preterite, a perfect, a participle, or be nominal. (3) *Whatever* occurs in between is to be considered to be temporal in meaning. Usually the intervening string is marked with some sort of temporal preposition or conjunction; but even when unmarked (cf. *hēm mĕrîqîm śaqqêhem* in Gen 42:35 above) the construction is to be taken as temporal. (4) Very frequently this construction functions as a backreference to previous material. In fact, such a reference is often found even in the rare instances where a temporal expression is not preceded by *wayhî*.

1.2.6. A chain of preterites may also be preceded by a clause with a negative verb. In this respect, 45:1, which contains a clause with a negated perfect, has already been cited under 1.2.3. above. A similar negated perfect comes after the first preterite of the chain 45:1–3. It is well to remind ourselves here that an on-the-line preterite cannot be negated, but must give way to an off-the-line perfect. A more complex example, again outside our *Joseph* corpus, is found in 16:1 where a negated perfect is followed by a pair of nominal clauses before the onset of a chain of preterites (in this case dialogue). Probably *ʾên*, 'there isn't, nothing of', and *yēš*, 'there is/was', can have occasional use in serving to precede a chain of preterites, but I do not have clear examples as yet of them in such functions.

1.3. *Complex links in a chain*

It is important to note that a chain of preterites is not necessarily a simple sequence. In that the chain is not necessarily a simple succession of links, we sometimes find that two or three links form a complex within the whole and have to be related to the whole as a complex link. Some such combinations are summarized here.

---

[2] Robert Bergen (private communication) believes that *hāyâ* is used in a nominal clause to introduce a significant (non-human) prop or what proves to be an important factor in the story.

1.3.1. With verbs of speech and sensation, a very common patterning is for the nature of a speech act to be described in a specific verb such as 'ask' or 'refuse' and for this to be followed by a form of the verb *ʾāmar*, 'say', in introductory function to a quotation. That is, we first are told the nature of the speech act; then we are told the words that are spoken in the implementation of the act. Thus, in 37:10 the use of the verb *gāʿar*, 'rebuke', before *ʾāmar* identifies the speech acts as one of rebuke/reproof; in 37:18 *nākal*, 'plot against', before *ʾāmar* identifies the speech act as conspiracy; while in both 37:9 and 40:9 *sāpar*, 'recount', before *ʾāmar* alerts us to expect a narration. Similar uses of specific verbs before *ʾāmar* are as follows: (*a*) 37:21: the niphil of *nāṣal*, 'snatch away, deliver', signifies a speech act of *salutary intervention*; (*b*) 37:33: hiphil of *nākar*, 'recognize', a speech act expressing recognition; (*c*) 39:8: *māʾān*, 'refuse', a speech act of refusal; (*d*) 40:18: *ʿānâ*, 'answer', a reply; (*e*) 43:27: *šāʾal*, 'ask', a question; and (*f*) 43:19–20: piel of *dābar*, 'speak', simply tells us that a conversation is taking place and is somewhat neutral as to the nature of the speech act.

Also, in a very similar manner, verbs of sensation may be followed by a verb that introduces what is perceived (as the object of the verb) or the field of vision (in a *hinnēh* construction). Consider, for example, the frequent idiom 'to lift up the eyes' followed by the verb 'see' as in 37:25 *wayyiśʾû ʿênêhem wayyirʾû wĕhinnēh ʾōrĕḥat yišmĕʿēʾlîm bāʾâ miggilʿād*, 'And they lifted up their eyes, and they saw, and behold, a caravan of Ishmaelites coming from Gilead'. Here the first clause, *wayyiśʾû ʿênê-hem*, 'they lifted up their eyes', tells us no more than 'they glanced up'— or something on that order. The second verb *wayyirʾû*, 'and they saw', is somewhat parallel to *wayyōʾmĕrû*, 'and they said', in that the former introduces the field of vision, that is, what was *seen*, while the latter introduces a quotation, that is, what was *said*. The field of vision is described in the third sentence that begins with *wĕhinnēh*, 'and behold', and in the following sentence: 'And their camels were bearing gum, balm, and myrrh, proceeding on their way down to Egypt.' Gen 22:13 is almost the exact structural parallel to this latter passage.

1.3.2. Certain verbs are sometimes used in tandem—almost as if they were one verb, and sometimes with the first functioning as a manner modifier of the second. The latter is very clear when *māhar*, 'hurry', is used before another verb, as in 43:30: *waymahēr yôsēp kî-nikmĕrû rahămāyw ʾel-ʾāḥiw waybaqqēš libkôt*, 'And Joseph hurried (for his emotions were stirred concerning his brothers). And he looked [for a place] to cry.' Frequently in such usage, the verb *māhar* occurs without any accompanying noun phrases and all the noun phrases cluster around the second verb, as in 44:11: *waymahărû wayyôridû ᵓîš ᵓet-ᵓamtaḥtô ᵓārĕṣâ*, 'And they hastened and they lowered [each] man his sack to the ground'. Compare also two similar uses of *māhar* in 24:18, 46. In all these cases *māhar* need not be rendered as a verb in English but rather as an adverb, 'hurriedly' or 'quickly'. Compare also 41:32 where a participial form of *māhar* is used with *le-* + infinitive construct of *ᶜāśâ*, 'do'.

Somewhat dissimilar is the combination *nûs*, 'flee', + *yāṣāᵓ*, 'go out', since the second verb is more adverbial in thrust relative to the first. Thus in 39:12 we have the sequence *wayyānos wayyēṣeᵓ haḥûsâ*, 'and he fled and he exited outside'. Here, while the second verb, 'to exit/go out', takes the adverbial modifier *haḥûsâ*, 'outside', which naturally collocates with it (cf. also 39:15), in the adverbial clause of 39:13, 'when she saw that he had fled outside', the sequence is shortened to *wayyānos haḥûsâ* with deletion of the verb *wayyēṣēᵓ*, 'exit', (cf. also 39:18). Apparently, then, the first verb is lexically dominant here rather than the second.

Other lexical combinations of preterites are *māšak*, 'draw, pull', + *ᶜālah* (hiphil), 'bring up' (in 37:28 where they pull Joseph up out of the pit) *šālaḥ*, 'send', + *wārāᵓ*, 'call' (in 'send and call [for someone]', as in 41:8 and 14); *šātâ*, 'drink', + *šākar*, 'get drunk' (in 43:34); *ᶜāśâ*, 'do', + hiphil of *bôᵓ*, 'come in' (in 43:17, where *ᶜāśâ* is the generic verb and the clause with *wayyābēᵓ*, 'and he brought in', is the nearer specification of the action involved).

1.3.3. Somewhat similar to the preceding is the use of a motion verb or a positional verb before another verb. The verb *hālak*, 'go', occurs in combination with *māṣāᵓ*, 'find', in 37:17: 'And he went off Joseph after his brothers. And he found them at Dothan'. The verb *bôᵓ*, 'enter/go', occurs before several verbs: *šaḥâ*, 'bow', in 42:6; *nāgad*, 'declare', in 42:29; and *nāpal*, 'fall down', in 44:14. The verb *nāgaš*, 'draw near' occurs typically before verbs of speech, as in 43:19 and 44:18. Not dissimilar is the use of *nāśag*, 'overtake', before a verb of speech in 44:6. In similar function, *qûm*, 'raise', occurs in 43:15; *nāpal*, 'fall down', in 45:14; *sābab*, 'turn aside', in 42:24; and *šûb*, 'return', in 37:29, 30. Perhaps none of the combinations mentioned here are as close as some of those mentioned under §1.3.2. above.

1.4. *Subject switches within a chain*

1.4.1. Local reciprocities may occur anywhere along the storyline. That is, we have a situation in which A does something and B in return performs an action. Usually the conditions are specific enough lexically that the change of subject need not be formally marked. Thus, we have in 37:14: 'He sent him from the valley of Hebron. And he [the latter] went.' Similarly, in 37:28: 'They sold Joseph to the Ishmaelites. And they [the latter] brought him on down into Egypt.' Again, in 40:4: 'He entrusted Joseph with them and he [Joseph] looked after them.' Likewise in 40:21: 'He restored the cupbearer to his place. And he [the cupbearer] put the cup in Pharaoh's hand.'

1.4.2. In some cases a change in number and/or gender, indicated in the verb affixes, signals overtly a subject switch, as in 42:25: 'And he ordered Joseph. And they filled the vessels with grain.' Or 43:24: 'And he gave water. And they washed their feet.' A noun phrase can be employed to signal the switch (but taking us further afield from this discussion of *implied* reciprocities). When, however, the implied reciprocity is sufficient to indicate the switch without an overt noun phrase and the latter occurs anyway, then the motivation for the occurrence of the noun phrase is to mark a thematic participant in some stretch of the discourse. Thus in 41:37–45, we have a long chain of preterites: from v 38 on, Pharaoh is the stated or assumed subject of all these preterites and Joseph is on the receiving end. But in the final preterite of the chain we are told: 'and Joseph went out over the land of Egypt', that is, as a result of all the semi-royal prerogatives, trappings, and powers that had been given to him, Joseph now goes out as overlord of all Egypt.

1.4.3. We commonly also have reciprocities of the sort involved in any dialogue situation where A speaks to B then B answers A, etc. These are common throughout *Joseph*.

1.4.4. There can also be a series of subject switches in a chain of command, such as we have in 40:1–4. We are told in the setting of this paragraph that the cupbearer and the baker sinned against Pharaoh; then (in a series of preterites): Pharaoh is angry at them, Pharaoh puts them in jail in the very place where Joseph is, the captain of the guard commits them to Joseph, and Joseph looks after them.

1.5. *Thematic subparagraphs*

We have talked in the previous sections about complex links in a chain of preterites. This is really a rather awkward and *ad hoc* ways of talking. Our basic assumption is: We consider the whole string of preterites to be the backbone of a narrative paragraph (Longacre 1979a). Then, wherever within such a unit we recognize a grouping of several preterites or group preterites with non-preterites, we, in effect, are positing a subparagraph embedded within the main paragraph. In place of a simple preterite link in the backbone chain of a paragraph we find a link that consists of a subparagraph involving two or more preterites plus possibly some non-preterites. Such paragraphing and subparagraphing are developed in the following chapter. In addition, Part 4, which is a constituent analysis display ranging over most of the Joseph story, attempts to make these matters explicit.

2. *Off-the-line material*

I now discuss the status and function of off-the-line material. In this section, special attention is given to introductory phrases and clauses of the sort already summarized in the previous section of this chapter. An attempt is made here to classify these constructions and clarify their functions. Constructions are also noted that occur internally within a paragraph but are off-the-line, or, that are off-the-line and occur at the end of the paragraph.

2.1. *The perfect with a preposed noun*

The purpose of the construction perfect with preposed noun is to introduce or feature a participant or a prop. The action that is represented in connection with this participant or prop is a secondary or preparatory action. Thus in 39:1, preceding the onset of a chain of preterites, we have a sentence that begins with the words *wĕyôsēp hûrad miṣrāyĕmâ*, 'and Joseph was brought down to Egypt'. Plainly, the reason for throwing Joseph to the fore is to refocus on him as a central participant of a story, which has been interrupted by the intervening material concerning Judah and Tamar in chap. 38. The verb in the perfect, 'was brought down to Egypt', recapitulates a fact already told at the end of chap. 37. In 44:19 and 41:10, we have tactful deference to the addressee on the part of people speaking to Joseph or to Pharaoh. In both examples, in telling an anecdote that will shortly shift into a chain of preterites, it is tactful to prepose a clause with 'my lord asked his servant saying' (44:19) or 'Pharaoh was angry with his servant' (41:10). Again, the actions pictured in both clauses by means of verbs in the perfect are presumably actions that are preliminary to getting a chain of preterites going. For example, 37:3: 'And Israel loved Joseph more than all his sons.' This is in a passage that strongly focuses on Joseph as the central participant of the story, which is just there getting under way. There is temporary focus on Israel, his father, and this is achieved by means of using a clause with the verb in the perfect with the noun (Israel) preposed.

2.2. *The prefect initial in its clause*[3]

Evidently, when the perfect verb is initial in a clause, the intent is not to focus on the subject of the verb but either to present a preliminary action or to focus on an object in connection with a preliminary action. Thus we have the perfect in 37:3: 'And he made him a special coat.' Here the perfect introduces a preliminary and fateful action on Jacob's part, and introduces the coat that was to prove so disastrous for Joseph. The clause 'and spake the man, the lord of the country harsh things to us' in 42:30, which is initial in a quotation, portrays a preliminary action before beginning a chain of preterites in the next clause: 'he gave us out to be spies'. Presumably, it is not highlighting Joseph so much as what he said.

2.3. *Participial clause*

The purpose of a participial clause preceding the preterite that initiates a chain is to present a simultaneous background activity or state.[4] It also presents a participant performing the activity or in that state (compare §2.4. below). In *Joseph*, instances of introductory participial clauses without *hinnēh*, 'behold', do not occur. They are found, however, in other part of the Hebrew Bible. For example, in Esth 2:21 a seemingly insignificant (but altogether important) incident is introduced in a rather elaborate way. It begins with a temporal phrase 'in those days,' continues with a participial clause sketching the background situation 'and Mordecai was sitting in the gate of the king', continues with a perfect 'and were angry Bigthan and Teresh,' and then switches into the initiatory preterite of the chain: 'and tried to lay hands on the king'. Here we see the conjunction of a temporal element and a participial clause that sketches the background activity or state in which Mordecai was engaged at the time. These are, in turn, followed with a preliminary action (the anger of the two courtiers) before the preterite 'and tried to lay hands on the king' takes the center of the stage.

2.4. *Participial clause with* hinnēh

Introductory participial clauses regularly take *hinnēh*, 'behold', in *Joseph*. The *hinnēh* is attention calling—perhaps a tacit invitation to

---

[3] This is of course the stereotyped view of the relation of perfect and preterite, i.e., that a chain begins with a perfect and continues with preterites.

[4] Occasionally, an imperfect (not a preterite, i.e., not *waw*-consecutive + imperfect) can occur to express a background activity. Since there is only one

conjure up the picture. Thus, *hinnēh* can directly precede the participle (inflected for number and gender) as in 37:15: *wĕhinnēh tōʿeh baśśādeh*, 'and there [he] was—wandering in the field'; and 41:1: *wĕhinneh ʿōmēd ʿal-hayʾōr*, 'and there [he] was—standing above the river'. Quite frequently the subject of the participle is expressed immediately following the *hinnēh*, as in 41:3: *wĕhinnēh šebaʿ pārôt ʾăḥērôt ʿōlôt*, 'and behold, seven other cows were coming up'. Here the background situation is more explicitly focused on the subject of the participle. In a verse such as 41:2, *wĕhinnēh min-hayʾōr ʿōlōt šebaʿ pārôt yĕpôt marʾeh*, 'and behold from the river there came up seven beautifully formed cows', the *hinnēh* highlights the fact that something is coming out of the river and then proceeds to identify it.

2.5. *Nominal clauses (including a few that have medial* hāyâ, *and existentials with* yēš *or* ʾên)

Nominal clauses are depictive and descriptive. They portray background situations. Thus, in 42:6, after the introductory phrase 'And Joseph' (*wĕyôsēp*) we find: 'He [*hûʾ*] [was] lord of the land. He [*hûʾ*] [was] the one selling grain to all the people of the lands.' These two clauses, which are nominal and participial respectively, are followed by the preterite: 'And they came in the brothers of Joseph to buy.' Gen 41:12 is not dissimilar. Here, in the speech of the cupbearer to Pharaoh just before Joseph is called before Pharaoh, we have the clause: 'And there with us [was] a Hebrew lad a servant to the captain of the guard.' Here this nominal clause portrays the situation preceding the first preterite of the cupbearer's story: 'And we told him our dreams.' Similarly in 40:11 the nominal clause *wĕkôs parʿōh bĕyādî*, 'and the cup of Pharaoh [was] in my hand', precedes the chain of three preterites in which the chief cupbearer presents the actions that he performed in his dream. Gen 41:46 presents a nominal clause, 'and Joseph [was] thirty years old when he stood before Pharaoh, king of Egypt', that precedes a chain of six preterites telling the course of events and actions of Joseph during the years of plenty.

2.6. *Negative verbs*

Negative verbs do not often occur in material that precedes a chain of preterites, but are more commonly found scattered somewhere in the

---

such use of the imperfect in the whole *Joseph* story (37:7: *wĕhinnēh tĕsubbênâ ʾălummōtêkem*, 'behold your sheafs were gathering around'), I do not at present have sufficient data to decide what contextual conditions call for such an imperfect as opposed to a participle when representing an ongoing activity.

interior of such a chain or at its close. Often they express a construction that could be called negated antonym paraphrase. That is, they express a situation negatively, followed by a more positive expression of it in a clause whose preterite is on the storyline of the paragraph. In 45:1 the negated antonym paraphrase is introductory: 'And wasn't able (Joseph) to control himself before his attendants [negated perfect]. And he cried out, "Have everyone leave my presence"' (clause whose verb is preterite and on the storyline of the paragraph). Thus, 40:23: 'And the chief cupbearer didn't remember Joseph [negated perfect]. But forgot him [preterite]'; this closes both a paragraph and an episode of the story.

2.7. *A perfect clause in paraphrase with a preterite clause*

When the perfect occurs paragraph medial, a preterite clause and a perfect clause constitute a chiastic sentence when the two verb forms are from the same or synonymous verbs and there is not intervening *wĕ-*, 'and'. Thus in 41:12 we have a chiastic sentence that begins with the preterite *wayyiptār*, 'and he interpreted', and ends with the perfect *pātār*, 'interpreted he': 'And he interpreted for us our dreams; according to each man's dream so he interpreted.' Notice also in 41:48 a chiastic sentence that begins with the preterite *wayyitten*, 'and he gave/put', and ends with the perfect *nātan*, 'he gave/put': 'And he stored food in the cities, the food of the fields that surrounded the city, he stored in its midst' (cf. also 41:11). Compare also 7:21–22 where we have a long chiastic sentence beginning with *wayyigĕwaᶜ*, 'perished', and ending with *mētû*, 'died'. The whole sentence goes as follows: 'And perished every living thing that moved on the earth: birds, livestock, wild animals, all the creatures that swarm over the earth and all mankind; everything on dry land that had the breath of life in its nostrils died.'

In other cases, when *wĕ-* occurs before the second sentence the whole structure might better be considered to be a chiastic paragraph (embedded within a larger paragraph unit). Thus 39:4b: *wayyapqidēhû ᶜal-bêtô wĕkol-yeš-lô nātan bĕyādô*, 'And he made responsible him over his house. And all [which] was to him gave he into his hand.' Here the verb *wayyapqidēhû*, 'and he made responsible him', (a preterite) and the rather synonymous verb *nātan*, 'gave he', + *bĕyādô*, 'in his hand', bracket the whole complex of two sentences.

2.8. *Other cases of off-the-line perfects*

Other cases of paragraph medial perfects are not so easy to classify as the above, but they constitute some of our more interesting examples. In these examples we see clearly how the narrator uses a perfect to put an action off the storyline when it is not an action of the same rank and importance to the story as the action indicated by a preterite on the storyline proves to be. Thus in 37:11, the incident of Joseph's dreams ends with two clauses, the first is a preterite and the second involves a verb in the perfect: 'And his brothers were jealous of him. But his father pondered the matter.'

In the total sweep and development of the story the brothers' jealousy is much more tied into the plot structure than the father's meditating as to what the dream might mean. The story moves along because the brothers are jealous of him and sell him into Egypt regardless of the father's attitude. So, interestingly enough, the verb that refers to the father's attitude is off-the-line and is reported by a preposed noun (which emphasizes the father as opposed to the brothers) and a verb in the perfect.

Similarly interesting is 40:22 where, after reporting the elevation of the cupbearer to his former duties by means of verbs in the preterite and therefore on the storyline of the paragraph, we find a clause whose verb is in the perfect: 'But the baker he hung.' Here in terms of the development of the story, what happens to the baker is comparatively unimportant. It was the cupbearer who finally recalled how Joseph had interpreted their dreams and this in turn led to Joseph's elevation to the lordship of Egypt. Again, the fateful circumstance of the cupbearer's being restored to duty is reported by a a verb in the preterite while the circumstances of the baker are disposed of by a verb in the perfect (although the baker is temporarily highlighted in contrast to the cupbearer by the fact that in the clause in which he is mentioned, the noun 'baker' is preposed).[5]

Notice also the peculiar structure of 41:51–52 regarding the naming of Joseph's sons Ephraim and Manasseh. The naming of the first-born is reported on the storyline by means of the preterite, presumably because the birth of the first-born and his naming was the greater event. Ephraim is mentioned off the storyline in a clause in which reference to him is preposed to a verb in the perfect. Clearly here Ephraim's name is singled out for local contrastive pointing. Note here that there is no set of antonyms in the passage and hence no notional contrast between the birth of the two sons or in the meaning of their names. Possibly, the

---

[5] Chapter 4, §1.6. regarding narrative antithetical paragraphs shows that the regular way to show contrast between two nouns in Hebrew is to adopt the chiastic pattern illustrated above in 37:11 and 40:22. Nevertheless, more far-reaching considerations of storyline and participant ranking are conveyed by the same construction as well. After all, the narrator had the option in Preterite + N_1, N_2 + Perfect construction of choosing which noun to put in the storyline clause and which to put in the accompanying clause.

import of this passage is that although the birth and the naming of the first born is the greater event, Ephraim is eventually to prove to be the more important personality. This inference, evidently, does not hold in 40:22 where the notional contrast between the fates of the cup-bearer and baker is to the fore, and where the demise of the latter is contrasted with the restoration of the former.

We also sometimes find perfect clauses in the terminus of a para-graph or closure of an episode. Thus in 37:36 at the end of the first main episode of the Joseph story, there is a clause that is somewhat dis-connected from the immediately preceding context and that, in fact, acts as an anticipatory link with the resumption of the story over in chap. 39. Its verb is in the perfect: 'And the Midianites sold him into Egypt, to Potiphar, a courtier of Pharaoh, the captain of the guard.'

There is a further use of the perfect quite distinct from all those mentioned thus far in this section. This is the use of a perfect in a pluperfect sense in subordinated clauses introduced by ᵓăšer (relative particle), kaᵓăšer (comparison particle), and kî (marker of complement). The event reported in the subordinated clause is clearly out of chrono-logical sequence with the preceding preterites and is a flashback to a ear-lier event. Thus 39:1: wĕyôsēp hûrad miṣrāyĕmâ wayyiqnēhû pôṭîpar . . . miyyad hayyišmĕᶜēᵓlîm ᵓăšer hôriduhû šāmmâh, 'and he purchased him Potiphar from the hand of the Ishmaelites which had brought him there'. Here wayyiqnēhû, 'and he purchased him', is subsequent to hûrad (per-fect), 'he was brought down', in the previous clause. In turn, however, the relative clause ᵓăšer hôriduhû šāmmâh harks back to this earlier event that temporally preceded the event reported in the preterite.

Likewise 40:21–22 reports the restoration of the cupbearer in two preterites. The fate of the baker is reported as a perfect in the next clause. To the latter is appended kaᵓăšer pātar lāhem yôsēp, 'as Joseph had interpreted to them'. This harks back to Joseph's predictions of three days before as reported in 40:12–19.

In 39:12, which reports Joseph's struggle to get free of the clutch of Potiphar's wife, we are told: 'He left his garment in her hand. And he fled. And he went outside.' All these are in the chain of preterites and are chronologically successive. Gen 39:13 reports, however, the way in which Potiphar's wife took the measure of the situation and responded to it: wayhî kirᵓôtāh kî-ᶜāzab bigdô bĕyādāh wayyānos haḥûṣâ wattiqrāᵓ leᵓanšê bêtāh, 'and when she saw that he had left his garment in her hand and had fled outside, then she cried out to the men of her house'. In this sentence everything from kirᵓôtāh to haḥûṣâ is a temporal ex-pression that occurs between wayhî 'and it happened', and its comple-ment wattiqrāᵓ 'then she cried out'. In this temporal expression kirᵓôtāh consists of kĕ, 'as', + infinitive construct of the verb 'see' + 3 s.f. ending 'in her seeing' (or better 'when she saw'). Both verbs ⁽ʿ⁾*āzab*, 'he left', and *wayyānos*, 'he fled', are dependent on the preceding infinitive; they constitute an embedded sequence of a perfect (necessary after *kî*) + preterite. Here, in this situation not only the perfect but the following preterite are both pluperfect in meaning.

2.9.   *Nominal and existential clauses in the interior of paragraphs*

We also find nominal and existential clauses within the interior of paragraphs. These pattern as comments and often are of an explanatory nature, relative to a clause that is on the storyline of the story. Thus in 37:24 'and they cast him into the pit' is on the main line of the narrative. The following comment is off-the-line: 'And the pit [was] empty. No water [was] in it.' Similarly, in 39:11 the clause 'and he went into the house' is a preterite and is on the storyline while the comment 'and none of the men of the house [were] there in the house' is a comment that is off-the-line.

2.10.   wayhî *clauses near paragraph end*

A feature of paragraph terminus is the occasional use of a *wayhî* clause in a paraphrase near the end of a paragraph. For example, 39:5: 'and Yahweh blessed the house of the Egyptian [clause with a verb in the preterite]. . . . *Wayhî* the blessing of the Lord on all he had both in house and field'. Here the *wayhî* clause is obviously a paraphrase and amplification of the previous clause. Again, the paraphrase and its amplification form a complex link (subparagraph) within the overall sequence of the narrative paragraph. We also have an instance in 39:23 of a participial clause as terminus in a paragraph: 'And whatsoever he did, Yahweh was making it to prosper.'

3.   *A verbal rank scheme*

At this point I have recourse again to the two clues concerning Hebrew discourse structure found in GKC (mentioned above in §0.): (1) the *waw*-consecutive is a special narrative tense and (2) the distinction of verb clause versus noun clause (as found in the Arab grammarians). In line with the first we have everywhere in this chapter treated clauses with a preterite as on the narrative line and all clauses with some other form of the verb as off-the-line. In line with the second, we have noted that preterites are verbal clauses par excellence—since any permutation of a noun to the fore of a preterite makes necessary a switch to another tense (regularly the perfect). We have also drawn a distinction between the

DIAGRAM 3. Verb Rank in Narrative Discourse

Band 1: Storyline	1. Preterite: primary[a]
Band 2: Backgrounded Actions	2.1. Perfect 2.2. Noun + perfect (with noun in focus)
Band 3: Backgrounded Activities	3.1. *hinnēh* + participle 3.2. Participle 3.3. Noun + participle
Band 4: Setting	4.1. Preterite of *hāyâ*, 'be' 4.2. Perfect of *hāyâ*, 'be' 4.3. Nominal clause (verbless) 4.4. Existential clause with *yēš*
Band 5:	5. Negation of verb clause: irrealis (any band)[b]

[a]1. demotes to 2.2. by preposing a noun. 1. demotes to 5. by preposing *lôʾ*, 'not' [Preterite > Perfect].

[b]"Momentous negation" promotes 5. to 2.1./2.2.

perfect initial in its clause and the use of a perfect with a preposed noun. The former we consider to report some sort of secondary activity while the latter foregrounds a noun relative to that activity. This is in accordance with the distinction of the Arab grammarians who labelled *any* verb initial clause a verb clause and *any* noun initial clause a noun clause. Fundamentally, I believe that the Arab grammarians here had a feel for the difference in discourse function between clauses that feature actions and those that feature participants or props. We have also noted a possibly similar distinction in participial clauses between, for example, *hinnēh* + participle and *hinnēh* + noun phrase + participle.

Nevertheless, I do not find per se that the grand dichotomy verb clause versus noun clause is useful. Rather I absorb it into a rank scheme that can be thought of as the *verbal spectrum for narrative* (see Diagram 3). In this scheme I assume a cline, a structural slope from clauses that are relatively dynamic to clauses that are relatively static. The preterite is at the top of the scheme (band 1) and the nominal clause strictly defined (i.e., clauses with zero verb or at the most *hāyâ*, 'be') is toward the bottom (band 4),—although negated clauses constitute the bottom band (5) as belonging to an alternative world from the world of the bands above it. Clause-initial perfects are outranked by preterites but in turn outrank clauses with perfects and preposed nouns.[6] Participles rank still lower. I have ranked nominal clauses with *hāyâ*, 'be', as slightly higher in the scheme than those with no verb at all. Possibly the insertion of *hāyâ* into noun clause injects a modicum of dynamism into the construction (representing a state as a pseudo event?).

This rank scheme includes only independent clauses and is applicable only to narrative. Subordinate clauses, whether or not they contain a verb, are closely backgrounded to the main clause. As we have shown above, under certain contextual conditions perfects in subordinate clauses have the thrust of pluperfects. In subsequent chapters rank schemes are presented for other discourse types.

Some further comments and observations on the rank scheme projected in Diagram 3: (1) There are essentially five major categories, as indicated on the cline. (2) Within a give category subrankings are indicated. Thus a perfect initial in its clause outranks a perfect with a preposed noun; a participial without a preposed noun (presumably) outranks one with it; and the preterite of *hāyâ* (*wayhî*, etc.), which cannot have a preposed noun, outranks the perfect of *hāyâ*, which can have a preposed noun. (3) Any negated clause falls into band 5, the irrealis band, except that a momentous negation that advances the narrative line is probably best considered to be promoted to band 2 (cf. the Flood Story where the dove fails to return to the ark).

The rank scheme as here elaborated will be confronted with the constituent structure of *Joseph* in the next chapter. In narrative sections of the story (as opposed, for example, to the structure of embedded hortatory discourses), the rank scheme will be seen to be a crucial criterion in deciding which parts of a discourse or paragraph are considered to be the most prominent (cf. Longacre 1982a).

---

[6] The scheme given here could be alternatively conceived (Longacre, in press) as embodying a storyline band in which the preterite is primary and the perfect is secondary. As long, however, as a cline is presented—a scheme symbolizing degrees of departure from the storyline—it makes little difference whether the perfect is conceived of as in the same band as the preterite or in the next lower band immediately contiguous to the preterite; in either case no element is closer to the primary storyline than is the perfect. At all events, it is a first degree departure from the mainline of the story.

CHAPTER FOUR

VERB RANK AND CONSTITUENT STRUCTURE

In the previous chapter we established that a story in Hebrew is carried forward largely by chains of preterites (*waw*-consecutives + prefixal tense) and suggested that attention to onset and closure of such chains could provide a criterion for dividing a Hebrew narrative into natural (i.e., structural) paragraphs. It was further indicated that such paragraphs often contained subparagraphs, that is, embedded paragraph units. Finally, a rank scheme of the various verb forms/clause types involved in narrative was suggested along with the promise that the rank scheme and the constituent structure would subsequently be given joint consideration, along with the consideration of further discourse types embedded within the narrative. These further considerations are the goal of this chapter.

0. *Paragraph, embedded discourse, and sentence*

As foundational to this chapter, I recapitulate briefly here certain points already made in the Introduction to Part 2: (1) The term *paragraph* as used here is a *structural* term, not simply an orthographic indentation unit. If, as frequently happens, there is a paragraph with embedded paragraphs ranging through several layers of embedding, it is impossible with the normal devices of punctuation and indentation to indicate the various layerings of paragraph structure. In the structural display in Part 4 of this book, such nested structures can be displayed for analytical purposes. (2) Just as a paragraph can contain embedded paragraphs so a discourse can contain embedded discourses. We have, therefore, given considerable attention (especially in chaps. 1 and 2) to the structure of *Joseph* as a whole and to the structure of its constituent discourses.

In the preceding chapter we have given an unpolished sketch of the constituent structure in terms of chains of preterites and other materials that relate to the chain. It remains, however, to develop the notion of paragraph in some useful way that is specifically related to Biblical Hebrew. One such further question has to do with paragraph constituents; that is, What are paragraphs made of? While we have indicated that paragraphs can contain subparagraphs, what are the building blocks of paragraphs that either (1) contain no subparagraphs, or (2) are at the deepest layer of embedding within a complex of embedded paragraphs? If seems simplest to call the basic building blocks of the paragraph *sentences*—although this may lead to a type of "sentence" somewhat different than our preconceptions might indicate.

In accordance with this assumption, a sentence in Hebrew is considered to be basically a unit with a main clause (and a main verb), to which may be attached such subordinate clauses as adverbial clauses and relative clauses. Normally, a sentence that follows another sentence will start with a conjunction, a *waw*-consecutive, or a temporal expression. It does not seem to be useful to assume that such English-type sentences as coordinated sentences (with medial "and") and antithetical sentences (with medial "but") characterize Hebrew. They are, at any rate, all but indistinguishable from sequences of two sentences. It is more to the point to interpret some sequences of two main clauses *without* any conjunction or *w-* as constituting juxtaposition sentences, as in Gen 40:10b: *wĕhî° kĕpōraḥat °ālĕtâ niṣṣāh hibšîlû °aškĕlōtêhā °ănābim*, 'and it, in its budding, came-up its blossom; ripened-they its clusters [into] grapes'. (Several such juxtaposed chiastic sentences are cited in chap. 3, §2.1.)

In addition to the above sentence structures, Hebrew also has the complementative structure, which was explained and illustrated in the previous chapter, namely, *wayhî* + temporal expression + main clause (i.e., *waw*-consecutive + prefixal tense). With the exception of this (and a few peculiarly close clusters of preterites as in chap. 3, §1.1.2), it seems best to consider that in an on-going story every preterite initiates a new sentence.

This sort of "sentence" is shorter and more contextually bound (less independent) than the English sentence; but the exaggerated independence of the latter is in part the accomplishment of generations of sentence-oriented grammarians. Admittedly, the Hebrew sentence as thus defined is a modest unit.[1] Many combinations of clauses that constitute compound sentences in Indo-European languages correspond

---

[1] Andersen (1974) in his pioneer work on Hebrew sentences and paragraphs handles many structures as sentences that I here treat as paragraphs. The main contribution of Andersen's work lies in its careful treatment of the semantics of clause combination in Biblical Hebrew, along with equally careful attention to the lexical and grammatical markings that characterize the surface structures. I

to combinations of sentences in Hebrew (i.e., lower level paragraph units). However, although the Hebrew sentence is relatively restricted in structure, it is nevertheless a significant unit of organization and an indispensable unit for the analysis of paragraph. For example, the distinction of main clause versus adverbial and relative clauses within the sentence unit is vital to the fitting of each sentence into its paragraph context, since it is the status of the *main* clause that is diagnostic of the status of the whole sentence.

1. *Narrative paragraphs*

Having (hopefully!) disposed of the sentence in this fashion, we are now ready to consider in detail the chains of preterites as various sorts of structural paragraphs in Hebrew. The nine paragraph types described here (sequence, simple, reason, result, comment, amplification, paraphrase, coordinate, and antithetical) are all considered to conform to the abstract basic types that occur in the various discourse genre (cf. Longacre 1980). While only the *narrative* variants of these abstract basic types are described here in this section, further discourse-conditioned variants are described in subsequent sections of this chapter and in chap. 5. For a paragraph of an abstract basic type to be further classified as *narrative*, the verb(s) of its predominating constituent(s) must be relatively high on the rank scale of verbs/clauses as arranged for narrative (as given at the conclusion of chap. 3).[2] Usually this means that such verbs are preterites. Occasionally, granted deep embedding, a lower ranking verb is found in the predominating constituent(s).

1.1. *The narrative sequence paragraph*

1.1.1. Consider Gen 40:1–4 as an example of narrative sequence paragraph:

40:1 Setting: *wayhî*   *ʾaḥar haddĕbārîm hāʾēlleh*
             and it happened that after things   these

             hāṭeʾu   *mašqēh*   *melek*   *-miṣrayim*
             they sinned the cupbearer of the King of Egypt

---

read Andersen's book a decade ago and was considerably impressed by it. My own work is in many ways indebted to him, in spite of my assigning less structure to the sentence and more to the paragraph in Biblical Hebrew.

[2] Cf. however, some examples cited under §3 of this chapter. The predominating constituents of a paragraph ultimately are recognizable on the assumption that the context makes clear whether story-telling, exposition, or what-have-you is the function of a given passage.

      wĕhā᾿ōpeh   la᾿ădōnêhem   lĕmelek
      and the baker against their lord against the King of

      -miṣrāyim
      Egypt

40:2 BU₁: *wayyiqṣōp   par῾ōh   ῾al   šĕnê*
          and he got angry Pharaoh against the two

          śārîsāyw   ῾al   śar   hammašqîm
          courtiers of him against the chief of the cupbearers

          wĕ῾al   śar   hā᾿ōpîm
          and against the chief of the bakers

40:3 BU₂: *wayyittēn ᾿ōtām -bĕmišmar bêt*
          and he put them   in jail   [in] the house of

          śar   haṭṭabbāḥîm ᾿el -bêt hassōhar mĕqôm
          the captain of the guard   into the prison   the place

          ᾿ăšer yôsēp   ᾿āsûr   šām
          where Joseph was imprisoned there

40:4 BU₃: *wayyipqōd   śar   haṭṭabbāḥîm*
          and he entrusted/appointed the captain of the guard

          ᾿et-yôsēp ᾿ittām
          Joseph   with them

      BUₙ: *wayšāret   ᾿ōtām*
          and he looked after them

    Terminus: *wayyihyû   yāmîm   bĕmišar*
            and they were [a number of] days in the jail

This paragraph consists of six Hebrew sentences. (1) Each sentence has one main verb—aside from 40:1, which has the *wayhî* + temporal + perfect construction, and thus has two verbs, *wayhî* and *ḥāṭĕ᾿û* 'sinned'. (2) As can be readily seen, however, a considerable complex of nominal structures can accompany the verb of a sentence, as in the first three sentences (40:1–3). This complexity answers to macrostructural constraints pointed out in earlier chapters; namely, the need to introduce and integrate into the story the cupbearer and the baker, and the need to make explicit (40:3) that their place of imprisonment was precisely the place where Joseph was. (3) The first sentences (40:1) and the last sentence (40:4c) are not part of the main body of the paragraph (the chain of preterites) but serve to preface and close that structure. Thus, the first sentence has a perfect as its main verb, preceded by a temporal expression that provides transition from the preceding episode (by means of a backreference). The last sentence has a form of *hāyâ*, 'be', that, while a preterite, does not report events or actions: 'And they were there for some time in the prison' (cf. chap. 3, §1.1 where forms of *hāyâ* are specifically excluded from the storyline). (4) In terms of the labeling of these constituents, I have considered sentence 1 to fill a *Setting* slot, and the last sentence to fill a *Terminus* slot. I consider that the body of the paragraph consists of a chain of Build-up slot-filler units (abbreviated BU), which are the predominating and diagnostic constituents. I have numbered these consecutively, but reserve the subscript $_n$ to mark the last of the series regardless of the number of units. This paragraph can be considered to be a *narrative sequence paragraph*; the diagnostic feature is the sequence of preterite clauses. Narrative sequence paragraphs must be distinguished from predictive sequence paragraphs (whose BUs are characterized by *waw* + the perfect, i.e., the suffixal tense) and hortatory sequence paragraphs (whose BUs are characterized by imperatives, cohortatives, and jussives; cf. chap. 5).

1.1.2. Before going on to further paragraphs I pause to examine in more detail the type of structures that characterize Setting and Terminus. When a complete sentence preceding the first preterite has a verb that is other than a preterite, it is clear that the former is in the Setting. In the paragraph just examined (40:1–4), the Setting sentence has a perfect as is also true in 37:17, 41:10, 41:50, 42:23, and 44:27. In 37:7 two perfects in an embedded coordinate paragraph occur in Setting; and in 32:20 an infinitive absolute precedes the perfect in Setting. A *wayhî* sentence (not the preposed *wayhî* + temporal) may also occur in Setting, as in 39:21 and 39:2 (where three coordinated *wayhî* sentences occur). Nominal clauses also occur in Setting, as in 41:12 and 41:46. In all these cases the preterites of the body of these paragraphs outrank the verbs/clauses that are considered to occur in Setting.

Under certain lexical conditions I have, however, considered that even certain clauses with initial preterites should be considered to belong to Setting rather than to the following chain of preterites. Preterites that are thus assigned to Setting are preterites of motion, sensation, or psychological state; they seem to be preparatory to what follows. Thus in 37:12 *wayyēlĕkû*, 'and they went', takes the brothers *off* the stage in this paragraph, which concerns first Jacob and Joseph, then Joseph and "the man" who found him wandering in the field. Not until the last preterite are we told that Joseph finally caught up with his brothers in Dothan. So not only is *wayyēlĕkû* a motion verb (which serves to get the brothers away from home so that Joseph can be sent to them) but it has as subject a referent that characterizes no other preterite in the paragraph. Conversely, in 37:28 the verb *wayyaᶜabrû*, 'and they passed by', serves to get the Midianites (formerly sighted in the distance as "Ishmaelites") *onto* the stage, so that Joseph's brothers can sell him into Egypt.

In 37:18 I consider the sensation verb *wayyirᵓû*, 'and they saw [him from afar]', to belong to the Setting of the paragraph. This is partly because this first sentence is explicitly set apart from the rest of the paragraph by the temporal clause *ûbĕterem yiqrab ʾălêhem*, 'and before he came near to them', which introduces the next preterite. Again, moreover, this first clause 'and they saw him from afar' seems to be preparatory to all that follows. In 41:8 a verb of psychological state *wattipāʿem* (*rûḥô*), 'and it was troubled (his spirit)', seems to be preparatory to all that follows. I would have no great argument with any who might suggest that a more consistent definition of Setting versus Body of a paragraph in terms of verb ranking would demand that all these examples be considered as constituting the first BUs in their chains instead of Setting. Nevertheless, on some level or other the peculiarity of these verbs as thus used needs to be accounted for.

A further example of a preterite in Setting seems to me, however, to look somewhat more persuasive. This is the occurrence of *wayyaʿăśû-kēn*, 'and they did thus', in 45:21—since the rest of the paragraph (which has a complicated nest of embedding (seems to report the carrying out of what the brothers did, thus making *wayyaʿăśû-kēn* a kind of a summary preview. Occasionally, a setting seems to contain a backgrounded sequence of events, as in 39:14: *hēbîʾ lānû ʾîš ʿibrî . . . bāʾ ʾēlay*, 'he brought in to us a Hebrew man . . . he came in to me'. Such sequences are only mildly sequential. I have considered such sequences (rare at best) to constitute narrative sequences whose preterites have been downgraded to perfects by virtue of the embedding of the paragraph in Setting.

1.1.3. With the exception of one special case to be discussed below, Terminus is clearly filled by verbs/clauses of lower rank than the chain of preterites that they close. Thus, in 39:20 we have a *wayhî* sentence in Terminus; in 41:15 and 41:57 we find perfects; and 39:10, and 41:13 the *wayhî* + temporal + perfect construction. Often, as to tense and subject matter, the Terminus bears little relation to what it terminates and is clearly cataphoric (37:36, where it closes an Episode and is called Closure rather than Terminus, and 39:6). This use of a cataphoric sentence at the end of a unit is, as we have seen, not uncommon in closing a *tôlĕdōt* section of Genesis. In 39:10 the Terminus is both summary and cataphoric; in 39:20 it is plainly summary (but even here the *šām*, 'there', is fateful of coming events).

In 41:53-54 I have considered two preterites (an embedded narrative sequence paragraph) to fill Terminus—without even being reduced to perfects. This is because the preterites involved ('And were finished the seven years of plenty. . . . And began the seven years of famine') are unrelated to the preceding body of the paragraph, which treats the naming of Joseph's sons, but are related somewhat to the Setting: 'And there were born to Joseph two sons before the years of the famine came in'

(41:50). In view of the frequent cataphoric function of Terminus, I have therefore assigned these two preterites to that slot.

1.1.4. One further quirk of the narrative sequence paragraph should be mentioned: The possibility of elevating a BU late in its paragraph (usually the BU_n) to the status of Climax by special marking. In 39:5 this is accomplished by using a midparagraph backreference, followed by a paraphrase unit. Gen 39:19 has a similar use of midparagraph backreference—in this case the longest and most involved backreference in the entire Joseph story. Semantically 39:5 is the climactic moment when Joseph reaches his zenith in Potiphar's house, while 39:19–20 marks his nadir: unjust imprisonment in Egypt through the false accusation of a woman.

Very probably, whenever a BU_n is elaborated considerably over the structure of the preceding BUs, the BU_n is meant to be climactic. This is especially true if the BU_n gives quoted speech or dialogue where such features are absent in the preceding BUs. Thus 37:30 voices Reuben's wail and is the first use of quoted speech in its paragraph. Similarly climactic is Jacob's wail at the end of a dialogue, which is BU_n in a series of six BUs (37:31–33). The striking threefold occurrence of Joseph's name in v 28 probably indicates that vv 26–28 are meant to be the climactic BU_n in a series of five BUs beginning in v 24.

Such climactic narrative sequence paragraphs are very distinct in structure from chiastic variants of this paragraph type, as in 37:34–35, where the key of the chiasmus (its *central* lines) are emphasized: 'And all his sons and daughters rose up to comfort him. And he refused to be comforted.' Similarly in 41:54b–57 the key lines refer to the severity of the famine—which is mentioned squarely in midparagraph *and* at both its extremities.

Different from both the climactic and the chiastic variants of the narrative sequence paragraph is such a long rambling unit as 43:15–25 in which the interactions of 'the men' (Joseph's brothers) and 'the man' (Joseph's steward) are described. Here and there occur BUs whose fillers are single sentences, namely, BU_3, BU_6, and BU_n. No evident pattern of prominence can be seen here; the treatment is simply unweighted and episodic.

1.2. *The narrative simple paragraph*

The narrative simple paragraph could be regarded as a specialized instance of the narrative sequence paragraph, but it is frequent enough that we single it out here for special description and exemplification.

Actually, when a narrative paragraph consists of only one sentence containing a preterite—whether or not another sentence that functions as Setting accompanies this sentence—it is impossible to assign the paragraph to any such specific paragraph type as Sequence, Reason, Result, Comment, or any of the paragraphs described in this chapter. Often we suspect that, since the preterite reports an event, we have simply a paragraph that consists of (Setting) BU_n. But the essence of a narrative sequence paragraph is reporting events in temporal order and no such sequence can occur when only one event is reported. For this reason I am considering the units described here to be simple paragraphs. The nucleus (excluding the Setting) of such paragraphs is simple and may be called the Text (as with the paragraphs described in subsequent sections of this chapter).

In such narrative simple paragraphs we sometimes find Setting expounded by sentences whose verb is a perfect as in 39:1, 44:3, 44:24, and 45:8. In 37:7 the Setting is an embedded paragraph whose sentences have two perfects and one imperfect. A participial clause expounds the Setting in 37:7, 41:2–3, 5–6, 18, 19–20, 22–23. A nominal clause expounds the Setting in 37:2. The Aperture of the entire Joseph story is a long nominal clause/sentence with the perfect of *hāyâ* plus a participle.[3] In all these examples the Text is a unit that contains a preterite, which thereby outranks all the other verb forms and clause types that have been mentioned.

1.2.1. In 40:5 a Text without an accompanying Setting figures as an Episode of the embedded narrative found in that chapter. As a whole Episode/Paragraph/Sentence, 40:5 is one of the longest sentences in the story:

> *wayyaḥalmû   ḥălôm   šĕnêhem   ʾîš*
> and they dreamed a dream   the two of them [each] man
>
> *ḥălōmô   bĕlāylâ   ʾeḥād   ʾîš*
> his dream in night   one   [each] man
>
> *kĕpitrôn   ḥălōmô   hammašqeh*
> according to the interpretation of his dream   the cupbearer
>
> *wĕhā ʾōpeh   ʾăšer   lĕmelek   miṣrayim*
> and the baker   which   [were] to the king of   Egypt
>
> *ʾăšer   ʾăsûrîm   bĕbêt hassōhar*
> which   [were] imprisoned   in the prison

There is also one instance where, in a succession of two preterites, the first has been called a Setting and the second the Text. This is parallel to

---

[3] Both Aperture and Stage on the discourse level are broadly similar to Setting on the paragraph level.

our treatment of setting in narrative sequence paragraphs. In this case, 41:37, 38, the preterite involved is a verb of psychological state that precedes action: *wayyîṭab haddābār bĕʿênê parʿōh . . . wayyōʾmer parʿōh*, 'And it seemed good the word in the eyes of Pharaoh. . . . And Pharaoh said. . . .'

1.2.2. We have also an example of a narrative simple paragraph (40:9–11) whose Setting is expounded by an embedded paragraph that consists of two noun clauses and whose Text is a juxtaposition sentence with two perfects. The *whole* functions as Setting in a still more inclusive unit. Here we see a nice example of verb ranking as it correlates with paragraph structure: (1) Perfects outrank nominal clauses, hence the latter are Setting to the former; but (2) preterite outranks perfect, so the whole embedded unit is Setting (in this case Stage) of an embedded narrative to a sequence of preterites (in this case an Episode).

Stage: (N) Simple Paragraph

    Setting: (E) Coordinate Paragraph

        Item $_1$: *baḥălômî   wĕhinnēh gepen lĕpānāy*
            in my dream behold   a vine [was] before me

        Item $_2$: *ûbaggepen   šĕlōšâ   śārîgim*
            and on the vine [were] three branches

    Text: *wĕhîʾ kĕpōraḥat   ʿālĕtâ   niṣṣāh* [3 f.s.]
        and it at its budding went up [burst into] bloom

        hibšîlû   ʾaškĕlōtêhā ʿănābîm [juxtaposed sentence]
        [and] ripened its clusters into grapes

Episode: (N) Sequence Paragraph

    Setting: *wĕkôs   parʾōh   bĕyādî*
        and the cup of Pharaoh [was] in my hand

    BU$_1$: *wāʾeqqaḥ   ʾet-hāʿănābîm*
        and I took the grapes

    BU$_2$: *wāʾeśḥaṭ   ʾōtām ʾel-kôs   parʿōh*
        and I pressed them into the cup of Pharaoh

    BU$_n$: *wāʾettēn   ʾet-hakkôs ʿal-kap   parʿōh*
        and I gave the cup   into the hand of Pharaoh

1.2.3. One slightly problematical example remains, namely, 40:16–17. Here, while the Setting is an embedded paragraph that consists of two nominal clauses, the putative Text is a participial clause/sentence. This passage recounts the baker's dream in which he is entirely passive; he performs no action. We might well then raise the question as to whether the paragraph is narrative or expository. In choosing the former, our analytical decision has been two-fold: (1) Since presumably the intent of the baker is to recount (narrate) his dream, we have decided to follow the rank scheme for narrative (no other rank scheme has been described as yet, but several more are to be posited). (2) According to this scheme, participles, which portray ongoing activities, outrank nominal clauses, which are simply descriptive of situations. Consequently, we have identified the participial construction as Text and the preceding nominal clauses as simply Setting.

1.3.   *The narrative reason and narrative result paragraphs*

Both reason and result paragraphs are somewhat scarce in narrative; most commonly they are found in hortatory and to a lesser degree in explanatory passages. A reason paragraph features an action/event or situation as its Text, then proceeds to give in the Reason the cause or reason that underlies the action/event or situation. A result paragraph likewise features in its Text an action/event or situation, then proceeds to give in the Result the outworking of the action/event or situation. The two are notional (semantic) inverses: A reason paragraph highlights the (Text) result over its cause/reason; a result paragraph highlights the (Text) cause/reason over its result.

The prevalence of these two paragraph types in hortatory passages is understandable: Hortatory discourse sets out to modify or influence behavior, and in achieving that goal the mentioning of reasons and results is strategic. But in narrative discourse? Here the rationale seems to be that at certain places in a story it is strategic to halt the flow of events for a moment and explain an action/event. Consequently, reason and result paragraphs are *not* found in random distribution through a discourse; rather they occur only at places where they serve to enhance the *staging* of a story (or some episode within it), or contribute to a *summary* or *crescendo* effect (in reference to a great moment of a story). Since only six instances of these paragraph types occur in narrative passages in the Joseph story they are all cited and discussed here.

1.3.1.   In the Stage of Ep₁ (the conspiracy against and selling of Joseph) both a reason (37:3) and a result (37:4) paragraph occur. This is a passage in which conflicting motivations on the part of Jacob and Joseph's brothers are described.

In 37:3, the reason paragraph, we construe the structure in accordance with the fact that the perfect outranks the N + perfect in the rank scheme of chap. 3—thus making the former (linearly second) the Text:

Reason: *wĕyiśrā⁾ēl ⁾āhab ⁾et-yôsēp mikkol   -bānāyw kî*
and Israel loved Joseph   more than all his sons for

-ben   -zēqunîm ∅   hû⁾ lô
a son of old age [was] he to him

Text: *wĕ⁽āśâ   lô   kĕtōnet passîm*
and he made him a "special" cloak

Here the sentence within the Reason slot starts out with N + perfect,
wĕyiśrā⁾ēl ⁾āhab, 'and Israel loved', and includes its own internal *kî*
clause, which expresses a further motivation: *kî-ben-zēqunîm ∅ hû⁾ lô*,
'for a son of old age he [was] to him' (a nominal clause). The presence
within this sentence of a Cause Margin (adverbial clause introduced with
kî) is evidence that the presentation of emotional predilections is the
order of the day in this passage. The Text narrate the concrete expression of Jacob's love, the special cloak that he had made for Joseph. This
sentence also serves to introduce the cloak, a prop of considerable importance throughout Genesis 37. This Reason paragraph functions as
Setting to a chain of two following preterites, which by virtue of being
preterites outrank the perfects of the Setting.

1.3.2. Immediately following the above examples are two sentences,
the first with a preterite and the second with a negated perfect, that
constitute a result paragraph (37:4). This unit, in turn, expounds the
BU_n of the larger framework (see pp. 210–11):

Text: *wayyiśnĕ⁾û   ⁾ōtô*
and they hated him

Result: *wĕlō⁾   yākĕlû   dabbĕrô   lĕśālōm*
and not they could speak [to him] decently

Here the fact that the brothers came to hate Joseph is on the storyline,
while the result—that they couldn't speak to him decently—is somewhat
routine and predictable from the hatred.

1.3.3. Two examples of these paragraph types—doubtful for different
reasons—are here cited from Genesis 43. The first example (43:32) is
doubtful solely because the sentence in the putative Reason is introduced with *kî*, 'because'. Most frequently, *kî* clauses are simply part of
the preceding sentence. The possibility exists, however, that granted
sufficient (!) complexity of the construction following *kî*, the whole may
be considered a separate sentence (cf., for example, *gar*, 'for', in Greek,
which sometimes determines a Cause margin that is part of the previous
sentence and sometimes begins a new sentence). No harm is done here in

citing this as an example of the narrative reason paragraph; if this seems to be undesirable and inconsistent with the general conception of sentence and paragraph in Hebrew (as above), then the whole can be collapsed into a sentence—provided that we are not sacrificing empirical reality to the consistency of a model. At any rate, after consideration of 43:33 below, we shall comment on this as an appropriate place in the Joseph story for citations of motivations.

1.3.4.   Gen 43:33, which immediately follows the above, is doubtful for a different reason, namely, both Text and Result have preterites. But as we have seen in the case of Setting versus Text (or versus a BU), we probably need to posit a notional classification of verbs, whereby action verbs outrank verbs of mental action or state—even when both are preterites. We have also had recourse to the assumption that motion verbs (which take participants on or off the stage or simply shift their locale) are outranked notionally by action verbs proper. The first assumption holds for 43:33:

Text: *wayyēšĕbû*   *lĕpānāyw   habbĕkōr*
         and they took their seats before him the first born

         kibkōrātô   *wĕhaṣṣāʿîr*
         according to his seniority and the youngest

         kiṣʿirātô
         according to his youth

Result: *wayyitmĕhû*   *hāʾănāšîm   ʾîš   ʾel -rēʿēhû*
         and they marveled the men   [each] man to his fellow

Here, *wayyēšĕbû*, 'they took their seats', even if simply translated 'they sat', is presented (by virtue of being a preterite) to us as an event. The marveling reported in the Result is the psychological effect of the seating arrangements described in the Text.

Both these examples, like 37:3 and 37:4, occur in the BU_n (climax) of a long paragraph—in this case, 43:26-34, which we might entitle "Dining with Joseph." Within this passage, 43:31b-34, preterites occur that picture events that are only loosely sequential; there is a strong depictive cast to the passage. This apparently correlates with the structural status of the passage as exponent of a BU_n (climax).[4] Furthermore, resort to explanation of motivations and results is peculiarly appropriate at such a juncture in story; this explanatory material is found in the embedded paragraphs we have just examined. This whole passage (43:26-34) just precedes the peak (chap. 44) of the embedded story, which is the whole of 43-45.

---

[4] Cf. the climax of the Flood story (Gen 7:6-10).

1.3.5. The narrative result paragraph found in 45:1 is part of the immediate structural crescendo that leads to Joseph's self revelation.

Text: *wayyiqrā*ʾ   *hôṣîʾû*   *kol*   -ʾîš *mēʿālāy*
        and he cried out clear out every man from before me

Result: *wělōʾ*   *ʿāmad*   *ʾîš*   *ʾittô*
        and not [there] stood [any] man with him

        běhitwaddaʿ   *yôsēp* *ʾel* -ʾeḥāyw
        in his making himself known Joseph to his brothers

Here the preterite of the Text *wayyiqrāʾ*, 'and he cried out', outranks the negated perfect, *wělōʾ ʿāmad*, 'and not [there] stood', of the Result. The former is an act (specifically a speech act), while the latter is a resultant state of affairs that is predictable from Joseph's command.

1.4. *The narrative comment paragraph*

A narrative comment paragraph makes possible, on the part of the narrator, a comment on or explanation of some event reported on the storyline. In the Joseph corpus every instance of Text in such paragraphs is expounded by a clause/sentence with a preterite, while the Comment varies from perfect to negated perfect, to participial clause, to nominal clause, to negated nominal clause. Again, the presence of such narrative comment paragraphs is not random. Explanatory or graphic details are not found willy-nilly, but serve to enhance great moments of the story or the crescendo to a great moment. I posit seven instances of such narrative comment paragraphs.

1.4.1. In 37:15 we have an incident from the paragraph (BU_n-climax?) in which a man finds Joseph wandering in the field and finally directs him (fateful contingency!) to his brothers in Dothan:

Text: *wayyimṣāʾēhû*   *ʾîš*
          and he found him a man

Comment: *wěhinnēh* *tōʿeh*   *baśśādeh*
          and behold [he] was wandering in the field

Here the comment is a participial clause, which is graphically introduced by *hinnēh*, 'behold'.

1.4.2. In 37:24 (part of the general Peak episode [37:23–28] of the embedded narrative which is chap. 37), after the seizure of Joseph, the paragraph embeds a narrative comment paragraph as the next BU:

Text: *wayyašlikû   ʾōtô habbôrâ*
          and they threw him   into the pit

Comment: (E) Paraphrase Paragraph

  Text: *wĕhabbôr   rēq*
            and the pit [was] empty

  Paraphrase: *ʾên   bô   māyim*
              [there was] no   in it water

Here the Comment is an explanatory paraphrase paragraph (yet to be described), whose nominal clauses are outranked in the over-all narrative structure by the preterite of the Text.

1.4.3. In 39:11, which I do not here present in detail, the narrator reports on the storyline that Joseph went into the house to perform some errand, then adds the Comment: 'And none of the men of the house [were] there in the house.' The first sentence with its preterite and the second with its negated nominal clause constitute a narrative comment paragraph that precedes and suspensefully anticipates the ensuing action between Potiphar's wife and Joseph.

1.4.4. In 41:7 at the end of Pharaoh's composite dream we are told on the storyline 'and he awoke Pharaoh', then, in an off-the-line Comment (not really new information to us, but valid to the psychology of one awakening from slumber), 'and-behold [it was] a dream'. Again, a narrative comment paragraph underscores the fateful contingency of this dream—which will catapult Joseph to the lordship of Egypt.

1.4.5. Gen 44:12 is an example of the skillful insertion of a narrative comment paragraph at a point of maximum tension (pre-paragraph climax):

Text: *wayḥappēś*
          and he searched

Comment: (N) Antithetical Paragraph

Thesis: *baggādôl   hēḥēl*
          with the oldest he began

  Antithesis: *ûbaqqāṭōn   killâ*
              and with the youngest he finished

The internal analysis of the narrative antithetical paragraph is considered in §1.6. Suffice it here to note that both verbs in the embedded paragraph found in the Comment are in clauses with noun + perfect—

and both are outranked by the preterite of the text. The artfulness of the introduction of a narrative comment paragraph at this junction in the story is seen at a glance by noticing the event reported in the following line: 'And the cup was found in Benjamin's sack.'

1.4.6.   Gen 44:28 contains a narrative comment paragraph embedded in a speech of Jacob's as retold by Judah. It precedes Jacob's outburst: 'You will bring down my grey hairs in sorrow to Sheol'—but the analysis of this complicated layering of quotations is beyond the purpose of this section.

1.4.7.   Finally, 41:21 has to do with a Comment of Pharaoh concerning one phase of his dream. I will not present this example here. It is probably symptomatic of Pharaoh's emotional distress at his grisly and foreboding vision.

1.5.   *The narrative amplification and paraphrase paragraphs*

Amplification paragraphs are paragraphs that consists of a Text and an Amplification, with the latter adding new information not contained in the former, while at the same time essentially incorporating the material found in it. In the paraphrase paragraph the additional information is nonexistent or at most minimal. The former are much more frequent than the latter. Both of these paragraph types can be regarded as encoding notional paraphrase of which I elsewhere distinguish seven varieties (Longacre 1983).

Narrative amplification paragraphs are amplification paragraphs that occur in narrative context. Most commonly the Text is expounded by a clause whose verb is a preterite; the amplification is either a verb/clause of lesser rank or a clause with a preterite of the sort discussed in chap. 3, §1.3. under "complex links in a chain." I will illustrate the former first then dispose somewhat summarily of the latter. Not all occurring examples can be discussed here, since the Amplification is the most frequently used device to add further information to the storyline, the examples are much too numerous to be discussed one-by-one.

1.5.1.   Gen 39:4–6 provides an example of three narrative amplification paragraphs in sequence. In 39:4 we have an example of a chiastically structured paragraph, which (like many such examples) is a narrative amplification paragraph. The verb of the Text is a preterite and on the storyline of the story. The verb of the Amplification—as is regular in

such chiastic structures where the noun precedes the verb in the second
sentence—is a perfect.[5]

Text: *wayyapqidēhû ʿal -bêtô*
                and he put him over his house

Amplification: *wĕkol -yeš-lô   nātan   bĕyādô*
                and all his substance he gave into his hand

Gen 39:6 is very similar to the above, but has a negated perfect in the
Amplification. The intervening paragraph 39:5, to which we have already referred several times, has the preterite of 'bless' in its Text and
has *wayhî birkat yhwh*, 'and was the blessing of the LORD', in the
Amplification, that is, a finite verb occurs in the Text, followed by
the verb 'be' + a nominalization of the first verb in the Amplification.
The series of three embedded narrative amplification paragraphs here
serves to mark the general region of the Climax of the embedding
paragraph.

1.5.2. A few narrative amplification paragraphs occur deeply embedded
in the narrative context and consequently do not have a preterite in their
Text: 39:22, 44:4, and 45:23. In 39:22 the Text has the perfect of *hāya* +
a participle while the Amplification has a negated participial clause. In
44:4 the Text has a perfect, the Amplification a negated perfect. Finally,
in 45:23 the Text has a perfect and the Amplification a participial clause.
In all these the verb/clause rank scheme of chapter 3 still serves to
identify the naturally prominent member of the series of two sentences.
In a further example, 37:33 (the *second* narrative amplification paraphrase in that verse), there is a less clear situation that involves noun +
perfect in the Text and infinitive absolute + perfect in the Amplification.
The data are few, however, in which infinitive absolutes reinforcing a
finite verb occur, so infinitive absolutes do not figure in our present
ranking scheme. At any rate, we have here in this paragraph a perfect
preceded by some other element in both sentences.

1.5.3. Most of the examples of narrative amplification paragraphs involve preterites in both the Text and the Amplification. I have presented
these in summary chapter 3, §1.3. complex links in a chain, under verbs
of speech and sensation. In accordance with what is stated there, narrative amplification paragraphs of this sort involve a Text that describes a
speech act by means of a specific preterite (e.g., 'ask', 'refuse', 'reprove',

---

[5] Note, however, that the two clauses are in a loose paraphrase relation and
are thus distinct from the contrastive arrangement of the antithetical paragraph,
which can also have a noun perfect in its second member.

'conspire', 'narrate', 'reply', etc.); then the Amplification introduces, by means of the preterite of *ʾāmar*, 'say', a quotation that gives the words used in implementing the speech act. Thus in 39:8 we have:

Text: *waymāʾēn*
and he refused

Amplification: *wayyōʾmer ʾel -ʾēšet ʾădōnāyw*
and he said to the wife of his lord

There follows in vv 8–9 the substance of Joseph's refusal: his master has entrusted all that he has to him—except *his wife*; how can Joseph violate this trust and sin against God? In 40:9 the speech act is *recounting*:

Text: *waysappēr śar -hammašqîm*
and he recounted the prince of the cupbearers

ʾet ḥălōmô lĕyôsēp
his dream to Joseph

Amplification: *wayyōʾmer lô*
and he said to him

There follows in 40:9–11, the recital of the cupbearer's dream. In 40:18, the speech act is less exactly characterized as a *reply*:

Text: *wayyaʿan yôsēp*
and he answered Joseph

Amplification: *wayyōʾmer zeh pitrōnô*
and he said this [is] the interpretation of it

There follows the interpretation of the baker's dream. In these three examples above, each quotation sentence backloops a paragraph (or even a short discourse as in 40:9) into its structure. This leads, of course, to considerable embedding. In viewing this complexity it is helpful to keep in mind that the whole quotation sentence with its more or less extensive quote is simply an Amplification of the Text. For more such examples, see the previous section already indicated.

1.5.4. As also mentioned in that same section, a clause that has a verb of sensation can be followed by a clause with a verb that indicates what is perceived, as in 37:25 where 'lift up the eyes' occurs in the Text and a clause with *raʾa*, 'see', occurs in the Amplification where what is seen is specified. Compare also 43:39, where the same structure occurs, and 42:27, which is not materially different. Perhaps the most interestingly divergent example here is 43:17, where the Text contains the generic preterite *ʿāśâ*, 'do', and the Amplification employs the more specific preterite *bôʾ*, 'bring in'.

It is interesting to note that narrative amplification paragraphs are used considerably more frequently than are narrative reason, result, and comment paragraphs—which are reserved for more selective and hence less frequent use.

1.5.5.   By contrast, what I have termed the narrative paraphrase paragraph is very infrequent. In fact, our sole example is in 40:23. Here negated antonym paraphrase is used. We are told in the Paraphrase that 'he didn't remember Joseph' and in the Text, 'but he forgot him'. I have here labeled the second sentence the Text because the preterite of 'forget' outranks the negated perfect of 'didn't remember'. How shall we evaluate such a construction as 40:23? It could be argued that it is simply a variant of the narrative amplification paragraph, but note: (1) it is notionally distinct in that it is simple paraphrase without amplification; and (2) the Paraphrase precedes the Text, while Amplification (of which we have many examples) always follows the Text. If this be a rare narrative paragraph type in its own right, we can assume that it is used here to mark the most frustrating period in Joseph's life—two full years of further waiting after he had had every reason to believe that things had already taken a turn for the better. A more abstract formulation of the function of this narrative paragraph must await examination of its usage in other contexts.

1.6.   *The narrative coordinate and narrative antithetical paragraphs*

Both the coordinate and the antithetical paragraph types are broadly coordinate in structure, that is, neither part is semantically subordinated to the other. In the narrative coordinate paragraph, of which there are only a handful of examples, the clauses that are coordinated have the verbs of equal rank; *gam*, 'also', frequently occurs in the second sentence. In narrative antithetical paragraphs, the component parts of the paragraph either have equal rank or the first member outranks the second. We refer to these two variants—which are about equally frequent—as equi-weighted or fore-weighted.

1.6.1.   In that most coordinate paragraphs occur in hortatory or expository context, only a few examples of narrative coordinate paragraphs can be cited. Consider, for example, 40:15:

Item$_1$: *kî-gunnōb gunnabtî   mē'ereṣ   hā'ibrîm*
       and surely was kidnapped from the land of the Hebrews

Item$_2$: *wĕgam -pōh lō' -'aśîtî   mĕ'ûmâ kî -śāmû   'ōtî*
       and also here not I have done anything that they put me

babbôr
in the dungeon

As to possible relative rank of the verbs involved here, the first sentence has an infinitive absolute with the perfect and the second a negated perfect. Furthermore the second has the particle *gam*, 'also', which I take to be basically a mark of coordination. Apparently sequence is not focal in this paragraph, although 'being kidnapped' from the land of the Hebrews obviously had to precede anything that Joseph did (or didn't do) in Egypt. Note also the prominence given to local references: 'the land of the Hebrews . . . here'. I believe that we have in this passage some evidence that perfects—even when occurring in successive sentences—are not as explicitly sequential as preterites. Granted the locational orientation of the passage and the presence of *gam* preceding the second verb, it would seem that the coordination is intended here rather than temporal sequence.[6] Compare also 37:7:

Item$_1$: *wĕhinnēh   qāmâ   ʾălummātî*
and behold arose my sheaf

Item$_2$: *wĕgam   -niṣṣābâ*
and also it stood up

Here again we have a sequence of perfects that could be interpreted to indicate temporal sequence. But, if we are to give any significance to the presence of *gam*, it would seem that it is coordination that is intended.

1.6.2. Other examples of narrative coordinate paragraphs have embedded paragraphs instead of sentences as exponents of Items. Thus 37:2c–4 is a narrative coordinate paragraph that couples a narrative simple paragraph (37:2c) and a narrative sequence paragraph (37:3–4). First Joseph and then Israel are thematic in the two halves of this paragraph. This narrative coordinate paragraph expounds the Stage of the story by presenting action and attitudes of first Joseph and then Israel—actions and attitudes that led to the development of a crisis within the family. Also, both the long structure in 41:1–7 (the narrator's account of Pharaoh's dreams) and the parallel structure in 41:17–24 (Pharaoh's own account of his dreams) can be considered to be narrative coordinate paragraphs in which awareness quote paragraphs (cf. chap. 8) are coordinate within each passage.

---

[6] *Gam* does not directly precede a preterite anywhere in the Joseph narratives. Cf. Gen 29:30: *wayyābōʾ gam ʾel-rāhēl wayyeʾĕhab gam-ʾet-rāhēl millēʾâ*, 'And he went in also to Rachel. And he loved also Rachel more than Leah'. Note here that although *gam* occurs in context with preterites it does not

1.6.3. Narrative antithetical paragraphs are somewhat more numerous, but are less than half as numerous as narrative amplification paragraphs— which are the most frequent means employed to hang clothes (additional, supportive information) on the (story)line. About half of our examples of narrative antithetical paragraphs are equi-weighted. Several of these are composed of noun + perfect in both parts of the paragraph. Gen 41:13 is a paragraph that backloops into the preceding sentence and is preceded by *kēn hāyâ*, 'thus it happened', (cataphoric):

Thesis: *ʾōtî hēšîb   ʿal -kannî*
              me   he restored   to   my pedestal

Antithesis: *wĕʾōtô   tālâ*
              and him   he hanged

Gen 44:12 has a narrative antithetical paragraph that is deeply embedded in several layers of paragraph structure; again, noun + perfect occurs in both parts of the paragraph:

Thesis: *baggādôl   hēḥēl*
              with the oldest he began

Antithesis: *ûbaqqāṭōn   killâ*
              with the youngest he finished

In 45:22 there occurs a similar example, also deeply embedded, with noun + perfect in both parts of the paragraph:

Thesis: *lĕkullām   nātan   lāʾîš   ḥălipôt   śĕmālōt*
              and to all of them he gave to each changes of raiment

Antithesis: *ûlĕbinyāmin   nātan   šĕlōš-mēʾôt   kesep*
              but to Benjamin   he gave three hundred pieces of silver

              wĕḥāmēš ḥălipōt   śĕmālōt
              and five changes of raiment

    In these three examples, contrast is featured in each narrative antithetical paragraph: (1) contrast between the fates of cupbearer and the baker; (2) contrast between the starting with the oldest and finishing with the youngest; and (3) contrast between the gifts given to the rest of his brothers and the more lavish gifts given to Benjamin. Also each of the three examples occurs towards the end of some unit. Thus, 41:13 is the end of the cupbearer's speech to Pharaoh and immediately precedes the pell-mell sending for Joseph, his audience with Pharaoh, and his sudden elevation to lordship of Egypt. Gen 44:12 is just before the

---

precede the preterites. Furthermore, in both sentences the *gam* seems to be associated with the noun Rachel instead of the verbs.

climax of its paragraph, that is, it immediately precedes the discovery of the cup in Benjamin's sack and the main crisis of the whole story. Finally, 45:22 is at the end of the long first post-peak Episode (in the overall unity of chaps. 43–45) and the precedes the dramatic confrontation of the brothers with Jacob as they tell him 'Joseph is still alive'. To these examples we can also add 42:38, where a backlooped narrative antithetical paragraph occurs as part of a sentence, has a perfect in both parts, and is towards the end of Jacob's speech, which in turn terminates the interpeak Episode (chap. 42) and precedes the whole massive development of 43–45 (the Peak).[7]

1.6.4. Still other equi-weighted narrative antithetical paragraphs have preterites in both halves of the paragraph. Gen 37:35a embeds such a paragraph at the "key" of the chiasmus found in 37:34–35.

Thesis: *wayyāqumû   kol -bānāyw wĕkol -bĕnōtāyw*
and they rose up all   his sons and all his daughters

lĕnaḥămô
to comfort him

Antithesis: *waymā'ēn   lĕhitnaḥēm*
and he refused to be comforted

Clearly, a contrast is indicated here between what the sons and daughters attempted and what they were able to carry out (expectancy reversal). Furthermore, this passage occurs in the Peak of the embedded narrative 37:29–35 concerning the attempt to conceal the crime of selling Joseph. Chiasmus in general provides closure to several episodes of the Joseph story; here the key of this chiasmus is a narrative antithetical paragraph, which, as we have pointed out above, often occurs towards the end of some unit. In brief, here both the chiasmus and the narrative antithetical paragraph found within its serve a closure function.

1.6.5. Other examples of equi-weighted paragraphs of this sort with preterites in the component sentences are 41:56 (where the narrative antithetical paragraph occurs in another chiastic paragraph, which serves to mark closure of the Peak episode of Joseph [chap. 41]) and 42:7a. The latter examples and 41:56 involve embedding of paragraphs in one

[7] To these examples we might further add 44:4, where two embedded paragraphs have noun + perfect in their dominant sentences, and where the brothers have left the city in blissful ignorance and Joseph bids his steward to pursue them and accuse them of stealing his cup. This, of course, is the apparent end of the brothers' second stay in the city as guests of Joseph, but the storm is about to break over their heads.

of both halves of each example. The 42:7a passage is peculiarly situated in that it occurs early in the episode and is more similar to the staging of an episode than to its Peak or Closure. There will be, however, other examples below of the narrative antithetical paragraph in this function.

1.6.6. Other examples of this paragraph type are fore-weighted. Gen 37:11 contains an examples that closes the account of Joseph's dreams, his telling of the dreams, and his brothers' reactions:

Thesis: *wayqanᵓû*   *-bô*   *ᵓeḥāyw*
           and they were jealous of him his brothers

Antithesis: *wĕᵓābîw*   *šāmar*   *ᵓet-haddābār*
            but his father pondered [kept] the word

Likewise, in "closing out," function is the narrative antithetical paragraph found in 40:21, 22:

Thesis: (N) Sequence Paragraph

  BU₁: *wayyāšeb*   *ᵓet-śar*   *hammašqîm*   *ᶜal -mašqēhû*
        and he restored the chief of the cupbearers to his office

  BU₂: *wayyittēn*   *hakkôs ᶜal -kap*   *parᶜōh*
        and he gave the cup to the hand of Pharaoh

Antithesis: *wĕᵓēt śar*   *hāᵓōpîm*   *tālâ*   *kaᵓăšer*
            and the chief of the bakers   he hanged just as

            pātar   *lāhem*   *yôsēp*
            had interpreted to them Joseph

Here the Thesis is expounded by a narrative sequence paragraph whose preterites outweigh the noun + perfect of the Antithessis. The fates of the two courtiers are contrasted (thus giving a certain *local* prominence to the chief baker), but the fate of the first is given greater prominence— as befits his subsequent importance to the story.[8] This paragraph expounds the next to the last BU in the final episode/paragraph of the narrative that constitutes chap. 40. Compare also 43:21, where a paragraph of this type occurs just short of the Terminus of the speech of 'the men' (Joseph's brothers) to the steward of Joseph's house.

1.6.7. Other fore-weighted examples of this paragraph type belong rather to staging than to closure (using both of these terms broadly).

---

[8] This affords an exquisite example of event prominence versus participant prominence. A lesser event can be reported in a clause that at the same time gives greater local prominence to a participant. Cf. also the birth of Ephraim and Manasseh (41:51–52) as discussed in chap. 3, §2.8.

Thus in 40:8 the two imprisoned courtiers broach the subject of what was troubling them by saying to Joseph, 'We've dreamed a dream, and there is no interpreter'; here the Thesis has a noun + perfect and the antithesis has a nominal clause. Compare also 41:15, where a very similar paragraph occurs recursively within another narrative antithetical paragraph:

Thesis: Narrative Antithetical Paragarph

   Thesis: *ḥălôm*   *ḥālamtî*
                 I've dreamed a dream

   Antithesis: *ûpōtēr*   *ʾên*   *ʾōtô*
                 and interpreter [there is] none of it

Antithesis: *waʾănî šamaʿtî ʿālêkā lēʾmōr tišmaʿ*   *ḥălôm*
           but I I heard concerning you that you hear a dream

           liptōr   *ʾōtô*
           to interpret it

Here the embedded paragraph is of the fore-weighted variety, while the embedding paragraph is equi-weighted (noun + perfect in Thesis of Thesis and in the main Antithesis). The whole unit serves Pharaoh as an opening to broach to Joseph the subject that is bothering him.

1.6.8. Gen 42:3–4 contains a narrative antithetical paragraph of fore-weighted structure with a preterite in the Thesis and a noun + perfect in the Antithesis: 'And they went down, the ten brothers of Joseph, to buy grain in Egypt. But Benjamin the brother of Joseph he did not send Jacob.' This occurs as a vital piece of information in Episode₁ of the embedded narrative that constitutes Gen 42 (unless indeed this whole Episode₁ were to be considered simply to be the Stage of the story found in chap. 42).

    We are told twice in the early part of chap. 42 that Joseph recognized his brothers. The first instance, 42:7a, was pointed out as an example of an equi-weighted variety of this paragraph type. In the second instance, 42:8, we have a narrative antithetical paragraph of the fore-weighted variety (preterite and noun + perfect): 'And he recognized Joseph his brothers. But *they* didn't recognize him.' This immediately precedes Joseph's beginning of a prolonged and acrimonious debate with them by accusing them (in v 9) of being spies.

1.6.9. For other fore-weighted examples of this paragraph type see 42:21, 42:22, and 41:51–52. The latter is part of a very short episode (the births of Joseph's sons) and is of obscure function. A further paragraph found in 45:14 probably also should be classified as a narrative antithetical paragraph—although semantic reciprocity rather than contrast is encoded here (Joseph embraced Benjamin and Benjamin embraced Joseph). Here, as always, linguistic constructions have their more frequent and usual uses and their less frequent and more peripheral functions. At any rate, 45:14 occurs very close to the *end* of the long paragraph (45:1–15) in which Joseph reveals himself to his brothers— and closure (broadly conceived) is a typical functions of the narrative antithetical paragraph.

2.   *Predictive paragraphs*

2.0.   *Verb rank in predictive discourse*

Stretches of embedded predictive discourse characterize some of the speeches of Joseph within the story. Verb rank in such predictive discourses is parallel in many respects to the scheme that has been posited for narrative discourse, specifically, (1) the highest ranking form of the verb is the *w* (cons) perfect (i.e., *waw*-consecutive perfect). This is parallel to the position of the preterite in narrative discourse, since the preterite is *waw*-consecutive imperfect. (2) The next highest ranking verb forms are forms of the imperfect (i.e., the imperfect, and preposed noun + imperfect). (3) The remaining verb forms, participles, *hāyâ* clauses, and nominal clauses occupy the same relative positions in verb rank in both discourse types (see Diagram 4).[9]

The general parallelism of prediction (events told in advance of their happening) and narration (recounting of events that have already transpired) is seen in the common adherence to a strict VSO (or VOS) ordering of storyline clauses and the restriction to the affirmative. In Prediction, the VSO in which the V consists of a *w* (cons) perfect gives way to the imperfect (backgrounded event), the imperfect with preposed noun (event relevant to a participant), or negated imperfect (events that won't come off), in much the same way that in narrative the preterite

---

[9] Procedural discourse (cf. the sacrificial prescriptions of Leviticus, e.g., 4:2–12) is broadly similar to predictive discourse (Longacre 1982b). There is, however, a variety of procedural discourse that can be called *enjoined procedure*. In the latter, a clause-initial imperative and noun announce the goal of the following procedures and enjoin its accomplishment. Cf. Gen 6:14: 'Make for yourself an ark', which is followed by instructions on how to make an ark. Consider also Exod 25:1; 28:1, 42; and 29:1. A new subtopic toward the middle or end of a set of procedures can call for another imperative, as in Gen 6:21: 'take for yourself food'. A further use of the initial imperative in procedural discourse is that of the imperative of a motion verb. The imperative form *lēk* of *hālak*, 'go', functions almost like a functional particle (Exod 3:16, 4:19, 7:15) in both procedural and hortatory discourse.

DIAGRAM 4. Verb Rank in Predictive Discourse

Band 1: Line of Pre- diction	1. *w* (consecutive) perfect[a]
Band 2: Backgrounded Predictions	2.1. Imperfect 2.2. Noun + imperfect (with noun in focus)
Band 3: Backgrounded Activities	3.1. *hinnēh* + participle 3.2. Participle 3.3. Noun + participle
Band 4: Setting	4.1. *w* (consecutive) perfect of *hāyâ*, 'be' 4.2. Imperfect of *hāyâ*, 'be' 4.3. Nominal clause (verbless) 4.4. Existential clause with *yēš*

[a]1. demotes to 2.1. by preposing *lô*, 'not', and to 2.2. by preposing a noun.

(*waw*-consecutive + imperfect) gives way to forms of the perfect (cf. above). The relation can be summarized as in the following chart:

	Storyline	Off-the-line
Narrative	Preterite (= *waw* consecutive + Impf)	Perfect
Predictive	*waw* consecutive + perfect	Imperfect

The scheme of verb rank can now be applied to predictive paragraphs in Biblical Hebrew—and to the Joseph story in particular. Most of the narrative paragraph types are seen to have their counterparts in predictive paragraph types. It is best to consider—in the interest of maximum generalization and overall simplicity—that there is one scheme of paragraph types and that these types have variants according to their distribution in different discourse types. Essential, then to the internal analysis of a paragraph is its identification as a N (Narrative), P (Predictive), E (Expository), or H (Hortatory) variant. Once a paragraph is so classified, then the appropriate scheme of verb rank can be applied to guide the analysis of the constituents of the paragraph.

2.1. *The predictive sequence paragraph*

Gen 40:13 exhibits an example of predictive sequence paragraph:

Setting: *bĕ⁽ôd šĕlōšet yāmîm yiśśā⁾   par⁽ōh   ⁾et-rō⁾šekā*
in just three days   he will lift up Pharaoh your head

BU₁: *wahăšîbĕkā*   *ʿal -kannekā*
        and he will put you on your pedestal

BUₙ: *wĕnātattā*   *kôs*   *-parʿōh   bĕyādô*
        and you will give the cup of Pharaoh into his hand

        kammišpāt   *hāriʾšôn   ʾăšer   hāyîtā*
        according to the custom former   which you were

        mašqēhû
        his cupbearer

Note that the Setting, which is peripheral to the body of the paragraph, has a verb that is an imperfect: *yiśśāʾ*, 'he will lift up'. The whole clause 'in yet three days Pharaoh will lift up you head' is preparatory to the following predicted events, which are given in BU₁ and BUₙ as *w* (cons) perfect clauses: 'And he will put you on your pedestal. And you will give the cup of Pharaoh into his hand according to the former custom which you were his cupbearer.' The main, initial verbs of these two sentences are *w* (cons) perfects.[10]

The paragraph that we have just presented is from Joseph's speech to the courtier (cupbearer) who has asked him to interpret his dream. Joseph's speech is a predictive discourse, but the second point that he makes, although formally predictive, is covertly hortatory (see chap. 6).

I note in passing that predictive simple paragraphs do not happen to occur in the Joseph story. Such units, consisting of a Setting (with some lower ranking verb) and a Text (*w* [cons] perfect) assuredly can and will be found in other parts of the Hebrew Old Testament since there is no good reason to believe that they cannot occur.

2.2.   *The predictive reason paragraph*

Two predictive reason paragraphs are found in the passage where Pharaoh installs Joseph as grand vizier of Egypt (apparently, predictive result paragraphs do not occur in the Joseph story). In 41:39–40 a complicated structure occurs in the Text (a predictive antithetical paragraph whose Thesis embeds a predictive coordinate paragraph). But for our purposes here it is sufficient to note that (1) the Reason is a negated participial clause ('no one [is] understanding and wise like you') and (2) the Text involves three instances of noun phrase + imperfect ('You shall be over all my house. And at your word shall all my people be marshalled. Only on the throne will I be greater than you.'). Thus, by verb

---

[10] A relative clause, which is final in the last sentence, contains a perfect. This element is not on the verb rank chart—since almost any non-consecutive structure can occur in a relative clause; its ranks somewhere down towards the bottom of the scale.

ranking, the element we have called Reason is clearly less salient than the complex of coordinated elements that follows (what we have considered to constitute the Text).

In 41:44 a less complex example occurs. Here the Reason is a nominal clause ('I [am] Pharaoh') and the Text is a simple sentence of noun + (negated) imperfect structure ('And without you he shall not raise [any] man his hand or his foot throughout the land of Egypt.'). While the noun + (neg) imperfect is not as salient as a *w* (cons) perfect, nevertheless it is more salient than the noun(verbless) clause here.[11]

These isolated bits of predictive discourse are appropriate to the installation passage. Pharaoh states what Joseph's powers are to be and appends reasons to his actions in so installing Joseph. Furthermore, as speech acts, these utterances of Pharaoh accomplish perlocutionarily what they set out to do, that is, they actually make Joseph lord of Egypt with the powers stated.

Another predictive reason paragraph occurs in 41:36; here the embedded reason paragraph occurs in the Conclusion of the hortatory part of Joseph's speech. Here the Reason unit is a sentence with a *w* (cons) perfect form of *hāyâ*, 'be'. While this tense form normally ranks highest in predictive discourse *wĕhāyâ*, 'and it will be', here (like the preterite of the same verb *wayhî* in narrative discourse) it ranks low in the scale by virtue of being a form of the verb 'be'. The following clause, with a negated imperfect of an action verb presumably ranks higher:

Reason: And the food will be for a reserve for the land against the seven years of famine which will be in the land of Egypt.

Text: And the land won't be destroyed by the famine.

2.3. *The predictive comment paragraph*

In the predictive part of Joseph's speech to Pharaoh two predictive comment paragraphs occur. In the first such paragraph (41:27–28) Joseph predicts in the Text several years of famine; the verb is the imperfect of *hāyâ*: 'There will be seven years of famine.' Joseph's comment is two-fold: (1) The first Comment is a nominal clause (whose relative clause contains a perfect): 'This [is] the word which I have

---

[11] For predictive discourse I have not assumed an irrealis band into which negated verbs automatically fit—unless promoted as "momentous negations" (cf. Diagram 3, p. 81 above). I have rather assumed that since predictive discourse is per se projected and hence in a sense irrealis, negated verbs rank much as their affirmative counterparts. When, however, a negated clause is a negated antonym paraphrase of an affirmative clause, it seems plausible to consider that the latter outranks the former.

spoken to Pharaoh.' (2) The second Comment has a perfect as its main verb and participle in its relative clause: 'That which God is doing he has revealed to Pharaoh.' Note in the above, that the perfect is seen as coordinated with a nominal clause in the structure of the two Comments. This is further evidence of the extremely low ranking of the perfect when not in the *w* (cons) perfect construction. In the second such paragraph (41:30c–31), the Text contains a *w* (cons) perfect construction: 'And the famine will consume the land.' The Comment contains a negated imperfect: 'And the abundance in the land shall not be remembered (known) in the face of the famine which will come afterwards—for great will be that famine.' Here the comment paragraphs serve to underline the importance and solemnity of Joseph's predictions.

2.4. *The predictive amplification paragraph*

There is one possible example of Amplification paragraph here, namely, 41:29. (In our limited corpus of predictive discourse in Joseph, predictive paraphrase paragraphs do not occur.) The Text contains a participle and the Amplification a nominal clause:

Text: Behold, seven years are coming.

Amplification: A great famine [shall be] in all the land of Egypt.

2.5. *The predictive coordinate and antithetical paragraphs*

Gen 41:39–40 seems to structure as a predictive antithetical paragraph that embeds within its Thesis a predictive coordinate paragraph. The Antithesis turns on a 'you'/'I' contrast:

Thesis: (P) Coordinate paragraph

  Item₁: You shall be [*tihyeh*] over my house.

  Item₂: And at your word (mouth) shall be marshalled [*yiššaq*] all my people.

Antithesis: Only on the throne shall I be greater [*ʾegdal*] than you.

Here all the verbs are imperfect and broadly of equal rank. Item₁ contains, however, the imperfect of *hāyâ*, which could in strict accordance with the rank scheme be considered to be of lower rank than *yiššaq*. If this line of reasoning were pushed, then the predictive coordinate paragraph might prove simply to be a predictive simple paragraph of Setting-Text structure. At any rate *yiššaq* in the Thesis and *ʾegdal* in the Antithesis are clearly of equal rank, and we have here an equi-weighted predictive antithetical paragraph.

2.6. *The predictive evidence paragraph*

I illustrate here a type of paragraph for which I have no corresponding examples of narrative paragraphs: predictive evidence paragraph. This is essentially an argumentative type of paragraph in which evidence is introduced and a conclusion drawn. Perhaps such a paragraph is to be expected in prediction rather than in narration, since in a sense there is burden of proof involved in making a prediction. I call the two parts of an evidence paragraph, Evidence and Text. The former is off the mainline of predictive discourse; the latter is on it (consistent with our usual use of Text).

A rather complicated example of this is found in 40:12-13. The first words *zeh pitrōnô*, 'this [is] its interpretation', can probably be set aside as Aperture of this discourse (speech of Joseph to the imprisoned courtier). It is at all events a nominal clause and not on the mainline of the predictive discourse that follows. The Evidence is likewise a nominal clause: 'The three branches-they [are] three days.' The Text is a predictive sequence paragraph with a Setting whose verb is imperfect and two BUs whose verbs are *w* (cons) perfect. (For the internal analysis of the latter, see 2.1.) For two other examples of the predictive evidence paragraph—in dream interpretation contexts—see 40:19 and 41:27.

3. *Expository discourse and expository paragraphs*

Bits and pieces of expository discourse also occur within the Joseph story—either in reported speech and/or in such slots as Setting or Comment within the narrative framework. I will not posit a new cline for ranking the verbs in these examples of expository discourse. My reluctance to construct such a cline at this time is based, for the most part, on the feeling that more expository discourse in the Hebrew Bible (e.g., in portions of the wisdom literature) needs to be explored before such a cline is constructed. Second, I feel that for the time being it is sufficient to note that as the inverse of narrative discourse (and to some degree of predictive as well), expository discourse can be defined as discourse in which the most static verb forms of a language predominate and have the highest ranking. For this reason, elements at the bottom of the clines for Narrative, Procedural, and Hortatory discourse have the highest ranking in Exposition.

Thus the nominal (verbless) clause is the static clause par excellence. Clauses with *yēš*, 'there is', and *ʾēn* 'there isn't', (also the negative of nominal clauses) have about the same ranking as nominal clauses. Clauses with copulative uses of *hāyâ*, 'be', rank a step lower; by virtue of having any sort of verb at all they are not as completely static as verbless clauses. Possibly, clauses with stative/denominative perfects rank next;

these verbs are essentially adjectival in function. Below all of these rank clauses with participials—since these encode activities in whatever discourse type they are found. Finite verbs rank lowest; they fill functions such as Reason, Result, Comment, and Amplification, rather than Text.[12] Note that the sort of clauses that predominate in expository discourse are the typical stuff, for example, of Setting in narrative paragraphs. Clearly, what is off-the-line in narrative is on-the-line in exposition.

In presenting expository paragraphs below, note that the failure to document the expository sequence paragraph is probably not a lacuna in the data but rather a systematic gap. Sequence implies action but expository discourse is by definition static. We do not, therefore, expect to find (temporal) sequence paragraphs in expository discourse.[13] All the other paragraph types that we have posited presumably have, however, expository variants. The failure to document any of these variants is either a fortuitous absence of such a variant from the Joseph corpus or a failure in the present analysis to recognize such a variant if it is present.

3.1.   *The expository result and reason paragraphs*

In 42:21–22 we have two paragraphs that probably should be construed as expository, one result and one reason. In both these examples, clauses are assumed as Text that contain elements more static than those found in the putative Result or Reason part of the paragraph. Conversely, of course, these paragraphs could be construed as narrative with application of the narrative cline in normal descending order (and with the putative Result or Reason made the Text). It seems to me, however, that in these paragraphs the brothers are explaining—or trying to understand—their present situation instead of simply recounting the past. Let us examine these paragraphs in detail.

42:21   (E) Result Paragraph

> Text: *ʾăbāl ʾăšēmîm ʾănaḥnû ʿal   -ʾāḥînû   ʾăšer*
>   truly are guilty we   on account of our brother whom

---

[12] Here again, however our data base is incomplete, e.g., in the expository-hortatory melange of Proverbs, imperfects very commonly occur as a sort of gnomic present.

[13] This does not, of course, rule out the possibility of an expository paragraph of the form: "First of all consider A. Next consider B. Finally, consider C." Here the speaker's/writer's order of presentation can determine an expository sequence paragraph in English and other European languages. As far as I know, Biblical Hebrew does not use this rhetorical structure.

[N Antithetical Paragraph backloops into Relative Clause]

Thesis: *rāînî   ṣārat   napšô   běhithaněnô   ēlênû*
we saw the distress of his soul in his beseeching us

Antithesis: *wělō   šāmā^cnû*
and not we harkened

Result: ^c*al-kēn   bāă   ēlênû haṣṣārâ hazzōt*
therefore has come on us distress this

The Text here is a nominal clause: 'Surely we [are] guilty on an account of our brother'. The relative clause, which depends on *āḥînû*, 'our brother,' backloops a narrative antithetical paragraph with verbs in the perfect. Here the action verbs are embedded within the nominal clause and, indeed, come in by way of explaining the word *ăšēmîm*, 'guilty'. The Result is a clause with a perfect: 'on account of this/therefore this distress has come upon us', with the explicit sequence signal ^c*al-kēn*, 'therefore'. This analysis considers the nominal clause of v 21a to be dominant in this paragraph, and the perfects to occur in elements that are in secondary function.

42:22   (Expository) Reason Paragraph

Reason: (Narrative) Antithetical Paragraph

Thesis: *hălô   āmartî ălêkem lēmōr al   -teḥeṭû*
did not I tell   you   saying don't harm

bayyeled
the lad

Antithesis: *wělō   šěmatem*
and not you would listen

Text: *wěgam   -dāmô   hinnēh*
and also his blood behold

nidrāš
is being required/sought after

Here again, the less dominant element, in this case the Reason unit, embeds a narrative paragraph—as Reuben recollects his warning to them so many years ago. I have construed the Text to be the clause: 'And also, his blood, behold it is required.' I assume here that the niphal participle *nidrāš* with its preceding *hinnēh*, 'behold', and the introductory noun phrase 'his blood' as a static element outranks the perfects found in Reuben's recollective anecdote.

It is noteworthy, however, that our initial decision that these paragraphs are expository determines the analysis. This decision in turn is based on the immediate context of these verses in chap. 41, that is, an inspection of the context makes it plausible that explanation rather than narration is intended.

3.2. *The expository comment paragraph*

In 41:25 there occurs a clear example of expository comment paragraph in which the Text is expounded by a nominal clause:

ḥălôm   parʿōh   ʾeḥād hûʾ
the dream of Pharaoh one   [is] it

The Comment is expounded by a clause whose verb is a perfect:

ʾēt ʾăšer hāʾĕlōhîm ʿōśeh higgîd   lĕparʿōh
that which God   is doing he has revealed to Pharaoh

This is the portion of Joseph's discourse to Pharaoh in which Joseph is explaining the meaning of Pharaoh's dream. The explanation forms the basis of prediction and suggestion, but this part of the speech seems clearly to be expository. Consequently we consider the first clause to be more prominent than the second.

In 41:19 an expository comment paragraph occurs in which the Text is expounded by a participial clause and the Comment by a clause whose verb is a perfect. There is, furthermore, a shift from third person to first person in going from Text to Comment, that is, the Comment is a break in the description of the scene of confronting Pharaoh—a break consisting of his personal interpretation and evaluation. The whole unit (Text + Comment) functions as Setting relative to the following action verb (cf. Part 4):

Text: wĕhinnēh   šebaʿ -pārôt ʾăḥērôt ʿōlôt
          and behold seven cows   others   were coming up

          ʾaḥărêhen dallôt wĕrāʿôt tōʾar   mĕʾōd wĕraqqôt
          after them wasted and bad looking very   and lean

          bāśār
          [in] flesh

Comment: lōʾ -rāʾîtî   kāhēnnâ bĕkol -ʾereṣ   miṣrayim
          not I have seen their like in all the land of Egypt

          lārōaʿ
          for ugliness

3.3. *The expository amplification and paraphrase paragraphs*

Paragraphs containing expository amplification and paraphrase are more plentiful and easier to document. In 39:3 we have an expository amplification paragraph that backloops into a sentence, 'And his master saw that. . . .' The Text is a nominal clause:

yhwh ∅ *ʾittô*
YHWH [was] with him

The Amplification is a clause with a hiphil (causative) participle:

wĕkōl *ʾăšer -hûʾ* *ʿōśeh* *yhwh*
and everything that he was doing YHWH

maṣlîaḥ *bĕyādô*
was making prosper in his hand

A similar examples occurs in 42:9. Again, the Text is a nominal clause:

mĕraggĕllîm ∅ *ʾattem*
spies [are] you

The Amplification contains a perfect as its main verb:

lirʾôt *ʾet-ʿerwat* *hāʾāreṣ* *bāʾtem*
to see the nakedness of the land you have come

Still another example (42:6) has a nominal clause in its Text and a participial clause in its Amplification:

Text: *wĕyôsēp* *hûʾ* ∅ *haššallîṭ* *ʿal -hāʾāreṣ*
and Joseph he [was] the governor over the land

Amplification: *hûʾ hammašbîr* *lĕkol -ʿam* *hāʾāreṣ*
he the one selling to all the people of the land

In the preceding examples the Text is in each case a nominal clause, that is, the most static of any verb form/clause type in Biblical Hebrew. The Amplifications are participial clauses or a clause whose verb is a perfect. Here we see plainly the inversion of the rank scheme that is applicable to narrative discourse where the most dynamic verbs/clauses rank highest.

In 37:24 an expository (negated antonym) paraphrase paragraph occurs:

Text: *wĕhabbôr* ∅ *rēq*
and the pit (∅) empty

Paraphrase: *ʾên bô* ∅ *māyim*
not in it (∅) water

Here the Text is a nominal clause, while the Paraphrase is, in effect, a negated nominal clause.[14] Very probably, it is best to consider that,

[14] *ʾên* is, of course, a negated existential counterpart of *yeš* 'there is'. However, a positive nominal clause *bô māyim* 'in it (was) water' is also negated with *ʾên* 'there isn't'. At any rate *yeš* clauses probably rank on about the same level as nominal clauses in the various verb rank schemes here suggested.

although the verb rank scheme for narrative is (roughly) inverted in expository discourse, affirmative clauses outrank negatives in paraphrase.

Another example of an expository paraphrase paragraph is found in 41:21. Here the affirmative-negative pair are found in inverted order:

Paraphrase: *wĕlō* *nôda^c* *kî* *-bā^ʔû* *ʔel*
and not it was known that they had gone into

-qirbenâ
their insides

Text: *ûmar^ʔêhen* ∅ *ra^c* *ka^ʔăšer battĕhillâ*
and their appearance (∅) ugly as before

Here the Text is again a nominal clause, while the Paraphrase is a perfect. The thrust of the paraphrase is: One couldn't tell (know) that they were any better off (by swallowing the good cattle). Their appearance was as bad as before. Here, 'not visibly better' = 'as bad as before.'

An expository paraphrase paragraph found in 42:11 is slightly different. While its Text is a nominal clause, its Paraphrase is a negated perfect of *hāyâ*, 'be'.

Text: *kēnîm* ∅ *ʔănahnû*
honest men (∅) we

Paraphrase: *lō^ʔ-hāyû* *^căbādêkā* *mĕraggĕlîm*
have not been your servants spies

3.4. *The expository coordinate paragraph*

Expository coordinate paragraphs coordinate two clauses of a relatively static nature. Thus, in 40:9–10, two nominal clauses are found:

Item₁: *bahălômî* *wĕhinnēh gepen lĕpānāy*
in my dream behold a vine [was] before me

Itemₙ: *ûbaggepen* *šĕlōšâ* *śārîgim*
and on the vine [were] three branches

In 42:13 we find a somewhat more complex example in which three items are coordinated and in which the first is an embedded expository amplification paragraph. All the sentences are nominal clauses.

Item₁: Expository Amplification Paragraph

Text: *šĕnêm ^căśār ^căbādêkā* *ʔahîm*
twelve [are] your servants brothers

Amplification: *ʔănahnû bĕnê* *ʔîš* *-ʔehād bĕ^ʔereṣ*
we [are] sons of man one in the land of

> *kĕnā⁻an*
> Caanan

Item₂: *wĕhinnēh   haqqāṭōn   ⁻et-⁻ābînû   hayyôm*
and behold the youngest [is] with our father today

Item₃: *wĕhā⁻eḥād   ⁻ênennû*
and the one none of him [= and the other no longer exists]

This seems, judging from the context, to be part of an earnest attempt on the part of the brothers to clear themselves of the charge of being spies by explaining their relatedness in the same family. I do not find a clear example of an expository antithetical paragraph in Joseph.

3.5. *The expository evidence paragraph*

In 41:25–26 an expository evidence paragraph occurs. Furthermore, it is *cyclic* in structure; there is not only an initial Text for which evidence is cited but the paragraph ends with a Text', that is, with a restatement of the Text (minus the Comment that accompanies the first occurrence of Text). Aside from the Comment embedded in the Text (cf. 3.2.), all clauses are nominal.

Text: Comment Paragraph

Text: *ḥălôm   par⁻ōh   ⁻eḥād hû⁻*
the dream of Pharaoh one   [is] it

Comment: *⁻ēt   ⁻ăšer   hā⁻ĕlōhîm ⁻ōśeh   higgîd*
that which God   is doing he has revealed

lēpar⁻ōh
to Pharaoh

Evidence₁: *šeba⁻   pārōt haṭṭōbōt šeba⁻ šānîm hēnnâ*
the seven cattle good   seven years [are] they

Evidence₂: *wĕšeba⁻   haššibolîm   haṭṭōbōt šeba⁻ šānîm*
and the seven ears of grain good   seven years

hēnnâ
[are] they

Text':   *ḥălôm   ⁻eḥād hû⁻*
the dream one   [is] it

4. *Summary*

In this chapter the twin concerns of verb/clause ranking and the constituent structure of discourse have been brought together in an attempt to show that (1) constituent structure analysis is necessary, and, while involving a certain inevitable subjectivity, can partially be guided objectively by considerations of verb/clause ranking, when the latter have been appropriately sorted out as to discourse type; and (2), on the other hand, the functional understanding of the various verb/clause types is incomplete until it is related to the constituent structure of various discourses.

CHAPTER FIVE

SOCIOLINGUISTIC DYNAMICS OF HORTATORY DISCOURSE

The *Joseph* narrative contains a number of interpersonal hortatory discourses, that is, discourses in which one person tries to influence the conduct of another. These discourses as portrayed in the narrative are spoken in a wide range of social situations. They include: a father talking to his son, brother to brothers, an imprisoned slaveboy to an imprisoned courtier, a commoner to a reigning monarch, a monarch to a commoner, etc. The hortatory discourses also contain a considerable variety of linguistic form—especially of mainline verbs. Thus, not only are imperatives, cohortatives, and jussives found, but also types of mitigated commands. An attempt is made in this chapter to relate the various linguistic forms found in hortatory discourse to the social situations in which they are employed.

The hortatory discourses found within *Joseph* are catalogued in Diagram 5. After each entry a single arrow going in a given direction or a double pointed arrow symbolizes the a priori sociological (hence, non-linguistic) appraisal of the situation in terms of social structure and dominance. In numbers 1, 2, 3, and 12 my judgment is that the hortatory discourse is delivered by the speaker to hearers who are his peers; there is no obvious dominance of either the speaker or the addressee. In numbers 4, 5, 9, and 11 it is assumed that the addressee is socially dominant over the speaker. In numbers 6, 7, 8, 10, and 13 it is assumed that the speaker is socially dominant over the addressee. Having made these sociological judgments, I now devote the balance of this chapter to the inspection of the hortatory discourses to see what (if any) linguistic indications of dominance are found, and how well (or how poorly) such linguistic marking correlates with these a priori sociological judgments.

To do this it will be necessary, first of all, to posit a further rank scale of the verb forms used in hortatory discourse and to correlate the relative salience of verb forms that are variously placed on that scale with particular constituents of hortatory paragraphs (cf. the rank scales

DIAGRAM 5. Hortatory Discourses in *Joseph*

1.	37:19–20	Brothers to each other (←→)
2.	37:21–22	Reuben to the brothers (←→)
3.	37:26–27	Judah to the brothers (←→)
4.	40:14–15	Joseph to courtier (—→)
5.	41:33–36	Joseph to Pharaoh (—→)
6.	42:14–16	Joseph (incognito) to his brothers (←—)
7.	42:18–20	Joseph (incognito) to his brothers (←—)
8.	42:33–34	Retelling of Joseph (incognito) to brothers (←—)
9.	43:8–10	Judah to Jacob (—→)
10.	43:11–14	Jacob to his sons (←—)
11.	44:33	Climax of long speech of Judah to Joseph (incognito) (—→)
12.	45:9–13	Joseph (known) to his brothers (←→)
13.	45:17–20	Pharaoh to Joseph to relay to the brothers (←—)

in chaps. 3 and 4). With this as a tool to understanding the embedded hortatory discourses it is then possible to compare them with each other sociolinguistically.

I do not specifically discuss in this chapter hortatory paragraphs as such nor illustrate the various types of such paragraphs in order. Hortatory paragraphs are simply hortatory variants of paragraphs types that have already been abundantly illustrated. Furthermore, most types of hortatory paragraphs are illustrated in the course of discussing the various types of hortatory discourse presented here.

I note here in passing that interpersonal hortatory discourse is possibly but one type of hortatory discourse. At all events, clearly distinct in type from the interpersonal hortatory discourses found in *Joseph* are discourses such as the Decalogue and the other legislation of the Hebrew Bible; these may well prove, however, to be a further hortatory type: jurisprudence.

1. *A rank scale of verb forms for hortatory discourse*

A rank scale of Biblical Hebrew verb forms relative to hortatory discourse is given in Diagram 6. In this diagram, as in those posited for other discourse types, forms are arranged on a cline: the forms that are most central to hortatory discourse appear at the upper lefthand corner and those that are more peripheral occur at the lower righthand corner. The lower the placement of a verb form on the cline the further are clauses that contain this verb form from what might be called the *line of exhortation* (this corresponds to the storyline in narrative discourse).

DIAGRAM 6. Verb Rank in Hortatory Discourse

Band 1: Primary line of Exhortation	1.1 Imperative (2p) 1.2. Cohortative (1p) 1.3. Jussive (3p)[a]	} unranked
Band 2: Secondary Line of Exhortation	2.1. ʾāl + jussive/imperfect 2.2. Modal imperfect	
Band 3: Results/Con- sequences (Motivation)	3.1. w (consecutive) perfect[b] 3.2. lôʾ/pen + imperfect 3.3. (Future) perfect	
Band 4: Setting (Problem)	4.1. Perfect (of past events) 4.2. Participles 4.3. Nominal clauses	

[a]1.3. substitutes for 1.1. in deferential avoidance of 2p.

[b]3.1. may substitute for band 1—but this possibly involves substitution of the form of predictive discourse.

As might be expected, command forms (band 1) are central to hortatory discourse, on whose line of exhortation they clearly lie. Commands in Biblical Hebrew are formally distinguished according to person. In the second person, (positive) commands are *imperative*. In the first person, *cohortatives* occur ('Let me do X'; 'Let's do X'). In the third person, *jussives* occur ('Let R do X'). With any of these command forms may occur the enclitic -nāʾ, 'submissive and modest request' (Gesenius 1859: 523), which mitigates somewhat the bluntness of the form.[1]

Space does not permit going into detail regarding the morphological nature of the forms just indicated. Any standard grammar of Biblical Hebrew contains this information. The same sources also indicate

[1] This is a somewhat simplified summary of a very complex situation. I quote GKC (§48b): "Along with the usual form of the imperfect, there exists also a lengthened form of it (the *cohortative*), and a shortened form (the *jussive*). The former occurs (with few exceptions) only in the 1st person, while the latter is mostly found in the 2nd and 3rd persons, and less frequently in the 1st person." Noticeably here, GKC assigns the cohortative mainly to first person. As far as the jussive goes—ignoring the very few occurrences of this in first person—it can be noted that most of the second-person jussives are in negative commands. In positive commands my general equation of imperative with second person apparently holds for the present corpus.

the (few) places where "hidden" cohortatives or jussives are posited—since occasionally, rules of inflection and prosody (vowel change and accentuation) result in ambiguous forms.[2]

There is a secondary band of exhortation (Band 2) in which negative commands and modal uses of the imperfect figure. In interpersonal hortatory discourses, *ʾāl*, 'not', + the jussive/imperfect is the normally expected form for negative command.[3] In Gen 37:21, however, *lôʾ* appears with what may be a hidden cohortative form: *lôʾ nakkennû nāpeš*, 'let's not kill him'. In juridical discourse (cf. the Decalogue) *lôʾ* thus used is an absolute prohibition, which is stronger than the *ʾāl* + V ('don't . . .') of interpersonal hortatory discourse.[4] I have not for the present included *lôʾ* + imperfect as a negative command in the rank scheme for hortatory discourse.

The role of the modal imperfect in hortatory discourse is, however, somewhat more clear (43:12, 42:20); it is plausible that 'should'/'must' forms should rank below overt commands and yet above other non-peremptory elements.

Band 3 expresses results/consequences of commands rather than the commands themselves. Presumably the role of elements in this band is motivational ('seek good results instead of bad results'). Positive results are expressed via *w* (cons) perfect while negative results are expressed with *lôʾ* or *pen* + imperfect. In addition the perfect with future

---

[2] The following summary from GKC (§48g) may be helpful:
 1. the jussive as distinct from the imperfect is found in
    a. the Hiphil of the strong verb (*yaktîl* 'he will kill' > *yaktēl* 'let him kill') and similarly in weak verbs with *î* in the second syllable
    b. the Qal of *ʿw* and *ʿy* verbs (*yāmût* 'he will die' > *yāmōt* 'let him die'; *yāgîl* 'he will rejoice > *yāgēl* 'let him rejoice')
    c. general in *lʾʾh* with rejection of final (Qal: *yigleh* 'he will uncover' > *yigel* 'let him uncover'; Hiphil: *yagleh* 'he will carry into exile' > *yegel* let him carry into exile'; Piel *yĕṣawweh* 'he will command' > *yĕṣaw* 'let him command')
 2. the jussive is indistinct from the imperfect in
    a. almost all plurals
    b. 2 f.s.
    c. all verbs taking object suffixes
[3] I quote here a relevant passage from GKC (§107p) regarding *ʾal* + jussive: "The *jussive*, which is to be expected after *ʾal-*, does not, as a rule . . . differ in form from the simple imperfect. That many supposed jussives are intended as simple imperfects is possible from the occurrences after *ʾal* of what are undoubtedly imperfect forms, not only from verbs *lʾʾh* . . . but also from verbs *ʿʾʾw* to express a prohibition or negative wish." In keeping with this remark, I have indicated *ʾal* + jussive/imperfect in Diagram 6 instead of just *ʾal* + jussive.
[4] In the Decalogue, not only are on-the-line negative commands encountered but also the infinitive absolute as a command form (GKC §113bb).

significance (not the *w* cons perfect) is found in a few cases (43:14; 40:14) where it may be broadly motivational but where it figures in Setting or Terminus of hortatory paragraphs and as part of a conditional or quasi conditional construction.

In band 4 occur elements that have to do with the setting broadly conceived. Participles and nominal clauses can be expected here as in the other discourse types. In addition the perfect of past events can be used to refer to a problem arising from the past (cf. Gen 40:15). Here the use of the perfect can be compared with the use of the perfect in indictments that accompany exhortation in the prophets.

The various bands of the hortatory rank scheme express, then, commands, elements, motivations, and review/description of the problem.

The role of the *w* (cons) perfect in hortatory discourse is, I believe, primarily as sketched above. This tense may be used, however, as a mitagative substitute for the imperative. One could consider that this promotes a band 3 element to band 1. I lean increasingly, however, to viewing this substitution as a switching of the hortatory form into the surface structure of the predictive form while retaining the hortatory intent. (See the argumentation below in §§3 and 4.)

2. *Basic form of the hortatory discourse (unmitigated)*

2.1. I assume the whole discourse found in 43:11–14 (Example 1) to be a *hortatory coordinate paragraph*, where the speaker urges several *Items* on his hearers (but without logical or temporal ordering of the items; hence they are assumed to be *coordinated*). Item$_1$ and Item$_3$ are, however, internally ordered as hortatory sequence paragraphs (each constituent of which is a Build-Up or sequential unit). Each BU of the hortatory sequence paragraph is signaled by an *imperative* verb form (underlined in the example). Item$_2$ is an embedded hortatory comment paragraph. The Comment, which is off the line of exhortation, is simply a noun clause ('Maybe it Ø an oversight'). The Text, that is, the unit concerning which the Comment is made, is an embedded hortatory amplification paragraph, (only the Text of which is on the line of exhortation: 'Take double silver . . .'). The Amplification of this command is by way of a modal imperfect ('The silver that was returned in the mouth of your bags you *must/should return* . . .').

The three Items are preceded by a Preliminary unit and followed by a Terminus unit. While the Preliminary unit is an imperative (and thus, strictly speaking, on the line of exhortation), it is *generic* and anticipates all that follows ('Do thus'). The Terminus no longer involves addressing the sons, but is, rather, an appeal to deity by way of a *jussive* ('And may God Almighty grant mercy'). When imperatives and jussives occur in the

EXAMPLE 1. Hortatory Coordinate Paragraph: Unmitigated Imperatives
Genesis 43:11–14

Jacob's speech to his sons after he capitulates (to the demand to take Benjamin), but takes charge of the arrangements for the journey: unmitigated imperatives.

Preliminary: N + **imperative** ['do']	if so, do as follows
Item₁: (hortatory) sequence paragraph	
BU₁: **imperative** + N	take some of the produce of the land
BU₂: **imperative** + N	and carry it down to the man as a gift
Item₂: (hortatory) comment paragraph	
Text: amplification paragraph	
Text: wN + **imperative**	and double silver take
Amplification: wN + imperfect	and the silver that was returned, give back
Comment: nominal clause	maybe it was an oversight
Item₃: (hortatory) sequence paragraph	
BU₁: wN + **imperative**	and your brother take
BU₂: w + **imperative**	and get up
BUₙ: **imperative**	return to the man
Terminus: (hortatory) antithetical paragraph	
Thesis: (hortatory) result paragraph	
Text: wN + jussive	and may God Almighty give you his mercy
Result: w (cons) perfect	and he will return your other brother and Benjamin
Antithesis: wN + (future) perfect	as for me, if I'm to be bereaved, I will be bereaved

same paragraph with shift of addressee, I assume that imperatives outrank jussives, which now fall into the periphery of the paragraph.

Internally within the Terminus unit, verb ranking continues to apply. (1) Jussive outranks w (cons) perfect, so that the former characterizes Text while the latter characterizes Result (further off the line of exhortation in the hortatory result paragraph). (2) Both these, in turn, outrank the (future) perfect, which falls into the Antithesis of a (front-weighted) hortatory antithetical paragraph: 'May God be merciful, but if he doesn't, I'll just have to accept the consequences.'

The social situation (as indicated briefly at the top of Example 1) is that of a father (clan head and patriarch) talking to his sons. As clan head, Jacob has come out on the losing side of a year-long debate about letting Benjamin go to Egypt along with his brothers. The beginning of the debate is recorded at the end of Genesis 42. Here Jacob terminated the argument with the words, 'My son *shall not* go down with you' (to Egypt to buy food on a projected trip). The better part of a year later, as represented at the beginning of chap. 43, the food purchased on the first trip to Egypt is exhausted, and fresh argument begins concerning taking Benjamin along with Jacob's other sons to a projected (and desperately necessary) second trip. The chief argument of Jacob's sons is that 'the man', 'the overlord of Egypt' (Joseph incognito), has categorically told them that they will not see him again (nor be able to buy grain) unless their youngest brother Benjamin accompanies them. In the face of this argument, vigorously propounded by Judah, Jacob at last has to give in—since the alternative is death by starvation for all of them. But, in capitulation, Jacob salvages his pride and dignity by taking charge of the proceedings: 'All right, if it must be so, then *do* as follows' (43:11).

In this situation—of a patriarchal clan head talking to his sons—it is not important who won or lost the last argument. Regardless of the immediately antecedent speech acts and exchanges, the appropriate forms (and their implied prerogatives) are employed in Jacob's speech to his sons. In addressing commands to them he uses bald, unmitigated imperatives (as we have just seen). Obviously, here the linguistic forms that are employed mirror the social situation.

2.2.   Example 2 is a speech of Joseph to his brothers on the occasion of their first descent into Egypt. Joseph, who is of course still incognito, speaks to his brothers through an interpreter (although he really understands Canaanite), and is giving them a hard time. He wants to find out if they have had a change of heart since they sold him into Egypt years before. Specifically, he wants to see his younger full brother Benjamin (all the others are his half brothers) brought to Egypt in order to see how the older brothers will treat Benjamin when they are threatened.

I consider the discourse again to be a one-paragraph unit, which I have labeled a hortatory sequence paragraph, that is, the brothers are not simply told to perform certain actions but the actions are presented as ordered in temporal sequence. The first few sentences, however, are simply the Preliminary unit (cf. Example 1). Again, the verb that is featured is generic ('do') and summarily anticipates (rather than chronologically precedes) all that follows. I consider that the Preliminary unit consists of an embedded hortatory reason paragraph. The Reason unit, given at the end of the Preliminary, is a participial clause ('I [am] one who fears God') that, in keeping with its position at the bottom of the verb rank cline, is some distance removed from the line of exhortation. The Text of the result paragraph is another embedded hortatory result paragraph. The Text and Result both employ imperatives; the second,

EXAMPLE 2. Hortatory Sequence Paragraph: Unmitigated Imperatives
Genesis 42:18–20

Joseph's speech (incognito) on the occasion of the brothers' first journey to Egypt: unmitigated imperatives.

Preliminary: (hortatory) reason paragraph	
Text: (hortatory) result paragraph	
Text: **imperative**	this do
Result: *w* **imperative**	and live
Reason: N + participle	I am one who fears God
BU_1: (hortatory) antithetical paragraph	
Thesis: N + jussive	let one of you remain bound
Antithesis: (hortatory) sequence	
paragraph	
BU_1: N + **imperative**	and the rest of you, go
BU_n: **imperative**	take famine relief to your households
BU_n: (hortatory) reason paragraph	
Reason: N + imperfect-modal	and your little brother you will bring to me
Text: (hortatory) result paragraph	
Text: *w* jussive	and let your words be confirmed
Result: *lôʾ* + imperfect	and you won't die

while not lower in rank than the first, seems to be semantically a result of the first. A strict following of verb ranking would result in our coordinating the two in a coordinate paragraph.

The first BU unit of the main (matrix) paragraph embeds a hortatory antithetical paragraph, that is, two contrary courses of action are urged on two differing participants. The Thesis employs a jussive rather than an imperative simply because the form of address, 'one of you', throws the usual second person plural into third person, which requires a jussive. Contrary to this course of action ('Let one of you remain bound here'), an opposite course of action is urged on the other brothers, who are now directly addressed in bald imperatives: 'As for the rest of you go, take famine relief to your households.' All these jussive and imperative forms are on the line of exhortation.

The second and final BU unit (Bu_n) represents a complex of actions that are to be performed chronologically subsequent to those represented in the BU_1. But only one command form is used, the jussive, which is found in the second sentence. I consider the whole unit to be a hortatory reason paragraph (cf. Preliminary) with the ordering Reason-Text instead of the more usual Text-Reason. The Reason unit consists of a clause that employs a modal imperfect ('And your little brother you will [/ must] bring to me'). This is backgrounded in reference to the next unit, which contains a jussive. This unit, the Text, in turn consists of an embedded hortatory result paragraph (only the Text of which is on the line of exhortation by virtue of containing a jussive: 'And let your words be confirmed'), while the Result embodies the natural conse-quence and is off the line of exhortation by virtue of containing a (negated) imperfect ('And you won't die').[5]

Notice that this example, like the first one, has unmitigated com-mand forms on its line of exhortation. The imperative predominates but gives way to the jussive where exigencies of reference and grammar require the latter. Thus, 'one of you' comes out as a third person instead of a second person plural, while 'your words' likewise necessitates such a shift.

The sociolinguistic situation is clearly one in which such unmiti-gated command forms are proper. Joseph, who is Pharaoh's number two, is talking to a band of wandering nomads who have come as supplicants to buy food for famine relief. It is not yet known to the brothers that the grand vizier is really their long-lost brother. He is simply the forbidding power with whom they have to deal.

3. *Partially mitigated hortatory discourse*

The third example (45:9–13) is a speech of Joseph to his brothers after he has revealed himself to them as Joseph. I have again assumed that the speech is a one-paragraph discourse. Like Example 2, Example 3 is a hortatory sequence paragraph. There are four BU units without Prelim-inary or Terminus. Joseph is talking, so the whole structure is quoted speech. It contains, however, two further levels of quotation in BU_2.

BU_1 is two closely associated imperatives: 'Hurry and go up to my father.' BU_2 contains, however, a mitigated command expressed as a *w* (cons) perfect ('And you will say to him'). The rest of the material in BU_2 consists of the words that the brothers are instructed to say to Jacob. The first clause here is a Quotation Formula on a still deeper level of embedding ('Thus has said your son Joseph'); the quotation formula is a perfect, with straight forward past reference and is off the line of exhor-tation. The Quotation of this deeper level of embedding is also a horta-tory sequence paragraph, which is found in vv 9–11. There is a sequence of three BUs, each of which consists of a Text and one further element. The first Text has an imperative, while the last two have *w* (cons) perfect forms. Apparently here we have a pattern analogous to that found in

[5] Note here the structural chiasmus: Text-Result/Reason/Thesis/Antithesis-Reason/Text/Result.

EXAMPLE 3. Hortatory Sequence Paragraph: Partially Mitigated Imperatives
Genesis 45:9-13

Joseph to his brothers after revealing himself to them as their brother: partially mitigated imperatives. (In each layer of quotation, initial imperatives are given that shift immediately into w [consecutive] perfects.)

BU₁: **imperative + imperative**	hurry and go up to my father
BU₂: *w* (cons) perfect	and you will say to him
Quotation formula: perfect	thus has said your son Joseph
Quotation: (hortatory) sequence paragraph	
Preliminary: perfect	God has made me lord of all Egypt
BU₁: (hortatory) negated antonym paraphrase paragraph	
Text: **imperative**	come down to me
Paraphrase: ʾāl + imperfect	don't delay
BU₂: (predictive) amplification paragraph	
Text: *w* (cons) perfect	and you shall dwell in the land of Goshen
Amplification: *w* (cons) perfect (*hāyâ*)	and you shall be near to me
BUₙ: (predictive) result paragraph	
Text: *w* (cons) perfect	and I will nourish you there
Result: *pen* + imperfect	lest you be brought to poverty
BU₃: (predictive) simple paragraph	
Setting: *hinnēh* N + participle	behold you are seeing
kî N + participle	that I am talking to you
Text: *w* (cons) perfect	and you shall declare to my father all my glory
BUₙ: *w* (cons) perfect + *w* (cons) perfect	hurry and bring my father here

v 9a, that is, a series of commands is given with the first have the form of an imperative and the subsequent command(s) mitigated to *w* (cons) perfect. Thus, in v 9b we have a negated antonym paraphrase (NAP) paragraph that gives a command in positive and negative form via imperative and ʾāl + imperfect: *rĕdâ ʾēlay*, 'come down to me', and *ʾal-taʿămōd*, 'don't delay'. But there are no further imperatives in the chain. Rather, BU₂ is an amplification paragraph whose Text is a *w* (cons) perfect amplified by a clause with the *w* (cons) perfect of *hāyâ*, 'be' (which is of lower rank than the Text): *wĕyāšabtā bĕ⁾ereṣ-gōšen*, 'and you shall dwell in the land of Goshen'; *wĕhāyîtā qārôb ⁾ēlay*, 'and you shall be near to me'. Finally, the BU_n of this embedded sequence paragraph is a result paragraph whose Text is a *w* (cons) perfect and whose Result is a *pen*, 'lest', + imperfect construction: *wĕkilkaltî ⁾ōtĕkā šām*, 'and I will nourish you there' (equivalent to let me nourish you there'); *pen-tiwwārēs ⁾attā*, 'lest you be brought to poverty'.

With the preceding, Joseph's words to his father—which are to be transmitted via his brothers—come to an end. Joseph returns to addressing his brothers directly. Thus in BU_3 of the main paragraph we have another mitigated command given as a *w* (cons) perfect. The command is preceded by a Setting with which it forms a simple paragraph. The Setting is a participial clause. The (mitigated) commands of Joseph to his brothers conclude with two closely associated verbs in 45:13b; again both verbs are *w* (cons) perfects (cf. 45:9a where *māhar*, 'hurry', is similarly used in close conjunction with a motion verb, but where both are imperative).[6]

This example, then, is strikingly different from the first two considered. Command forms such as imperatives and cohortatives are relatively infrequent and give way to the *w* (cons) perfect construction, which is used in the internal structure of the paragraph exactly where we would expect command forms (as in the first two examples). Plainly, then, the *w* (cons) perfect is used as a surrogate for command forms; it is here considered to indicate mitigated commands. On both levels of quotation, (Joseph telling his brothers what to do and Joseph through the brothers telling Jacob what to do) we find first an imperative and the *w* (cons) perfect as mitigated command. Thus Joseph's instruction to his brothers begins with 'hurry and go up to my father' (imperatives) and continues with *w* (cons) perfect in BU_2, BU_3, and BU_n. In parallel fashion, Joseph's words to be relayed to his father through the brothers begin with 'come down to me' (imperative) and continue with *w* (cons) perfect in the embedded hortatory sequence paragraph found within BU_2.

What then? We have here a pattern of partial mitigation in which the onset of the hortatory discourse is marked by an initial imperative, but with subsequent shift to *w* (cons) perfect as surrogate and mitigated command form. It is probably misleading to translate these *w* (cons) perfect forms as futures (I did so only to assist the reader by tagging this

---

[6] There is a loose chiastic structure discernible here in which the initial 'hurry and go up' corresponds to the final 'hurry and bring down my father', with the references to Joseph's office and splendor forming another inner bracketing.

construction via translation gloss). The intent is to signal command—
but at the same time to avoid brusqueness, rudeness, or impertinence.
There remains, however, an alternative possibility, namely, that Joseph's
partial mitigation of command forms simply substitutes one entire discourse for another, in this case an (enjoined) procedural discourse for
hortatory discourse (cf. chap. 4 n. 9). According to this alternative
analysis the initial imperatives in the two levels of quotation would
announce the discourse topic, that is, going to Canaan and bringing
Jacob down to Egypt, while the rest of the discourse gives the specific
procedures and accompanying materials. If this latter analysis were to be
adopted, the imperatives would probably go into a distinctive functional
slot while the *w* (cons) perfect forms would bear the mainline of the
embedded discourse. At any rate, even partial mitigation as presupposed
here heavily entails features of procedural discourse.

Note the social situation here pictured. Joseph here no longer
speaks as the forbiddingly distant grand vizier of Egypt but as their
forgiving and reconciled brother (although he still is in charge of
things!). The change from straight use of command forms in Example 2
to mitigated command in Example 3 correlates, therefore, with the
change in social relationship. As for Joseph's words to Jacob his father,
again bald command forms would scarcely be appropriate.

We have left a problem in the above analysis, however: when in the
course of a mitigated hortatory discourse we come across an embedded
paragraph whose Text is a *w* (cons) perfect, do we call the paragraph
type hortatory or predictive? Plainly the intent is hortatory, but just as
plainly the form is identical with that of the corresponding predictive
paragraph type as described in the preceding chapter. Two analytical
options are open here: to consider that we simply shift here to the
surface structure of predictive discourse; or to consider that at some
points in partially mitigated hortatory discourse the contrast between
predictive and hortatory discourse is neutralized. There is much to be
said in favor of the latter option. It recognizes the fact of language that
sometimes the identical surface structure is generated from two non-
identical starting points. I have, however, adopted the first option since
it seems to be a more straightforward handling of the surface structures
which are involved there. I consider therefore that in vv 9–11 above the
amplification paragraph, the result paragraph, and the simple paragraph are all predictive in form (although clearly hortatory in intent).
Note, however, that in each sequence of commands in this example BU_1
employs imperatives; specifically the BU_1 of the embedded hortatory
paragraph emerges as a hortatory negated antonym paragraph. This
leads us to posit: in partially mitigated hortatory discourse, if the first
BU contains an embedded paragraph it will be hortatory in form, but

EXAMPLE 4. Predictive Reason Paragraph: Completely Mitigated Imperatives
Genesis 40:14–15

Joseph's speech to the chief cupbearer after he interpreted his dream: completely mitigated imperatives ("covert" hortatory = predictive).

Text: (predictive) sequence paragraph	
Setting: (future) perfect	[no thanks] only you will remember me when it's well with you
BU$_1$: w (cons) perfect + nā$^{\jmath}$	and you'll do me a favor, please
BU$_2$: w (cons) perfect	and you'll remember me to Pharaoh
BU$_n$: w (cons) perfect	and you'll get me out of this prison
Reason: (narrative) coordinate paragraph	
Item$_1$: infinitive absolute + perfect	for truly I was kidnapped from the land of the Hebrews
Item$_2$: lô$^{\jmath}$ + perfect	and even here I've done nothing that they should have placed me in this hole

paragraphs that are embedded in subsequent BUs will be predictive in form; nevertheless, the intent of the whole remains hortatory.

4. *Completely mitigated hortatory discourse*

Example 4, which is from an earlier episode of *Joseph* (40:14–15) contains no imperative forms; rather all commands are reduced to the w (cons) perfect form. The only surface structure trace of the hortatory intent is the presence of the particle nā$^{\jmath}$, "used in submissive and modest request" (Gesenius 1859: 523), with the first w (cons) perfect construction. Aside from this feature, the discourse is identical with 1 Samuel 10:2–6, which is clearly predictive.

In keeping with the general identity of this passage with the predictive discourse I have considered 40:14–15 to be predictive. The surface form of one discourse is sometimes put to work to fulfill the intent of another discourse type. In such fashion, for example, a narrative may be told with hortatory intent and compromise the surface structure to the extent of appending a *moral* (Longacre 1983).

Consequently, I have labeled this one-paragraph discourse a predictive reason paragraph. The Text is a predictive sequence paragraph, as follows: Setting is an elliptical sentence beginning with kî $^{\jmath}$im[7] which

---

[7] Literally, kî is a particle 'that', which often introduces complements; the customary meaning of $^{\jmath}$im is 'if'.

seems to indicate turning down some sort of proffered reward and saying: '[No.] It's just that you'll remember me when all's well with you'. The verb is a (future) perfect in a kind of stipulatory clause.[8] The BU_1, BU_2, and BU_n are all *w* (cons) perfect form (with the particle *-nā*, 'please', attached to the first. The Reason unit is a narrative coordinate paragraph whose two Items both employ perfects in constructions other than *w* (cons) perfect. Since the latter is on the backbone of predictive discourse, other uses of the perfect rank lower in the rank scheme, which is proper to that discourse. Even in reference, however, to the rank scheme of hortatory discourse, *w* (cons) perfect outranks other uses of the perfect. Clearly, then, these two sentences are subsidiary to those of the previous verse. Their subsidiary status is recognized in relegating them to a Reason unit. Within the coordinate paragraph of the Reason unit, the perfects apparently have past force and picture weakly consecutive actions—thus leading me to consider that the paragraph is actually narrative.

This discourse is characterized by careful mitigation of its hortatory intent. Requests are still formulated—as in the previous examples—but are put in the mildest manner possible. One might freely render it as follows:

> No don't worry about a reward. I'd rather have you keep me in mind when everything turns out good for you. You'll do me a favor, won't you? You'll remember me to Pharaoh. You'll get me out of this prison. For surely I was kidnapped from the land of the Hebrews. And even here I've done nothing to deserve being put into this hole.

Why the careful mitigation? The social disparity between Joseph and the imprisoned courtiers is crucial to the structure here. Joseph is a foreigner, a slave, and furthermore, a degraded slave. The man that he addresses is the cupbearer to the most powerful monarch of his day. Although temporarily in disfavor the cupbearer is (by Joseph's own prediction) to be restored in three days. Joseph therefore addresses the courtier with extreme care. Again, the linguistic forms that are used closely reflect the social reality.

5. *Deferential hortatory discourse*

In contrast to the types of hortatory discourse illustrated in the above four examples, ranging from unmitigated to partially mitigated to

DB 475b considers this use of a bare perfect after *kî ʾim* to be rather
ꭒus.

EXAMPLE 5. Hortatory Coordinate Paragraph: Deferential Imperatives
Genesis 41:33–36

Third point of Joseph's speech to Pharoah. Deferential, by avoidance of second person.

Item$_1$: (hortatory) sequence paragraph	
BU$_1$: **jussive**	and *now*, let Pharaoh find a wise man
BU$_2$: *w* **jussive**	and let him set him over the land of Egypt
Item$_2$: (hortatory) result paragraph	
Text: amplification paragraph	
Text: **jussive** (or: ingressive/ inchoative)	let Pharaoh *act*
Amplification: *w* **jussive**	and let him appoint overseers over the land
Result: *w* (cons) perfect	and he will take a fifth of the produce during the plenty
Item$_3$: *w* **jussive**	and let them gather food during the good years
Item$_4$: (hortatory) result paragraph	
Text: **jussive**	and let them heap up grain under the hand of Pharaoh
Result: *w* (cons) perfect	and they will guard [it]
Conclusion: (predictive) reason paragraph	
Reason: *w* (cons) perfect (*hāyâ*)	and it will be a food reserve for the land
Text: *w lô$^{\circ}$* + imperfect	then the land won't be destroyed by the famine

wholly mitigated hortatory discourse, there is a further type of hortatory discourse that moves along a different parameter, that of *deference* rather than that of mitigation. This further type is illustrated in Example 5. Here Joseph, a commoner, is addressing royalty in the person of Pharaoh. Pharaoh may not be spoken to in the second person; rather it is necessary to shift to the third person. Beyond this shift to third person— and the consequent use of the jussive (instead of imperative)—no further adjustment apparently takes place. Consequently, we have again in Example 5 the basic form of the hortatory discourse. Notice, however, that while in other types of hortatory discourse the jussive is used only with a *bona fide* third person referent, here it is used with a pseudo third person referent, which is actually avoidance of second person.

The one paragraph discourse represented in Example 5 is a hortatory coordinate paragraph (cf. Example 1), which consists of four Items and a Conclusion. Item$_1$ is a hortatory sequence paragraph with two BUs, both of which are sentences with *jussives*: 'And now let Pharaoh find a wise man. And let him set him over the land of Egypt.' Item$_2$ is a hortatory result paragraph whose Text is two closely related jussives (which are here considered to be a hortatory amplification paragraph): 'Let Pharaoh act [vigorously]. And let him appoint overseers over the land.'[9] The Result, which is off the line of exhortation, is a sentence whose verb is a *waw* (cons) perfect: 'And he will take a fifth of the produce during the plenty.' The latter is taken here to be a result of implementing the former. Item$_3$ is, again, a hortatory result paragraph, whose Text has a jussive and whose Result has a *w* (cons) perfect: 'And let them heap up grain under the hand of Pharaoh [who continues to be addressed obliquely]. And they will guard (it).'[10] The Terminus (off the line of exhortation) is a predictive reason paragraph. Its Reason is a *w* (cons) perfect of *hāyâ*, 'be', and its Text is a negative imperfect: 'And [since] it will be a food reserve for the land, then the land won't be destroyed by the famine.'[11]

[9] Alternatively, the first verb 'do' may simply be ingressive in reference to the second: 'Let Pharaoh proceed to appoint overseers over the land of Egypt.'

[10] My interpretation of the *w* (cons) perfects in vv 34, 35 as expressing result has been questioned by some on the grounds that these verbs should be interpreted as expressing further commands which are consecutive on explicit commands expressed by preceding jussives (or modal imperfects). In support of my present analysis, it can be argued: (1) the random sprinkling of a few *w* (cons) perfect forms with imperative force in a chain that otherwise consists of jussives/modal imperfects does not look plausible or well-motivated structurally. (2) On the other hand, there are some relatively clear examples of *w* (cons) perfect forms that express *result* after a command form. Thus, e.g., Gen 8:16–17 and Exod 5:1, where the *w* (cons) perfects are translated as purpose/result in all English versions. (3) Speiser's translation (1964: 311) of 41:34–35 also makes *w* (cons) perfects to express purpose/result. For v 34 he suggests (313) that the verb *wĕhimmēš* should be considered to come from a root *ḥmš*, 'organize, (as found in Josh 1:14, 4:12; Judg 7:11; and Exod 13:18). He translates this verse, 'And let Pharaoh take steps to appoint overseers for the land so as to organize the country of Egypt for the seven years of plenty.' His translation of v 35 also makes a purpose clause out of the *w* (cons) perfect form *wĕšāmārû*,' . . . to be stored in the towns for food'. As for purpose versus result, I find no cause for concern here. Text-Result structures found in hortatory discourse become in effect Exhortation-Purpose by shaping to the requirement of the discourse type.

[11] This analysis, as given here and in chap. 4 §2.2. is inconsistent with that given in the constituent structure display Part 4, where 41:36 is considered to be a predictive result paragraph. The analysis here given seems preferable on the grounds that any form of an active verb (in narrative or predictive discourse) should be considered to outrank any form of *hāyâ*, 'be'. This discrepancy was

This deferential hortatory discourse of Joseph to Pharaoh is the third (and climactic) point that he is making. His whole speech can be summarized: 'I'm explaining to you X as a prediction of Y, in order to urge Z'—where X is interpretation of Pharaoh's dreams, Y is a prediction of severe famine, and Z is a program of food conservation and storage. Of the perlocutionary effects of Joseph's speech we are not kept in the dark; Joseph himself is chosen as economic czar and the program is carried out. It was an extremely effective piece of persuasion. In form, however, it conforms to the court etiquette of addressing the Pharaoh in third person.

The brothers similarly address Joseph (incognito) in third person on the occasions of their first and second trips to buy grain. Judah's speech in Genesis 44 is especially worth studying in this regard. Here Judah refers to Joseph in third person as 'my Lord' and to himself as 'your servant'. Even Jacob is referred to as 'your servant, our father'. Again, the social situation is obvious: Joseph is Pharaoh's number two and must be treated with much the same deference as Pharaoh.

6. *Conclusion*

An initial question in this chapter concerned how well linguistic structures that are found in hortatory discourses in *Joseph* would confirm my a priori sociological judgments regarding the relative dominance of speaker and addressee—as summarized in a simple three-way distinction in Diagram 5 (peer to peer, addressee dominant, speaker dominant). In testing for this correlation, five of the lengthier hortatory discourses were singled out for special presentation and discussion. Examples 1 and 2 (numbers 10 and 7 in Diagram 5) have linguistic structures that clearly imply speaker dominance. Examples 4 and 5 (numbers 4 and 5 in Diagram 5) just as clearly express the dominance of the addressee. This dominance is expressed in two linguistic structures (complete mitigation in Example 4 and deference via shift to third person in Example 5). It is less easy to maintain that there is a distinct structure for peer to peer exhortation. To be true, Example 3 (number 12 in Diagram 5) reflects partially mitigated discourse via limitation on the incidence of imperatives. Probably, however, this is not uncomplicated peer to peer exhortation; Joseph is still the authority figure, although he is trying to be gracious rather than imperious. It is rather numbers 1–3 in Diagram 5 that reflect peer to peer exhortation (with prominence of cohortatives and jussives along with imperatives and negative commands). Even

---

discovered too late in the preparation of the constituency structure display to make feasible its correction.

Judah's speech to Jacob (number 9 in Diagram 5) is not markedly different. Of the remaining numbers in Diagram 5, 6 and 8 are similar to 7, 11 is similar to 5, and 13 to any of the speaker dominant examples.

Therefore, it can be concluded that, while the original a priori sociological judgments given at the beginning of the chapter are correct in broad outline, the sociolical reality and the consequent encodings in discourse are more complex than the three-way distinction envisioned at the outset of the investigation.

I have tried to demonstrate here that hortatory discourse, like narrative, has a mainline versus supportive/background distinction. In narrative we have a storyline, and in hortatory discourse we have a comparable line of exhortation versus supportive/background. In addition, variations in tense/mood/aspect on the mainlines of differing hortatory discourses alert us to the fact that hortatory discourse is, in many languages, the most immediately responsive of any main discourse type to the social context.

PARTICIPANTS, SPEECH ACTS, AND DIALOGUE

PART 3

INTRODUCTION

This part of our treatment of *Joseph* is meant to supply a lack and to correct an imbalance which would result if the volume were to consist only of Parts 1 and 2. Part 1, the overview and macrostructures, is absolutely essential to the text theoretical treatment of any discourse, narrative or otherwise, in Hebrew or in any other ancient or modern language. The structure of the whole and its overall conception act as a control on the content and relative elaboration of parts within a discourse.

Part 2 features in particular the role of variant forms of the Hebrew verb in differing types of discourse. It confronts the realities of the Hebrew verb with local constituent structure (the structural paragraph). Within Part 2, chapter 5 is somewhat broader in outlook, since hortatory discourse is particularly sensitive to social constraints. Here the approach is of necessity sociolinguistic rather than strictly linguistic or even textlinguistic. Furthermore, the sociolinguistic constraints on the structure of hortatory discourse largely cluster around the social position of the speaker relative to that of the hearer(s).

Except for the latter emphasis in chapter 5, Part 2 deals largely with only one strand of the double helix of discourse, that is, the role of verbs in marking discourse types and structures within each type. Part 3, among other concerns, deals with the noun phrase, pronouns, verbal affixes, and other elements (including zero anaphora), such as, noun phrases or other items that substitute for or cross-reference noun phrases. This is the other strand of the double helix of discourse. Let us for convenience call these matters participant reference (allowing "participant" to cover *prop* and *theme* as well).

But participants not only figure in actions and events, but in a very important subset of actions that have come to be termed speech acts. Central to speech act theory is the notion that speech acts, quite as much as any action, accomplish certain ends. A rather extensive body of publication has grown up around speech act theory, beginning with

Austin (1962) and on up to the present. Searle (1969), Cole and Morgan (1975), and van Dijk's summary (1977: 167–247) are only a few rather obvious bibliographical citations here where we have to do with an embarrassment of riches. It seems obvious that, granting the typically large incidence of quoted speech and dialogue that characterizes most narrative, textlinguistic analysis of stories must give a broad place to such concerns.

Therefore, in this third part of the volume, I address the matters of participants, speech acts, and dialogue. Participant reference in general is the subject of chapter 6. Here the discussion of participant reference in *Joseph* is organized around the notions of participant reference resources, participant ranking, and the various operations that are loosely subsumed under participant reference.

In chapter 7 I consider participant reference in speech acts. Here general grammatical roles such as subject and indirect or direct object can be redefined as *speaker* versus *hearer* (whether treated as indirect or as direct object). One does not, however, proceed far into a study of references to speaker and hearer, which along with speech verbs constitute *formulas of quotation* (e.g., John said to Mary, "——"), before one is confronted with the considerable variety of form and reference in formulas of quotations within a Biblical Hebrew narrative such as *Joseph*. Our non-randomness assumption requires that we take such variation to have some pragmatic import. Furthermore, as we study variation in formulas of quotation we come to feel that factors are at work here that outrun the simple requirements of participant identification and tracking—hence chapter 7.

A further chapter is required, however, to treat dialogues as they need to be treated. In Part 2 various sorts of paragraph types are introduced, in some of which reported speech figures in minor ways. Dialogue paragraphs, however, constitute a further sort of paragraph type and belong, in fact, to an even broader category of paragraph structure, which can be termed interactional. A story moves forward quite as much (sometimes more) by virtue of verbal and quasi verbal interchanges as it does by other actions/events. Hence chapter 8, where an effort is made to describe and evaluate the role of such interactional paragraphs in pushing the narrative line forward in our story.

I personally believe that the in-depth study of interactional units can potentially open up a new exegetical frontier in our understanding of the Hebrew Scriptures. I hope that chapters 7 and 8 of this volume can be a beginning in this direction.

CHAPTER SIX

PARTICIPANT REFERENCE

Considering a text to be essentially a high-level interweaving of noun phrases and verb phrases, I begin here to discuss noun phrases and the elements that can stand in for them in Biblical Hebrew. What the Hebrew verb does in discourse has been the subject of preceding chapters in Part 2.

Noun phrases and the elements that stand in for them index the dramatis personae, that is, the participants, as well as props, locales, and time intervals. The focus of this chapter is on the referencing of participants and props in *Joseph*, a third person narrative (as opposed to first-person narrative, and to third-person-as-told-to-first-person narrative). Except within reported speech (which is especially considered in chapters 7 and 8), all participant references in *Joseph* are third-person references. In sections of (direct) reported speech the "I" or "thou" of the quotation must, of course, be correctly matched with proper third-person reference within the narrative framework itself.

1. *An apparatus for participant reference*

Before considering in detail participant references in *Joseph*, it is helpful to sketch a general apparatus for participant reference in Biblical Hebrew. This apparatus summarizes the resources of Biblical Hebrew for participant identification, the ranking of participants within narratives, and the operations that participant reference must fulfill. While the first two considerations can be hierarchically ranked, the last approximates more the order of operations within a story.

1.1. *Participant reference resources*

The participant reference resources of Biblical Hebrew are:

1. nouns (including proper names) + qualifiers such as adjectives, relative clauses (with *ʾăšer*), and descriptive sentences (clauses with *hāyâ*, 'be', or nominal clauses)

2. nouns (including proper names) without such qualifiers
3. surrogate nouns as substitutes for (1) and (2), especially by resort to terms for kinship or occupation/role (sometimes, especially with minor participants, this may be the usual level of participant identification, e.g., a relative clause may simply be part of a job or role description
4. pronominal elements
   a. independent subject pronouns
   b. object pronouns (*ʾet* + pronominal element)
   c. preposition + pronominal element
5. pronominal object suffixes on verbs
6. subject and possessor affixes
7. nul references, e.g., in regard to objects that are implied in the context but not stated in a given clause

While the participant reference resources of Biblical Hebrew are, as a whole, of the sort that might be found in any language, there are some idiosyncracies, especially in regard to ranks (4) and (5). In regard to (4a) note that independent subject pronouns are (*a*) frequently found as subjects of nominal or participial clauses and (*b*) relatively infrequent with finite verbs, where their occurrence always has some sort of contrast/pointing function. As for (4b) and (5), I will attempt to show at the end of this chapter that a semantic and functional distinction needs to be posited here between these two ways of indicating the object.

I have not included here front shifting of nouns before finite verbs; this has been considered in connection with clause ranking and paragraph structure (chaps. 3 and 4).

1.2. *Ranking the participants*

Granted the above participant reference resources, Biblical Hebrew, like any language, must employ those resources in accordance with the following hierarchically ranked distinctions among participants in narrative. The scheme below is general rather than specific to Biblical Hebrew.

α. major participants (the slate of participants for the whole story):
   1. central (protagonist)
   2. other(s)
      a. antagonist
      b. helpers/bystanders
β. minor participants (participants whose role is restricted only to particular episodes in the story)

γ. props
1. human
2. animate
3. inanimate
4. natural forces

In the *Joseph* story, Joseph is the protagonist (the central character), while the brothers constitute the antagonists—with foregrounding of Reuben and of Judah in certain passages. Jacob is a bystander; he is not engaged in the struggle between Joseph and his brothers—although his own unwise policies are partly responsible for provoking the struggle. Jacob's trauma and healing are described toward the beginning and the end of the story, respectively. Minor participants are, for example, 'the man' in Gen 37:15-17, the cupbearer and the baker in Gen 40, Potiphar's wife in chap. 39, and the steward of Joseph's house in chap. 41. Pharaoh may be a minor participant or possibly a major participant (helper of Joseph) in that he occurs several places in the story (chaps. 40, 41, 45, and 46).

Benjamin is a human prop, the donkeys are animate props, the cloak of Joseph and the piece of clothing left in the hands of Potiphar's wife are inanimate props, along with the paraphernalia of the installation ceremony in 41:42-43.

1.3. *The operations of participant reference*

Granted the resources of Biblical Hebrew for referencing participants within a story, the following operations of participant referencing are carried out within a narrative:

Q: introduction into the story, i.e., the first mention of a participant or prop
R: integration into the story as central in a narrative (whether main or embedded) or as thematic participant of a paragraph
S: tracking, i.e., tracing references to participants through the text so as to keep track of who-does-what-to-whom, and other such considerations.
T: reinstatement (applicable if a participant has been off-stage)
U: indication of confrontation (e.g., at the climax of a story) and/or role change, i.e., flip in dominance patterns (at a denouement)
V: marking locally contrastive status (accomplished by fronting a noun in the second sentence of an antithetical paragraph (chap. 4, §1.6.)
W: an intrusive narrator evaluation

In *Joseph* the latter is not often found, that is, the narrator does not intrude with comments such as 'Joseph was a righteous man' or 'the brothers were wicked'. Possibly, however, 39:7 is such a narrator evaluation.

The task of participant reference in a story is to match the set (1–7) with the set [α–γ] with the set [Q–W], that is, to use the resources of a language (in this case, Biblical Hebrew), in accordance with distinctions of participant rank, so as to carry out the necessary narrative operations.

2.   *The centrality of Joseph*

Gen 37:2-4, which contains the *tōlĕdôt yaʿăqōb* title and which serves as a stage for the *Joseph* story, establishes Joseph as central (operation R) in a very explicit way—by the use of level 1 of the reference resources. The proper name Joseph and a descriptive phrase immediately follow the *tōlĕdôt* title in the first sentence of the staging paragraph: 'Joseph, a lad of 17 years, was pasturing the flocks along with his brothers.' The next sentence refers to him by the means of an independent pronoun *wĕhûʾ* (a nominal clause must have an explicit noun/pronoun subject): 'And he was/had been a servant along with the sons of Bilhah and the sons of Zilpah, wives of his father.' Joseph is reintroduced by name in the next sentence (level 2 of the referencing system): 'And he brought Joseph their evil gossip to their father.' Next follow two off-the-line verbs (perfects), both of which have Israel as subject while Joseph is named as the object of the first verb: 'As for Israel, he loved Joseph more than all his sons, for a child of his old age/or a natural leader [was] he. And made he a special coat for him.' Following this the brothers became subjects of storyline verbs in 37:4 and Joseph, by now introduced (operation Q) and integrated (operation R) into the story is referred to only by pronouns (level 4) and affixes (level 6). The careful introduction of Joseph with attention to his age and attendant circumstances as well as to the attitude of his father and his brothers towards him clearly marks him as central (i.e., as rank α1).

In 37:5-11, Joseph continues to be central. He is named as the dreamer of the first dream (37:5) and consequently does not need to be so identified in reference to the second dream where 'and he dreamed another dream' (level 6) is sufficient. In the paragraph 37:12-17, where he searches for his brothers, the proper name Joseph (level 2) brackets the paragraph by occurring in 37:13 and 37:17, while level 6 elements suffice again in 37:18-22. On the other hand, the arrival of Joseph on the scene and the violent reception that he received from his brothers correlates with two uses of the proper name (level 2) in adjacent clauses:

'And it came to pass when Joseph came to his brothers, they stripped Joseph of his special coat' (37:23). Likewise, at the apex of the action (as I noted above) the name Joseph occurs three times (37:28) in describing the nefarious transaction of selling the little brother. The name Joseph occurs only three times more in chap. 37: (1) when Reuben returns to the pit and 'no Joseph [was] there'; (2) at the beginning of the cover-up, 'and they took the special coat of Joseph'; and (3) in Jacob's outcry, 'Surely Joseph is torn!' It is plain from the above that the central participant, once carefully introduced, is referred to more often than not by pronoun (level 4) and by affixes (level 6), but it is equally plain that at crucial transitions and climaxes the proper name (level 2) is reinforced.

In 39:1 the *Joseph* story resumes. Considerable care is taken here to reestablish Joseph as central (operation T). The chapter begins: *wĕyôsēp* (level 2): 'Now as for Joseph, he was brought down to Egypt.' Again, while a pronoun or affix suffices to refer to Joseph in most places, at several crucial points he is named (level 2): (1) in the first sentence of the setting of the main paragraph: 'And Yahweh was with Joseph' (39:2); (2) 'And he found Joseph grace in the eyes of his lord' (39:5); (3) 'And he abandoned all that he had to the hand of Joseph' (39:6); and finally (4) 'And he was Joseph good looking and well formed' (39:7). The first three occurrences trace stages in Joseph's rise to increasing esteem in his master's eyes. Possibly the frequency of the name may be partially conditioned by the necessity of reestablishing Joseph as central. Potiphar is not named after v 1, but is referred to as 'the Egyptian' or as 'his [Joseph's] lord'. That Potiphar is thus societally identified (level 3) in reference to Joseph further increases the centrality of the latter. The fourth occurrence above is a pregnant sentence that anticipates the next episode, 'Joseph's ruin' (this sentence is possibly operation W, i.e., an author comment).

I have traced through here, somewhat meticulously, the variation between noun, pronoun, and verb affix in reference to Joseph. The pattern of noun/pronoun/affix alternation well illustrates Hebrew usage in respect to identification and tracking of a central participant. In what follows, I will deal in more summary fashion with continuing participant references to Joseph.

In the struggle (temptation scene) between Joseph and Potiphar's wife, 'Joseph' is only sparingly named. While Joseph as central participant brackets fore and aft the paragraph found in 39:7b–10, he is not named in the following paragraph (39:11–12), where apparently Potiphar's wife is thematic. Here, the 3d masculine singular versus 3d feminine singular endings of the verbs (level 6) keep the subjects straight in this action-oriented passage. The name 'Joseph' does not recur until v 20, where Potiphar is identified at reference level 3 as 'Joseph's master' and where the partnership between the two men is broken. In v 21, we are told again that 'Yahweh was with Joseph' and in v 22 we are told that 'the keeper of the prison committed all the prisoners to Joseph'. Thus, use of Joseph's name (level 2) shifts again the thematic spotlight to Joseph at the end of chap. 39.

I pass over here chap. 40 (where the two courtiers are central) and most of 41, except to note two things: (1) When the cupbearer finally gets around to mentioning Joseph to Pharaoh in 41:12, he refers to him rather slightingly as 'a Hebrew lad, a slave of the captain of the guard' (level 3). (2) In Joseph's audience with Pharaoh all the quotation formulas involve *both* proper names without resort to pronoun for either:

    And said Pharaoh to Joseph (41:15)
    And answered Joseph to Pharaoh (41:16)
    And spoke Pharaoh to Joseph (41:17)
    And said Joseph to Pharaoh (41:25)

Here, in spite of the overwhelming social dominance of Pharaoh, the centrality of Joseph to the whole narrative is maintained by persistent use of his name (level 2). To the narrator, while Pharaoh was a great potentate of this world, Joseph, as one of the founding fathers of the nation, is no whit inferior. Furthermore, as we note in chapter 7, this is a momentous interview between two men and in such confrontation both names are customarily mentioned.

In chap. 42, the first paragraph has to do with Jacob and his family in Canaan. Even here, however, the brothers (see below) are identified as 'Joseph's brothers' (level 3); Benjamin in particular is so labeled. In brief, the centrality of Joseph to the story is assumed even here where others are identified relative to him. In the next paragraph, however, the centrality of Joseph is made even more explicit in that the brothers are pictured as entering Joseph's domain: 'And *Joseph*, he [was] governor. He [was] the one selling grain to all the peoples of the land. And they came in the brothers of Joseph. And he saw *Joseph* his brothers. And he recognized them' (42:6–7).

Especially interesting here is the initial *wĕyôsēp*, which reintroduces Joseph after a digression (operation T; cf. 39:1). The recurrence of Joseph in the rest of this chapter seems to emphasize his dominance of the situation in which the brothers found themselves (e.g., 42:8–9). This is especially marked in the use of the quotation formula 'And he said to them Joseph' in 42:14, 18, where the brothers are referred to by pronoun (level 4), but Joseph by name (level 2): the pronouncements of Joseph that follow convey the crucial piece of information that the brothers will carry back to Canaan. In all this Joseph has the whip hand, and the very selection of quotation formula demonstrates this (cf. chap. 7).

Joseph is largely off-stage in 42:29–43:25. His brothers, in speaking of Joseph (incognito) to their father, refer to him as 'the man' or 'the lord of the land' (at reference level 3) in 42:30,33; in 43:1–14 both the brothers and Jacob so refer to him. Joseph is briefly on stage in 43:15–16, where it is mentioned that the brothers 'stood before Joseph' (v 15) and Joseph recognized Benjamin (v 16). He is off-stage again in the subsequent passage (43:17–25), where the men are brought to 'Joseph's house' and have dealings with 'the one over Joseph's house' (the steward, identified at level 3). Significantly, although Joseph is off-stage, the locale and the person dealing with the brothers are both identified relative to him. The balance of the chapter—even after Joseph comes back on stage—is rather parsimonious in the use of his name, which occurs only in v 26 (his arrival) and v 30 (his weeping at seeing Benjamin). The absence of the name Joseph in vv 31b–34 serves to establish 'the men' (i.e., the brothers) as thematic in this local environment (operation R).

Patterns of interaction between Joseph and his brothers in chap. 44 are much like those already illustrated. In the highly dramatic passage, 45:1–4, the name Joseph occurs rather frequently in keeping with the use of the name at other high points of the story (cf. 37:28).

Beyond this point, I will not trace further references to Joseph, the central participant. As we have seen, the narrator uses great care to make and keep Joseph central in the narrative as a whole—although in local sections of it Joseph may be off-stage, or on-stage but non-thematic. At great moments of the story the proper name (level 2) is liberally used. He deals with Pharaoh as an equal—in spite of Pharaoh's station and in spite of Joseph's deferential speech before him (chap. 7). He dominates his brothers as he puts them to the test before revealing himself.

3. *References to Joseph's brothers*

There is some significant variation in the references to Joseph's brothers from episode to episode of the story. In the Stage, Ep $_1$, and the Interpeak Ep (with the others off-stage in what intervenes) the brothers are referred to as 'Joseph's/his brothers' (level 3) with only a few exceptions occasioned by restricted passages in which Israel/Jacob, Reuben, Judah, or Benjamin are temporarily thematic and the brothers are referred to relative to such local themes (all at level 3). Thus in 37:3 we read of Israel and 'his sons' in an off-the-line sentence in the stage where Israel is temporarily thematic. In 42:5 we are told that 'the sons of Israel came to buy'. This comes at the end of a paragraph (42:1–5) in which Jacob/Israel is thematic throughout. Admittedly, we have a reference in 42:3 to 'Joseph's ten brothers', and in 42:4 to 'Benjamin, Joseph's brother', but in 42:5 the reference to the brothers as 'sons of Israel' closes the paragraph by referring to them again in reference to the thematic participant. This is in accordance with the convention whereby the name of the thematic participant often brackets the paragraph (operation R). The paragraph medial explicit reference to Joseph's *ten* brothers is presumably used to prepare us for the exclusion of Benjamin (Joseph's *special* brother) in v 4.

Two other instances of reference to the sons of Israel occur. One is very brief, occurs in the Stage, and indicates a subset of Jacob's sons: 'He was a lad/apprentice along with the sons of Bilhah, and with the sons of Zilpah, his father's wives.' The other passage indicates the union of the sons of Israel with the daughters of Israel in a larger set: 'And all his sons and all his daughters rose up to comfort him' (37:35).

Just as Joseph's brothers are characterized as sons of Israel/Jacob in local contexts where the thematic spotlight rests temporarily on Israel/Jacob, so there are passages where: (1) the set X of the brothers is partitioned into a set A and X–A where A is either Reuben or Judah and X–A is 'his [Reuben's or Judah's] brothers'. In these passages, Reuben (37:21–22, 29–30) and Judah (37:26–27) are thematic. By virtue of their being made thematic (operation R), the other brothers are referred to in relation to them at level 3.

In summary: in the Stage, Ep$_1$, and Interpeak Ep (earlier parts of the story in which the brothers are on stage), they are quite regularly identified relative to the central participant as 'Joseph's/his brothers'. In local contexts where someone else in the family is thematic, they are identified relative to the thematic participant. All these references to the brothers are all level 3, and can be regarded as part and parcel of operation R (establishing someone else as the thematic participant in a passage).

However, the long Peak' Ep (chaps. 43–45) where Joseph gives his brothers the third degree, where Judah desperately intercedes for Benjamin, and where Joseph finally reveals himself to them, the references to Joseph's brothers vary according to their placement in the episodes of this embedded discourse.

In 43:1–14, there is no overt reference by noun to Joseph's brothers. In 43:15 through the end of chap. 43, wherever the brothers are referred to by a noun phrase, they are called 'the men'. Here we have an abandonment of the kinship term at level 3 for a noun reference at level 2. We can readily understand this usage in 43:16 where Joseph commands his steward concerning 'the men', in that they are not yet revealed as his brothers, he could scarcely have spoken of them differently. But this usage occurs also in 43:15: 'And they arose, and they went down to Egypt. And they stood before Joseph' (as well as in 43:17–18, and in 43:24).

Thus, in 43:17: 'And he brought the man *the men* to the house of Joseph'; in 43:18: 'And they feared *the men* because they were brought to Joseph's house'; and again, in 43:24, which is much like 43:17. Clearly, the figure of the steward of Joseph's house dominates the scene; to him the brothers of Joseph are simply a group of men who have come to buy grain and for some reason excite the interest of his master Joseph. Furthermore, it appears that the narrator in referring to Joseph's brothers adopts the same stance as the steward who is central to the scene and thematic. Apparently, 43:15, as part of this span in which the steward is thematic, likewise refers to the brothers as 'the men', even though the steward himself is mentioned for the first time in the following verse.

Likewise, in the next embedded episode where the brothers dine with Joseph (where, however, the brothers, not Joseph, are locally thematic) the narrator still refers to the brothers as 'the men' (v 33). Indeed, the brothers are not called 'Joseph's/his brothers' again until Joseph reveals himself to them in the early part of chap. 45.

In terms, therefore, of the development of this embedded discourse (chaps. 43–45) towards its own peak it appears that referring to Joseph's brothers as 'the men' serves to heighten the dramatic suspense. The fraternal relationship is held, as it were, in abeyance, while the remorseless testing of 'the men' proceeds to its successful climax. Meanwhile, at the supreme crisis of the testing (47:14–34), Judah is indicated as central (operation R). Thus, in 44:14 the phrase 'Judah and his brothers' (cf. 37:36). Here as elsewhere, participants are societally identified relative to a local thematic participant (operation R by use of level 3). The local thematic status of Judah is further confirmed in his proper name (level 2) in 44:16 and 44:18, where he functions as spokesman for the brothers and makes the longest speech in the entire story.

4. *References to Israel/Jacob*

As we have said, Israel/Jacob is (in most of the story) a bystander, that is, neither antagonist nor protagonist. He is, however, locally thematic in some passages and even dominant in a passage or two. Here we are faced with the use of two names for the same personage (a split at reference level 2). Why, after the change of name in 35:10, is Jacob not consistently called Israel—as Abram becomes consistently Abraham after his change of name? While this problem affects Gen 35:9–29 and 37:1 (as the end of the previous *tŏlĕdôt*) I will confine discussion here to choice of one name versus the other within *Joseph*.

Apparently, 'Jacob' emphasizes more Joseph's father as a suffering, feeling human being, while 'Israel' accords better with passages where his office and dignity are in view.[1] Thus, we find 'Israel' in 37:3 and 13, before the sale of Joseph into Egypt, but 'Jacob' in 37:34, where Jacob mourns his son. In both parts of the chapter, of course, Jacob can be referred to as 'his father' (where Joseph as central participant is in view), or as 'their father' (where the brothers are local theme)—in which case 'Israel/Jacob' of level 2 gives way to level 3.

In 42:1–4, in the brief dialogue that introduces the first descent of the brothers into Egypt, we find 'Jacob'. In v 5 we have a reference to 'the sons of Israel'. Perhaps, the name 'Jacob' is fitting to describe the measures taken by a man to obtain food for himself and his family. Again, perhaps, the reference to 'the sons of Israel' in v 5 is a reminder of the dignity and historical importance of the one whose sons come to buy grain at this juncture in the nation's history.

In the dialogue that ensures on the occasion of the first return with grain (42:29–32), Jacob is 'Jacob' again; a frustrated, troubled, somewhat petulant old man.

It is somewhat surprising, therefore, to find 'Israel' on the stage again in the dialogue of 43:1–14. Nevertheless, this dialogue is somewhat different in that Israel, even in acceding to his sons' demands that Benjamin must go with them, comes through the passage with a certain dignity. Thus, at the end (43:11–14) he, as clan head, finalizes the terms on which they are to go: with a present for 'the man' (Joseph), with double money, and with Benjamin. In the end, he commits his case to God Almighty and resigns himself to whatever may happen (43:14). Perhaps it is not strange therefore that the narrator should dub him Israel in vv 6, 8, and 11, since he takes hold of things in his fashion (a flip in dominance, operation U).

[1] Doris Myers (personal communication), to whom I am again indebted, referred me to E. H. Kantorowicz, *The King's Two Bodies*, who points out how medieval tombs make a distinction between the king's representation on top of the tomb and the actual remains inside. According to the former, he is king in robes with no sign of death and decay, while inside the tomb is the king, naked and skeletal. Here the contrast between the public and private person of the king is graphically portrayed. In some degree also our story here represents Israel as the public person and Jacob as the private person.

Joseph, once he has revealed himself to his brothers seems to relish referring to Jacob as 'my father' (45:3, 9, and 13 [2x]).

Again, in 45:21, we find the 'sons of Israel' setting out on their journey to tell the good news to 'Jacob their father' (45:25, 27). Consequently, 'Israel' in v 28 makes his decision as clan-head. Thus, chap. 46 records 'Israel' taking his journey and God's speaking to him. Note, however, that 'God spoke to *Israel* in the visions of the night and said, "Jacob, Jacob"'. The narrator calls him Israel, but God in the vision calls him by his old familiar name, Jacob.

In the balance of the chapter 'Jacob' and 'Israel' both occur. The latter is found again in the title 'the sons of Israel' (v 5, where, interestingly enough, 'the sons of Israel carried *Jacob* their father . . .'; and in the genealogy of 'the children of Israel' (v 30). Elsewhere, 'Jacob' seems to suffice for the narrator's purposes.

In chap. 47, we find the name 'Jacob' used for the interview with Pharaoh—where they discuss life and its brevity. Finally, in 47:27, the number of years that 'Jacob' lived in Goshen and the total years of his life are given, while in 47:29 the time draws near for 'Israel' (clan-head) to die (cf. v 31).

I do not pretend to have made a solid and closed case that variety such as is found here in referring to Joseph's father can be summarily and in detail explained without reference to the devices of source criticism (which explains variations as characteristic of different documents). But I believe that a careful sympathetic reading of the story makes it highly plausible that a skillful narrator has been at work and his use of Israel/Jacob is neither random nor unmotivated. Certainly it is less difficult to see a pattern here than in some Russian novels where, for example, the same person can be referred to as 'Boris Boturin' in one passage and 'Ivanovich' (patronymic) in another—much to the confusion of the English-speaking reader!

5. *References to further participants*

The remaining participants discussed here are relatively minor since the narrative is mainly concerned with Joseph, Jacob, and the brothers.

5.1. Pharaoh is never referred to by pronoun (level 4), whether in the third or second person, but by name (level 2) or by verb affix or affix of possessor (level 6). Usually, he is referred to simply as 'Pharaoh'. In 39:40 he is referred to as 'the king' (level 3) in explaining that the king's prisoners were kept in the same jail that Joseph was put into. In 40:1, 5 he is referred to as 'the king of Egypt'—somewhat interchangeably with

'Pharaoh' (40:2,7). In the rest of the story, we find only 'Pharaoh', except for the complete title, 'Pharaoh, King of Egypt' in 41:46. The latter title occurs in the paragraph that immediately follows the installation passage (41:37–45). The use of the complete title (level 1) may inject a certain solemnity into the (post-peak) summary: 'And Joseph [was] thirty years old in his standing before Pharaoh, the King of Egypt. And he went out Joseph from the presence of Pharaoh. And he passed-through all the land of Egypt.'

5.2 In 37:15–17, an unidentified man answers Joseph's inquiry about his brothers and redirects him from Shechem to Dothan. The role of this participant is brief but crucial. He is first introduced as an indefinite noun *ʾîš*, 'a man', 'a certain man' (operation Q). In the next reference (the next preterite after an intervening participial clause), he is referred to as *hāʾîš*, 'the man'. Similarly, after Joseph's reply we're told: 'And he said the man, "They've left here. I heard them saying, 'Let's go to Dothan.'"' In this passage Joseph is referred to only by object affix *-hû* (level 5) and as *y-* subject of the preterite (level 6), but 'the man' is named three times (level 2). It seems that by these devices the newly introduced (albeit anonymous) man is made thematic for a brief span (operation R). Note that the participant who is introduced in the clause 'and he found him a man' is also made the subject of the next finite verb: 'And he asked him the man.' It is not simply assumed that the newly introduced participant will naturally be subject of the next preterite; rather the noun is repeated here and yet once again in v 17; this seems to be regular procedure in regard to operation R. Although this minor participant is anonymous and no detail is given concerning him, he is integrated into the paragraph and made thematic by being doubly mentioned at its beginning again at its end so as to bracket the span wherein he is local theme.

5.3. Potiphar is also duly introduced and identified (operations Q and R) but the two references to him are split—one at the end of chap. 37 and the other at the beginning of chap. 39—so as to provide back-reference and resumption of the interrupted story (operation T). Thus, 37:36 states, 'And they sold him into Egypt, to Potiphar, a courtier of Pharaoh, the captain of the guard' (level 1). The backreference in 39:1 is not materially different: 'As for Joseph, he was brought down to Egypt and he bought him Potiphar, a courtier of Pharaoh, captain of the guard, and Egyptian man' (still at reference level 1). The further phrase 'an Egyptian man' in 39:1 is a significant addition since the proper name Potiphar does not occur again. In 39:2–6, he is variously referred to as 'his master the Egyptian', 'his master', or 'the Egyptian'. The dual presentation of Potiphar, in spite of its secondary purpose of recapitulation, is similar to the dual presentation of the cupbearer and the baker in 40:1–2, and of the man in 37:15–17. In each case, the repeated reference integrates and thematizes a participant according to operation R.

5.4. Potiphar's wife dominates the scenes in 39:7ff. (level 3). From here on, the alternation between third masculine singular and third feminine singular verb affixes (level 6) would have been sufficient to clear the ambiguity (operation S) between the words and actions of Joseph and the words and actions of the woman—as would also the gender of the pronouns used to express the indirect object (level 4). Nevertheless, in v 8 we read: 'But he refused. And he said to his master's wife.' Here apparently in repetition of the phrase 'his master's wife' (at level 3) we see operation R at work, that is, the integration and thematization of a participant by dual presentation as we have seen in the previous cases. Masculine and feminine verb morphology (level 6) and pronouns (level 4) continue to untangle the ambiguity (operation S) in the remainder of the scene (without either 'Joseph' or 'his master's wife' occurring). In v 9, however ('and it came to pass when his master heard the words of his wife') the woman is again explicitly mentioned at the end of the span. (For this reaffirmation of her thematicity, subsumed under operation R, cf. 42:5 as discussed in §3 above, and 37:14 as discussed above in this section.)

5.5. Chapter 40 is an embedded narrative with its own participant structure. Here Joseph's interpreting of the dreams of two of Pharaoh's courtiers provides (eventually) for the interview of Joseph with Pharaoh. This chapter takes the courtiers as the central participants. They are introduced as such in 40:1–2 (operation Q). The narrator signals their centrality by introducing them *twice* (operation R): (1) They are subject in 40:1 (paragraph setting expounded by a sentence whose verb is in the perfect): 'And it came to pass after these things, sinned they the cupbearer of the King of Egypt and the baker against their lord, the King of Egypt.' (2) They are oblique object in the clause that has the first storyline verb of the passage: 'And he got angry Pharaoh against the two of his servants, against the chief of the cupbearers and against the chief of the bakers.' Note here that for mere purposes of tracking, v 2 need have been no more than: 'And he got angry Pharaoh against the two of his servants.' The additional material goes over much of the same ground as is found in v 1—although it adds the further information that it is the *chief* of the cupbearers and the *chief* of the bakers that is meant. Thus, twice identified, the two courtiers are made central to the following narrative. To be true, Joseph as central participant of the *main* story, dominates the interaction with them (he interprets their dreams), but the narrative spotlight is temporarily on them.

5.6. The close of chap. 40 is a masterful paragraph (40:20–23) in which all the strands of participant reference are gathered up in preparation for the return to the main story. Pharaoh, off-stage in 40:4–19, now dominates the scene and is thematic (operation R), preparing us for the next scene where *he* has dreams. The cupbearer and the baker are despised by the narrator, so that we are told on the storyline that the cupbearer is restored to his office and resumes his duties; off-the-line we are told, in a clause with preposed noun and its verb in the perfect, 'But the baker, he hanged.' Here the preposing of the noun 'the baker' emphasizes the contrast of his fate with that of the cupbearer (operation V). At the same time the reporting of the event off-the-line accords with his irrelevance to all that follows (he never comes on stage again, although he is mentioned in 41:10ff.). The final participant referred to is Joseph (v 23), who as central participant in the main story is forgotten by the chief cupbearer for two long years (41:1).

5.7. The steward of Joseph's house is introduced in 43:16 in a welter of participant references: Joseph, Benjamin, 'the man', and the steward— three of whom would be referred to as third masculine singular in the morphology of the verb (at reference level 6) and in the pronominal structure (at level 4), while 'the men' calls for the third masculine plural on both levels. There is therefore no possibility of confusing the latter with any of the three other participants in the passage. Benjamin, moreover, does not act as such; he is more of a prop than a participant. Joseph and his steward are clearly distinguished as to subject references (operation S) by the pragmatic fact that Joseph gives the orders and the steward carries them out.

With all this in mind it is of some interest that the steward is introduced as 'the one over his house' (v 16), is referred to three times as 'the man' (vv 17, 24) and as 'the man who [was] over the house of Joseph' (v 19). Here we see operation R: integration and thematization by overt-multiple-mention (more than is needed for unambiguous reference) and by the bracketing nature of references to a thematic participant (as cited several times in the previous discussion).

It is also of some interest here that the steward is referred to by a definite noun phrase on first mention of him (unlike 'a man' who finds Joseph and becomes 'the man' in subsequent references); this usage probably reflects the assumption that a great lord like Joseph would surely have such a seneschal. In that his presence can be assumed, he is, in a sense, *not* introduced at all but simply comes on stage to participate in the action and be integrated into the story.

The steward also figures in the action of 44:1–2, where he is referred to as 'the one over his house' (level 3) in 44:1 and 44:4, but otherwise by verb ending and pronoun (lower levels of reference). In his dealings with 'the men', the third masculine singular versus third masculine plural morphology (at level 6) suffices for clear reference in most instances. Furthermore, the steward has already been integrated and made thematic. Aside from reintroducing him, there is no need to emphasize his thematicity or his dominance.

5.8. This brings us again to the Ishmaelite/Midianite question (which I discussed in chap. 1, §3.2.1.). Without recapitulating here the arguments of that section, I want to suggest that if the Midianites of 37:28 were meant to be a separate and new group of participants (distinct from the Ishmaelites), we have every right to expect that Hebrew participant introduction and integration (operations Q and R) would introduce them *not once* but twice and in the process would name them as the unambiguous subject of the verbs 'draw out' and 'pull up'. If, on the other hand, the Midianites of v 28 are the same as the Ishmaelites of v 25, then all falls into line quite well. While the Ishmaelites/Midianites are eventually mentioned twice (as befits their prominence in the story), the separation between the first and second mentioning of them is part of the narrator's art in supplying suspense at peak.

6. ʾet + *pronoun versus object suffixes on verbs*

One cannot read *Joseph* carefully without being puzzled by the alternation between references on level 4 (pronouns) and on level 5 (verb affixes) in relation to expressing the object (which is almost entirely a matter of the third person object since *Joseph* is a narrative told in third person). I propose here the view that resort to level 5 (the object suffix) rather than to level 4 (sign of accusative ʾet + pronoun) has to do not with thematicity as such but rather with dominance patterns (and related therefore to operation U). Succinctly, level 5 is used rather than level 4 to express a dominance pattern in which the participant(s) referred to by the object suffix is under the dominance of someone else. Often this implies a flip, that is, someone formerly dominant is no longer dominant (operation U). Indication of the object participant via ʾet + pronoun is the more neutral or unmarked form; it may be used to remind us that a participant indicated as dominant in the context (reference level 5) is still central and thematic. I illustrate these claims via chap. 37.

In the stage (37:2b–4) and in the Inciting Incident, Joseph, when object, is referred to as ʾet-yôsēp or ʾōtô. Here, as central participant, he is thematic and, while at odds with his brothers, he has a relatively high status as Jacob's favorite. In 37:12–14, Jacob sends Joseph off to visit (spy on) his brothers. Jacob as clan-head clearly dominates Joseph in an interaction paragraph where *both* are probably thematic. The next to the last verb of v 14 refers to Joseph as -*hû*, an object suffix on the verb *send*: 'And he sent him.' Here there is a flip of sorts; while Joseph is not presented as dominated in the preceding passages (2b–11), where he interacts with his brothers, here in interaction with his father, the clan-head, he is depicted as in the lower position.

In 37:15–17, 'a man' finds Joseph wandering in the field. The man is introduced, integrated, and made thematic in this section. He finds Joseph and authoritatively tells him that the brothers have gone to Dothan. Joseph not only is nonthematic here but replies to the questions and accepts the directive of the other participant. In this situation he is referred to as -*hû* on both the verb *find* and *ask*: 'And he found him. . . . And he asked him.'

Notice, however, what is marked at the end of the above passage and in the ensuring context. At the end of v 17, the brothers are referred to by the object affix -*ēm*: 'And he found *them* in Dothan.' Joseph at this point is still pictured as the special emissary from his father, posing perhaps something of a treat to this brothers—on whom he had previously informed Jacob (37:2c). At this point Joseph is dominant over his brothers and the use of -*ēm* at reference level 5 accords with his position. All this abruptly changes in the next passages (v 18 to the end of the chapter). In v 18, where the brothers see Joseph coming from afar and plot to kill him, he is still referred to as *ʾōtô*, 'him' (the neutral form), but in the reported speech of the brothers, in a bit of interspersed narrative comment (37:21), and in the first part of Reuben's speech, he is repeatedly referred to as -*hû*: 'Let's kill *him*'; 'Let's cast *him* into a pit'; 'Let's say, "A wild animal has eaten *him*."' (This also occurs in the interspersed narrative comment, 'He [Reuben] saved *him* from their hand.') Reuben's speech, in which he prevented the outright murder of Joseph, is marked by two features: (1) use of the more emphatic -*nnû* for the third person verbal affix; and (2) reversion to *ʾōtô* in his speech ('cast *him* into the pit') and in the narrative comment ('in order that he might rescue *him* from their hands'). Here we see that while in 37:14 Joseph was depicted as dominant over his brothers, there is a reversal of the dominance pattern in the way the brothers talk about him—apart from Reuben's references to him in accordance with Reuben's role as one who tried to rescue Joseph.

In 37:23–28 Joseph is completely at the mercy of his brothers. The proper name 'Joseph' is (as we have seen) used twice in v 23 and three times in v 28. He is certainly thematic in the passage as a whole, although off stage (in the pit) in the center of the paragraph. In v 24 he is referred to by -*hû*, object suffix on the verb 'and they seized *him*', but

ʾōtô in 'and they put *him* in the pit'. While the use of the former represents his changed fortunes (from top to bottom) the use of ʾōtô in the next clause may perhaps contribute to maintaining his thematic status. In Judah's speech when he refers to Joseph as 'our brother' and 'our flesh', Joseph is referred to once as -nnû, the more emphatic (whatever that means!) third-person object suffix.

I see nothing in the balance of *Joseph* to contradict the claim here made, that is, when the narrator wants to represent someone in a position where he is dominated by somebody else, verb object suffixes are used.[2] Uses of ʾōtô, 'him', and ʾōtām, 'them', do not on the other hand need to be explained or justified—aside from the matter already discussed of the usage of noun versus pronominal element.

[2] Further research is needed to see whether this claim can be extended to Biblical Hebrew narrative as a whole. Whatever the outcome of this question, it seems clear that this claim cannot be made in regard to certain non-narrative discourses, e.g., the poetry of the Psalms.

CHAPTER SEVEN

VARIATIONS IN FORMULAS OF QUOTATION

While in previous chapters there has been examination of the structure of various monologue discourse types—narrative, predictive, expository, and hortatory—no attempt has as yet been made to describe the nature of dialogue or even of those places in *Joseph* where someone is reported as having said something even though it did not initiate a dialogue. This chapter examines the structure of reported speech in reference to constraints on formulas of quotation. The following (and last) chapter will consider in a more global way the structure of dialogue. The concerns of this chapter are, of course, related to matters of participant reference presented in chapter 6. Here, however, we are specifically studying references to participants in *speech acts*.

In view of the relative novelty of the claims made here the argument will proceed in two stages: (1) assembling of observations regarding variations in the formulas of quotation that are found in *Joseph*; and (2) examination of further data from other portions of the Hebrew Scriptures in an attempt to supply a more adequate data base, and to make more solid whatever claims are made in §1, as well as to modify those claims in certain particulars.

1. *A preliminary sketch*

In Biblical Hebrew narrative (as in many languages) there is considerable variety in the structure of quotation formulas. Thus, on the storyline of a Hebrew narrative[1] we may find the following:

[1] The comparison of on-the-line varieties of quotation formulas that contain the preterite of *ʾāmar* is the scope of this study. Nevertheless, *ʾāmar* in quotation formulas is subject to the same range of formal variation that characterizes other Hebrew verbs. Thus, we sometimes find a preposed noun and *ʾāmar* (instead of *wayyōʾmer*) or *lēʾmōr* (*lĕ* + infinitive construct of *ʾāmar*) after a speech act verb or even after *wayyōʾmer*. Robert Burgen (oral communi-

wayyō²mer, 'and he said'

wayyō²mer yôsēp, 'and Joseph said'

wayyō²mer ²ĕlêhem yôsēp, 'and Joseph said to them'[2]

wayyō²mer ²ĕlêhem, 'and he said to them'

wayyō²mer lĕ²eḥāyw, 'and he said to his brothers'

wayyō²mer yôsēp lĕ²eḥāyw, 'and Joseph said to his brothers'

These are the on-the-line possibilities for this verb. Interestingly enough we do not find in this story examples in which the subject occurs as a pronoun: *wayyō²mer hû²*, 'and he said', or the use of this sequence plus the specification of the addressee of a speech act. I do not think that this formula of quotation is intrinsically impossible. Rather, the situation simply is that subject pronouns are used much more sparingly in Biblical Hebrew than in English—indeed, so sparingly that, although we can conceive of a context where the conditions of local contrast could justify this formula as opposed to what *someone else* said, this construction occurs nowhere in *Joseph*.

In terms of the participant referencing resources of Biblical Hebrew as summarized in chapter 6, we note that both the speaker and the addressee can be referenced at level 2 (by noun), that either speaker or addressee can be referenced at this level and the other at level 6 (verb affix for the speaker) or at level 7 (nul for the addressee), or the addressee can be indicated at level 4 (prepositional element + pronoun) while the speaker is referenced either at level 2 (by noun) or at level 6 (by verb affix). It would be strange indeed if the choice running from noun to pronoun to verb affix or nul did not tell us something about the relative importance of the speech act and/or its participants as thus referenced.

Nevertheless, granted the considerable variety in the structure of the formula of quotation, the question naturally arises as to the precise nature of the contextual constraints that call forth one variant of the quotation formula rather than another.[3] The immediate aim of this

---

cation) has has been especially concerned with explicating discourse implications of *lē²mōr* and such couplets and triplets as I include under the rubric *expanded quotation formula*.

[2] For the ordering of "indirect objects" (specification of addressee) when a preposition and pronoun occur in the V___S slot, see remarks under §1.2.5. (cf. also Longacre 1961).

[3] As far as I know the first to raise such a question were Carol Koontz (1977) in reference to Teribe (Panama); Stephen Levinsohn (1976) in reference to Inga (Quechua) and Aileen Reid (1979) in reference to Northern Totonac (Mexico).

section is to sketch in a rather *ad hoc* way an hypothesis that accounts for constraints in formulas of quotation within *Joseph*; this hypothesis is then extended and generalized in §2 on the basis of broader data. The full apparatus of participant reference in chapter 6 will not be regularly invoked here. I have noted above, however, the general parallelism of our work here to that of the earlier chapter.

1.1.   In seeking to account for the variations in formulas of quotation, several factors must be kept in balance.

1.1.1.   Quotation formulas *proper* consist of some form of the verb *ʾāmar*, 'say', +/- nouns and/or pronouns. Very frequently, however, the clause that contains the verb 'say' is preceded by another clause that has either a *motion* verb ('and they drew near to him, and they said'); a verb of *psychological* orientation ('and they feared greatly, and they said'); or a *verb* that is more specific in relation to the speech act ('and he refused, and he said'). Furthermore, the clause with the verb 'say' may be preceded by two or three such preparatory clauses. In such a situation the whole sequence of two to four clauses with whatever nouns and pronouns that it contains is relevant to the specification or nonspecification of speaker and addressee; it functions as an *expanded quotation formula*.[4] Wherever, therefore, in the following formulations I refer to the presence of a noun or pronoun that identifies a speech act participant, I may be referring to such presence even in clause(s) that come before the quotation formula narrowly conceived (this presence is taken to be equivalent to presence in that clause itself). Thus, 'and they drew near to him his brothers, and they said' is taken to be an example of a quotation formula in which the speaker is specified by a noun and the addressee by a pronoun. Therefore, anywhere that "quotation formula" is not explicitly used in the more restricted sense it is to be understood in this expanded sense.

1.1.2.   Secondly, it needs to be remembered that basic needs of continuing participant identification and tracking (operation S of chap. 6) must be met in passages that contain reported speech, as well as in those that do not. We must, of course, know who is talking to whom, and if the context does not clarify these matters the passage itself must so specify. This is especially true in initiating dialogue.

---

[4] Much of the justification for doing this is that it is possible to work out a rationale of variation in quotation formulas if and only if such an enlarged view of the introduction of quotations is taken. I see no discernible patterning in variation in quotation formulas narrowly defined.

Basic needs of participant identification and tracking are often fulfilled by the person-number-gender affixes on the verb. Thus, in a dialogue that involves a man and a woman (cf. Joseph and Potiphar's wife in 39:7–12) or in one that involves a man and a group of men (cf. Joseph and his brothers in chaps. 42 and 43), distinctions of gender in the one case and number in the other fill the need for routine participant tracking in a dialogue. Obviously, the areas of potential ambiguity are those in which the speaker and addressee are of the same person-number-gender category (e.g., 3 masc. sg.).

A further characteristic of Hebrew narrative discourse is of relevance here. This is the requirement that to introduce a participant and integrate him into the story (operation R) he must be presented explicitly more than once. Thus in 37:21–22 Reuben is thematic in a passage in which he saves Joseph from immediate death at the hands of his brothers. Verse 21 presents Reuben initially in this role: 'And Reuben heard. And he saved him from their hands. And he said, "Don't kill him."' In v 22 Reuben's speech act is further represented: 'And Reuben said to them, "Don't shed blood. Throw him into one of these pits that [are] in the desert. But let's not lay our hands on him"—in order to rescue him from their hands and return him to his father.' While all this fits the rules of §2 quite well, note than a re-presentation of Reuben is required somewhere in the context in that he is central to this passage. Therefore, the presence of the noun 'Reuben' in the quotation formula in 37:22 may be due to the more basic concerns of participant introduction and integration than to the operation of more particular rules as 1–7 below. In fact, the reporting of Reuben's intervention in two sections of reported speech instead of in one continuous monologue (with but one quotation formula) may well be to facilitate the dual presentation of him as thematic participant.

Likewise there is a brief passage (37:15–17) in which Joseph talks with a man who found him wandering around in the fields. The man, who is thematic to this passage (Joseph is reduced to an affix -*hû*, 'him', on the verbs 'find' and 'ask' as discussed in §7 of chap. 6) is presented twice, pursuant to his thematic role:

wayyimṣāʾēhû	*ʾîš*	*wayyišālēhû*	*hāʾîš*	*lēʾmōr*
and he found him	a man	and he asked him	the man	saying

Here in the quotation formula the speaker is indicated by a noun and the addressee by a pronominal affix on the verb. This superficially fits the pattern given in §1.2.5. below (attempted decisiveness). However, it seems hardly to be applicable to the situation here, and at any rate, the reintroduction of the noun 'the man' can be considered to be required by the usual device of re-presentation of a participant in establishing him as thematic.

1.1.3. Conventions of deferential address probably constitute separate but intersecting concerns from those sketched below under §§1.2.1.–1.2.7. According to these conventions 'your servant' substitutes for 'I, me' and 'my Lord' for 'you'. In initiating a dialogue the substitution is total and the verb morphology is changed accordingly, as in 44:18–19: 'Oh *my Lord*, let *your servant* speak a word in the ears of *my Lord*. And don't let your anger be kindled against *your servant*. *My Lord* asked his servants saying. . . .' In the last sentence when *ʾădōnî*, 'my Lord', substitutes for 'you' as subject the verb also becomes third person singular and the addressee is 'his servants' instead of 'your servants'. In continuing the dialogue these deferential constraints are relaxed to the extent that only the addressee is deferentially adjusted. Thus in 44:20 *wannōʾmer ʾel-ʾădōnî*, 'And we said to my lord', is found; and in 44:21 *wattōʾmer l-ʿăbādêkā*, 'And you said to your servants', is found.

1.2. Some tentative observations regarding variations in formulas of quotation follow. While I discuss these under seven captions, they are not a simple linear sequence. In §§1.2.1. and 1.2.2. I suggest some basic patterns and functions that initiate and continue a dialogue. In §§1.2.3. and 1.2.4. other functions of the pattern presented in §1.2.1. are discussed, since that pattern is not limited to initiating a dialogue. Sections 1.2.5., 1.2.6., and 1.2.7. describe other patterns of continuing dialogue than that presented in §1.2.2. and summarize our current understanding of the functions of those patterns. Throughout this discussion, *Sp* stands for speaker and *Add* for addressee; an intervening colon may be read as "specified by"; and *N*, *pr*, and ∅ stand for noun, pronoun, and nul respectively. In specifying Sp:∅, it is to be understood that there is no further indication of speaker (subject) beyond that specified by the verb morphology (in effect, reference levels 6 and 7 of chap. 6 are combined here). In specifying Add:∅ no indication of any sort of the addressee is found in the formula of quotation.

1.2.1. Sp:N + Add:N functions in *dialogue initiation* where it also reflects the basic need for participant identification and tracking (operation S of chap. 6). Thus, in 37:13 we find *wayyōʾmer yiśrāʾēl ʾel-yôsēp*, 'and Israel said to Joseph', in initiating a dialogue with Joseph about the latter's going to Shechem to see how his brothers were getting along. In 37:26 we find *wayyōʾmer yĕhûdâ ʾel-ʾēḥāyw*, 'and Judah said to his brothers', in initiating a dialogue in which he proposed selling Joseph to the Ishmaelites. In 39:7–8 Potiphar's wife ('the wife of his lord') and Joseph are both mentioned in the clause of psychological predisposition just before the bare verb *wattōʾmer*, 'and she said' (v 7); the complex of two clauses by thus mentioning explicitly the speaker and the addressee, regularly initiates the dialogue in which Potiphar's wife tries to seduce Joseph. In 41:9 the chief cupbearer and Pharaoh are both mentioned in the quotation formula in the initiation of the dialogue in which pharaoh learns about Joseph's ability to interpret dreams. This device serves to initiate dialogues also in 41:37, 42:1, 44:4, 45:17, 46:2, 46:30, 46:31, 47:1, 47:3, and 47:5.

The example in 47:1 is especially interesting in that the complex of clauses, that is, the extended quotation formula, that introduces speaker and addressee here contains three clauses rather than two. Here occur both a clause with motion verb and a clause that identifies the nature of the speech act; the former has the Sp:N, and the latter has the Add:N.

wayyābô$^{\circ}$	*yôsēp*	*wayyaggēd*	*lĕpar^{c}ōh*	*wayyō$^{\circ}$mer*
and he went in	Joseph	and he declared	to Pharaoh	and he said

1.2.2. Sp:∅ and Add:N/pr are the basic forms of quotation formula for a *continuing dialogue*. It is assumed at this point in the dialogue that the participants in the speech act are identified. It is, however, a convention of Biblical Hebrew to specify the addressee (most usually by pronouns). In calling this usage the basic form for continuing dialogue, it is assumed that the special conditions in §§1.2.3.–1.2.7. below do not apply in the passages cited here.

A clear instance of this is found in 37:13 where, after the initial *wayyō$^{\circ}$mer yiśrā$^{\circ}$ēl $^{\circ}$el-yôsēp*, 'and he said Israel to Joseph', the dialogue simply proceeds with *wayyō$^{\circ}$mer lô*, 'and he said to him', with alternation of speaker and addresses so that *lô* refers first to Israel and next to Joseph.

The dialogue initiated in 42:7 also shows this pattern for a portion of its length (for the special use of Sp:∅ and Add:N/pr in initiating a dialogue see immediately below). The brothers first reply to Joseph according to §1.2.6. below (social amenities). The next three quotations formulas, however, have the normative structure for continuing dialogue according to this rule. This continues until 42:13 where §1.2.6. (stalemate) applies and 42:14 where §1.2.5. (decisive intervention) applies.

This same pattern can also be used in initiating a dialogue whose first speaker is contextually well identified. Just as a dialogue can continue with Sp:∅ when the speaker is well identified, so it may be similarly initiated.

Thus, in 37:9 Joseph recounts his second dream. In most respects this passage is parallel to that which precedes it (in which Joseph recounts his first dream). Here Joseph as speaker is not reidentified:

wayyaḥălōm	*^{c}ôd*	*ḥălôm*	*$^{\circ}$aḥēr*	*waysappēr*	*$^{\circ}$ōtô*
and he dreamed	still	dream	another	and he recounted	it

lĕʾeḥāyw   wayyōʾmer
to his brothers and he said

In 42:7b (as mentioned above) a similar initiating formula of quotation occurs in which the speaker is not identified in the formula itself but is clearly identified in the not-so-remote context. Thus in 42:6 we are told 'Now *Joseph* was the governor of the land. He was the one who sold grain to all the people of the land. And the brothers of *Joseph* came in. And they bowed down to him with their faces to the ground.' Verse 7 begins: 'And *Joseph* saw his brothers.' With Joseph thus named three times in this fashion (cf. chap 1, § 3.3.1.) the rest of the verse does not mention him again: 'And he recognized them. And he pretended to be a stranger to them. And he spoke harsh to them. And he said to them, "Where do you come from?"' Thus, the clause with the verb 'say' (i.e., the quotation formula itself) omits the name of the speaker, and to recover his name we must go back four clauses (i.e., further back than what we normally include in the extended quotation formula). This is a clear instance of sufficient identification in context making identification of the speaker unnecessary in the quotation formula that initiates a dialogue.

In 42:29 we have another instance of initiating a dialogue with a quotation formula that does not identify the speaker:

wayyābōʾû   ʾel -yaʿăqōb ʾābîhem   ʾarṣâ   kĕnāʿan
and they came in to Jacob   their father to the land of Canaan

wayyaggîdû   lô   ʾēt kol -haqqōrōt   ʾōtām lēʾmōr
and they declared to him all   that had befallen them   saying

Here 'the brothers' have not been mentioned as such since 42:8. Nevertheless, they have been central in the chapter, are the only available third person plural subject in the context, and are in center stage throughout. Furthermore, they are referred to obliquely in various ways in the preceding context. Thus, in 42:13 they identify themselves as 'twelve brothers, sons of one man, who lives in the land of Canaan'. In 42:19 Joseph proposes 'let one of you, you *brothers*, stay bound here'. Finally in 42:28 the man who first finds the payment money in his sack says *to his brothers*, 'My money's been returned', while at the end of the same verse we are told that 'they turned trembling, each to his *brother*'. Thus, in the last episode of this story, when 'they' finally return to 'their' father in Canaan there can be no doubt as to the identification of those referred to.

A somewhat more aberrant example in 43:19–20 involves the brothers, contextually well identified, on the occasion of their second trip to Egypt. Here, however (as noted in chap. 5, §3.3.2.), the brothers are referred to as *hāʾănāšîm*, 'the men'. They are, in fact, so referred to in v 18: *wayyîreʾû hāʾănāšîm kî hûbĕʾû bêt yôsēp*, 'And the men feared because they were brought to the house of Joseph.' This clause of psychological orientation is followed by *wayyōʾmĕrû* and a quotation. In vv 19-20 another expanded quotation formula introduces another quotation. Three clauses occur: one containing a motion verb, one containing a more specific speech act verb, and finally a clause consisting of *wayyōʾmĕrû*, 'and they said':

wayyiggĕšû		*ʾel*	*-hāʾîš*	*ʾăšer*	*ʿal*	*-bêt*
and they drew near		to	the man	who [was]	over	the house of

yôsēp	*waydabbĕrû*	*ʾēlāyw*	*petaḥ*		*habbāyit*
Joseph	and they spoke	with him	[at] the door of		the house

wayyōʾmĕrû
and they said

This example finds the speaker not indicated even in the expanded quotation formula of the second quotation. Rather, the identification of the speaker(s) in the second quotation unit is dependent upon prior identification in the first unit. (For regular examples of this usage, see 44:1, 44:7, 45:24, and 45:25-26.)

1.2.3. Sp:N + Add:N in *dialogue medial* signals that the utterance thus introduced *redirects* the dialogue so that it takes a sudden and important turn, much like a fresh beginning. The assumption behind this claim and that made in §1.2.4. is that, since Sp:N + Add:N normally signal dialogue initial, the occurrence of this pattern anywhere else in a dialogue has special significance.

An outstanding and dramatic instance of this usage is Joseph's redirecting of the long see-saw dialogue that begins in 44:14 by his startling announcement in 45:3: *wayyōʾmer yôsēp ʾel-ʾeḥāyw ʾănî yôsēp*, 'And he said Joseph to his brothers "I [am] Joseph."' Indeed, here the context in 45:11-12 makes clear a discontinuity of sorts in the dialogue; Joseph is having difficulty maintaining his composure and orders all of his attendants to leave the room. But it is necessary to repeat and elaborate in 45:4 because the brothers were too terrified to speak; so a fresh beginning is made in which the whole unreduced formula of quotation again occurs: *wayyōʾmer yôsēp, ʾel-ʾeḥāyw gĕšû-náʾ ʾēlay*, 'And he said Joseph to his brothers, "Come close, I pray, to me."'

While other examples are less dramatic, the import of Sp:N + Add:N remains the same in *dialogue medial*. In 40:9 such an instance of dialogue redirection occurs in which Joseph's dialogue with the two courtiers is narrowed to a dialogue with the chief cupbearer. In the preceding verses (6-8) Joseph has noticed that the courtiers are very evidently troubled and preoccupied. He ask them what is wrong and

receives the reply, 'We have dreamed dreams. And there is no interpreter.' Joseph remarks to the two of them that 'interpretation of dreams
belong to God', then proceeds to suggest that they tell him their dreams.
At this point the chief cupbearer decides to accept Joseph's offer:

waysappēr	*śar*	*-hammašqîm*	*ʾet-ḥălōmô*	*lĕyôsēp*
and he recounted	the chief of	cupbearers	his dream	to Joseph

wayyōʾmer	*lô*
and he said	to him

Here the preliminary sparring is over and the serious part of the
transaction begins. Note also that the dialogue, which began as one
between Joseph and the two of them, is here narrowed to one of them—
and such a transition is customarily indicated in the quotation formula
(and indeed needed by the ordinary demands of participant tracking).

In 43:2–7 there is an acrimonious debate between Israel and his
sons over their going back to Egypt to buy grain, the sons' insistence
that Benjamin must go with them, and Israel's continuing reluctance to
let Benjamin go. This dialogue starts off with Judah as spokesman
answering his father (3), but becomes more general (v 7). Everything
takes a new turn in 43:8–9 because here Judah assumes personal
responsibility for Benjamin and goes surety for him:

wayyōʾmer	*yĕhûdâ*	*ʾel*	*-yiśrāʾēl*	*ʾābîw*	*šilḥâ*	*hannaʿar*
and he said	Judah	to	Israel	his father	send	the lad

ʾittî...	*ʾānōkî*	*ʾeʿerbennû*	*mîyyādî*
with me ...	I	will go surety for him	from my hand

tĕbaqšennû
you may require him

Here this new development in the (deadlocked) argument is heralded by
resort to the use of nouns for both speaker and addressee in the
quotation formula. (For a further instance of this construction see 42:37.)

1.2.4. Sp:N + Add:N, when found consistently throughout a dialogue
(as distinct from initiating a dialogue or signaling a significant turning
point within it), indicates that the narrator regards the speaker and the
addressee as of *equal status*.[5] Again we note here an unusual use of the
pattern presented in §1.2.1. We also note here a specialized convention
of dialogue that clearly outruns the normal need for participant
identification and tracking.

---

[5] An alternative suggestion by Doris Myers is "that repetition of names
could be a way of communicating formality and solemnity of a court scene"
(private communication). See §2.1. below.

There are two instances of this structure in *Joseph*: the dialogue of Joseph with Pharaoh on the occasion of Joseph's interpreting Pharaoh's dreams, and the brief dialogue of Jacob with Pharaoh on the occasion of Joseph's royal presentation of his father. Apparently the narrator here places both Joseph and Jacob on the same place of importance as Pharaoh in spite of the superior social status of the latter in the world of his day. Although Joseph uses deferential speech within the dialogue and thus recognizes his own inferior social status, the narrative framework by its choice of quotation formula refuses to subordinate the worthy progenitors of the nation, Jacob and Joseph, to even the high and mighty Pharaoh. Thus in the dialogue in which Joseph stands before Pharaoh and interprets his dreams—and emerges as overlord of Egypt—the quotation formulas run as follows:

41:15 *wayyō'mer par'ōh   'el -yôsēp*
      and he said Pharaoh to   Joseph

41:16 *wayya'an   yôsēp 'et-par'ōh lē'mōr*
      and he answered Joseph Pharaoh   saying

41:17 *waydabbēr   par'ōh   'el -yôsēp*
      and he spoke Pharaoh to Joseph

41:25 *wayyō'mer yôsēp 'el -par'ōh*
      and he said Joseph to Pharaoh

The quotation formulas in the dialogue of Jacob and Pharaoh in 47:7–10 are similar:

47:7 *waybārek   ya'ăqōb 'et-par'ōh*
      and he blessed/greeted Jacob   Pharaoh

47:8 *wayyō'mer par'ōh   'el -ya'ăqōb*
      and he said Pharaoh to Jacob

47:9 *wayyō'mer ya'ăqōb 'el -par'ōh*
      and he said Jacob   to Pharaoh

47:10 *waybārek   ya'ăqōb 'et-par'ōh*
      and he blessed/took leave of Jacob   Pharaoh

1.2.5. Sp:N + Add:pr represents a speech act as a *decisive intervention*, or a speech act that the speaker attempts to make so. It is often equivalent to a kind of rank pulling on the part of the speaker. The assumption here is: since Sp:∅ + Add:N/pr is the normal form of quotation formula for continuing dialogue, any departure from this norm is significant. Here the departure from the norm consists in promoting the speaker from ∅ to N, thus underscoring the importance of him and his utterance, while the addressee is referred to only by pronoun.

Before citing examples of this usage, a word is in order about the form of the exponent of the addressee. It may be marked by *lĕ-* or *el-*, both meaning 'to'; by *bĕ*, 'with' (for example, with the verb *gā⁽ar*, 'rebuke'); or by direct object pronominal suffix (for example, *-hû*, 'him', with *šā²al*, 'ask' (but this has special implications, cf. chap. 6, §6). Its normal position when the pronoun follows a prepositional element is to occur between the verb and its subject—and, of course, a pronominal suffix necessarily occurs between the verb and its noun subject.

To return to the 42:7–17 passage, in v 14 Joseph breaks in impatiently and in the strikingly chiastic fashion already mentioned as indicative of the episodic closure winds up the matter. There is no back talk from the clearly out-maneuvered brothers who are bundled off to jail in v 17. All of this is introduced in v 18 by a quotation formula of the Sp:N + Add:pr variety: *wayyō²mer ²ălēhem yôsēp*, 'And he said to them Joseph.'

For further examples of a decisive intervention represented in this fashion, note 40:8 where Joseph decisively asserts that God can give interpretation of dreams; 40:12 where in a similarly decisive manner he says, 'This is the interpretation [of the cupbearer's dream]' and proceeds to give that interpretation; and in 44:18 where Judah decisively and effectively intervenes with his offer to stay as a slave in place of Benjamin and thus provokes Joseph to reveal himself to them.[6]

In other places Sp:N + Add:pr seems to indicate a attempt on someone's part to be decisive or to "pull rank." Thus in 37:8 the older brothers, incensed at Joseph's recountal of his dream, remind him of their superior station:

wayyō²merû   lô   ²eḥāyw   hămālōk timlōk   ⁽ālênû
and they said to him his brothers will you really reign over us

²im -māšōl timšol   bānû
or   will you really rule us?

[6] So pronounced is this use of Sp:N + Add:pr to represent decisive speech acts that in several instances it apparently initiates a dialogue in which the person so initiating lets it be known that the course of action he is advocating is not to be contested. In these instances, however, the "bone of contention" in the dialogue is not a new one. Thus in 42:18 Joseph hauls his brothers out of jail, tells them he has a different plan, and orders them to implement it. But the goal is the same as that previously enunciated: to force the brothers to bring Benjamin on the next trip. It is a continuation of the former discussion. Similarly, in 43:2 Jacob, attempting to ignore all the former discussion about sending Benjamin to Egypt, tries (unsuccessfully) to tell the brothers to go get food again—and makes no mention of sending Benjamin. Both of these apparent exceptions in which Sp:N + Add:pr is dialogue initial instead of dialogue medial are characterized by the renewal of a former discussion. Somewhat less typical is

On the occasion of Joseph's telling of his second dream—where he was to rule not only over his brothers but over his parents as well—even Jacob protests (37:10): *wayyigʿar-bô ʾābîw*, 'And he rebuked him his father' (going on to say: 'What is this dream that you have dreamed? Do you surely think that I and you mother and your brothers will bow down to the earth before you?').

Often such attempts to "pull rank" are futile. Thus in 42:22 Reuben's "I-told-you-so" doesn't accomplish much: *wayyaʿan rĕʾûbēn ʾōtām lēʾmōr*, 'And he answered Reuben them saying.' Here the oldest brother, attempting to show the follow of the others in not following his counsel goes on to say: 'Didn't I tell you not to harm the lad? But you wouldn't listen. And now today there is an accounting for his blood.' Somewhat similar in 42:36 Jacob complains as an outraged authority figure at what his boys have done to him.

1.2.6. Sp:∅ + Add:∅ apparently has two functions: (1) introducing a speech act that amounts to *an expression of social amenities*, which is meant to be non-aggressive and reassuring; and (2) introducing a speech act that marks a *stalemate* in an argument (before someone says something to break the stalemate). Both of these usages are characteristic of continuing dialogue and constitute a further exception to §1.2.2., the norm of continuing dialogue, by reducing the addressee to ∅—and perhaps marking thereby the relative triviality or ineffectiveness of the speech act thus introduced. In the first function indicated above, *civility* is the keyword; in the second, *stalemate*. Putative examples of the working of this rule must be rigorously inspected for possible indication of speaker and/or addressee in the immediately preceding clauses—in which case the examples are not relevant at this point.

The following examples all come from Genesis 43 and 44, reflecting exchanges that occur between Joseph (still incognito) and his brothers, and Joseph's steward and the brothers (alias 'the men'). In these chapters speaker and addressee are unambiguously clear from the context but the complete omission of reference to them, even in extended formulas of quotation is unusual and is taken here to have the semantic impact of function 1 suggested above: exchange of civilities, reassurance.

In 43:27 Joseph inquires concerning them and the welfare of their families. His initiation of the dialogue is presented according to the conventions of §1.2.2.: Joseph, the speaker, is well identified in the

---

44:14, where Joseph, who has had the brothers brought back when they were setting out to go home, unabashedly accused the brothers of stealing his cup. Even here, however, Joseph's action is an (unexpected) renewal of dialogue with them.

context (three clauses back in v 26) and the addressee is referred to by pronoun in the speech act identification clause, which precedes the quotation formula proper:

> *wayyiš²al   lāhem lĕšālôm   wayyō²mer hăšālôm*
> and he asked them concerning their welfare and he said how is
> *²ăbîkem*
> your father?

The dialogue continues, however, with Sp:∅ + Add:∅ instead of the more usual form of continuing dialogue (§1.2.2.):

> *wayyō²mĕrû šālôm   lĕ²abdĕkā   lĕ²ābînû*
> and they said [he is] well your servant our father

In 43:29, which follows the passage just considered, the social amenities center around the person of Benjamin:

> *wayyiśśā²   ᶜênāyw wayyar²   ²et-binyāmîn ²āḥîw*
> and he lifted up his eyes and he saw Benjamin   his brother
> *ben   -²immô   wayyō²mer hăzeh   ²āḥîkem   haqqāṭōn . . .*
> son of his mother and he said [is] this your brother little . . .
> *wayyō²mer ²ĕlōhîm yoḥnĕkâ   bĕnî*
> and he said God   may he be gracious to you my son

Notice that although the first two clauses introduce Benjamin he is not the addressee in the third clause but rather the topic of the (germinal but undeveloped) dialogue. Benjamin is addressed in the fourth clause but separated from the clause in which he is identified by another quotation where he is topic rather than addressee. At any rate, neither speaker nor either of the successive addressees are identified here by the usual conventions. In this whole passage Joseph is attempting to be casual, to say all the socially correct things—but in what is for him an emotion-packed situation (cf. vv 30–31).

In 43:31b another such utterance occurs with the bare unadorned verb 'say': *wayyō²mer śîmû lāhem*, 'And he said, "Serve the meal."' Here the utterance is the routine action of a host in signalling that the food can now be served.

Three other examples of this usage seem to involve not so much exercise of the social amenities as an attempt to say something soothing and reassuring in a threatening situation. Thus in 43:23 after the brothers have expressed to the steward their anxiety regarding the money that had been returned in their sacks on the occasion of their first trip down to Egypt, the steward tries to reassure them. He begins as follows: *wayyō²mer šālôm lākem ²al-tîrā²û*, 'And he said, "Peace [be] with you. Don't be afraid."' He goes on to say that the God of their fathers must have been the one that returned the money in their sacks since he himself had received his payment.

In 44:10 we have part of the ongoing dialogue that began when the steward overtook the brothers on the road and accused them of stealing Joseph's silver cup. The accusation itself is given in indirect speech in 44:6 and is followed in 44:7–9 by the brothers' indignant denial and the suggestion that whoever the cup is found with will be put to death, while all the rest of them will remain in Egypt as slaves. The steward comes on reassuringly in 44:10, taking them up on their suggestion but modifying it significantly:

wayyō°mer gam -ᶜattâ kĕdibrêkem   ken -hû°
and he said also now   according to your words thus [let] it [be]

°ăšer   yimmāṣē°   °ittô   yihyeh   -llî   ᶜābed
[he] whom it will be found with him let him be to me a slave

wĕ°attem   tihyû   nĕqîyim
and the rest of you will be innocent

In 44:17 there is a similar exchange, which involves Joseph and the brothers after they are hailed back to his house on discovery of the cup in Benjamin's sack. The dialogue begins in 44:15 with Joseph's indignant denunciation and continues in v 16 with Judah's terrified and cringing agreement—and the offer for all of them to remain in Egypt as slaves. Joseph—again the picture of civility—indignantly rejects this in 44:14 and says that only the one who has stolen the cup will remain as a slave. Again, Joseph's speech is introduced simply with *wayyō°mer*, 'and he said'. Again this seems to be a feature of continuing dialogue when the social veneer is thickly applied. Throughout Joseph's interactions with his brothers and those of the steward with the brothers, a certain fiction of civility is maintained in the midst of a deadly game (as the brothers conceive it). The frequent use of quotation formulas of Sp:∅ + Add:∅ seems to correlate with this.

Three further examples indicate the second function of this quotation formula. In 42:13 the debate between the brothers and Joseph has come to somewhat of a stalemate with the brothers, in effect, repeating and amplifying in v 13 what they had said in v 11. Joseph will break the stalemate by what he says in vv 14–16, plus his action of bundling them off to jail in v 17. Meanwhile, v 13, which marks the standoff, simply has *wayyō°mĕrû*, 'and they said', as its quotation formula.

In 42:38 the argument between Jacob and his sons reaches a stalemate after Reuben's ineffectual attempt to get consent to take Benjamin with them. Here Jacob (unidentified in the quote formula) proves to be utterly recalcitrant:

wayyōʾmer lōʾ -yērēd   běnî   ʿimmākem kî . . .
and he said not shall go down my son with you because . . .

This, to be true, looks semantically like some examples under §1.2.7. below. But the dialogue is not over, only discontinued and is quickly renewed in chap. 43.

Meanwhile, everything is on hold. In 43:7 we find the stalemate of the renewed debate about sending Benjamin. The stalemate will be broken in the next verse by Judah's offer to go surety for Benjamin. Meanwhile in 43:7 the brothers counter their father's querulous complaint, 'Why did you tell the man that you had a younger brother', with their reply:

wayyōʾmerû šāʾōl šāʾal   -hāʾîs lānû
and they said carefully questioned the man concerning us

ûlěmôladtēnû
and concerning our families

Maybe the two functions of this quotation formula have something in common: civilities (which can approach banalities) and utterances that mark a stalemate in an argument are perhaps examples of speech acts that accomplish little. In such speech acts nobody is accomplishing much—and nobody is named. As indicated in §2.2. below, further dialogue material of a sort not found in *Joseph* indicates some further functions of this type of quotation formula.

1.2.7. Sp:N + Add:∅ indicates that the speech is intended to be *final* and does not anticipate answer or contradiction; this also includes expressions of puzzlement and outrage (where again no real answer is expected). Note that this pattern of quotation formula in continuing dialogue is an extreme of departure from the norm presented in §1.2.2. (Sp:∅ + Add:N/pr). Here the speaker is promoted (from ∅ to N) and the addressee is demoted (to ∅). In brief, speech acts so introduced are speaker-centered and, in a sense, leave the addressee out of account. Perhaps one of the clearest expressions of the first functions of this type of quotation formula is in 45:28, where Joseph in effect says, 'Don't tell me any more, I get it.'

wayyōʾmer yiśrāʾēl rab   ʿōd -yôsēp běnî   hāy
and he said Israel   enough still Joseph my son [is] alive

ʾēlěkâ   wěʾerʾennû   běṭerem ʾāmût
let me go and I will see him before   I die

Other examples follow. In 37:17 the dialogue between 'the man' (who found Joseph wandering in the fields) and Joseph closes out with

the crucial piece of information given by the man to the effect that he
had heard the brothers say 'Let's go to Dothan'. Here the quotation
formula is *wayyō᾽mer hā᾽îš*, 'and he said the man'. This is not answered
by Joseph and it closes out the dialogue. In 40:18 Joseph, replying to the
chief cupbearer's recital of his dream, gives its interpretation presumably
not as something tentative but as something definitive and final. Again,
the quotation formula is *wayyaᶜan yôsēp wayyō᾽mer*, 'And he answered
Joseph. And he said.' Probably in this same category is the brief
reporting in 42:4 of how Jacob, on the first going of the brothers to
Egypt, didn't send Benjamin. *That* time he managed to make his refusal
to send Benjamin stick: This examples has Jacob in the main clause as
speaker of the verb *᾽āmar* in the cause clause.

wĕ᾽et-binyāmîn	*᾽ăḥî*		*yôsēp*	*lō᾽*	*-šālaḥ*	*yaᶜăqōb*	*᾽et*
and Benjamin	the brother of Joseph			not	he sent	Jacob	with

-᾽eḥāyw	*kî*	*᾽āmar*	*pen*	*-yiqrā᾽ennû*	*᾽āsôn*
his brothers	for	he said	lest	overtake him	evil

In other cases this kind of quotation formula pictures commands
that do not expect contradiction. Thus in 44:25 Judah in his speech
pictures Jacob as trying to force through his command, 'Go, buy for us
a bit of food', without implementing his sons' often repeated insistence
that Benjamin must go with them:

wayyō᾽mer	*᾽ābînû*	*šubû*	*šibrû*	*-lānû*	*mĕ᾽aṭ*	*-᾽ōkel*
and he said	our father	go back	buy	us	a bit of	food

Finally, in 45:9 Joseph relays through the brothers a command to Jacob
to come to Egypt; again, a negative response is not anticipated:

koh	*᾽āmar*	*binkā*	*yôsēp*	*śāmanî*		*᾽ĕlōhîm*	*lĕ᾽ādôn*
thus	has said	your son	Joseph	he has set me	God		as lord

lĕkol	*-miṣrāyim*	*rĕdâ*	*-᾽ēlay*	*᾽al*	*-taᶜămōd*
to all Egypt		come down	to me	don't	delay

Still other uses of this type of quotation formula reflect the second
function mentioned above, that is, expression of emotional outrage or
puzzlement where no answer is necessarily solicited or expected. Thus in
43:18 the speaker is expressed in a clause of psychological orientation
and the quotation formula has only the verb 'say'—the two adding up,
of course, to the Sp:N + Add:∅ structure here being exemplified:

wayyîrĕ᾽û	*hā᾽ănāšîm*	*kî*	*hûbĕ᾽û*
and they feared	the men	because	they were brought

bêt	*yôsēp*	*wayyō᾽merû*
[to] the house of	Joseph	and they said

Here the substance of what they said was an expression of acute anxiety: 'It's all on account of the money which was returned in our sacks. He's seeking an excuse to fall upon us, to take us as slaves and confiscate our donkeys.'

In 44:16 Judah, on behalf of all the brothers, expresses his consternation and utter dismay at the finding of Joseph's cup in Benjamin's sack.

wayyō᾽mer yĕhûdâ mah -nnō᾽mar la᾽dōnî   mah
and he said Judah what can we say to my Lord? what

-nnĕdabbēr   ûmah   nniṣṭaddāq
can we speak? and how can we justify ourselves

2. *Toward a more adequate theory of variation in quotation formulas*

I here suggest a broader and more comprehensive theory of variation in quotation formulas than can be obtained by restricting the analysis to dialogues found only in *Joseph*. By resort to a broader corpus of biblical dialogues it is possible not only to put the understanding of these matters on a broader basis but to clarify and validate (with certain necessary modifications) the claims made in the first part of this chapter.[7] Similarly, in chapter 6 it proved necessary to resort to a broader corpus in order to elaborate the narrative functions of verbs.

Even in the light of a broader corpus, dialogue initiation can be viewed much as described above (§1.2.1.). Again, Sp:N + Add:N continues to be the norm, for simple and compelling reasons of participant identification. If, however, the participants who are about to engage in dialogue are already well identified, the form for continuing dialogue, Sp:∅ + Add:pr, is more probable. Dialogues that are initiated with a Sp:N + Add:pr formula (several of which are noted in n. 6 above) indicate speaker-dominance (rank/rank-pulling; decisiveness or attempted decisiveness) in initiating the dialogue. All of this is much as noted above in § 1.2.1.

Dialogue continuation is found to employ Sp:∅ + Add:N/pr much as indicated above (§1.2.2.). Again, we must specify that this formula is employed only when no other special implications are to be communicated. Since under special conditions Sp:∅ + Add:∅ can also func-

---

[7] This section is based on an examination of dialogues found in the following passages: Gen 3:1–5; 3:8–19; 18:22–32; 22:6–8, 11ff.; 24:15ff., 31:26–53; 33:1–16; 38:15–18; Exod 3:1–4:17; Num 16:1–25; 22:7–34; Josh 2:8–21; Judg 4:6–20; 6:11–24; 16:4–20; 1 Sam 1:14–18; 14:4–20; 15:13–31; 20:1–23; 26:14–25; 28:8–20; 2 Sam 1:1–16; Ruth (whole book).

tion extensively in dialogue continuation, we now regard the formula Sp:∅ + Add:pr as indication of dialogue continuation in a somewhat *neutral key*.

Dialogue redirection signaled by Sp:N + Add:N is still seen to function as described above (§1.2.3.). One immediate modification is that Sp:∅ + Add:∅ is used to introduce the last utterance of a dialogue with the implication of *compliance* on the part of the speaker. This is, however, not unlike the social amenities use of this formula as noted above in 1.2.6.

In regard to mid-dialogue dynamics the picture given above in §1.2.3. is incomplete rather than incorrect. As already hinted, it is essentially necessary to give a larger role to Sp:∅ + Add:∅ than is deducible from the dialogues found in *Joseph*. It is also necessary to broaden the understanding of what Sp:N + Add:N implies when it occurs other than in dialogue initial or is other than redirective in force. In *Joseph* the only examples of Sp:N + Add:N used throughout a dialogue are in the interviews of Joseph with Pharaoh and of Jacob with Pharaoh. In fact, however, a useful starting point in sketching a more broadly based theory of quotation variation is to begin by contrasting Sp:N + Add:N with Sp:∅ + Add:∅—since these are apparently the polar extremes of a system.

2.1. Quotation formulas with Sp:N + Add:N imply balance/tension/confrontation between Sp and Add. Often the implication is balance with mild tension, that is, "A significant interview between two important people" (cf. Joseph and Pharaoh, Jacob and Pharaoh in §1.2.4. above). Confrontation can occur (even across a considerable social gap). Thus Jacob and Laban have an angry confrontation in Genesis 31, and Moses and the party of Korah in Num 16:1–16. Moses' subsequent intercession for Israel with an angry Yahweh in Num 16:20–24 is also presented as a confrontation. Balaam, in Numbers 22, has successive confrontations with God (vv 9–12), with the chiefs of Moab (vv 13–14), with his donkey (!) (vv 28–30), and with the angel of Yahweh (vv 34–35).

Without the anger component we also find confrontation (or at least tension) underlying the dialogues between the woman and the serpent (Gen 3:1–5), between Abraham and the Hittites regarding buying the field and the cave of Machpelah (Genesis 23), between Saul and his servant regarding going to see the seer (1 Sam 9:5–10), and between Jonathan and a very distraught David (1 Sam 20:1–24). Fragmentary stretches of dialogue in which Sp:N + Add:N prevails are found scattered through other dialogues, which as a whole are not pitched in this key. In dialogue-medial, however, one must always be on guard to distinguish the use of this quotation formula as *redirection* from its use in balance/tension/confrontation.

2.2. By contrast, Sp:∅ + Add:∅ implies (much as I posit above) no-struggle-no-victory, that is, dialogue so characterized is in a much lower emotional key than dialogue characterized by Sp:N + Add:N. The main further specification that we need to make is that Sp:∅ + Add:∅ does not indicate no-struggle-no-victory per se, so much as at least a show or pretense of the same. Consider, for example, passages in *Joseph* where Joseph puts on an outward show of great politeness and civility to his brothers even though—from the brothers' point of view—a deadly verbal dual is in progress (e.g., over the fate of Benjamin in chap. 44).

What we need to add to the picture regarding the use of Sp:∅ + Add:∅ is the fact that whole dialogues or the larger part of a dialogue can be pitched in the no-struggle-no-victory key by use of this quotation formula. We do not need to look further afield than Genesis 38, Judah and Tamar, to find a prime example of such a low-pitched dialogue. Here Judah, seeing a prostitute by the wayside and not knowing that she is his daughter-in-law, arranges to avail himself of her services. The alternation in speakers is, of course, identified by the alternation of *wayyōʾmer*, 'and he said', with *wattōʾmer*, 'and she said', but no nouns are used in the quotation formulas. Here there is, presumably, a large social gap between Judah and the anonymous, veiled prostitute with whom he has a clandestine encounter. Furthermore, once she is engaged there is presumably no struggle or doubtfulness as to the outcome—although there is some routine bargaining over the price and assurances that it will be paid.

Somewhat similar is the midnight encounter of Ruth and Boaz on the threshing floor at Bethlehem (Ruth 3:7–15). Significantly enough, Boaz becomes *hāʾîš*, 'the man', in this passage and Ruth *hāʾiššâ*, 'the woman'. That there is a certain element of furtiveness and secrecy is also seen in v 14. At any rate, there is also a decided social gap between Boaz, the wealthy respected citizen of Bethlehem, and Ruth and Moabitess who is a foreigner, destitute, and without much social standing. Furthermore, not only is not much struggle expected on the part of an inferior towards a superior, but Boaz is not in the least inclined to resist the charms of this attractive young woman!

Lest we think, however, that this type of quotation formula works exclusively in man-woman dialogues characterized by a social gap and furtiveness, consider the dialogue of Jacob and Esau in Genesis 33. Jacob is ridden with guilt and fear at the prospect of meeting Esau, who is coming with four hundred armed men. Having taken every precaution humanly possible and having gained a measure of poise from his mysterious wrestling match with God, he now finally meets his brother. The first two exchanges (vv 5–8) of their dialogue are completely cast into the key indicated by quotation formulas with Sp:∅ + Add:∅. Here, civilities and Jacob's taking the lower place are much to the fore:

Esau:	Who are these with you?
Jacob:	They are the children that God has graciously given your servant.
Esau:	What do you mean by all these droves that I met?
Jacob:	To find favor in your eyes, my lord.

The context is full of bowings and scrapings on the part of Jacob and his family towards Esau. In the balance of the dialogue, a few sporadic further uses of Sp:∅ + N:∅ occur along with some polite see-sawing and attempted finality in vv 9–10, where Sp:N + Add:∅ is found.

God-man dialogues are also frequently characterized by the use of this quotation formula. Here a sizable "social gap," so to speak, exists, and presumably the encounters indicated are somewhat private affairs. Abraham's intercession with Yahweh for Sodom (Gen 18:22–32) is a good example of this. Although some more specialized structures (such as are described below) come at the beginning of the dialogue, it soon shakes down into the consistent use of Sp:∅ + Add:∅. Apparently, early in the dialogue the main point is granted—that Yahweh will spare Sodom if enough righteous people are found there—and the rest of the dialogue is a piece of somewhat routine bargaining. Abraham emphasizes the distance between Yahweh and himself by comments that introduce his requests in vv 27, 30, 31, and 32. Compare here also the beginning of God's interrogation of Adam after the fall in Gen 3:10–11, before more specialized structures (speaker-centered shifting of blame and addressee-centered judgments) take over the balance of the dialogue. Moses' dialogue with Yahweh at the burning bush (Exod 3:1–4:17) contains stretches of Sp:∅ + Add:∅ in the parts of the dialogue that are not in the main stream of Moses' attempts to evade God's call to lead Israel out of Egypt; especially in 3:5–6 (where the issue is not yet joined) and in 4:2–31 (which is a routine set of instructions about Moses' performing a miracle with his staff).

In many dialogues there are brief stretches of Sp:∅ + Add:∅ or even isolated instances of it. (Compare my claims about this indicating stalemate in certain dialogues in *Joseph* and the claim made above that it often indicates compliance at the end of the dialogue.) I believe that characterizing this as the polar opposite of Sp:N + Add:N is insightful. Just as Sp:N + Add:N tells us that there is an important interview/debate/confrontation afoot, so Sp:∅ + Add:∅ tells us that either not much tension is involved or that there is an attempt to play down tensions (cf. Jacob and Esau, as well as banalities/civilities in *Joseph*). While the keynote here seems to be no-struggle-no-victory, this quotation formula also seems to imply a social gap between the two parties to the dialogue and often an element of privacy/furtiveness. The contrast between the quotation formula for confrontation/important interview and the quotation formula for no-struggle-no-victory turns on mentioning *both* names versus mentioning *neither*. This seems to be intuitively satisfying. When a struggle of sorts is afoot it seems plausible to mention the participants; when no struggle is afoot but the whole thing is somewhat routinized, the naming of the participants is not of equal interest. Also in furtive encounters, where one or both parties is unknown to the other, it may also be artful narrative style not to identify speaker and addressee. To summarize in tabular form:

Sp:N + Add:N	Sp:$\emptyset$ + Add:$\emptyset$
1. balance/tension/confrontation	1. no tension present or tension glossed over
2. parties are socially equal or are treated as such	2. emphasis on the social gap
3. parties are known to each other	3. one or both may be unknown to the other

2.3. The quotation formula, Sp:$\emptyset$ + Add:pr is, as stated in the earlier part of this chapter, (§1.2.2.), the normal form for continuing dialogue. "Normal" does not mean this quotation formula is more frequent than others; rather it is to this quotation formula that the narrator resorts where there is no special effect to be achieved by using another (very often the latter holds true). A possible exception to this is the occasional use of Sp:$\emptyset$ + Add:pr in what appears to be a Sp:$\emptyset$ + Add:$\emptyset$ dialogue; examples of this are at present too rare to permit proper evaluation. The book of Ruth contains examples of the use of Sp:$\emptyset$ + Add:pr in the somewhat neutral way I posit here (Ruth 1:8, 19; 2:2, 4, 10; and 3:5).

Likewise the quotation formula Sp:N + Add:pr, even in the light of the broader corpus, is seen to function much as described in the earlier part of this chapter (§1.2.5.). It is now possible, however, to define its central meaning and thrust as *speaker-dominance*. He/she may be dominant because of higher social rank; he/she may be attempting to "pull rank" in a social situation where the precise ranking is ambiguous or at least somewhat fluid; he/she may be in *effective control* of a situation regardless of rank; or a person of lower rank may, with the indulgence of the ranking person, engage in repartee (verbal dueling) with his/her superior. In the latter case the person of lower rank is making a bid for *control of the dialogue*. Quotations that are introduced with this formula are characteristically *directive* or represent *decisive* interventions or an *attempt to be decisive.*

A succession of Sp:N + Add:pr with alternative speakers (as in 1 Samuel 28) indicates a struggle for dominance. Thus, in the opening exchange between Saul incognito and the medium of Endor, after the regular dialogue initiation (Sp:N + Add:N) introduces Saul's words, 'Bring me up whom I will', the medium replies in effect to her client, 'You're trying to get me killed', to which Saul replies solemnly (possibly in a way that gave a clue to his identity), 'No, as Yahweh lives you won't be punished.' The latter two utterances, which are introduced with Sp:N + Add:pr, reflect the medium's bid for control of the dialogue and Saul's successful reassertion of control as her client.

A similar struggle for dominance is seen in a brief but bitter dialogue between Saul and his son Jonathan in 1 Sam. 20:30-32. In the first exchange of the dialogue Saul questions Jonathan as to the whereabouts of David and receives an answer that Jonathan has let David skip the feast and go to Bethlehem. Saul is enraged and the following dialogue, marked by Sp:N + Add:pr ensues:

Saul: You S.O.B., David must die if you're ever to be
          king. Go get him so I can kill him.
Jonathan: Why should he be put to death: What has he done?

In many cases this formula of quotation, especially when used in initiating a dialogue (where it can replace the more usual Sp:N + Add:N), clearly indicates social dominance of the speaker. Thus Yahweh speaks to Moses at the burning bush in Exod 3:4, in the initiation of dialogue plus further occurrences of Yahweh to Moses in the interior of the same dialogue (4:2, 6, 11). Also, Naomi, as mother-in-law and native Bethlehemite, to Ruth, as daughter-in-law and foreigner, and as older woman to younger in Ruth 3:5. In 2 Sam 1:3 the use of this quotation formula characterizes King David's words to the Amalekite fugitive who claimed to have dispatched Saul (also, David's words to the same, vv 4, 14, and 16). In Judg 16:5 the same formula introduces the words of the Philistine lords to Delilah instructing her to trap Samson. (See also Judg 6:12, 16, and 23 for the words of the angel of Yahweh/Yahweh to Gideon.) Even in the case of Deborah and Barak (Judg 4:6), Deborah's initial orders to Barak ('Yahweh commands you to gather an army, fight Sisera, and win') are so introduced. Presumably as a prophetess she outranked Barak as general.

In some cases this formula apparently indicates that someone is attempting to pull rank. Thus Saul as King attempted, with disastrous results, to pull rank on Samuel, the prophet and king-maker in 1 Sam 15:13. Similarly, Korah, Nathan, Abiram, and others attempted to pull rank (rebel) against Moses and Aaron in Num 16:3: 'You've gone too far! The whole community is holy. . . . Why then do you set yourselves above the Lord's assembly?' Here the attempt of the rebels to cut Moses down to size is a kind of rank-pulling on their own part (exalting the common man?).

In some other cases Sp:N + Add:pr does not so much indicate rank or rank-pulling as the person in effective control of a situation. Thus Jael offers Sisera refuge in her tent in Judg 4:18. He is a defeated general of a king who has—up to the time of the battle that has just been fought—controlled northern Canaan. She, although simply the wife of a nomadic chieftain, is hiding him in her tent and is in *de facto* control of the situation (she, in fact, kills him while he is sleeping). Consider also the case of Jonathan and David in 1 Sam 20:1–23. They have a spirited dialogue (David is close to despair) regarding the intent of Jonathan's father, Saul, to kill David. At the very end of the dialogue Jonathan announces a plan whereby he will test his father's intent and inform David as to the outcome. This last utterance of Jonathan's (1 Sam 20:18–23) is introduced by Sp:N + Add:pr, in accordance with Jonathan's *de facto* control of the situation, even though the two men are on easy-going terms of intimacy and on a somewhat equal footing.

In still other cases, this formula of quotation is used more loosely to indicate a counter-utterance or retort. Used in this sense Sp:N + Add:pr is used regardless of social rank, that is, if a social superior decides to engage in argumentation with a social inferior, speech of *either* may be introduced by this formula of quotation. Actually these instances are relatively rare since this formula of quotation is usually responsive to social rank, rank-pulling, or actual control as stated and illustrated above. The usage here described is more a matter of a bid for control of a dialogue, than of social rank.

Note, however, Judg 6:12–13. Here the angel of Yahweh greets Gideon with the words 'Yahweh is with you, mighty warrior,' which is appropriately introduced with Sp:N + Add:pr. But Gideon comes back with the words (similarly introduced): 'If Yahweh is with us, how come we're oppressed here? Indeed he's given us into the hand of Midian.' Here the angel of Yahweh's word, 'God is with you,' is countered with Gideon's words: 'I can't see that he is with us'. Consider also Barak's reply to Deborah in Judg 4:6–8. I speculate above that Deborah as prophetess and judge presumably outranked Barak. The latter, however, felt free to make his obedience of her injunction conditioned on the stipulation that she would come along with him to battle. Both

Deborah's injunction in vv 6–7 and Barak's interposing a stipulation are introduced by the Sp:N + Add:pr formula.

2.4. If the formula Sp:N + Add:pr indicates dominance or attempted dominance on the part of the speaker, the formula Sp:N + Add:∅—in which the addressee is not referred to at all—indicates a speaker-centered utterance. In *Joseph*, as indicated above, this formula often introduces a quotation that is (1) either an emotional outburst, and hence not necessarily directed at anyone so much as at circumstances, or (2) attempted finality, that is, the speaker would like to have the last word and shut down the dialogue. In both cases the absence of any reference to the addressee in the formula of quotation correlates with the fact the utterance is not addressee-oriented but is speaker-centered. To these uses can be added instances where Sp:N + Add:∅ signifies a pronouncement on the part of the speaker, somewhat as if the quotation were to prepose, 'Now for *my* part, I have the following to say. . . .'

For examples of Sp:N + Add:∅ expressing something on the order of an emotional outburst see Gideon's outcry at the end of his dialogue with the angel (Judg 6:22): 'Oh Lord God, I've seen the angel of Yahweh face to face.' Here Gideon registers fear. Cf. also Ruth (Ruth 2:21) where she remarks: 'Why he even said to me "Stay with my workers until they've finished harvesting the grain."' Here presumably the motivating emotion is surprise: 'Now what do you think of *that?*'

Finality or attempted finality is possibly the most frequent and regular use of this construction. Dathan and Abiram, by refusing to come at Moses' summons, attempt a kind of finality (Num 18:12). But Moses' statement, 'Now watch and see them die in a highly unusual way,' achieves finality and closes the dialogue in vv 28–30.

The words of King David and of the wise woman of Tekoa are both reported with this formula several places in 2 Sam 14:4–20. In v 10 David thinks that he has disposed of her case when he says, 'If anyone bothers you bring him to me, and he won't do it again.' But the woman is not so easily disposed of. After requesting and getting the King's oath in v 11 (reported as a somewhat routine interchange by means of Sp:∅ + Add:∅), the woman says in v 12: 'May your handmaid ask you one more thing, O my Lord, the King?' Here the wise woman of Tekoa is approaching her punchline as carefully rehearsed with Joab. She hopes to finish the conversation on this note—and presumably take her leave with the King left to ponder her words. The punchline itself is reported in vv 13ff. and like the "last word" request in v 12 is also introduced with this Sp:N + Add:∅ formula. David, however, after strictly admonishing her to be truthful and receiving her assurance to that effect himself, tries for finality (v 19): 'Tell me, is Joab behind all this?' The wise woman of Tekoa, who, although defeated (exposed) could argue still, finishes with something that is somewhat of an emotional outburst but also reflects attempted finality (she does get the last word *this* time!): 'He sure is. Oh my Lord, you are as discerning as an angel.' The above dialogue illustrates the way that two speakers in a dialogue may struggle to have the last word, that is, to have their plan or viewpoint prevail without subsequent modification.

Often emotional outburst can characterize such a see-saw struggle as well. Consider, for example, the dialogue between Hannah and Eli the priest in 1 Sam 1:14-18. Although the dialogue begins routinely, Eli's words, 'Stop drinking, woman; sober up,' provokes Hannah's outburst: 'Oh my Lord, I'm not drunk. I'm pouring out my heart in prayer. Don't think of me as base.' Eli's blessing, also introduced with Sp:N + Add:∅, smacks at once of *finality* and a pronouncement (for so Hannah understood): 'Go in peace, and may the God of Israel grant you your request.'

Consider also Saul's final interview with the alleged shade of Samuel that the medium called up. Again the dialogue begins regularly with Sp:N + Add:N wherein Samuel addresses Saul: 'Why have you disturbed me?' Saul's answer is probably an emotional outburst (and is Sp:N + Add:∅): 'I'm in great distress. Yahweh won't answer in any way; I'm asking you what's going to happen.' Samuel's reply (likewise Sp:N + Add:∅) is the final pronouncement: 'You shouldn't ask me, since Yahweh has forsaken you. Yahweh is going to give the kingdom to David. Tomorrow you will be here with me.'

Finally, consider Gen 3:12-13, which occurs within the context of God's interrogation of Adam and his wife after their disobedience. This dialogue begins regularly enough with Sp:N + Add:N, then shifts into Sp:∅ + Add:∅ for two utterances (as mentioned above). But in vv 12 and 13, first Adam, and then Eve, try to justify their transgression by blaming someone else. Adam blames his wife and she blames the serpent. In these two utterances the formula of quotation Sp:N + Add:∅ is used. Apparently here the idea of *speaker-centeredness* is extended to include the attempt to shift blame by evading responsibility: 'For *my* part, I insist that I'm not to blame because. . . .'

2.5. If an utterance can be reported as speaker-centered, should we not also find utterances that are addressee-centered? If so, we should expect them to be Sp:∅ + Add:N. A prime instance of this seems to be the conclusion of God's interrogation of Adam and his wife in Gen 3:16-17. God's words to the woman in v 16 are a delayed response to her attempt to evade responsibility in v 13b; while God's words to Adam in v 17 are a delayed response to Adam's attempt to evade responsibility in v 12. The whole paragraph from v 12 through v 17 is an abeyance paragraph with discontinuous exchanges. As a chiasmus, the judgment on the serpent in vv 14–19 is the key. At any rate, the material in vv 16 and 17 reaches back to pick up previous material across intervening verses. The formulas of quotation found in these verses mention only the addressee— as might seem appropriate to their judgment-centered nature. Furthermore, there is an emphatic left shift in which, instead of getting *wayyōᵓmer* + specification of the addressee, we find *ᵓel-hāᵓiššâ ᵓāmar*, 'to the woman said [he]', in v 16 and *ûlĕ ᵓādām ᵓāmar*, 'and to the man said [he]', in v 17. Here, instead of the usual narrative preterite, we find the perfect of the verb with the noun of addressee preposed. Here, not only does the formula of quotation focus on the addressee but quite strongly so. Again, however, part of the peculiar structure found here may simply be a reflex of the backreference nature of these references in an abeyance (chiastic) paragraph.

Ruth 2:19, a portion of a dialogue between Naomi and Ruth, provides an example without the special complications found in the passage just considered. Naomi's words to Ruth are introduced with Sp:N + Add:pr, which, as we observed above, indicates Naomi's superior social position and her dominance of this dialogue. Ruth's reply is introduced with Sp:∅ + Add:N, which maintains the spotlight on Naomi—who is named as 'her mother-in-law'—first as speaker, then as addressee, while Ruth is referred to first as a pronoun, then as zero. Verse 20 preserves the same dominance pattern, for, while Sp:N + Add:N is regularly used for redirecting the dialogue, in the next utterance Naomi as speaker is again identified by name, while Ruth is referred to only by a pronoun.

Thus, although addressee-centered utterances are apparently not regularly indicated, they do occur and are marked somewhat as we might anticipate.

3. *Conclusion*

In conclusion, an expansion of the study of the semantic import of variation in quotation formulas from the narrow based in *Joseph* to a broader base does not lead to the overthrow of the observations and claims presented in the first part of this chapter, but does lead to some expansion or revision. Note the following summary table, which is based both on material found within *Joseph* and on material found within other parts of the Hebrew Scriptures. These summary observations reflect the pragmatic choices made by the narrator in reporting speech. I do not presume to predict the narrator's choices in advance. Rather my study has been concerned with explaining *ex post factum* the semantic import of the narrator's choices once that they have been made. This is, however, much the role of discourse analysis in general—which is *exegetical* rather than predictive.

The summary table is divided into dialogue initiation, dialogue continuance, redirection, and mid-dialogue dynamics. The five "rules" under the last category are perhaps of the greatest interest to the exegete of dialogue in the Hebrew Scriptures.

In the next (and last) chapter these considerations and others will be brought to bear explicitly on such exegesis of dialogue—which is, at present, an exegetical frontier.

SUMMARY TABLE OF VARIATION IN
FORMULAS OF QUOTATION

"The reason why a speech act participant is mentioned is. . . . "

A. *Dialogue Initiation*: any way that is contextually adequate to identify Sp and Add; very often N + N or $\emptyset$ + pr/N, but even here N + pr may be according to *D.3*.

B. *Dialogue Continuance* (normal, uncomplicated):
  1. between peers: $\emptyset$ + pr
  2. emphasis on a social gap (often sizeable): $\emptyset$ + $\emptyset$

C. *Dialogue Redirection* (fresh beginning, whether or not Sp/Add is changed): N + N

D. *Mid-dialogue Dynamics:*
  1. N + N (other than *C.*): balance/tension/confrontation between Sp and Add; often ="important interview of two important people"
  2. $\emptyset$ + $\emptyset$ (possibly overlapping somewhat with *B.2.*): plays down tension and confrontation between Sp and Add; no struggle; stalemate, civilities, working out details of already accepted plan; compliance at end of dialogue
  3. N + pr: speaker-dominant (or trying to be); rank/rank-pulling; decisive utterance; attempt to gain control of dialogue
  4. N + $\emptyset$: speaker-centered; emotional outburst; strong assertion of point of view; often attempted finality
  5. $\emptyset$ + N: addressee-dominant

CHAPTER EIGHT

THE ROLE OF DIALOGUE IN *JOSEPH*

It is obvious, even on cursory examination, that much of the narrative we have been examining is carried forward via sections of dialogue. A story moves along not only by virtue of what people are reported to do, but also by what they say. Saying is indeed a kind of doing for which we reserve the special name *speech act*. Speech acts have, however, not only an actional but an *interactional* nature, that is, speech acts typically occur in larger sections that we customarily have called dialogue. These sections of dialogue can be considered to constitute another category of paragraph, dialogue paragraphs.[1] Dialogue paragraphs are, in turn, part of a broader category that can be entitled interaction paragraphs—to which belong execution paragraphs and stimulus-response paragraphs, as well as dialogue. These two additional types will be considered at the end of this chapter.

The model of dialogue (and other interaction) paragraphs here employed (similar to that presented in Longacre 1968 in reference to Philippine languages and more widely developed in Longacre 1976 and 1983) emphasizes the dynamics of dialogue, that is, initiation, continuance, and closure in terms of speaker dominance and bids for dominance. The description proceeds from the simpler to the more complicated varieties of dialogues. It is the purpose of this chapter to combine insights from this apparatus with considerations of the sort raised in the previous chapter and in chapter 5.

Thus, for every dialogue found in *Joseph* we not only take account of *patterns of control* in terms of the apparatus here to be presented, but also the *nuances* conveyed in choice of certain quotation formulas over against others (as in the preceding chapter) and the general *tone* of the

---

[1] That such paragraphs, although clearly structural units, are broken up in such a language as English via the convention of indentation for speaker alternation is simply a feature of standard orthography.

component utterances of the dialogue. Is one speaker deferential toward
the other? If hortatory discourse (chap. 5) is involved, is the exhortation
mitigated or unmitigated? Are rhetorical questions or irony used by one
speaker to scold another? In short, the purpose of the chapter is to
understand as best we can the contributions of each dialogue to personal
interchanges among the participants of the story—the *inner dynamics* of
each dialogue.

1.   *Simple dialogue paragraphs*

1.1.   *Simple resolved dialogue paragraphs.*

According to my apparatus for the description of dialogue, it is
considered that a reported dialogue opens with an Initiating Utterance
(IU) whose notional structure can be a question (Q), a proposal
(PROP), or a remark (REM). With speaker change, a Resolving
Utterance (RU) can follow immediately on the Initiating Utterance. The
Resolving Utterance is an answer (A) if the IU was a question, a
response (RES) if the IU was a proposal, and an evaluation (EVAL) if
the IU was a remark.

It is evident that in a simple exchange between two speakers the
speaker of the IU controls the nature and course of the dialogue. The
speaker of the RU simply accepts the dialogue along the lines thus
suggested by answering a question, responding to a proposal, or evaluat-
ing a remark. It remains, however, that subtle nuances in such a
dialogue can be indicated by the choice of the quotation formula that
introduces RU. Here the regular formula for continuing dialogue can be
varied according to rules C.–D. (see the table of rules set at the end of
the previous chapter, p. 184). As already stated, we will also note the
tone of each simple dialogue.

The simple resolved dialogue paragraph found in Gen 37:32b–33
follows a string of five preterites beginning in v 31: the brothers took the
cloak of Joseph, slaughtered a goat, dipped the cloak in its blood, sent it
off to Jacob, so that 'they' (someone? who?) brought it in to Jacob. The
IU (= Q) is introduced with *wayyōᵓmĕrû* but the addressee ('their
father') is identified in the previous clause; hence we parse this quotation
formula as being S:∅ + Add:N (i.e., a way to initiate a dialogue when
the speaker is already identified in the previous context). If the speaker
is taken to be the brothers, then we must go back considerably in the
previous context to find them. It may be, however, that the speakers are
not given, that the construction is intentionally impersonal: 'and they
said'. In this case the omission of the speaker simply correlates with the
fact that they are not specified (and, as mere tools of the brothers, are

irrelevant). We can further note that the lack of specificity in regard to the speaker contributes in no small degree to establishing a certain *dreadful impersonality* at this part of the story. At any rate, what 'they' say is carefully phrased:

> *zōᵓt māṣāᵓnû   hakker   -nāᵓ hakkĕtōnet binkā*
> this we have found look it over please the cloak of your son
>
> *hiwᵓ   ᵓim -lōᵓ*
> [is] this or   not?

The one imperative of the passage *hakkĕr*, 'look over, examine', is mitigated with *-naᵓ*, 'entreaty'. The following question is proposed as an open one.

The RU (= A) is structured as an amplification paragraph, that is, *wayyakkîrāh*, 'and he recognized it', is followed by *wayyōᵓmer* + the content of the quotation:

> *kĕtonet   bĕnî   ḥayyâ rāᶜâ ᵓăkālātĕhû*
> [it is] the cloak of my son a beast evil has devoured him
>
> *ṭārōp ṭōrap   yôsēp*
> is surely torn in pieces Joseph

The addressee is omitted in the quotation formula that reports Jacob's reply. This may be due to a lack of specification by the narrator of the identity of those who brought in the cloak to Jacob. The intensity of Jacob's emotional outburst here is such that we might have expected Sp:N + Add:∅ in this verse, but instead we have a modification of the Sp:∅ + Add:N/pr of continuing dialogue to Sp:∅ + Add:∅—a modification possibly resultant from the lack of identity of the immediate addressee.

Our next example of simple resolved dialogue paragraph is from 39:7-10, the dialogue between Potiphar's wife and Joseph. Here the IU is PROP and the RU is a (negative) RES. Although the quotation formula proper is *wattōᵓmer*, 'and she said', both 'the wife of the lord' and Joseph are mentioned in the preceding clause: 'And it happened after a time that the wife of his lord took notice of Joseph.' Here the expanded quotation formula specifies both speaker and hearer. This is the customary form of dialogue initiation where the speaker is not previously specified. Her words are terse: *šikbâ ᶜimmî*, 'lie with me'. The verb is an emphatic imperative (GKC §48 k) with no attempt at coaxing or mitigation.

Joseph's response, the RU (= RES), is lengthy and moderate in tone but nonetheless firmly negative. First of all a speech act verb occurs: *waymāᵓēn*, 'And he refused.' This is followed by *wayyōᵓmer ᵓel-ᵓēšet ᵓădōnāyw*, 'And he said to the wife of his lord.' We have here the regular form of continuing dialogue with specification of the addressee only, but as previously noticed, the integration of Potiphar's wife into the story at this point required her re-presentation, which is accomplished by specifying her as the addressee in the quotation formula. Joseph's words, which we do not cite here verbatim, emphasize his position of confidence under Potiphar, and his unwillingness to harm his master and sin against his God by getting involved with his master's wife. Potiphar's wife controls the course of the dialogue; she makes the initial thrust in the verbal duel and Joseph is obliged to parry that thrust as best he can. She is preremptory in her attitude; Joseph is respectful but firm.

Our next example is from an early part of the story, where Joseph tells his dreams, thus eliciting the evaluation of his brothers. Gen 37:5-8 is the account of the recital of his first dream and his brothers' reaction to it. Here the dialogue proper is preceded by three preterites that I have grouped together into a narrative sequence paragraph that acts as *lead-in* to the dialogue; to summarize briefly: 'And Joseph dreamed a dream. And he declared it to his brothers. And they hated him all the more.' Here both speaker and addressee are specified before the dialogue begins (in a sort of preview of what will happen). The dialogue begins with *wayyōᵓmer ᵓălêhem*, the form of dialogue initiation where the speaker is well identified (cf. dialogue continuance by means of this formula). In the IU (= REM) Joseph starts off his dream recital with an imperative mitigated with *-naᵓ* 'entreaty':

šimᶜu-nāᵓ haḥălôm hazzeh ᵓăšer   ḥālāmĕtî
hear now dream   this   which   I've dreamed

In spite, however, of the respectful beginning, the brothers are outraged by the content of the dream he recites. The form of quotation formula used (Sp:N + Add:pr) to introduce their reply indicates rank-pulling. Who is this *younger* brother to say such things, and isn't it time to put him where he belongs? Their outraged reply employs infinitive absolutes + finite verbs to convey their ironic disgust in terms of pseudo certainty; in addition the IU (= EVAL) is put in the form of a rhetorical question, which adds the sense of scolding:

hămālōk timlōk   ᶜālênû   ᵓim
so, it's certain then that you'll reign over us, or

-māšōl timšōl bānû
it's certain that you'll order us [around]

Here, *ᵓim* does not express alternation as such but merely an alternative wording. Joseph, of course, controls this dialogue. By initiating the dialogue he *acts*, the brothers can only *react*.

In these three examples of simple resolved dialogue paragraphs we have illustrated pairing of question-answer, proposal-response, and remark-evaluation. For further examples of simple resolved dialogue paragraphs see 43:26–28 (of question-answer structure) and 43:18–23 (of remark-evaluation structure).

Still further examples of this paragraph type occur, embedded in structures such as the compound dialogue paragraph (see below). Thus, in 37:13 there occurs a brief proposal-response exchange. Israel controls in what is a sort of 'Go', 'Aye, aye, Sir' exchange between himself and Joseph. In 40:7–8 Joseph controls a question-answer exchange with the two courtiers. In 41:15–16 Pharaoh controls a proposal-response exchange with Joseph. In the latter, quotation formulas (Sp:N + Add:N) mark the interview as a fateful one! Pharaoh is respectful and interested; Joseph, modest and deferential. In spite of Joseph's disclaimer ('It's not in me') the whole thing comes out somewhat as follows:

Pharaoh: Interpret my dream.
Joseph: I will with God's help.

In 41:17–36, which immediately follows, Pharaoh again is in control; this time the exchange is remark-evaluation, in that Joseph is interpreting Pharaoh's dreams. Again the quotation formulas (Sp:N + Add:N) mark the interview as fateful. In tone, Pharaoh is informal, almost chatty, while Joseph is properly deferential throughout but speaks with confidence as God's spokesman.

In 42:7b there is a question-answer exchange between Joseph (incognito) and his brothers. Joseph is in control and the quotation formula of the RU (= A) is Sp:∅ + Add:∅, as befits the exchange of social amenities. In 42:9–10 Joseph controls a remark-evaluation exchange with his brothers. Joseph is brusque; the brothers, deferential. Further on, in 42:12–13, another such similar remark-evaluation exchange occurs. Here the quotation formula of the RU (= EVAL) indicates a stalemate (see the analysis below of the whole compound dialogue, 42:6–17).

In 42:21–22 there is a remark-evaluation interchange among the brothers themselves. The quotation formula of the RU (= EVAL) is Sp:N + Add:pr, here indicative of Reuben's attempt to pull rank (as first-born) with an 'I told you so' statement.

In 44:19–20 there is a second order quotation, that is, the narrator reports Judah's reporting of his earlier dialogue with Joseph. The tone is deferential throughout on the part of the brothers. Interestingly enough, in 42:30–32 there is another second order quote in which the narrator reports the brothers' reporting to Jacob what 'the man' (Joseph) had said to them down in Egypt. Here, however, in reporting to Jacob the

conversation with Joseph, all the deferential features that had characterized the conversation as originally reported are now omitted (compare
42:7–20 with 42:19, 30–32). To be true, the report to Jacob is represented
as being quite abbreviated. Nevertheless, the complete omission before
Jacob of all the deferential forms that the brothers used in talking to 'the
man' (Joseph) possibly should have some sociolinguistic rationale, for
example, did the brothers hesitate to disclose to the merchant-prince
Israel how low his sons had had to grovel in kowtowing to a foreign
potentate?

1.2. *Simple unresolved dialogue paragraph*

Sometimes an IU does not evoke a RU. In this case the dialogue
paragraph is considered to be unresolved. Two such unresolved simple
dialogue paragraphs occur in succession in 45:1–15, where Joseph makes
himself known to his brothers. The unresolved dialogue found in 45:1–3
has an elaborate build-up to the point where Joseph drops his verbal
bombshell *ʾănî yôsēp*, 'I [am] Joseph' (I have commented on this in
chap. 2). There is a Setting ('and Joseph could not control himself
before all those standing about him') and two Lead-ins.[2] In the first
lead-in Joseph calls out for his courtiers to leave him and they exit; in
the second it is recorded that Joseph wept loudly and was heard all over
the palace. Such an elaborate preparation for dialogue is unique and
befits the dramatic quality of this high point of the story. Joseph's IU
(= REM) is not replied to; rather we have a Terminus (which by
definition does not contain a preterite and thereby is similar to Setting)
in which we are told that the brothers were too terrified to answer him.

In 45:4–15 Joseph tries again to establish his identity and open up
communication with them. The Lead-in here is an execution paragraph
(see below) in which Joseph tells his brothers to come near and they
come near. The quotation formula in v 4, like that above in the former
unresolved simple dialogue paragraph, in Sp:N + Add:N, that is, full
specification of both Sp and Add as frequently found in dialogue
initiation. The use of this form of quotation formula a second time in
45:4 signals not simply continuation of the former dialogue, but a fresh
beginning.

The general tone of Joseph's speech in this second unresolved
simple dialogue is not strikingly different from the way in which he had
talked to them when he was *hāʾîš*, 'the man', the capricious blow-hot,

---

[2] The distinction between Setting and Lead-in is simple and consistent:
Setting precedes Lead-in and does not contain a preterite; Lead-in contains a
preterite.

blow-cold Lord of Egypt. To begin with, he mitigates the imperative (in the execution paragraph) with *-nāʾ*: *gĕšû-nāʾ ʾēlay*, 'Come close, I pray, to me.' Point 1 of his discourse is largely explanation; the command that occur are negative (*ʾal* + imperfect) and are reassuring: 'Don't be distressed', 'Don't be angry with yourselves.' Point 2, which is instructional, conforms to the pattern of mitigated hortatory discourse in which an initial imperative is followed by *w*-cons + the perfect. (For a detailed analysis of the passage see chap. 5, §3.)

Again, there is no reply recorded for us. Rather this unresolved dialogue has a Step-down—a narrative sequence paragraph—that records Joseph embracing, weeping over, and kissing his brothers.[3] The paragraph has a Terminus with a verb in the perfect: 'And after that, his brothers talked with him.' So, we are told indirectly, communication was finally reestablished and a broken relationship healed. In portraying this process of reestablishing the relationship, the use of simple unresolved dialogue paragraphs graphically pictures Joseph's, at first unsuccessful, attempts to build a bridge out from his side of the chasm.

A few other examples of simple unresolved dialogue paragraphs occur in *Joseph*. One such structure occurs at the end of Joseph's long compound dialogue with his brothers on their first trip down to Egypt (42:6-17). Here Joseph breaks off the dialogue at v 17, tells them what he is going to do, and bundles them off to jail. No reply is elicited or would have been tolerated. In an immediately following passage in 42:19-34, a somewhat parallel compound paragraph occurs—but here the brothers are reporting all this to Jacob and we have a second order quote. Again the last exchange of the dialogue is a simple unresolved dialogue paragraph: unresolved because 'the man' will brook no contradiction or comment.

These dialogues are here left unresolved for quite a different reason than that found in the dialogues of chap. 45. Joseph incognito in chap. 42 discourages comment or reaction from the brothers; his attitude is, 'This is how we will do it or else.' In chap. 45 he is attempting to change his role and is rather desperately trying to elicit comments and reaction from men too shocked and numbed to respond.

2. Complex dialogue paragraphs

It is an observable fact that not all dialogues can be structured as simple paired utterances (question-answer, proposal-response, remark-evaluation). Dialogues that structure as simple paired utterances need

[3] Step-down is material at the end of a dialogue in which the clauses contain preterites (while Terminus has no preterites).

not be brief (witness Pharaoh's careful description of his dreams and Joseph's interpretation of them in 41:17–36), but in such dialogues the second speaker is content to accept the dialogue along the lines indicated by the first speaker. The second speaker answers, responds to, or evaluates material given him by the first speaker. But what if the second speaker is not inclined to accept the dialogue in this form, or to reply as expected? In this case we have a structure that I have termed the complex dialogue. The second speaker does not reply with an RU, but employs a Continuing Utterance (CU) with three possible counter-tokens: counter-question (Q), counter-remark (REM), and counter-proposal (PROP). The counter-tokens are not necessarily evoked by the primary tokens (question, proposal, remark) nor necessarily paired with them. Thus, a question can be followed by a counter-question, a counter-proposal, or a counter-remark. Consider the following hypothetical dialogue:

IU (= Q):   What do you think about seventeenth-century French literature?

CU (= Q):   Well, what do *you* think about it?

or: Why do you ask *me* that question?

Note that the original question could have been followed by a counter-proposal.

CU (= PROP):   Look, go ask Professor LaPelle questions like that.

It could also have been followed by a counter-remark:

CU (= REM):   I don't think my thoughts on the subject are worth much.

In similar fashion, a proposal or a remark can be followed by any of the three counter tokens. In this way, on occasion, long chains of CUs (with an initial IU) can be built up as speaker 1 and speaker 2 contest for control of the conversation. Such a chain can end with an RU if one speaker (acknowledging, as it were, defeat) deigns to answer the last counter-question, respond to the last counter-proposal, or evaluate the last remark. Otherwise, such a complex dialogue remains unresolved.

A further variant of the complex dialogue is one in which the CU is itself complex, so that, for example, it starts off as if it were an RU (answer, response, or evaluation) but appends a question, proposal, or remark in the same utterance. Thus, to return to our hypothetical dialogue above, we could have such an exchange as:

IU (= Q):   What do you think about seventeenth-century French literature?

CU(= A,REM): I'm not overly fond of that period; I really prefer
nineteenth-century French literature.

In 37:15–17 there is a complex resolved dialogue paragraph whose
CU is somewhat similar to that found in our last hypothetical example
above. Here, however, the CU answers a previous question and appends
a fresh question to the answer. The Lead-in to this dialogue is a
narrative comment paragraph, which introduces a new (and focal)
participant and describes Joseph's circumstances at the time of the
appearance of the new participant:

wayyimṣāʾēhû   ʾîš   wĕhinnēh   tōʿeh
and he found him a man and behold [he] was wandering

baśśādeh
in the field

The form of the quotation formula, Sp:N + Add:pr, alerts us that the
speaker is decisively intervening. It is unusual to have this type of
quotation formula in an IU, but there is no doubt that 'the man's'
intervention will prove decisive. I also assume that his initial question to
Joseph is simply the thing anyone would say to someone whom he
met wandering around as if looking for something: IU (= Q): *mâ-
ttĕbaggēš*, 'What are you looking for?' Consequently, Joseph's reply is
introduced simply by *wayyōʾmer*, 'and he said', rather than by the usual
wayyōʾmer lô, 'and he said to him', of continuing dialogue. Probably,
here this formula indicates again (as in other places) exchange of social
amenities.[4] Joseph, however, does not simply reply routinely to the
stranger that has greeted him but appends a question of his own:

CU (=Q, A): *ʾet-ʾaḥay   ʾānōkî   mĕbaqqēš   haggîdâ-nnāʾ*
my brothers I   am seeking please tell I pray

lî   ʾêpōh   hēm   rōʿîm
to me where they [are] pasturing

Here Joseph courteously (witness the *-â* on the imperative and the *-nāʾ*
entreaty particle) bids for control of the conversation by changing it
from a routine exchange to a serious inquiry concerning the whereabouts of his brothers.

The man, accepting Joseph's restructuring of the dialogue, proceeds
to give Joseph the desired information. The answer has the ring of
authority and finality (witness the Sp:N + Add:∅) in that the speaker

---

[4] In similar fashion such semi-formulaic utterances as 'What are you doing?'
or 'Where are you going?' are standard greetings among speakers of many contemporary Mesoamerican languages.

had personally overheard the brothers express their intention of going to Dothan:

RU (=A): *nāsĕ°û*   *mizzeh*   *kî* *šāma°tî*
          they've gone away from here for I heard

          °ōmĕrîm   *nēlĕkâ* *dōtāyĕnâ*
          [them] saying let's go to Dothan

Another example of a simpler sort of complex dialogue paragraph is found in 40:8b–15, but here the dialogue paragraph is unresolved. The complex dialogue is part of a compound dialogue whose first Exchange (40:6–8a) was a simple question-answer unit. Joseph, again taking control in the second Exchange, continues the dialogue with a quotation formula (Sp:N + Add:pr), which indicates a decisive intervention on his part. The imprisoned courtiers have complained that they have had troublesome dreams and have no clues as to their meaning. Joseph is going to set about to do something about this situation:

IU (=PROP): *hălô°*   *lē°lōhîm*   *pitrōnîm*
             do not [belong] to God dreams?

             sappĕrû-nā°   *lî*
             tell [them] I pray to me

Joseph's proposal is given with a mitigated imperative (*sappĕrû* + *nā°*) and is preceded by a disclaimer of his own ability; he offers himself as God's spokesman (cf. his audience with Pharaoh).

The chief cupbearer responds to the proposal by submitting his dream for Joseph's evaluation, that is, we have CU (= RES/REM). In a sense here the dialogue is redirected because, while Joseph had addressed the two of them, one comes to the fore in the reply. The quotation formula (Sp:N + Add:N) is of the sort used in such mid-stream redirection of dialogue:

     waysappēr   *śar-hammišqîm*   *°et-ḥalōmô* *lĕyôsēp*
     and he recounted the chief cupbearer his dream to Joseph

This speech act verb is followed (according to very regular but not entirely predictable usage) by a form of the verb 'say': *wayyō°mer lô*, 'And he said to him.' The account of the dream then follows; it is a narrative with an explanatory paragraph as stage. The narrative part has a rather unusual sequence of three first-person-singular preterites (v 11); we do not have many such first-person accounts in the Hebrew Scriptures.

Joseph's reply is not a simple evaluation of the CU. Such a strategy on Joseph's part would simply have resolved the dialogue on the terms prescribed by the chief cupbearer, who had recounted a dream for Joseph to interpret. Instead Joseph comes on with a CU (= EVAL,PROP), that is, he evaluates (interprets) the dream but appends a proposal of his own—a personal plea for help in getting out of prison. As we notice in analyzing this hortatory discourse in chapter 4: Joseph brushes aside some unrecorded offer of a reward with *kî ʾim-zĕkartanî ʾittĕkā kaʾăšer yîṭab lāk*, 'Rather [i.e., all that I'm asking is] you will remember me when it is well with you.' The request itself is carefully couched in a hortatory discourse mitigated to the surface form of predictive discourse—except for the *nāʾ* of entreaty on the first *w*-cons perfect. Thus, we have in this complex dialogue a sequence that reflects alternating bids for control:

IU (= PROP)	Joseph
CU (= RES/REM)	the chief cupbearer
CU (= EVAL,PROP)	Joseph

If the cupbearer responded to Joseph's proposal it is not recorded, so the dialogue is left unresolved. Perhaps the response was not worth recording since the restored courtier promptly and conveniently forgot Joseph on return to power, until Pharaoh's troublesome dream two years later prodded him into reluctantly speaking of Joseph to Pharaoh (40:23, 41:1, and 41:9).

One of the dialogues that is the most crucial to the development of the story is that found in 44:14–34. This dialogue represents the last climactic verbal struggle of Joseph incognito with his brothers. Its internal climax is Judah's final speech, which finally convinces Joseph that the brothers are indeed 'honest men' (as they had often averred), that they would not sacrifice Benjamin to save themselves, and that now it was time to reveal himself and attempt a reconciliation.

After a brief Lead-in, which structures as a narrative comment paragraph (44:14), the dialogue is initiated by Joseph. The quotation formula Sp:N + Add:pr, which indicates decision or rank-pulling, matches well the arrogant tone of what Joseph says (notice his use of a rhetorical question for scolding):

IU (REM):   *mâ -hammaʿăśeh hazzeh ʾăšer ʿăśîtem   hălôʾ*
               what [is] deed   this   that you've done? don't

               yĕdaʿtem kî -naḥēš yĕnaḥēš   ʾîš
               you know that surely practices divination a man

               ʾăšer kāmōnî
               such as I

Judah's counterploy, as spokesman for the brothers, is an attempt to placate Joseph by wholesale capitulation. Indeed, the form of quotation formula used here (Sp:N + Add:∅) is that used in introducing an utterance that the speaker hopes will achieve finality. Judah is making a desperate bid for control here: making the abysmal best of a bad situation by suggesting that they *all* (not just Benjamin) remain as slaves. Perhaps also he is desperately hoping to circumvent the implementation of an earlier proposal of the brothers': 'Whosoever it [the missing cup] is found with among your servants, let him die' (44:9). In spite of the fact that Judah and the brothers had every reason to believe that the cup had been planted in Benjamin's sack, the speech of Judah's is deferential to the point of groveling:

CU (PROP):[5]   *mâ   -nnōʾmar   laʾdōnî   mâ   -nnĕdabbēr*
         what shall we say to my lord? what shall we speak?

         ûmâ   -nniṣṭaddāq   hāʾĕlōhîm
         and how shall we justify ourselves? God

         māṣāʾ   ʾet-ʿăwōn   ʿăbādêkā
         has found out the iniquity of your servants

         hinnennû   ʿăbādîm   laʾdōnî   gam -ʾănaḥnû
         behold we [are] slaves to my lord both we

         gam ʾăšer   -nimṣāʾ   haggābîaʿ bĕyādô
         and [he] which was found the cup in his hand

Joseph's reply in v 17 is unctuous and well soaped-over with civility—as indicated by the choice of quotation formula (Sp:∅ + Add:∅). His CU (PROP) is exactly what the brothers do not want: Benjamin is to remain as a slave and the rest of them are to go scot-free:

   hālîlâ -llî   mēʿăśôt zōʾt   hāʾîš   ʾăšer
   far be it from me to do   such a thing the man who

   nimṣāʾ   haggābîaʿ bĕyādô   hûʾ yihyeh -llî   ʿābed
   was found the cup   in his hand he shall be to me a slave

   wĕʾattem   ʿălû   lĕšālôm   ʾel -ʾăbîkem
   but the rest of you go on up in peace to your father

In turn, this provokes Judah to heroic heights in his CU (PROP). He makes a lengthy speech in which, after recounting the dealings of Joseph with them and pinpointing the problem (namely, the loss of Jacob's last son by Rachel would probably bring about his death from grief), Judah boldly proposes to stay as a slave in Benjamin's place. This crucial speech of Judah's is carefully introduced with a motion verb clause: *wayyiggaš ʾēlāyw yĕhûdâ*, 'And he drew near to him Judah,' followed by simple *wayyōʾmer*. It adds up, however, to a quotation of the Sp:N + Add:pr form as customary in introducing a decisive intervention (or rank-pulling, which is not appropriate here). Because of the

---

[5] The layers of constituent embedding that characterize this structure are left out here (cf. the display in Part 4).

length of Judah's speech (the longest in the whole story, 44:18–34) I will reproduce here only the punch-line (vv 33–34), that is, his proposal at the end (again the layers of paragraph embedding are not indicated):

wĕ°attâ   yēšeb-nā°   °abdĕkâ   tahat   hanna°ar
and now let dwell I pray your servant in place of the lad

°ebed   la°dōnî   wĕhanna°ar   ya°al   °im   °eḥāyw
a slave to my lord and the lad he shall go up with his brothers

kî -°êk   °e°ĕleh   °el -°ābî   wĕhanna°ar   °ênennû
for how can I go up to my father and the lad none of him

°ittî   pen °er°eh bārā°   °ăšer yimṣā°   °et -°ābî
[is] with me lest I look on the evil that shall befall my father

It is of some interest that, while the first part of the passage (and the preceding parts of Judah's speech) are duly deferential in tone—with 'your servant' for 'I' and 'my Lord' for 'you' in v 33a—no further deferential forms occur in the passage. It is as if under the emotional fervor of the moment Judah was partially forgetting his court etiquette.

It is best to consider that this dialogue ends here and is unresolved. The initial verses of chap. 45 indicate a dramatic break with a new beginning in 45:3. The dialogue has reached a point where Joseph evidently figures that there is no point to continuing the dialogue along its see-saw course any longer; better to make a new and wonderful beginning. The structure of this dialogue with its alternative bids for control is:

IU (REM)   Joseph (implacable and arrogant)
CU (PROP)   Judah (groveling and desperate)
CU (PROP)   Joseph (forced civility)
CU (PROP)   Judah (heroic intervention)

Another example of a complex dialogue paragraph is analyzed in the next section as part of the compound dialogue paragraph found in 43:1–14.

3. *Compound dialogue paragraphs*

Compound dialogue paragraphs are dialogues that, although one unit, articulate into clear subdivisions, which can be called Exchanges. Each Exchange consists of a single or a complex dialogue, whether resolved or unresolved. At the seam between Exchanges, exclusion of a former speaker or inclusion of a new speaker can occur.

Some such dialogues simply contain a sort of preliminary Exchange (almost equal to greetings), followed by another Exchange that is more substantive. Thus, 37:13–14 has Exchange$_1$ in which Jacob says to

Joseph, 'Aren't your brothers pasturing the flocks in Shechem? Go, I'll send you to them.' Joseph's reply is a sort of 'Aye, aye, sir', that is, *hinnēnî*, 'Behold me [at your orders].' This Exchange is an IU (PROP) followed by an RU (RES). In Exchange$_2$, Jacob's instructions are reiterated and amplified. No reply of Joseph is recorded, but simply that his father sent him and he went. I do not analyze this second exchange as a dialogue paragraph but rather as an execution paragraph (see §4.1 below) of two parts: Plan (Jacob's instructions) and Execution (putting the plan into action).

Consider also the compound dialogue found in 40:6–19: Joseph's talking to the imprisoned courtiers about their dreams. Here in Exchange$_1$, Joseph—who has come in to the courtiers in the morning (Lead-in$_1$) and observed the look of distress on their faces (Lead-in$_2$)— asks them what is wrong and gets their answer. The Exchange is a simple IU (Q) followed by an RU (A). But on receiving their answer, 'We've dreamed dreams and there is no interpreter,' Joseph initiates a second Exchange that, as we have analyzed above, proves to be a complex unresolved dialogue paragraph in which Joseph hears the chief cupbearer's dream, interprets it, and appends a plea for the courtier to help him get out of jail.

The reporting of Joseph's crucial audience with Pharaoh is of somewhat parallel structure. The first Exchange between Pharaoh and Joseph is an IU (PROP) and RU (RES) interchange that broaches the subject (interpreting Pharaoh's dreams) and sets the atmosphere (Pharaoh is interested in Joseph and his reputed ability; Joseph is deferential but confident). It is in Exchange$_2$ that the real work of the dialogue is accomplished. Pharaoh recites his dream and Joseph interprets it. Joseph's interpretation does not, however, pattern itself simply as an RU (EVAL). Rather it patterns as a CU (EVAL,PROP) because Joseph explains the dream in order to predict a famine and to urge Pharaoh to adopt a food conservation program. There is no verbal resolution of this dialogue, but in the extensive section that follows—41:37–45, which I consider to be a Step-down from the dialogue—Pharaoh's actions show that he has enthusiastically taken Joseph's advice.

Without attempting to summarize exhaustively all compound paragraphs in Joseph, I terminate this section with the examination of two examples of peculiar interest. The first is the compound dialogue paragraph found in 43:1–14—the acrimonious debate between Jacob and his sons over their going to Egypt a second time to buy grain and their taking Benjamin with them. The Setting is simple: 'And the famine was severe in the land.' Israel initiates. His IU (PROP) is introduced with a quotation formular of the form Sp:N + Add:pr, that is, the narrator represents Jacob as trying to be decisive, perhaps pulling rank as clanhead. His words are:

šubû   šibrû   -lanû mē͑at -ʾōkel
return [and] buy us   a bit of food

This initiates a complex dialogue—for Jacob the clan-head was not to
be permitted to ignore the oft-repeated claim that they could not go a
second time without taking Benjamin. Jacob's attempt to ignore this—to
pull rank and get his way—does not work.

Judah comes back with the by now familiar counter-proposal,
which is stated more forcibly than ever. Benjamin must go or there is
no point in their going. If they go without Benjamin 'the man' won't
even see them. The quotation formula that introduces the CU (PROP) is
the same as that used to introduce Jacob's IU: Sp:N + Add:pr. While
we could argue here that Judah has to be identified anyway if he is the
one who spoke (how otherwise would we know?), Judah manages to be
decisive. He counters his father's proposal to the point that Jacob gives
up getting involved in a chain of proposal and counter-proposal. He
resorts rather to a querulous counter-question, which is introduced by
Sp:N + Add:∅, since emotional outbursts of this sort are spoken more
to *fatum perversum* than necessarily to anyone, regardless of the
apparent addressee:

CU (= Q):   Why did you do me the wrong of even telling the man that
you had another brother?

Whether this was a real or a rhetorical question (= You shouldn't have
done that!) the brothers take it up and try to answer it, explaining that
the man had carefully questioned them regarding their family connections, especially regarding their father and any further brothers. They go
on to say that they told the man what he asked, for 'How were we surely
to know that he would say, "Bring down your brother"?' The form of
the quotation formular that introduces this RU (A) is Sp:∅ + Add:∅,
which probably (as I have said before concerning this passage) signifies a
stalemate. They are going over all the old ground again and resolution
of the issue seems far removed. Thus ends the first Exchange, which we
can summarize as:

IU (PROP)   Jacob (attempted finality)
CU (PROP)   Judah (vigorous refutation)
CU (Q)   Jacob (querulous complaint)
RU (A)   the brothers (who attempt again to explain it all)

In Exchange₂ Judah breaks the deadlock in the negotiations by
personally promising to take charge of and go surety for Benjamin,
commenting at the end, 'For if we hadn't delayed like this we could have
gone there and returned twice by now.' The form of quotation formula
for this initiating utterance of the new exchange is Sp:N + Add:N—as is
regular in dialogue redirection, especially where it is not absolutely

certain who is speaking. The brothers had been the last speakers in the previous exchange.

Jacob hauls up the white flag—but with due ceremony. Furthermore, he does not simply agree in a RU (RES), rather he takes control by means of a CU (RES,PROP): 'If so it must be, then do as follows . . .' (43:11). The form of the quotation formula is Sp:N + Add:pr, which is quite fitting: the clan-head pulls rank and takes charge, although he has lost the main point for which he was contending. (Jacob's talk is analyzed as a specimen of unmitigated hortatory discourse in chapter 5.) The speech is very prescriptive of detail and in fact unveils a quite sensible strategy: take 'the man' gifts, and return the money that you found in your bags. The Terminus, however, reveals the personal cost to Jacob as he resignedly says, 'And may God Almighty extend you mercy in the eyes of the man. . . . As for me, if I am to be bereaved, I will be bereaved.'

Finally, consider the long compound dialogue in 42:6–17 where there are four Exchanges. This is on the occasion of the first going down to Egypt. The Setting (42:6a) and Lead-in (42:6b–7a) set the tone: Joseph is governor of the land, the brothers come in and grovel before him, he recognizes them, and decides to give them a hard time. The first Exchange (7b) is, however, presumably pacific in that he simply asks them in the IU (Q) where they are from and they answer him. The Sp:∅ + Add:∅ of the RU (A) probably suggests that all this is routine (social amenities or regular border-crossing procedure?).

The second Exchange has its own Lead-in, where we are told again that Joseph recognized them—but they didn't recognize him—with the added information that Joseph remembered 'his dreams that he had dreamed concerning them'. The Exchange consists of an IU (REM) and and RU (EVAL), that is, Joseph accuses them of being spies and they deny the accusation, reaffirm that they have come only to buy grain, and drop the information that they are 'all sons of one man'. The quotation formulas here conform to the norms for regular dialogue initiation and continuance.

In Exchange$_3$ Joseph repeats the accusation in an IU (REM) and receives again their denial in an RU (EVAL). The form of the quotation formula in the RU (EVAL) is Sp:∅ + Add:∅, thus suggesting that the dialogue has reached a stalemate. And indeed it has, although that is hardly the exclusive fault of the brothers who, finding themselves accused again, repeat and amplify information regarding their family. They even refer at one point to their lost brother (Joseph): *wĕhā²eḥād ²ênennû*, 'and this one—nothing of him' ('and one no longer exists'). At this point—possibly because his emotional control was threatened—Joseph breaks in and begins Exchange$_4$.

Exchange$_4$ is a simple unresolved dialogue paragraph: Joseph brusquely tells his brothers what to do (IU = PROP) and throws them in jail three days to soften them up and give them a chance to think it all over. The passage is chiastic (as described in chap. 1). The plan is: Joseph will find out whether or not they are spies by keeping all of them bound in prison except one who will go and fetch Benjamin to prove the truthfulness of their 'cover' story.[6] This last speech of Joseph at the initiation of Exchange$_4$ is introduced with Sp:N + Add:pr, as befits the status of this utterance as decisive (by one able to pull rank).

4. *Other interaction paragraphs*

4.1. *Execution paragraphs*

Execution paragraphs are similar to a simple dialogue paragraph in that they involve a proposal and a response. There is, however, no true dialogue because, although a Plan is proposed verbally, the reported Execution of the plan is non-verbal. A rather straightforward example of this paragraph type occurs in 37:14 where Jacob sends Joseph off to Shechem to see how his brothers are doing:

Plan: quotation = hortatory sequence paragraph

> *wayyō'mer lô*
> and he said to him

BU$_1$: *lek-nā' rĕ'ēh 'et-šĕlôm 'aḥêkā*
and now see to the well being of your brothers

wĕ'et-šĕlôm haṣṣō'n
and the well being of the flocks

BU$_n$: *wahăšibēnî dābār*
and bring me back word

Execution: (narrative) sequence paragraph

BU$_1$: *wayyišlāḥēhû mē'ēmeq ḥebrôn*
and he sent him from the valley of Hebron

BU$_n$: *wayyābō' šĕkemâ*
and he came to Shechem

Here Jacob in a hortatory discourse tells Joseph what to do. It is then recorded that the Plan was carried out by sending Joseph from Hebron

---

[6] Actually, after three days of "softening" in jail, Joseph reverses this plan, and keeps one bound in Egypt while the others take supplies back to Canaan and go for Benjamin. This is typical of Joseph's blow-hot, blow-cold tactics, as a competent interrogator.

to Shechem. This execution paragraph occurs between two stretches of dialogue: Jacob and Joseph (v 13) and Joseph and *hāʾîš*, 'the man' (vv 15–17). It seems evident here and elsewhere that execution paragraphs function much like dialogue paragraphs in advancing the story line.

Extended and recursive use of execution paragraphs characterizes 44:1–13. Its use is quite appropriate here for in this part of the story Joseph is rather fiendishly manipulating things off stage. This chapter, which is the Peak (climax of tension) in the embedded narrative found in chaps. 43–45, and which is itself a narrative, begins with a Stage expounded by an execution paragraph (44:1–2). The Plan is given by Joseph to his steward and constitutes a hortatory sequence paragraph in which the steward is commanded to fill the brothers' sacks with grain, return the money in the top of each sack, and put Joseph's silver cup in Benjamin's sack. The Execution is reported in one tense sentence *wayyaʿaś kidbar yôsēp ʾăšer dibbēr*, 'And he did according to the word of Joseph which he had said.'

Episode $_1$, which follows this stage is one extended execution paragraph (44:3–13). Here, after due dramatic build-up in the Setting (v 3), the Plan is presented in an antithetical paragraph: while the relieved brothers are leaving the city and starting their journey back to Canaan, Joseph is briefing his steward and dispatching him in hot pursuit of the brothers. The speech that the steward is to use in apprehending them is put into his mouth by Joseph and ends (v 5) with a final near-insult of a comment: 'You've really done a lousy, rotten job of it (Couldn't even a thief have been more subtle?).' The Execution of this Plan, as recorded in 44:6–13, is itself an execution paragraph. The steward goes along as planned, apprehends them, accuses them, and finally discovers the cup in Benjamin's sack. Internally, however, in 44:6–13 there is a dialogue in vv 6–10 in which the steward and the brothers work out a plan: the man (if any!) in whose sack the cup is found will remain in Egypt as a slave; the rest of the brothers will go free. The Plan is (partially) executed in 44:11–13 in a stimulus-response paragraph in which the search is made, the cup is found, and the utterly demoralized brothers shuffle back into the city to face Joseph.

4.2. *Stimulus-response paragraphs*

It is especially useful to posit the stimulus-response paragraph in passages where the string of preterites that characterizes a narrative paragraph is split by a subject referent switch. In 37:10 Joseph is so rash as to tell his second dream not only to his brothers but to his father also. The father's response is one of outraged dignity (quotation formula

Sp:N + Add:pr, as well as the verb 'rebuke', and the resort to a rhetorical question):

Stimulus: *waysappēr*   *ʾel -ʾābîw*   *wĕʾel -ʾeḥāyw*
          and he recounted [it] to his father and to his brothers

Response: amplification paragraph

    Text: *wayyigʿar*   *-bô ʾābîw*
        and he rebuked him his father

    Amplification: *wayyōʾmer lô*   *mâ*   *hahălôm*   *hazzeh ʾăšer*
               and he said to him what [is] dream this   which

           ḥālāmĕtā   *hăbôʾ nābôʾ*   *ʾănîʾ*
           you've dreamed will we surely come in I

           wĕʾimmĕkā   *wĕʾaḥêkā*   *lĕhištaḥăwōt*
           and your mother and your brothers to bow

           lĕkā   *ʾārĕṣâ*
           before you to the earth?

All told, the general import of this passage is that Joseph was somewhat rash in telling the dream in front of his father—who never, however, forgot the matter, but was profoundly impressed by it (37:11).

In 42:6-7 occurs another such stimulus-response paragraph where the dream of the young Joseph is fulfilled in the occasion of the brothers' first descent into Egypt to buy grain. Here there is no reported speech; rather the entrance of the brothers is the Stimulus and Joseph's reaction to seeing them after so many years is the Response.

Stimulus: (narrative) sequence paragraph

   BU₁: *wayyābōʾû*   *ʾăḥê*   *yôsēp*
      and they came in the brothers of Joseph

   BUₙ: *wayyištaḥăwû* *-lô*   *ʾappayim ʾārĕṣâ*
      and they bowed to him faces   to the ground

Response: (narrative) antithetical paragraph
   Thesis: (narrative) sequence paragraph

     BU₁: *wayyarʾ*   *yôsēp*   *ʾet-ʾĕḥāyw*
        and he saw Joseph his brothers

     BUₙ: *wayyakkirēm*
        and he recognized them

   Antithesis: (narrative) amplification paragraph

     Text: *wayyitnakkēr*   *ʾălêhem*
         and he acted as stranger to them

     Amplification: *waydabbēr*   *ʾittām*   *qāšôt*
                and he spoke with them harsh things

Here the brothers come in and bow 'faces to the ground' before Joseph
(not just 'to the ground' as in the dream: does the narrator delight in
putting in this extra humiliating detail?). Joseph's Response is mixed:
On the one hand, he recognizes them as his brothers. On the other hand
he feels that he cannot at this time let them know who he is but decides
to put them through a time of testing. Hence the 'acting as a stranger to
them' and 'speaking harshly'. Obviously this encounter sets the tone for
much of what is to follow in chaps. 42 and 43.

Perhaps the most effective use of stimulus-response paragraphs is
the sequence of two such paragraphs found in 45:25–28, the scene where
the brothers tell Jacob their father that Joseph is still alive. I have traced
earlier (chap. 1, §3.2.7.) the chiastic nature of this passage and its
simultaneous strophic structuring. All that is necessary to add here is
that each strophe has the structure of a stimulus-response unit in which
the brothers say something to their father and get his response. In the
first such unit the Stimulus is an embedded narrative sequence paragraph while the Response is but one sentence. In the second, quite the
opposite, the Stimulus is but one sentence and the Response is a
narrative sequence paragraph. I indicate all this briefly here in translation without reference to the layerings of the constituent structure:

Stimulus: And they went up from Egypt. And they came in to the land
            of Canaan, to Jacob their father. And they declared to him
            saying "Joseph is still alive. And he is Lord of all Egypt."
Response: And his heart went numb because he really couldn't believe
            them.
Stimulus: And they spoke to him all the words that Joseph had said to
            them.
Response: And he saw the carts that Joseph had sent to convey him.
            And the heart of Jacob their father revived. And Israel said,
            "That's enough! Joseph, my son, is still alive. I will go and
            see him before I die."

Finally, there is another paragraph that I have labeled stimulus-
response even though it does not involve a subject referent switch but
rather a different sort of break in a chain of preterite. In the passage in
question, 43:29–31a, Joseph catches sight of Benjamin and utters a few
socially approved things (Sp:∅ + Add:∅), first to the brothers then to
Benjamin. So much for the Stimulus. In the second half of the paragraph Joseph has to withdraw from the room, weep in the solitude of his
quarters, wash his face, compose himself, and return. I've called this part
the Response. It involves motion verbs and a change of location.

Note again that both execution paragraphs and stimulus-response
paragraphs are sparingly used. They seem to feature in especially
dramatic parts of the story.

5. *Conclusion*

In backing away a bit from the mass of detail presented in this chapter and in considering again the constituent structure of the story as a whole, I note that the narrative sequence paragraph and the simpler sort of dialogue paragraph carry in a somewhat routine way the burden of propelling the story forward. Most other paragraph types (excluding probably the narrative amplification paragraph) have other more specialized uses. Among the paragraphs that picture interaction patterns, the complex dialogue, the execution, and the stimulus-response paragraphs especially serve to underscore the more dramatic parts of the story. These paragraph types have, therefore, been analyzed with special attention to details of their structure; they are too important to the structure of the whole to be passed over lightly and summarily.

A CONSTITUENT DISPLAY OF *JOSEPH*

Part 4

INTRODUCTION

The purpose of this display is to exhibit in detail the constituent structure of *Joseph*, while at the same time relating that structure to broader concerns. The main device used to exhibit the constituent structure is indentation. I do not expect the reader who is unacquainted with the first three parts of this volume to be able to follow this display.

The constituent structure of the whole story is necessarily much more complex and involved than that of some small part extracted from it. To begin with, the main story has its stage, episodes, and peaks. But these in turn may be expounded by embedded narratives with their own stages, episodes and peak(s). Ultimately, discourse slots, such as those summarized above, are expounded by paragraphs. But paragraphs may also have multiple levels of embedding. To help the reader (or user) of the apparatus keep track of the appropriate level of indentation from the main story to the lowest level of embedded discourse, each page of the display is provided with a calibrative scale at the top and bottom. Thus, level one is reserved for slots of the major story, level two marks slots of narratives on the first level of embedding, and so forth.

In addition, different type fonts assist the user of the apparatus for the first several layers of embedding, and a peculiar typefont is reserved for N, P, H, and E, which label various embedded discourses and constituent paragraphs as narrative, predictive, hortatory, and expository respectively (cf. chap. 4 and 5).

For abbreviations used in this constituent display I refer the reader to the list found on p. vii–viii. In the transliterated Hebrew all preterite forms (*waw*-consecutive + the preformative tense) are italicized to help the user of the apparatus to correlate the main narrative line of the story with the constituent structure.

37:2b   **APERTURE** (of whole DISC/of embedded DISC): yôsēp$_1$ ben-
             šěba^c-^{c}eśrēh$_2$ šānâ$_3$ hāyâ$_4$ rō^{c}eh$_5$ $^\supset$et-$^\supset$eḥāyw$_6$ baṣṣō$^\supset$n$_7$.
37:2c-36   ***INCITING INCIDENT (EPISODE$_1$)*: N** DISCOURSE
37:2c-4   **STAGE: N** COORDINATE ¶
37:2c   **ITEM$_1$: N** SIMPLE ¶
                     SETTING: wěhû$^\supset$$_1$ (Ø) na^{c}ar$_2$ $^\supset$et-běnê bilhâ$_3$ wě$^\supset$et-běnê
                     zilpâ$_4$ něšê$_5$ $^\supset$ābîw$_6$.
                     TEXT: wayyābē$^\supset$$_1$ yôsēp$_2$ $^\supset$et-dibbātām$_3$ rā^{c}â$_4$ $^\supset$el-$^\supset$ăbîhem$_5$.
37:3-4   **ITEM$_2$: N** SEQUENCE ¶
37:3   SETTING: **N** REASON ¶
                        REASON: wěyiśrā$^\supset$ēl$_1$ $^\supset$āhab$_2$ $^\supset$et-yôsēp$_3$ mikkol$_4$-
                        bānāyw$_5$ kî-ben-zěqunîm$_6$ (Ø) hû$^\supset$$_7$ lô$_8$.
                        TEXT: wě^{c}āśâ$_1$ lô$_2$ kětōnet passîm$_3$.
37:4   BU$_1$: wayyir$^\supset$û$_1$ $^\supset$eḥāyw$_2$ kî-$^\supset$ōtô$_3$ $^\supset$āhab$_4$ $^\supset$ăbîhem$_5$ mikkol$_6$-
                        $^\supset$eḥāyw$_7$.
                     BU$_n$: **N** RESULT ¶
                        TEXT: wayyiśně$^\supset$û$_1$ $^\supset$ōtô$_2$.
                        RESULT: wělō$^\supset$$_1$ yākělû$_2$ dabběrô$_3$ lěšālōm$_4$.
37:5-11   ***INCITING INCIDENT (EPISODE$_1$)*: N** SEQUENCE ¶
             (Joseph's dream)
37:5-8   **BU$_1$:** SIMPLE RESOLVED DIALOGUE ¶
37:5   LEAD-IN: **N** SEQUENCE ¶
                     BU$_1$: wayyaḥălōm$_1$ yôsēp$_2$ ḥălôm$_3$.
                     BU$_2$: wayyaggēd$_1$ lě$^\supset$eḥāyw$_2$.
                     BU$_n$: wayyôsipû$_1$ ^{c}ôd$_2$ śěnō$^\supset$$_3$ $^\supset$ōtô$_4$.
37:6-7   IU (REM): QUOTE=**N** DISC/**N** SIMPLE ¶
37:6   wayyō$^\supset$mer$_1$ $^\supset$ălêhem$_2$:
                     APERTURE (OF DISC): «šim^{c}û-nā$^\supset$$_1$ haḥălôm$_2$ hazzeh$_3$
                     $^\supset$ăšer$_4$ ḥālāmětî$_5$.
37:7   SETTING (OF ¶): wěhinnēh$_1$ $^\supset$ănaḥnû$_2$ (Ø) mě$^\supset$allěmîm$_3$
                     $^\supset$ălummîm$_4$ bětôk$_5$ haśśādeh$_6$.
                     TEXT: **N** SIMPLE ¶
                        SETTING: **N** COORDINATE ¶
                        ITEM$_1$: **N** COORDINATE ¶
                           ITEM$_1$: wěhinnēh$_1$ qāmâ$_2$ $^\supset$ălummātî$_3$.
                           ITEM$_2$: wěgam$_1$ niṣṣābâ$_2$.
                        ITEM$_2$: wěhinnēh$_1$ těsubbênâ$_2$ $^\supset$ălummōtêkem$_3$.
                        TEXT: wattištaḥăwênā$_1$ la$^\supset$ălummātî$_2$.»
37:8   RU (EVAL): wayyō$^\supset$měrû$_1$ lô$_2$ $^\supset$eḥāyw$_3$:
                     QUOTE=ALTERNATIVE S: «hămālōk$_4$ timlōk$_5$ ^{c}ālênû$_6$
                     $^\supset$im$_7$ māšōl$_8$ timšōl$_9$ bānû$_{10}$?»
                     STEP-DOWN: wayyôsipû$_1$ ^{c}ôd$_2$ śěnō$^\supset$$_3$ $^\supset$ōtô$_4$ ^{c}al-
                     ḥălōmōtāyw$_5$ wě^{c}al-děbārāyw$_7$.

37:2b	Joseph$_1$, seventeen years old$_{2-3}$, was$_4$ shepherding$_5$ with his brothers$_6$ among the flocks$_7$.
37:2c	He$_1$ (was) a lad/apprentice$_2$ with the sons of Bilhah$_3$ and with the sons of Zilpah$_4$ wives of$_5$ his father$_6$.
	And-he-brought-in$_1$ Joseph$_2$ their evil words$_{3-4}$ to their father$_5$.
37:3	As for Israel$_1$ he-loved$_2$ Joseph$_3$ more than all$_4$ his sons$_5$ because a son of old age (or 'born leader')$_6$ (was) he$_7$ to him$_8$.
	And-he-made$_1$ for him$_2$ a 'special' cloak$_3$.
37:4	*And-they-saw$_1$* his brothers$_2$ that (it was) him$_3$ their father$_5$ loved$_4$ more than all$_6$ his brothers$_7$.
	And-they-hated$_1$ him$_2$.
	And not$_1$ they-could$_2$ speak-to-him$_3$ peaceably/decently$_4$.
37:5	*And-he-dreamed$_1$* Joseph$_2$ a dream$_3$.
	And-he-declared (it)$_1$ to his brothers$_2$.
	And-they-added$_1$ still$_2$ to hate$_3$ him$_4$.
37:6	*And-he-said$_1$* to them$_2$
	«Hear now$_1$ this dream$_{2-3}$ which$_4$ I-haved-dreamed$_5$.
37:7	Behold$_1$ we$_2$ (were) sheaving$_3$ sheaves$_4$ in the middle of$_5$ the field$_6$.
	And behold$_1$, arose$_2$ my sheaf$_3$.
	And also$_1$ it-stood-up$_2$.
	And behold$_1$, they-were-gathering-around$_2$ your sheaves$_3$.
	And-they-bowed-down$_1$ to my sheaf$_2$.»
37:8	*And-they-said$_1$* to him$_2$ his brothers$_3$: «You will surely reign$_{4-5}$ over us$_6$ or$_7$ you will surely rule$_{8-9}$ among us$_{10}$?»
	And-they-added$_1$ still$_2$ to hate$_3$ him$_4$ on account of his dream$_5$ and on account of$_6$ his words$_7$.

1 2 3 4 5 6 7 8 9

37:9-11   **BU$_2$:** COMPOUND DIALOGUE ¶
            LEAD-IN: **N** SEQUENCE ¶
37:9   BU$_1$: *wayyaḥălōm$_1$* ^{c}ôd$_2$ hālôm$_3$ $^{\circ}$aḥēr$_4$.
            BU$_n$: *waysappēr$_1$** $^{\circ}$ōtô$_2$ lĕ$^{\circ}$eḥāyw$_3$.
            EXCHANGE$_1$: (SIMPLE UNRESOLVED DIALOGUE) ¶
            IU (REM): *wayyō$^{\circ}$mer$_1$:* QUOTE=AWARENESS
            QUOTE ¶
            AW Q F: «hinnēh$_1$ ḥālamtî$_2$ ḥălôm$_3$ ^{c}ôd$_4$.
            AW Q: wĕhinnēh$_1$ haššemeš$_2$ wĕhayyārēaḥ$_3$ wĕ$^{\circ}$aḥad$_4$
            ^{c}āśār$_5$ kôkābîm$_6$ mištaḥăwîm$_7$ lî$_8$.»
37:10   EXCHANGE$_2$: (STIMULUS-RESPONSE ¶)
            STIMULUS: *waysappēr$_1$* $^{\circ}$el-$^{\circ}$ābîw$_2$ wĕ$^{\circ}$el-$^{\circ}$eḥāyw$_3$.
            RESPONSE: **N** AMPL ¶
            TEXT: *wayyig^{c}ar-b*ô$_1$ $^{\circ}$ābîw$_2$.
            AMPL: *wayyō$^{\circ}$mer$_1$* lô$_2$: QUOTE=**P** SIMPLE ¶
            SETTING: «mâ$_1$ haḥălôm$_2$ hazzeh$_3$ $^{\circ}$ăšer$_4$
            ḥālāmĕtā$_5$?
            TEXT: hăbô$^{\circ}_1$ nābô$^{\circ}_2$ $^{\circ}$ănî$_3$ wĕ$^{\circ}$immĕkā$_4$ wĕ$^{\circ}$aḥêkā$_5$
            lĕhištaḥăwôt$_6$ lĕkā$_7$ $^{\circ}$āṛṣâ$_8$?»
37:11   STEP-DOWN: **N** ANTI ¶
            THESIS: *wayqan$^{\circ}$û-b*ô$_1$ $^{\circ}$eḥāyw$_2$.
            ANTI: wĕ$^{\circ}$ābîw$_1$ šāmar$_2$ $^{\circ}$et-haddābār$_3$.

* *waysappēr* rather than *wayĕsappēr* (see Lambdin 1971: 197).

1 2 3 4 5 6 7 8 9

37:9   *And-he-dreamed₁* yet₂ another₄ dream₃.
          And-he-told₁ it₂ to his brothers₃.
          And-he-said₁:
          «Behold₁ I-dreamed₂ another dream₃₋₄.
          And behold₁ the sun₂ and the moon₃ and eleven₄₋₅ stars₆ were
          bowing down₇ to me₈.»
37:10   *And-he-told (it)₁* to his father₂ as well as to his brothers₃.
          And-he-rebuked-him₁ his father₂.
          And-he-said₁ to him₂:
          «What₁ (is) this dream₂₋₃ which₄ you-have-dreamed₅?
          Surely will-we-come₁₋₂ I₃ and your mother₄ and your brothers₅ to
          bow down₆ before you₇ to the ground₈!?»
37:11   *And-they-envied-him₁* his brothers₂.
          But his father₁ pondered₂ the matter₃.

1 2 3 4 5 6 7 8 9

37:12-17 **EPISODE₂: N** SEQUENCE ¶ (Joseph seeks his brothers)
37:12 **SETTING:** *wayyēlēkû₁* ᵓeḥāyw₂ lirᶜôt₃ (ᵓet-)ṣōᵓn₄ ᵓăbîhem₅ biškem₆*.
37:13-14 **BU₁:** COMPOUND DIALOGUE ¶
37:13 EXCHANGE₁: SIMPLE RESOLVED DIALOGUE ¶
  IU (PROP): *wayyōᵓmer₁* yiśrāᵓēl₂ ᵓel-yôsēp₃:
  QUOTE =**H** SIMPLE ¶
  SETTING: «hălôᵓ₁ ᵓaḥêkā₂ rōᶜîm₃ biškem₄?
  TEXT: lĕkâ₁
  wĕᵓešlāḥăkā₂ ᵓălêhem₃.»
  RU (RES): *wayyōᵓmer₁* lô₂ «hinnēnî₃».
37:14 EXCHANGE₂: **N** EXECUTION ¶
  PLAN: *wayyōᵓmer* lô₂: QUOTE =**H** SEQUENCE ¶
  BU₁: «lek-nāᵓ₁
  rĕᵓēh₂ ᵓet-šĕlôm₃ ᵓaḥêkā₄ wĕᵓet-šĕlôm₅ haṣṣōᵓn₆.
  BUₙ: wahăšibēnî₁ dābār₂.»
  EXEC: **N** SEQUENCE ¶
  BU₁: *wayyišlāḥēhû₁* mēᶜēmeq₂ ḥebrôn₃.
  BUₙ: *wayyābōᵓ₁* šĕkemâ₂.
37:15-17 **BUₙ:** COMPLEX RESOLVED DIALOGUE ¶
  LEAD-IN: **N** COMMENT ¶
37:15 TEXT: *wayyimṣāᵓēhû₁* ᵓîš₂
  COMMENT: wĕhinnēh₁ tōᶜeh₂ baśśādeh₃.
  IU (Q): *wayyišᵓālēhû₁* hāᵓîš₂ lēᵓmōr₃:
  «mah₄-tĕbaqqēš₅?»
37:16 CU (A,Q): *wayyōᵓmer₁*: QUOTE =**H** SIMPLE ¶
  SETTING: «ᵓet-ᵓaḥay₂ ᵓānōkî₃ mĕbaqqēš₄.
  TEXT: haggîdâ-nnāᵓ₁ lî₂ ᵓêpōh₃ hēm₄ rōᶜîm₅.»
37:17 RU (A): *wayyōᵓmer₁* hāᵓîš₂:
  «nāsᶜᵉû₃ mizzeh₄ kî₅ šāmaᶜtî₆ ᵓōmĕrîm₇ ''nēlĕkâ₈ dōtāyĕnâ₉.''»
  STEP-DOWN: **N** SEQUENCE ¶
  BU₁: *wayyēlek₁* yôsēp₂ ᵓaḥar₃ ᵓeḥāyw₄.
  BUₙ: *wayyimṣāᵓēm₁* bĕdōtān₂.

* *biškem* rather than *bišĕkem* (see Lambdin 1971: xx).

1 2 3 4 5 6 7 8 9

37:12   *And-they-went ('had gone')$_1$* his brothers$_2$ to shepherd$_3$ the flock
of$_4$ their father$_5$ in Shechem$_6$.

37:13   *And-he-said$_1$* Israel$_2$ to Joseph$_3$:
«Aren't$_1$ your brothers$_2$ shepherding$_3$ in Shechem$_4$?
Come$_1$ and-I'll-send-you$_2$ to them$_3$.»
And-he-said$_1$ to him$_2$ «Behold me =('At your orders')$_3$»

37:14   *And-he-said$_1$* to him$_2$
«Go now$_1$
See$_2$ the peace of ('how they are doing')$_3$ your brothers$_4$ and the
peace of$_5$ the flock$_6$.
And-bring-me-back$_1$ word$_2$.»
And-he-sent-him$_1$ from the valley of$_2$ Hebron$_3$.
And-he-went-off$_1$ towards Shechem$_2$.

37:15   *And-he-found-him$_1$* a man$_2$;
And behold$_1$ (he) was wandering$_2$ in the field$_3$.
And-he-asked-him$_1$ the man$_2$ saying$_3$:
«What$_4$ are you looking for$_5$?»

37:16   *And-he-said$_1$:*
«(It's) my brothers$_2$ I$_3$ am looking for$_4$.
Tell me now$_{1-2}$ where$_3$ (are) they$_4$ shepherding$_5$?»

37:17   *And-he-answered$_1$* the man$_2$
«They-have-gone-away$_3$ from here$_4$ for$_5$ I-heard$_6$ (them) saying$_7$
"Let's go$_8$ to Dothan$_9$."»
And-he-went$_1$ Joseph$_2$ after$_3$ his brothers$_4$.
And-he-found-them$_1$ in Dothan$_2$.

216   1 2 3 4 5 6 7 8 9

37:18-22   **EPISODE$_3$: N** SEQUENCE ¶/N ANTITHETICAL ¶ (The Conspiracy)
37:18   **SETTING:** *wayyir$^\supset$û$_1$* $^\supset$ōtô$_2$ mērāḥōq$_3$.
    BU$_1$ (THESIS): N AMPLIFICATION ¶
    TEXT: ûbĕterem$_1$ yiqrab$_2$ $^\supset$ălêhem$_3$ *wayyitnakkĕlû$_4$* $^\supset$ōtô$_5$ lahămîtô$_6$.
37:19   AMPL: *wayyō$^\supset$mĕrû$_1$* $^\supset$îš$_2$ $^\supset$el-$^\supset$āḥîw$_3$: QUOTE =**H** SEQUENCE ¶
    SETTING: «hinneh$_1$ ba^{c}al$_2$ haḥălōmôt$_3$ hallāzeh$_4$ bā$^\supset$$_5$.
37:20   BU$_1$: wĕ^{c}attâ$_1$ lĕkû$_2$ wĕnahargēhû$_3$.
    BU$_2$:**H** RESULT ¶
    TEXT: wĕnašlikēhû$_1$ bĕ$^\supset$aḥad$_2$ habbōrôt$_3$.
    RESULT: wĕ$^\supset$āmarnû$_1$: "ḥayyâ$_2$ rā$^\supset$â$_3$ $^\supset$ăkālātĕhû$_4$."
    BU$_n$: wĕnir$^\supset$eh$_1$ mâ-yyihû$_2$ ḥălōmōtāyw$_3$.»
    BU$_2$ (ANTI?): N AMPLIFICATION ¶
37:21   SETTING: *wayyišma^c$_1$* rĕ$^\supset$ûben$_2$
    TEXT: *wayyaṣṣilēhû$_1$* miyyādām$_2$.
    AMPL$_1$: *wayyō$^\supset$mer$_1$*: «lō$^\supset$ nakkennû$_2$ nāpeš$_3$.»
37:22   AMPL$_2$: *wayyō$^\supset$mer$_1$* $^\supset$ălēhem$_2$ rĕ$^\supset$ûben$_3$:
    QUOTE=CYCLIC **H** ANTITHETICAL ¶ (END-WEIGHTED), BUT QUOTATION SENTENCE CONCLUDES WITH A PURPOSE MARGIN.
    THESIS: « $^\supset$al-tišpĕkû$_1$-dām$_2$
    ANTI: hašlîkû$_1$ $^\supset$ōtô$_2$ $^\supset$el-habbôr$_3$ hazzeh$_4$ $^\supset$ăšer$_5$ bammidbār$_6$.
    THESIS′: wĕyād$_1$ $^\supset$al-tišlĕḥû$_2$-bô$_3$»
    —lĕma^{c}an$_1$ haṣṣîl$_2$ $^\supset$ōtô$_3$ miyyādām$_4$ lahăšîbô$_5$ $^\supset$el-$^\supset$ābîw$_6$.

1 2 3 4 5 6 7 8 9

37:18	*And-they-saw$_1$* him$_2$ from afar$_3$.
	And before$_1$ he-came-near$_2$ to them$_3$
	they-plotted-against$_4$ him$_5$ to kill him$_6$.
37:19	*And-they-said$_1$* each (man)$_2$ to his brother$_3$
	«Behold$_1$ this$_4$ master-of$_2$ dreams$_3$ is coming$_5$.
37:20	So, now$_1$ come on$_2$
	let's-kill-him$_3$.
	And let's-throw-him$_1$ into one of$_2$ the pits$_3$.
	And-we'll-say$_1$ ''An evil$_3$ beast$_2$ has-eaten-him$_4$.''
	And we'll see$_1$ what-will-come-of$_2$ his dreams$_3$.»
37:21	*But-he-heard$_1$* Reuben$_2$
	And-he-saved-him$_1$ from their hands$_2$.
	And-he-said$_1$ «Don't smite-him$_2$ life$_3$='Don't take his life.'»
37:22	*And-he-said$_1$* to them$_2$ Reuben$_3$
	«Don't shed$_1$ blood$_2$
	Cast$_1$ him$_2$ into this$_4$ pit$_3$ which$_5$ (is) in the desert$_6$.
	And don't lay$_2$ hand$_1$ on him$_3$ »
	in order that$_1$ he might rescue$_2$ him$_3$ from their hands$_4$ to-return-him$_5$ to his father$_6$.

218   1 2 3 4 5 6 7 8 9

37:23-28   **PEAK EPISODE: N** SEQUENCE ¶
37:23   **BU₁:** wayhî₁* kaʾăšer-bāʾ₂ yôsēp₃ ʾel-ʾeḥāyw₄
            wayyapšîṭû₅ ʾet-yôsēp₆ ʾet-kuttontô₇ ʾet-kĕtōnet happassîm₈
            ʾăšer₉ ʿālāyw₁₀.
            BU₂: N SEQUENCE ¶
37:24   BU₁: wayyiqqāḥuhû₁
                BU₂: **N** COMMENT ¶
                TEXT: wayyašlikû₁ ʾōtô₂ habbōrâ₃.
                COMMENT: **E** PARAPHRASE ¶
                TEXT: wĕhabbôr₁ rēq₂.
                PARA: ʾên₁ bô₂ mayim₃.
37:25   BU₃: wayyēšĕbû₁ leʾĕkol₂-leḥem₃.
                BU₄: **N** AMPLIFICATION ¶
                TEXT: wayyiśʾû₁ ʾênêhem₂.
                AMPL: AW QUOTE ¶
                AW Q F: wayyirʾû₁.
                AW Q: **E** COORDINATE ¶
                ITEM₁: wehinnēh₁ ʾōrĕḥat₂ yišmĕʿēʾlîm₃ bāʾâ₄
                miggilʿād₅.
                ITEM₂: ûgĕmallêhem₁ nōśēʾîm₂ nĕkōʾt₃ ûṣĕrî₄
                wālōṭ₅ hôlĕkîm₆ lĕhôrîd₇ miṣrāyĕmâ₈. (or=ITEM₃?)

        * wayhî rather than wayĕhî (see Lambdin 1971: 123).

        1 2 3 4 5 6 7 8 9

37:23   And-it-happened-that$_1$ when arrived$_2$ Joseph$_3$ to his brother$_4$
         they-stripped$_5$ Joseph$_6$ his cloak$_7$ his special cloak$_8$ which$_9$ (was)
         on him$_{10}$.

37:24   *And-they-siezed-him$_1$*
         And-they-put-in$_1$ him$_2$ (into) the pit$_3$.
         The pit$_1$ (was) empty$_2$.
         Nothing of$_1$ water$_3$ in it$_2$.

37:25   *And-they-sat-down$_1$* to eat$_2$ bread$_3$.
         And-they-lifted-up$_1$ their eyes$_2$.
         And-they-saw$_1$.
         And behold$_1$! a caravan$_2$ of Ishmaelites$_3$ coming$_4$ from Gilead$_5$.
         And their camels$_1$ were carrying$_2$ spices$_3$ and balm$_4$ and myrrh$_5$
         proceeding$_6$ to go down$_7$ to Egypt$_8$.

1 2 3 4 5 6 7 8 9

BU$_n$: (CLIMAX) EXECUTION ¶
PLAN: SIMPLE RESOLVED DIALOGUE ¶

37:26   IU (PROP): *wayyō$^{\rangle}$mer$_1$* yĕhûdâ$_2$ $^{\rangle}$el-$^{\rangle}$ēhāyw$_3$:
QUOTE=*H* ANTITHETICAL ¶
SETTING: «mah$_1$-beṣa$^c_2$ kî$_3$ [*P* SEQUENCE ¶ as
Subject of a nominal clause]
BU$_1$: nahărōg$_1$ $^{\rangle}$et-$^{\rangle}$āḥînû$_2$
BU$_n$: wĕkissînû$_1$ $^{\rangle}$et-dāmô$_2$?

37:27   THESIS: lĕkû$_1$
wĕnimkĕrennû$_2$ layyišmĕ^{c}ē$^{\rangle}$lîm$_3$.
ANTI: wĕyādēnû$_1$ $^{\rangle}$al-tĕhî$_2$-bô$_3$, kî$_4$-$^{\rangle}$āḥînû$_5$
bĕśārēnû$_6$ hû$^{\rangle}_7$».
RU (RES): *wayyišmĕ^{c}û$_1$* $^{\rangle}$eḥāyw$_2$.

EXEC: *N* SEQUENCE ¶

37:28   SETTING: *wayya^{c}abrû$_1$* $^{\rangle}$ănāšîm$_2$ midyānîm$_3$
sōḥărîm$_4$.
BU$_1$: *wayyimšĕkû$_1$*
wayya^{c}ălû$_2$ $^{\rangle}$et-yôsēp$_3$ min-habbôr$_4$.
BU$_2$: *wayyimkĕrû$_1$* $^{\rangle}$ĕt-yôsēp$_2$ layyišmĕ^{c}ē$^{\rangle}$lîm$_3$
bĕ^{c}eśrîm$_4$ kāsep$_5$.
BU$_n$: *wayyābî$^{\rangle}$û$_1$* $^{\rangle}$et-yôsēp$_2$ miṣrāyĕmâ$_3$.

37:29-35   **POST-PEAK EPISODE$_1$: *N* DISC (Cover-up)**
37:29-30   **INCITING INCIDENT (EPISODE$_1$): *N* SEQUENCE ¶**
37:29   BU$_1$: AWARENESS QUOTE ¶
LEAD-IN [no Q F]: *wayyāšob$_1$* rĕ$^{\rangle}$ûben$_2$ $^{\rangle}$el-habbôr$_3$.
AW Q: wĕhinnēh$_1$ $^{\rangle}$ēn$_2$-yôsēp$_3$ babbôr$_4$.
BU$_2$: *wayyiqra$^{c}_1$* $^{\rangle}$et-bĕgādāyw$_2$.
37:30   BU$_3$: *wayyāšob$_1$* $^{\rangle}$el-$^{\rangle}$eḥāyw$_2$.
BU$_n$ **(CLIMAX):** *wayyō$^{\rangle}$mar$_1$* (pausal): QUOTE=*E*
RESULT ¶
TEXT: «hayyeled$_1$ $^{\rangle}$ênennû$_2$
RESULT: wa$^{\rangle}$ănî$_1$ $^{\rangle}$ānâ$_2$ $^{\rangle}$ănî$_3$-bā$^{\rangle}_4$?»

1 2 3 4 5 6 7 8 9

37:26   *And-he-said$_1$* Judah$_2$ to his brothers$_3$:
                    «What$_1$ profit$_2$ (is it) that$_3$
                    we-should-kill$_1$ our brother$_2$
                    and-cover$_1$ his blood$_2$?

37:27   Come$_1$ let's-sell-him$_2$ to the Ishmaelites$_3$
                    And-let-not-be$_2$ our hand$_1$ on him$_3$ for$_4$ our brother$_5$ our flesh$_6$ (is)
                    he$_7$.»
                    And-they-hearkened$_1$ his brothers$_2$.

37:28   *And-they-passed-by$_1$* men$_2$ Midianites$_3$ merchants$_4$.
                    And-they-pulled-up$_1$
                    and-they-raised$_2$ Joseph$_3$ from the pit$_4$.
                    And-they-sold$_1$ Joseph$_2$ to the Ishmaelites$_3$ for twenty (pieces)$_4$ of
                    silver$_5$.
                    And-they-brought$_1$ Joseph$_2$ into Egypt$_3$.

37:29   *And-he-returned$_1$* Reuben$_2$ to the pit$_3$.
                    And-behold$_1$! nothing of$_2$ Joseph$_3$ (was) in the pit $_4$.
                    And-he-tore$_1$ his clothes$_2$.

37:30   *And-he-returned$_1$* to his brothers$_2$.
                    And-he-said$_1$
                    «The lad$_1$—nothing of him$_2$.
                    And-I$_1$ where$_2$ (shall) I$_3$ go$_4$?»

222   1 2 3 4 5 6 7 8 9
            ┌─┬─┬─┬─┬─┬─┬─┬─┐

37:31-33   **EPISODE₂: N** SEQUENCE ¶
37:31   BU₁: *wayyiqḥû₁* ᵓet-kĕtōnet₂ yôsēp₃.
                BU₂: *wayyišḥāṭû₁* śĕᶜîr₂ ᶜizzîm₃.
                BU₃: *wayyiṭbĕlû₁* ᵓet-hakkuttōnet₂ baddām₃.
37:32   BU₄: *wayšallĕḥû₁* ᵓet-kĕtōnet happassîm₂.
                BU₅: *wayyābîᵓû₁* ᵓel-ᵓābîhem₂.
                BUₙ: SIMPLE RESOLVED DIALOGUE ¶
                    IU (Q): *wayyōᵓmĕrû₁:* QUOTE=AWARENESS
                    QUOTE ¶
                       PRELIM: «zōᵓt₁ māṣāᵓnû₂.
                       AW Q F: hakker-nāᵓ₁
                       AW Q: hakkĕtōnet₁ binkā₂ hiwᵓ₃ ᵓim₄-lōᵓ₅?»
                    RU (A): **N** AMPL ¶
37:33   TEXT: *wayyakkîrâh₁* (dagesh in h =₃fs).
                    AMPL: *wayyōᵓmer₁:* QUOTE=**N** AMPLIFICATION
                    ¶
                       PRELIM: «kĕtōnet₁ bĕnî₂.
                       TEXT: ḥayyâ₁ rāᶜâ₂ ᵓăkālātĕhû₃.
                       AMPL: ṭārōp₁ ṭōrap₂ yôsēp₃.»
37:34-35   **PEAK: N** SEQUENCE ¶ (SIMPLE CLOSURE?)
                CHIASMUS
37:34   BU₁: *wayyiqraᶜ₁* yaᶜăqōb₂ śimlôtāyw₃.
                BU₂: *wayyāśem₁* śaq₂ bĕmotnāyw₃.
                BU₃: *wayyitᵓabbēl₁* ᶜal-bĕnô₂ yāmîm₃ rabbîm₄.
                BU₄: **N** ANTI ¶
37:35   THESIS: *wayyāqumû₁* kol-bānāyw₂ wĕkol₃-bĕnōtāyw₄
                    lĕnaḥămô₅.
                    ANTI: *waymāᵓēn₁* lĕhitnaḥēm₂.
                    BU₅: *wayyōᵓmer₁* kî₂-«ᵓērēd₃ ᵓel-bĕnî₄ ᵓābēl₅ šĕᵓōlâ₆.»
                    BUₙ: *wayyēbk₁** ᵓōtô₂ ᵓābîw₃.
37:36   **CLOSURE (OF EMBEDDED DISC=CHAPTER 37):**
                wĕhammĕdānîm₁ mākĕrû₂ ᵓōtô₃ ᵓel- miṣrāyim₄ lĕpôṭîpar₅ sĕrîs₆
                parᶜōh₇ śar₈ haṭṭabbāḥîm₉.

                * *wayyēbk* rather than *wayyēbĕk* (see Lambdin 1971: xxvii).

                ┌─┬─┬─┬─┬─┬─┬─┬─┐
                1 2 3 4 5 6 7 8 9

37:31   *And-they-took[1]* the cloak of[2] Joseph[3].
And-they-slaughtered[1] a ram[2] of the goats[3].
And-they-dipped[1] the cloak[2] in the blood[3].

37:32   *And-they-sent[1]* the 'special' cloak[2].
And-they-had-it-brought-in[1] to their father[2].
And-they-said[1]:
«This[1] we have found[2].
Look carefully[1]
The cloak of[1] your son[2] (is) it[3] or[4] not[5]?»

37:33   *And-he-recognized-it[1].*
And-he-said[1]:
«(It is) the cloak-of[1] my son[2].
An evil[2] beast[1] has eaten him[2].
Surely is torn to pieces[1-2] Joseph[3].»

37:34   *And-he-tore[1]* Jacob[2] his clothing[3].
And-he-put-on[1] sackcloth[2] on his loins[3].
And-he-mourned[1] for his son[2] many[4] days[3].

37:35   *And-they-rose-up[1]* all his sons[2] and all[3] his daughters[4] to comfort him[5].
And-he-refused[1] to be comforted[2].
And-he-said[1] that[2] «I-will-go-down[3] mourning[5] for my son[4] to Sheol[6].»
And-he-wept[1] him[2] his father[3].

37:36   As for the Midianites[1] they-sold[2] him[3] into Egypt[4] to Potiphar[5] a courtier of[6] Pharoah[7], captain of[8] the guard[9] (or 'Lord High Executioner'.)

1 2 3 4 5 6 7 8 9
┌─┬─┬─┬─┬─┬─┬─┬─┐

39:1-6   ***EPISODE$_2$: N*** DISC WHICH CONSISTS OF (RE-)STAGE &
PEAK. (SINCE THIS IS A ONE-¶ DISC, FEATURES OF ¶ &
DISC ARE COLLAPSED). (Joseph in Potiphar's house)
     RE-STAGE: *N* SIMPLE ¶
39:1   **SETTING:** wĕyôsēp$_1$ hûrad$_2$ miṣrāyĕmâ$_3$.
       TEXT: *wayyiqnēhû$_1$* pôṭîpar$_2$ sĕrîs$_3$ par^{c}ōh$_4$ śar$_5$ haṭṭabbāḥîm$_6$
       $^?$îš$_7$ miṣrî$_8$ miyyad$_9$ hayyišmĕ^{c}ē$^?$lîm$_{10}$ $^?$āšer$_{11}$ hôriduhû$_{12}$
       šāmmâh$_{13}$.
     EPISODE$_n$ (PEAK): *N* SEQUENCE ¶
     SETTING: *E* COORDINATE ¶
39:2   **ITEM$_1$:** wayhî$_1$ yhwh$_2$ $^?$et-yôsēp$_3$.
       ITEM$_2$: wayhî$_1$ $^?$îš$_2$ maṣlîaḥ$_3$.
       ITEM$_3$: wayhî$_1$ bĕbêt$_2$ $^?$ădōnāyw$_3$ hammiṣrî$_4$.
     BU$_1$: AW Q WHOSE QUOTE =***E*** AMPL ¶
39:3   *wayyar$^?_1$* $^?$ădōnāyw$_2$ kî$_3$
       TEXT: yhwh$_1$ $^?$ittô$_2$.
       AMPL: wĕkōl$_1$ $^?$āšer-hû$^?_3$ ^{c}ōśeh$_4$ yhwh$_5$ maṣlîaḥ$_6$ bĕyādô$_7$.
39:4   **BU$_2$:** *wayyimṣa$^?_1$* yôsēp$_2$ ḥēn$_3$ bĕ^{c}ênâyw$_4$.
     BU$_3$: *wayšāret$_1$* $^?$ōtô$_2$.
     BU$_4$: *N* AMPL ¶
       TEXT: *wayyapqidēhû$_1$* ^{c}al-bêtô$_2$.
       AMPL: wĕkōl$_1$-yeš$_2$-lô$_3$ nātan$_4$ bĕyādô$_5$.
     BU$_n$ (CLIMAX): *N* AMPLIFICATION ¶
39:5   **TEXT:** wayhî$_1$ mē$^?$āz$_2$ hipqîd$_3$ $^?$ōtô$_4$ bĕbêtô$_5$ wĕ^{c}al$_6$ kol$_7$-
       $^?$āšer$_8$ yeš$_9$-lô$_{10}$ (BACK REFERENCE) *waybārek$_{11}$* yhwh$_{12}$
       $^?$et-bêt$_{13}$ hammiṣrî$_{14}$ biglal$_{15}$ yôsēp$_{16}$.
       AMPL: wayhî$_1$ birkat$_2$ yhwh$_3$ bĕkol$_4$ $^?$āšer$_5$-yeš$_6$-lô$_7$
       babbayit$_8$ ûbaśśādeh$_9$.
     BU$_{n+1}$: *N* NEGATED ANTONYM PARAPHRASE ¶
39:6   **TEXT:** *wayya^{c}ăzōb$_1$* kol$_2$-$^?$āšer$_3$-lô$_4$ bĕyad$_5$ yôsēp$_6$.
       PARA: wĕlō$^?_1$-yāda$_2$ $^?$ittô$_3$ mē$^?$ûmâ$_4$ kî$_5$ $^?$im$_6$ halleḥem$_7$
       $^?$āšer$_8$-hû$_9$ $^?$ôkēl$_{10}$.
     TERMINUS: wayhî$_1$ yôsēp$_2$ yĕpēh$_3$ tō$^?$ar$_4$ wîpeh$_5$ mar$^?$eh$_6$.

└─┴─┴─┴─┴─┴─┴─┴─┘
1 2 3 4 5 6 7 8 9

39:1 And Joseph$_1$ was brought down$_2$ to Egypt$_3$.
And-he-purchased-him$_1$ Potiphar$_2$, a courtier$_3$ of Pharaoh$_4$, the captain of$_5$ the guard$_6$, an Egyptian$_8$ man$_7$ from-the hand of$_9$ the Ishmaelites$_{10}$ which$_{11}$ brought him down$_{12}$ there$_{13}$.

39:2 And YHWH$_2$ was$_1$ with Joseph$_3$.
And-he-was/became$_1$ a man$_2$ (who) prospers$_3$.
And-he-was$_1$ in the house-of$_2$ his master$_3$ the Egyptian$_4$.

39:3 *And-he-saw$_1$* his master$_2$ that$_3$
YHWH$_1$ (was) with him$_2$.
And everything$_1$ which$_2$ he$_3$ was-doing$_4$ YHWH$_5$ caused to prosper$_6$ in his hand$_7$.

39:4 *And-he-found$_1$* Joseph$_2$ grace$_3$ in his eyes$_4$.
And-he-served$_1$ him$_2$ (=became his personal attendant).
And-he-appointed-him$_1$ over all his house$_2$.
And everything$_1$ (that) was$_2$ to-him$_3$ he-gave$_4$ in his hand$_5$.

39:5 And-it-happened that$_1$ from when$_2$ he-appointed$_3$ him$_4$ over his house$_5$ and over$_6$ all$_7$ that$_8$ was$_9$ to him$_{10}$
he-blessed$_{11}$ YHWH$_{12}$ the house$_{13}$ of the Egyptian$_{14}$ on account of$_{15}$ Joseph$_{16}$.
And-it-was$_1$ the blessing of$_2$ YHWH$_3$ on all$_4$ which$_5$ was$_6$ to him$_7$ in-the house$_8$ and in the field$_9$.

39:6 *And-he-abandoned$_1$* all$_2$ which$_3$ (was) to him$_4$ in the hand$_5$ of Joseph$_6$.
And not$_1$ he-kept-account$_2$ with him$_3$ anything$_4$ except$_{5-6}$ the bread$_7$ which$_8$ he$_9$ ate$_{10}$.
And-he-was$_1$ Joseph$_2$ shapely$_3$ of form$_4$ and-fair$_5$ of face$_6$.

1 2 3 4 5 6 7 8 9

39:7-23   **EPISODE$_3$:** *N* DISC (Joseph's ruin)

39:7-10   **EPISODE$_1$ (INCITING INCIDENT):** SIMPLE RESOLVED DIALOGUE ¶

        IU (PROP): *N* SEQUENCE ¶

39:7   BU$_1$: wayhî$_1$ $^{\supset}$aḥar$_2$ haddĕbārîm$_3$ hā$^{\supset}$ēlleh$_4$

        [BACKREFERENCE]

        wattiśśā$^{\supset}_5$ $^{\supset}$ēšet$_6$- $^{\supset}$ădōnāyw$_7$ $^{\supset}$et-^{c}ênêhā$_8$ $^{\supset}$el-yôsēp$_9$.

        BU$_n$: *wattō$^{\supset}$mer$_1$:* «šikbâ$_2$ ^{c}immî$_3$.»

        RU (RES): *N* AMPLIFICATION ¶

39:8   TEXT: *waymā$^{\supset}$ēn$_1$.*

        AMPL: *wayyō$^{\supset}$mer$_1$ $^{\supset}$el$_2$-$^{\supset}$ēšet$_3$-$^{\supset}$ădōnāyw$_4$:* QUOTE = *H* REASON ¶

          REASON: *E* COORDINATE ¶

            ITEM$_1$: *E* AMPLIFICATION ¶

              TEXT: «hēn$_1$ $^{\supset}$ădōnî$_2$ lō$_3$ yāda$^c_4$ $^{\supset}$ittî$_5$ mah$_6$-babbāyit$_7$.

              AMPL: wĕkol$_1$ $^{\supset}$ăšer$_2$-yeš$_3$-lô$_4$ nātan$_5$ bĕyādî$_6$.

39:9   ITEM$_2$: $^{\supset}$ênennû$_1$ gādōl$_2$ babbāyit$_3$ hazzeh$_4$ mimmennî$_5$.

            ITEM$_3$: wĕlō$^{\supset}_1$ ḥāśak$_2$ mimmennî$_3$ mĕ$^{\supset}$ûmâ$_4$ kî $^{\supset}$im$_5$-$^{\supset}$ôtāk$_6$ ba$^{\supset}$ăšer$_7$ $^{\supset}$att$_8$-$^{\supset}$ištô$_9$.

            TEXT: *H* AMPLIFICATION ¶

              TEXT: wĕ$^{\supset}$êk$_1$ $^{\supset}$e^{c}ĕśeh$_2$ hārā^{c}â$_3$ haggĕdōlâ$_4$ hazzō$^{\supset}$t$_5$.

              AMPL: wĕḥāṭā$^{\supset}$tî$_1$ lē$^{\supset}$lōhîm$_2$.»

39:10   **TERMINUS:** wayhî$_1$ kĕdabbĕrâ$_2$ $^{\supset}$el-yôsēp$_3$ yôm$_4$ yôm$_5$ wĕlō$^{\supset}_6$-šāma$^c_7$ $^{\supset}$ēlêhā$_8$ liškab$_9$ $^{\supset}$eṣlāh$_{10}$ (h = 3fs) lihyôt$_{11}$ ^{c}immāh$_{12}$.

39:11-12   **EPISODE$_2$:** *N* SEQUENCE ¶

        BU$_1$: *N* COMMENT ¶

39:11   TEXT: wayhî$_1$ kĕhayyōm$_2$ hazzeh$_3$ *wayyābō$^{\supset}_4$* habbaytâ$_5$ la^{c}ăśôt$_6$ mĕla$^{\supset}$ktô$_7$.

        COMMENT: wĕ$^{\supset}$ên$_1$ $^{\supset}$îš$_2$ mē$^{\supset}$anšê$_3$ habbayit$_4$ šām$_5$ babbāyit$_6$.

39:12   **BU$_2$:** *wattitpĕśēhû$_1$ bĕbigdô$_2$ lē$^{\supset}$mōr$_3$:* «šikbâ$_4$ ^{c}immî$_5$.»

        BU$_3$: *wayya^{c}ăzob$_1$ bigdô$_2$* bĕyādāh (3fs)$_3$.*

        BU$_n$: *N* SEQUENCE ¶

        BU$_1$: *wayyānos$_1$.*

        BU$_n$: *wayyēṣē$^{\supset}_1$ haḥûṣâ$_2$.*

* *bigdô* rather than *bigĕdô* (see Lambdin 1971: xx, 77–78).

1 2 3 4 5 6 7 8 9

39:7	And-it-happened (that)$_1$ after$_2$ these$_4$ things$_3$,
	she-lifted-up$_5$ the wife-of$_6$ his lord$_7$ her eyes$_8$ to Joseph$_9$.
	And-she-said$_1$: «Lie$_2$ with me$_3$.»
39:8	*And-he-refused* (her)$_1$.
	And-he-said$_1$ to$_2$ the wife of$_3$ his lord$_4$:
	«Look$_1$ my master$_2$ doesn't$_3$ keep account of$_4$ with me$_5$ what$_6$ (is) in the house$_7$.
	And everything$_1$ which$_2$ is$_3$ to him$_4$ he-has-given$_5$ into my hand$_6$.
39:9	No one$_1$ (is) greater$_2$ in this$_4$ house$_3$ than me$_5$.
	And not$_1$ he-(has)-kept-back$_2$ from me$_3$ anything$_4$ except$_5$ you$_6$— in that$_7$ you$_8$ (are) his wife$_9$.
	How then$_1$ can-I-do$_2$ this$_5$ great$_4$ evil$_3$?
	And-shall-I-sin$_1$ against God$_2$?»
39:10	And-so-it-was$_1$ in her speaking$_2$ to Joseph$_3$ day by day$_{4-5}$ that didn't$_6$ he-hearken$_7$ to her$_8$ to lie$_9$ at her side$_{10}$ to be$_{11}$ with her$_{12}$.
39:11	And-it-happened$_1$ on a certain$_3$ day$_2$ (that) *he-went-in$_4$* to the house$_5$ to discharge$_6$ (some) errand-of-his$_7$.
	And no one$_1$ man of$_2$ the men of$_3$ the house$_4$ (was) there$_5$ in the house$_6$.
39:12	*And-she-caught-hold-of-him$_1$* by his clothing$_2$ saying$_3$ «Lie$_4$ with-me$_5$.»
	And-he-abandoned$_1$ his clothing$_2$ in her hand$_3$.
	And-he-ran$_1$.
	And-he-exited$_1$ outside$_2$.

39:13-20   **PEAK: N** SEQUENCE ¶
            BU₁: N AMPLIFICATION ¶
39:13   TEXT: wayhî$_1$ kir$^\jmath$ôtāh$_2$ kî$_3$ ^{c}āzab$_4$ bigdô$_5$ bĕyādāh$_6$
                wayyānos$_7$ haḥûṣâ$_8$ (BACKREFERENCE)
39:14   *wattiqrā$^\jmath_9$* lē$^\jmath$anšê$_{10}$ bêtāh$_{11}$.
                AMPL: *wattō$^\jmath$mer$_1$* lāhem$_2$ lē$^\jmath$mōr$_3$: QUOTE =**N**
                SEQUENCE ¶ or **N** DISC
                    APERTURE: «rĕ$^\jmath$û$_1$
                    SETTING: **N** SEQUENCE ¶/**N** COORDINATE ¶
                    BU₁: hēbî$^\jmath_1$ lānû$_2$ $^\jmath$îš$_3$ ^{c}ibrî$_4$ lĕṣaḥeq$_5$ bānû$_6$.
                    BUₙ: bā$^\jmath_1$ $^\jmath$ēlāy$_2$ liškab$_3$ ^{c}immî$_4$.
                    BU₁: *wā$^\jmath$eqrā$^\jmath_1$* bĕqōl$_2$ gādôl$_3$.
                    BUₙ: **N** SEQUENCE ¶
39:15   BU₁: wayhî$_1$ kĕšāmĕ^{c}ô$_2$ kî$_3$ hărîmōtî$_4$ qōlî$_5$ *wā$^\jmath$eqrā$^\jmath_6$*
                    (BACKREFERENCE) *wayya^{c}ăzōb$_7$* bigdô$_8$ $^\jmath$eṣlî$_9$.
                    BUₙ: **N** SEQUENCE ¶
                        BU₁: *wayyānos$_1$*.
                        BUₙ: *wayyēṣē$^\jmath_1$* haḥûṣâ$_2$.»
39:16   **BU₂:** *waṭṭanaḥ$_1$* bigdô$_2$ $^\jmath$eṣlāh$_3$ ^{c}ad-bō$^\jmath_4$ $^\jmath$ădōnāyw$_5$ $^\jmath$el-bêtô$_6$.
39:17   **BU₃:** *wattĕdabber$_1$* $^\jmath$ēlāyw$_2$ kaddĕbārîm$_3$ hā$^\jmath$ēlleh$_4$ lē$^\jmath$mōr$_5$:
            QUOTE =**N** SEQUENCE ¶
                SETTING: «bā$^\jmath_1$ $^\jmath$ēlay$_2$ hā^{c}ebed$_3$ hā^{c}ibrî$_4$ $^\jmath$ăšer$_5$ hēbē$^\jmath$tā$_6$
                lānû$_7$ lĕṣaḥeq$_8$ bî$_9$.
39:18   BU₁: wayhî$_1$ kahărîmî$_2$ qôlî$_3$ *wa$^\jmath$eqrā$^\jmath_4$* *wayyā^{c}ăzōb$_5$* bigdô$_6$
                $^\jmath$eṣlî$_7$.
                BUₙ: *wayyānos$_1$* haḥuṣâ$_2$.»
            BUₙ: (CLIMAX) N SEQUENCE ¶
39:19   BU₁: wayhî$_1$ kišmōa$^c_2$ $^\jmath$ădōnāyw$_3$ $^\jmath$et-dibrê$_4$ $^\jmath$îstô$_5$ $^\jmath$ăšer
                dibbĕrāh$_7$ $^\jmath$ēlāyw$_8$ lē$^\jmath$mōr$_9$: «kaddĕbārîm$_{10}$ ha$^\jmath$ēlleh$_{11}$ ^{c}āśâ$_{12}$
                lî$_{13}$ $^\jmath$abdekā$_{14}$,» (BACK REFERENCE) *wayyiḥar$_{15}$*
                $^\jmath$appô$_{16}$.
39:20   BU₂: *wayyiqqaḥ$_1$* $^\jmath$ădōnê$_2$ yôsēp$_3$ $^\jmath$ōtô$_4$.
                BUₙ: *wayyittĕnēhû$_1$* $^\jmath$el-bêt$_2$ hassōhar$_3$ mĕqôm$_4$ $^\jmath$ăšer$_5$
                $^\jmath$ăsîrê$_6$ hammelek$_7$ $^\jmath$ăsûrîm$_8$.
            TERMINUS: wayhî$_1$ šām$_2$ bĕbêt$_3$ bassōhar$_4$.

39:13   And-it-happened-that$_1$ when she saw$_2$ that$_3$ he-had-abandoned$_4$ his clothing$_5$ in her hand$_6$ *and-he-had-run$_7$* outside$_8$,

39:14   then *she-cried-out$_9$* to the men of$_{10}$ the house$_{11}$
     And-she-said$_1$ to them$_2$ saying$_3$:
     «Look$_1$.
     He's-brought-in$_1$ to us$_2$ a Hebrew$_4$ man$_3$ to mock$_5$ us$_6$.
     He-came-in$_1$ to me$_2$ to lie$_3$ with me$_4$.
     And-I-cried-out$_1$ with a great$_3$ voice$_2$.

39:15   And-it-happened$_1$ when he heard$_2$ that$_3$ I-raised$_4$ my voice$_5$ *and-I-cried-out$_6$ then-he-left$_7$* his garment$_8$ by me$_9$.
     And-he-ran$_1$.
     And-he-exited$_1$ outside$_2$.»

39:16   *And-she-put-up$_1$* his clothing$_2$ by her$_3$ until-should come$_4$ his lord$_5$ to his house$_6$.

39:17   *And-she-told$_1$* to him$_2$ according to these$_4$ words$_3$ saying$_5$:
     «He-came$_1$ to me$_2$ the Hebrew$_4$ slave$_3$ which$_5$ you-brought-in$_6$ to us$_7$ to mock$_8$ me$_9$.

39:18   And-it-happened that$_1$ when I raised up$_2$ my voice$_3$ and *I-cried-out$_4$ then-he-abandoned$_5$* his clothing$_6$ by me$_7$.
     And-he-ran$_1$ outside$_2$.»

39:19   And-it-happened-that$_1$ when his lord$_3$ heard$_2$ the words of$_4$ his wife$_5$ which$_6$ she-spoke$_7$ to him$_8$ saying$_9$: «According of these$_{11}$ words$_{10}$ he-did$_{12}$ to me$_{13}$ your slave$_{14}$»
     then-he-got-hot$_{15}$ his anger$_{16}$.

39:20   *And-he-took$_1$* the lord of$_2$ Joseph$_3$ him$_4$.
     And-he-put-him$_1$ in the house-of$_2$ the prison$_3$ the place$_4$ where$_5$ the prisoners of$_6$ the king$_7$ are confined$_8$.
     And-he-was$_1$ there$_2$ in the house of$_3$ the prison$_4$.

39:21-23   **EPISODE (P_{+1}): N** SEQUENCE ¶

39:21   **SETTING:** wayhî$_1$ yhwh$_2$ ᵓet-yôsēp$_3$.

     BU$_1$: *wayyēṭ$_1$* ᵓēlāyw$_2$ ḥāsed (pausal)$_3$.

     BU$_2$: *wayyittēn$_1$* ḥinnô$_2$ bĕᶜênê$_3$ śar$_4$ bêt-hassōhar$_5$.

     BU$_n$: N AMPLIFICATION ¶

39:22   TEXT: *wayyittēn$_1$* śar$_2$ bêt-hassōhar$_3$ bĕyad$_4$-yôsēp$_5$ ᵓēt-kol$_6$-hāᵓāsîrim$_7$ ᵓăšer$_8$ bĕbêt-hassōhar$_9$.

     AMPL: **E** AMPLIFICATION ¶

     TEXT: weᵓēt$_1$ kol$_2$-ᵓăšer$_3$ ᶜōśîm$_4$ šām$_5$ hûᵓ$_6$ hāyâ$_7$ ᶜōśeh$_8$.

39:23   AMPL: ᵓên$_1$ śar$_2$ bêt-hassōhar$_3$ rōᵓeh$_4$ ᵓet-kol$_5$-mĕᵓûmâ$_6$ bĕyādô$_7$

     baᵓăšer$_1$ [**E** AMPLIFICATION ¶ BACKLOOPS INTO THE CAUSE MARGIN]*

       TEXT: yhwh$_2$ (was) ᵓittô$_3$†.

       AMPL: waᵓăšer$_1$ hûᵓ$_2$ ᶜōseh$_3$ yhwh$_4$ maṣlîaḥ$_5$.

* This classification disregards the position of the *athnach* following *ᵓittô* (marked with † above); to take it into account may require that the last clause of v. 23 be treated as a result (practical outworking) of all that precedes in vv. 22 and 23.

1 2 3 4 5 6 7 8 9

39:21   And-he-was$_1$ YHWH$_2$ with Joseph$_3$.
               And-he-extended$_1$ to him$_2$ favor$_3$.
               And-he-gave$_1$ favor to him$_2$ in the eyes of$_3$ the warden of$_4$ the
               prison$_5$.
39:22   *And-he-gave$_1$* the warden of$_2$ the prison$_3$ into the hand of$_4$ Joseph$_5$
               all$_6$ the prisoners$_7$ which$_8$ (were) in the prison$_9$.
               And$_1$ everything$_2$ which$_3$ (they) were doing$_4$ there$_5$ he$_6$ was$_7$ the-
               doer$_8$.
39:23   Nothing$_1$ (did) the warden of$_2$ the prison$_3$ concern himself with$_4$—
               not anything$_{5-6}$ (which was) in his hand$_7$
               inasmuch as$_1$ YHWH$_2$ (was) with him$_3$.
               And whatsoever$_1$ he$_2$ did$_3$ YHWH$_4$ made it prosper$_5$.

232   1 2 3 4 5 6 7 8 9

40:1-23   **EPISODE₄: N** DISC [OF SPECIAL GENRE, 'DREAM
           INTERPRETATION'=STAGE, EPISODE₁ (DREAM),
           EPISODE₂ (INTERPRETATION), EPISODE₃
           (FULFILLMENT)]

40:1-4   **STAGE: N** SEQUENCE ¶

40:1   **SETTING:** wayhî₁ ꜣaḥar₂ haddĕbārîm₃ hā\}ēlleh₄ (BACK
           REFERENCE) ḥāṭĕꜣû₅ mašqēh₆ melek₇-miṣrayîm₈
           wĕhāꜣōpeh₉ laꜣădōnêhem₁₀ lĕmelek₁₁-miṣrāyîm₁₂.

40:2   **BU₁:** *wayyiqṣōp₁* parᶜōh₂ ᶜal₃ šĕnê₄ sārîsāyw₅ ᶜal₆ śar₇
           hammašqîm₈ wĕᶜal₉ śar₁₀ hāꜣôpîm₁₁.

40:3   **BU₂:** *wayyittēn₁* ꜣōtām₂ bĕmišmar₃ bêt₄ śar₅ haṭṭabbāḥîm₆
           ꜣel₇-bêt hassōhar₈ mĕqōm₉ ꜣăšer₁₀ yôsēp₁₁ ꜣāsûr₁₂ šām₁₃.

40:4   **BU₃:** *wayyipqōd₁* śar₂ haṭṭabbāḥîm₃ ꜣet-yôsēp₄ ꜣittām₅.
       BUₙ: *wayšāret₁* ꜣōtām₂.
       TERMINUS: wayyihyû₁ yāmîm₂ bĕmišmar₃.

40:5   **EPISODE₁ (DREAM):N** SIMPLE ¶
       TEXT: *wayyaḥalmû₁* ḥālôm₂ šĕnêhem₃ ꜣîš₄ ḥālōmô₅ bĕlāylâ₆
           ꜣeḥād₇ ꜣîš₈ kĕpitrôn₉ ḥălōmô₁₀ hammašqeh₁₁ wĕhāꜣōpeh₁₂
           ꜣăšer₁₃ lĕmelek₁₄ miṣrayîm₁₅ ꜣăšer₁₆ ꜣăsûrîm₁₇ bĕbêt₁₈
           hassohar₁₉.

40:6-19   **EPISODE₂ (INTERPRETATION) COMPOUND
           DIALOGUE** ¶

40:6   **LEAD-IN₁:** AWARENESS QUOTE ¶
       wayyābō₁ ălênem₂ yôsēp₃ babbōqer₄.
       AW Q F: *wayyarꜣ₁* ꜣōtām₂.
       AW Q: wĕhinnām₁ zōᶜăpîm₂.

1 2 3 4 5 6 7 8 9

40:1 And-it-happened-that$_1$ after$_2$ these$_4$ things$_3$, they-sinned$_5$ the cupbearer of$_6$ the King of$_7$ Egypt$_8$ and the baker$_9$ against their lord$_{10}$ against the King of$_{11}$ Egypt$_{12}$.

40:2 *And-he-got-angry$_1$* Pharaoh$_2$ against$_3$ the two$_4$ courtiers of him$_5$ against$_6$ the chief of$_7$ the cupbearers$_8$ and against$_9$ the chief of$_{10}$ the bakers$_{11}$.

40:3 *And-he-put$_1$* them$_2$ in jail$_3$ (in) the house of$_4$ the captain of$_5$ the guard$_6$ into$_7$ the prison$_8$ the place$_9$ where$_{10}$ Joseph$_{11}$ was imprisoned$_{12}$ there$_{13}$.

40:4 *And-he-entrusted /appointed$_1$* the captain of$_2$ the guard$_3$ Joseph$_4$ with them$_5$.
And-he-looked-after$_1$ them$_2$.
And-they-were$_1$ (a number of) days$_2$ in the jail$_3$.

40:5 *And-they-dreamed$_1$* a dream$_2$ the two of them$_3$ (each) man$_4$ his dream$_5$ in one$_7$ night$_6$, (each) man$_8$ according to the interpretation of$_9$ his dream$_{10}$ the cupbearer$_{11}$ and the baker$_{12}$ which$_{13}$ (were) to the King of$_{14}$ Egypt$_{15}$, (they) which$_{16}$ (were) imprisoned$_{17}$ in the prison$_{18-19}$.

40:6 *And-he-went-in$_1$* to them$_2$ Joseph$_3$ in the morning$_4$.
And-he-saw$_1$ them$_2$.
And behold$_1$ (they were) sad$_2$.

1 2 3 4 5 6 7 8 9

40:7-8 **EXCHANGE$_1$:** SIMPLE RESOLVED DIALOGUE ¶
40:7 IU (Q): *wayyiš⊃al*$_1$ ⊃et-sĕrîsê$_2$ par⊂ōh$_3$ ⊃ăšer$_4$ ⊃ittô$_5$
bĕmišmar$_6$ bêt$_7$-⊃ădōnāyw$_8$ lē⊃mōr$_9$: «maddûa⊂$_{10}$ pĕnêkem
rā⊂îm$_{11}$ hayyôm$_{12}$?»
40:8a RU (A): *wayyō⊃merû*$_1$ ⊃ēlāyw$_2$: QUOTE =**N**
ANTITHETICAL ¶
THESIS: «ḥălôm$_1$ ḥālamnû$_2$
ANTI: ûpōtēr$_1$ ⊃ên$_2$ ⊃ōtô$_3$.»
40:8b-15 **EXCHANGE$_2$:** COMPLEX UNRESOLVED DIALOGUE ¶
40:8b IU (PROP): *wayyō⊃mer*$_1$ ⊃ălēhem$_2$ yôsēp$_3$: QUOTE =**H**
REASON ¶
REASON: «hălô⊃$_1$ lē⊃lōhîm$_2$ pitrōnîm$_3$?
TEXT: sappĕrû-nā⊃$_1$ lî$_2$.»
CU (RES/REM): **N** AMPLIFICATION ¶
40:9 TEXT: *waysappēr*$_1$ śar$_2$-hammašqîm$_3$ ⊃et-ḥălōmô$_4$
lĕyôsēp$_5$.
AMPL: *wayyō⊃mer*$_1$ lô$_2$: QUOTE =**N** DISC
STAGE: **N** SIMPLE ¶
SETTING: **E** COORDINATE ¶
ITEM$_1$: «baḥălōmî$_1$ wĕhinnēh$_2$ gepen$_3$ lĕpānāy$_4$.
40:10 ITEM$_2$: ûbaggepen$_1$ šĕlōšâ$_2$ śārîgim$_3$.
TEXT: wĕhî⊃$_1$ kĕpōraḥat$_2$ ⊂ālĕtâ$_3$ niṣṣāh$_4$ (3fs)
hibšîlû$_5$ ⊃aškĕlōtêhâ$_6$ ⊂ănābîm$_7$ (=JUXTAPOSED
SENTENCE?).
EPISODE: **N** SEQUENCE ¶
40:11 SETTING: wĕkôs$_1$ par⊂ōh$_2$ bĕyādî$_3$.
BU$_1$: *wā⊃eqqaḥ*$_1$ ⊃et-hā⊂ănābîm$_2$.
BU$_2$: *wā⊃eśḥaṭ*$_1$ ⊃ōtām$_2$ ⊃el-kôs$_3$ par⊂ōh$_4$.
BU$_n$: *wā⊃ettēn*$_1$ ⊃et-hakkôs$_2$ ⊂al kap$_3$ par⊂ōh$_4$.»

1 2 3 4 5 6 7 8 9

40:7   *And-he-asked$_1$* the servants of$_2$ Pharaoh$_3$ which$_4$ (were) with-him$_5$
            in the jail$_6$, the house$_7$ of his lord$_8$ saying$_9$: «Why$_{10}$ (are you) out of
            sorts$_{11}$ today$_{12}$?»
40:8a   *And-they-said$_1$* to him$_2$:
            «A dream$_1$ we have dreamed$_2$.
            And (there is) no$_2$ interpreter$_1$ of it$_3$.»
40:8b   *And-he-said$_1$* to them$_2$ Joseph$_3$:
            «Do not$_1$ interpretations$_3$ (belong) to God$_2$?
            Tell$_1$ (them) to me$_2$.»
40:9   *And-he-recounted$_1$* the chief of$_2$ the cupbearers$_3$ his dream$_4$ to
            Joseph$_5$.
            And-he-said$_1$ to him$_2$:
            «In my dream$_1$ behold$_2$ a vine$_3$ (was) before me$_4$.
40:10   And on the vine$_1$ (were) three$_2$ branches$_3$.
            And it$_1$ at its budding$_2$ went up (burst into)$_3$ its bloom$_4$ (and)
            ripened$_5$ its clusters$_6$ into grapes$_7$.
40:11   And the cup of$_1$ Pharaoh$_2$ (was) in my hand$_3$.
            And-I-took$_1$ the grapes$_2$.
            And-I-pressed$_1$ them$_2$ into the cup$_3$ of Pharaoh$_4$.
            And-I-gave$_1$ the cup$_2$ into the hand of$_3$ Pharaoh$_4$.»

1 2 3 4 5 6 7 8 9

40:12-15;40:12   CU (EVAL/PROP): *wayyō$^{\supset}$mer$_1$* lô$_2$ yôsēp$_3$:
QUOTE=PREDICTIVE DISC='COVERT' *H* DISC
POINT$_1$: EVIDENCE ¶
SETTING/APERTURE (OF DISC): «zeh$_1$ pitrōnô$_2$.
EVIDENCE: šēlōšet$_1$ haśśārigîm$_2$ šēlōšet$_3$ yāmîm$_4$
hēm$_5$.
TEXT: *P* SEQUENCE ¶
40:13   SETTING: bĕ^{c}ôd$_1$ šēlōšet$_2$ yāmîm$_3$ yiśśā$^{\supset}_4$ par^{c}ōh$_5$
$^{\supset}$et-rō$^{\supset}$šekā$_6$
BU$_1$: wĕhăšîbĕkā$_1$ ^{c}al-kannekā$_2$.
BU$_n$: wĕnātattā$_1$ kôs$_2$-par^{c}ōh$_3$ bĕyādô$_4$ kammišpat$_5$
hāri$^{\supset}$šôn$_6$ $^{\supset}$āšer$_7$ hāyîtā$_8$ mašqēhû$_9$.
POINT$_2$: *P* REASON ¶
TEXT: *P* SEQUENCE ¶ ['COVERT' *H*]
40:14   SETTING: —kî $^{\supset}$im$_1$-zĕkartanî$_2$ $^{\supset}$ittĕkā$_3$ ka$^{\supset}$āšer$_4$
yîtab$_5$ lāk$_6$.
BU$_1$: wĕ^{c}āśîtā-nnā$^{\supset}_1$ ^{c}immādî$_2$ ḥāsed$_3$ (pausal).
BU$_2$: wĕhizkartanî$_1$ $^{\supset}$el$_2$-par^{c}ōh$_3$.
BU$_n$: wĕhôṣē$^{\supset}$tanî$_1$ min$_2$ habbayit$_3$ hazzeh$_4$.
REASON: *N* COORDINATE ¶
40:15   ITEM$_1$: kî$_1$-gunnōb$_2$ gunnabtî$_3$ mē$^{\supset}$ereṣ$_4$ hā^{c}ibrîm$_5$.
ITEM$_2$: wĕgam$_1$-pōh$_2$ lō$^{\supset}_3$-^{c}aśîtî$_4$ mĕ$^{\supset}$ûmâ$_5$ kî$_6$-śāmû$_7$
$^{\supset}$ōtî$_8$ babbôr$_9$.»

1 2 3 4 5 6 7 8 9

40:12   *And-he-said₁* to him₂ Joseph₃:
«This₁ (is) the interpretation₂.
The three₁ branches₂, three₃ days₄ (are) they₅.

40:13   In just₁ three₂ days₃ he-will-lift-up₄ Pharaoh₅ your head₆.
And-he-will-put-you₁ on your pedestal₂.
And-you-will-give₁ the cup of₂ Pharaoh₃ into his hand₄ according to the former₆ custom₅ which₇ you were₈ his cupbearer₉.

40:14   —Only₁ you will remember me₂ with-you₃ according to the time when₄ it-will-be-well₅ with you₆.
And-you-will-do₁ with me₂ favor₃.
And-you-will-remember-me₁ to₂ Pharaoh₃.
And-you-will-get-me-out₁ from₂ this₄ house₃.

40:15   For₁ surely I was kidnapped₂₋₃ from the land of₄ the Hebrews₅.
And-also₁ here₂ I haven't₃ done₄ anything₅ that₆ they-should have placed₇ me₈ in the dungeon₉.»

40:16-19   **EXCHANGE$_3$:** SIMPLE RESOLVED DIALOGUE ¶
40:16   LEAD-IN: *wayyar$^{\supset}_1$ śar$_2$ hā$^{\supset}$ōpîm$_3$ kî$_4$ ṭōb$_5$ pātār$_6$.*
             IU (REM): *wayyō$^{\supset}$mer$_1$* $^{\supset}$el$_2$-yôsēp$_3$: QUOTE=**N** SIMPLE ¶
             SETTING: **E** COORDINATE ¶
             ITEM$_1$: «$^{\supset}$ap$_1$-$^{\supset}$ănî$_2$ baḥălômî$_3$ wĕhinnēh$_4$ šĕlōšâ$_5$ sallê$_6$
             ḥōrî$_7$ ^{C}al$_8$ rō$^{\supset}$šî$_9$.
40:17   ITEM$_2$: ûbassal$_1$ hā^{C}elyôn$_2$ mikkol$_3$ ma$^{\supset}$ăkal$_4$ par^{C}ōh$_5$
             ma^{C}ăśēh$_6$ $^{\supset}$ōpeh$_7$.
             TEXT: wĕhā^{C}ôp$_1$ $^{\supset}$ōkēl$_2$ $^{\supset}$ōtām$_3$ min$_4$-hassal$_5$ mē^{C}al$_6$
             rō$^{\supset}$šî$_7$.»
             RU (EVAL): **N** AMPLIFICATION ¶
40:18   TEXT: *wayya^{C}an$_1$ yôsēp$_2$*
             AMPL: *wayyō$^{\supset}$mer$_1$:* QUOTE=**P** EVIDENCE
             ¶/PREDICTIVE DISC
             SETTING/APERTURE (OF DISC): «zeh$_1$ pitrōnô$_2$:
             EVIDENCE: šĕlōšet$_1$ hassallîm$_2$ šĕlōšet$_3$ yāmîm$_4$ hēm$_5$.
             TEXT: **P** SEQUENCE ¶
40:19   SETTING: bĕ^{C}ôd$_1$ šĕlōšet$_2$ yāmîm$_3$ yiśśā$^{\supset}_4$ par^{C}ōh$_5$
             $^{\supset}$et-rō$^{\supset}$šĕkā$_6$ mē^{C}ālêkā$_7$.
             BU$_1$: wĕtālâ$_1$ $^{\supset}$ôtĕkā$_2$ ^{C}al$_3$-^{C}ēṣ$_4$.
             BU$_n$: wĕ$^{\supset}$ākal$_1$ hā$^{\supset}$ôp$_2$ $^{\supset}$et-bĕśārĕkā$_3$ mē^{C}ālêkā$_4$.»
40:20-23   **EPISODE$_3$ (FULFILLMENT):** **N** SEQUENCE ¶
40:20   **BU$_1$:** wayhî$_1$ bayyôm$_2$ haššĕlîšî$_3$ yôm$_4$ hulledet$_5$ $^{\supset}$et-par^{C}ōh$_6$
             wayya^{C}aś$_7$ mišteh$_8$ lĕkol$_9$ ^{C}ăbādāyw$_{10}$.
             BU$_2$: *wayyiśśā$^{\supset}_1$* $^{\supset}$et-rō$^{\supset}$š$_2$ śar$_3$ hammašqîm$_4$ wĕ$^{\supset}$et-rō$^{\supset}$š$_5$ śar$_6$
             hā$^{\supset}$ōpîm$_7$ bĕtôk$_8$ ^{C}ăbādāyw$_9$.
             BU$_3$: **N** ANTITHETICAL ¶
             THESIS: **N** SEQUENCE ¶
40:21   BU$_1$: *wayyāšeb$_1$* $^{\supset}$et-śar$_2$ hammašqîm$_3$ ^{C}al$_4$-mašqēhû$_5$.
             BU$_2$: *wayyitten$_1$* hakkôs$_2$ ^{C}al$_3$ kap$_4$ par^{C}ōh$_5$.
40:22   ANTI: wĕ$^{\supset}$et-śar$_1$ hā$^{\supset}$ōpîm$_2$ tālâ$_3$ ka$^{\supset}$ăšer$_4$ pātar$_5$ lāhem$_6$
             yôsēp$_7$.
             BU$_n$: **N** NEGATED ANTONYM PARAPHRASE ¶
40:23   PARA: wĕlō$^{\supset}_1$ zākar$_2$ śar$_3$-hammašqîm$_4$ $^{\supset}$et-yôsēp$_5$.
             TEXT: *wayyiškāḥēhû$_1$.*

40:16   *And-he-saw$_1$* the chief of$_2$ the bakers$_3$ that$_4$ good$_5$ (was) the interpretation$_6$.
And-he-said$_1$ to$_2$ Joseph$_3$:
«Also$_1$ I$_2$ in my dream$_3$: And behold$_4$ three$_5$ baskets of$_6$ white bread$_7$ (were) on$_8$ my head$_9$.

40:17   And in the top$_2$ basket$_1$ (were) from all$_3$ the food of$_4$ Pharaoh$_5$ the work of$_6$ a baker$_7$.
And the bird(s)$_1$ were eating$_2$ them$_3$ from$_4$ the basket$_5$ from off$_6$ my head$_7$.»

40:18   *And-he-answered$_1$* Joseph$_2$.
And-he-said$_1$:
«This$_1$ (is) the interpretation$_2$:
The three$_1$ baskets$_2$ three$_3$ days$_4$ (are) they$_5$.

40:19   In just$_1$ three$_2$ days$_3$ will-lift-up$_4$ Pharaoh$_5$ your head$_6$ from off you$_7$.
And-he-will-hang$_1$ you$_2$ on$_3$ a tree$_4$.
And-will-eat$_1$ the birds$_2$ your flesh$_3$ from off you$_4$.»

40:20   *And-it-happened-that$_1$* on the third$_3$ day$_2$ the day$_4$ that was born$_5$ Pharaoh$_6$
he-made$_7$ a feast$_8$ for all$_9$ his servants$_{10}$
And-he-lifted-up$_1$ the head of$_2$ the chief of$_3$ the cupbearers$_4$ and the head of$_5$ the chief of$_6$ the bakers$_7$ in the midst of$_8$ his servants$_9$.

40:21   *And-he-restored$_1$* the chief of$_2$ the cupbearers$_3$ to$_4$ his cup-bearer-ship$_5$.
And-he-gave$_1$ (again) the cup$_2$ into$_3$ the hand of$_4$ Pharaoh$_5$.

40:22   But the chief of$_1$ the bakers$_2$ he-hanged$_3$ just as$_4$ had interpreted$_5$ to them$_6$ Joseph$_7$.

40:23   And not$_1$ he-did-remember$_2$ the chief of$_3$ the cup-bearers$_4$ Joseph$_5$.
But-he-forgot-him$_1$.

41:1-57   **PEAK: N** DISC (Joseph's Rise to Power)
41:1-7   **STAGE (INCITING INCIDENT?): N** COORDINATE ¶
             ITEM₁: AWARENESS QUOTE ¶
41:1   AW Q F: wayhî₁ miqqēṣ₂ šĕnātayim₃ yāmîm₄ ûparᶜōh₅
             ḥōlēm₆.
             AW Q: AWARENESS QUOTE ¶
             AW Q F: wĕhinneh₁ ᶜōmēd₂ ᶜalₐ₃-hayᵓōr₄.
             AW Q: **N** SEQUENCE ¶
             BU₁: **N** SIMPLE ¶
41:2   SETTING: wĕhinnēh₁ min₂-hayᵓōr₃ ᶜōlôt₄ šebaᶜ₅
             pārôt₆ yĕpôt₇ marᵓeh₈ ûbĕrîᵓôt₉ bāśār₁₀.
             TEXT: wattirᶜênâ₁ bāᵓāḥû₂.
             BU₂: **N** SIMPLE ¶
41:3   SETTING: wĕhinnēh₁ šebaᶜ₂ pārôt₃ ᵓăḥērôt₄ ᶜōlôt₅
             ᵓaḥārêhen₆ min₇-hayᵓōr₈ rāᶜôt₉ marᵓeh₁₀
             wĕdaqqôt₁₁ bāśār₁₂.
             TEXT: wattaᶜămōdĕnâ₁ ᵓēṣel₂ happārôt₃ ᶜal₄-śĕpat₅
             hayᵓōr₆.
41:4   BUₙ (CLIMAX): wattōᵓkalnâ₁ happārôt₂ rāᶜôt₃
             hammarᵓeh₄ wĕdaqqôt₅ habbāśār₆ ᵓēt-šebaᶜ₇
             happārôt₈ yĕpôt₉ hammarᵓeh₁₀ wĕhabbĕrîᵓôt₁₁.
             END OF QUOTE: wayyîqaṣ₁ parᶜōh₂.
             ITEM₂: AWARENESS QUOTE ¶
41:5   LEAD-IN: wayyîšān₁
41:5   AW Q F: wayyaḥălōm₁ šēnît₂.
             AW Q: **N** SIMPLE ¶
             SETTING: COORDINATE ¶
             ITEM₁: wĕhinnēh₁ šebāᶜ₂ šibbŏlîm₃ ᶜōlôt₄ bĕqāneh₅
             ᵓeḥād₆ bĕrîᵓôt₇ wĕṭōbôt₈.
41:6   ITEM₂: wĕhinnēh₁ šebāᶜ₂ šibbŏlîm₃ daqqôt₄ ûšĕdûpôt₅
             qādîm₆ ṣōmĕḥôt₇ ᵓaḥārêhen₈.
41:7   TEXT: wattibla ᶜnâ₁ haššibbŏlîm₂ haddaqqôt₃ ᵓēt-šebaᶜ₄
             haššibbŏlîm₅ habbĕrîᵓôt₆ wĕhammĕlēᵓôt₇.
             END OF QUOTE: **N** COMMENT ¶
             TEXT: wayyîqaṣ₁ parᶜōh₂.
             COMMENT: wĕhinnēh₁ ḥălôm₂.

41:1   And-it-happened$_1$ at the end of$_2$ two full years$_{3-4}$ now Pharaoh$_5$ was dreaming$_6$.

             And behold$_1$ (he) was standing$_2$ above$_3$ the river$_4$.

41:2   And behold$_1$ from$_2$ the river$_3$ were coming up$_4$ seven$_5$ cows$_6$ beautiful of$_7$ form$_8$ and well-filled-out$_9$ (in) flesh$_{10}$.

             And-they-grazed$_1$ among the reeds$_2$.

41:3   And-behold$_1$ seven$_2$ other$_4$ cattle$_3$ were coming up$_5$ after them$_6$ from$_7$ the river$_8$ bad$_9$ looking$_{10}$ and wasted of$_{11}$ flesh$_{12}$.

             And-they-took-their-stand$_1$ beside$_2$ the cows$_3$ on$_4$ the bank of$_5$ the river$_6$.

41:4   *And-they-ate-up$_1$* the bad$_3$ looking$_4$ and wasted of$_5$ flesh$_6$ cows$_2$ the seven$_7$ fair of$_9$ form$_{10}$ fleshed out$_{11}$ cows$_8$.

             And-he-woke-up$_1$ Pharoah$_2$.

41:5   *And-he-went-to-sleep$_1$*.

             And-he-dreamed$_1$ a second time$_2$.

             And-behold$_1$ seven$_2$ ears of grain$_3$ springing up$_4$ on one$_6$ stalk$_5$, full$_7$ and good$_8$.

41:6   And behold$_1$ seven$_2$ ears$_3$ bedraggled$_4$ and smitten$_5$ (by) the east (wind)$_6$ were sprouting$_7$ after them$_8$.

41:7   *And-they-swallowed$_1$* the bedraggled$_3$ ears$_2$ the seven$_4$ full$_6$ and rounded-out$_7$ ears$_5$.

             And-he-awoke$_1$ Pharaoh$_2$.

             And behold$_1$ (it was) a dream$_2$.

1 2 3 4 5 6 7 8 9

41:8-13 **EPISODE$_1$: N** SEQUENCE ¶

41:8 **BU$_1$ (or SETTING?):** *wayhî$_1$ babbōqer$_2$ wattippāᶜem$_3$ rûḥô$_4$.*

BU$_2$: N AMPLIFICATION ¶

TEXT: *wayyišlaḥ$_1$.*

AMPL: *wayyiqrā⁾$_1$ ⁾et-kol$_2$-ḥarṭummê$_3$ miṣrayim$_4$ wĕ⁾et-kol$_5$-ḥăkāmêhā$_6$.*

BU$_3$: N ANTITHETICAL ¶ (EXPECTANCY REVERSAL)

THESIS: *waysappēr$_1$ parᶜōh$_2$ lāhem$_3$ ⁾et-ḥălōmô$_4$.*

ANTI: *wĕ⁾ên$_1$ pôtēr$_2$ ⁾ôtām$_3$ lĕparᶜōh$_4$.*

41:9 **BU$_n$:** *waydabbēr$_1$ śar$_2$ hammašqîm$_3$ ⁾et-parᶜōh$_4$ lē⁾mōr$_5$:*

QUOTE=**N** SEQUENCE ¶/**N** DISC

APERTURE: «*⁾et-ḥăṭā⁾ay$_1$ ⁾ănî$_2$ mazkîr$_3$ hayyôm$_4$.*

41:10 SETTING: *parᶜōh$_1$ qāṣap$_2$ ᶜal$_3$ ⁾ăbādāyw$_4$.*

BU$_1$: *wayyittēn$_1$ ⁾ōtî$_2$ bĕmišmar$_3$ bêt$_4$ śar$_5$ haṭṭabbāḥîm$_6$ ⁾ōtî$_7$ wĕ⁾ēt śar$_8$ hā⁾ōpîm$_9$.*

41:11 BU$_2$: *wannaḥalmâ$_1$ ḥălōm$_2$ bĕlaylâ$_3$ ⁾eḥād$_4$ ⁾ănî$_5$ wāhû⁾$_6$* (pausal) *⁾îš$_7$ kĕpitrôn$_8$ ḥălōmô$_9$ ḥālāmnû$_{10}$.*

BU$_n$: **N** SEQUENCE ¶

41:12 SETTING: *wĕšām$_1$ ⁾ittānû$_2$ naᶜar$_3$ ᶜibrî$_4$ ᶜebed$_5$ lĕśar$_6$ haṭṭabbāḥîm$_7$.*

BU$_1$: *wannĕsappēr$_1$-lô$_2$*

BU$_n$: *wayyiptār$_1$ -lānû$_2$ ⁾et-ḥălōmōtênû$_3$ ⁾îš$_4$ kaḥălōmô$_5$ pātār$_6$.*

41:13 TERMINUS/CLOSURE OF DISC: *wayhî$_1$ ka⁾ăšer$_2$ pātar$_3$-lānû$_4$ kēn$_5$ hāyâ$_6$:* [¶ BACKLOOPS WITHIN THIS SENTENCE; **N** ANTITHETICAL ¶]

THESIS: *⁾ōtî$_1$ hēšîb$_2$ ᶜal-kannî$_3$.*

ANTI: *wĕ⁾ōtô$_1$ tālâ$_2$.»*

1 2 3 4 5 6 7 8 9

41:8 And-it-happened-that$_1$ in the morning$_2$ *and-was-troubled$_3$* his spirit$_4$.
And-he-sent$_1$.
And-he-called$_1$ all$_2$ the magicians of$_3$ Egypt$_4$ and all$_5$ her wisemen$_6$.
And-he-told$_1$ Pharaoh$_2$ to them$_3$ his dream$_4$.
And (there was) no$_1$ interpreter$_2$ of them$_3$ to Pharaoh$_4$.

41:9 *And-he-said$_1$* the chief of$_2$ the cupbearers$_3$ to Pharaoh$_4$ saying$_5$: «My sins$_1$ I$_2$ am remembering$_3$ today$_4$.

41:10 Pharaoh$_1$ was angry$_2$ at$_3$ his servants$_4$.
And-he-put$_1$ me$_2$ in custody$_3$ (in) the house of$_4$ the captain$_5$ of the guard$_6$, me$_7$ and the chief of$_8$ the bakers$_9$.

41:11 *And-we-dreamed$_1$* dream(s)$_2$ in the same$_4$ night$_3$, I$_5$ and he$_6$; (each) man$_7$ according to the interpretation$_8$ of his dream$_9$ we dreamed$_{10}$.

41:12 And (there was) there$_1$ with us$_2$ a Hebrew$_4$ lad$_3$, a slave of$_5$ the captain of$_6$ the guard$_7$.
And-we-told$_1$ him$_2$ (our dreams).
And-he-interpreted$_1$ to us$_2$ our dreams$_3$; (each) man$_4$ according to his dream$_5$ he-interpreted$_6$.

41:13 And-it-happened$_1$ just as$_2$ he-interpreted$_3$ to us$_4$ so$_5$ it-was$_6$: Me$_1$ he-restored$_2$ to my place$_3$.
And him$_1$ he-hanged$_2$.»

244

41:14-45   **PEAK:** COMPOUND DIALOGUE ¶ (Joseph before Pharaoh)
            LEAD-IN: N SEQUENCE ¶
               BU$_1$: N AMPLIFICATION ¶
41:14   TEXT: *wayyišlaḥ$_1$* par^{c}ōh$_2$.
                  AMPL: *wayyiqrāʾ$_1$* ʾet-yôsēp$_2$.
               BU$_2$: *wayrîṣuhû$_1$* min-habbôr$_2$.
               BU$_3$: *waygallaḥ$_1$*.
               BU$_4$: *wayḥallēp$_1$* śimlōtāyw$_2$.
               BU$_n$: *wayyābōʾ$_1$* ʾel-par^{c}ōh$_2$.
41:15-16   **EXCHANGE$_1$:** SIMPLE RESOLVED DIALOGUE ¶
41:15   IU (PROP): *wayyōʾmer$_1$* par^{c}ōh$_2$ ʾel-yôsēp$_3$: QUOTE=N
                ANTITHETICAL ¶
                  THESIS: N or ANTITHETICAL ¶
                    THESIS: «ḥalôm$_1$ ḥālamtî$_2$.
                    ANTI: ûpōtēr$_1$ ʾên$_2$ ʾōtô$_3$.
                    ANTI: waʾănî$_1$ šāma^{c}tî$_2$ ^{c}ālêkā$_3$ lēʾmōr$_4$ ''tišma$^c_5$ ḥălôm$_6$
                    liptōr$_7$ ʾōtô$_8$.''»
41:16   RU (RES): *wayya^{c}an$_1$* yôsēp$_2$ ʾet-par^{c}ōh$_3$ lēʾmōr$_4$:
                QUOTE=P NEGATED ANTONYM PARAPHRASE ¶
                  PARA: «bilādāy$_1$.
                  TEXT: ʾĕlōhîm$_1$ ya^{c}ăneh$_2$ ʾet-sĕlôm$_3$ par^{c}ōh$_4$.»

41:14   *And-he-sent₁* Pharaoh₂.
             And-he-called₁ Joseph₂.
             And-they-hurried-him₁ from the dungeon₂.
             And-he-shaved₁.
             And-he-changed₁ his clothing₂.
             And-he-came-in₁ unto Pharaoh₂.
41:15   *And-he-said₁* Pharaoh₂ to Joseph₃:
             «A dream₁ I-have-dreamed₂.
             And no one₂ interpreting₁ it₃.
             And I₁ have-heard₂ concerning you₃ saying₄, "You-hear₅ a dream₆
             to interpret₇ it₈."»
41:16   *And-he-answered₁* Joseph₂ Pharaoh₃ saying₄.
             «It's not me₁.
             God₁ will-answer₂ the welfare of₃ Pharaoh₄.»

41:17-36   **EXCHANGE$_2$:** COMPLEX UNRESOLVED DIALOGUE ¶
41:17   IU (REM): *waydabbēr$_1$* par^{c}ōh$_2$ $^{\ni}$el-yôsēp$_3$:
              QUOTE=**N** COORDINATE ¶
              ITEM$_1$: AWARENESS QUOTE ¶
              AW Q F: «baḥălōmî$_1$ hinĕnî$_2$ ^{c}ōmēd$_3$ ^{c}al-śĕpat$_4$
              hay^{c}ōr$_5$.
              AW Q: **N** SEQUENCE ¶
              BU$_1$: **N** SIMPLE ¶
41:18   SETTING: wĕhinnēh$_1$ min-hay$^{\ni}$ōr$_2$ ^{c}ōlōt$_3$ šeba$^c{}_4$
                   pārōt$_5$ bĕrî$^{\ni}$ōt$_6$ bāśār$_7$ wîpōt$_8$ tō$^{\ni}$ar$_9$.
                   TEXT: *wattir^{c}ênâ$_1$* bā$^{\ni}$āḥû$_2$.
              BU$_2$: **N** SIMPLE ¶
41:19   SETTING: **E** COMMENT ¶
                   TEXT: wĕhinnēh$_1$ šeba$^c{}_2$ pārōt$_3$ $^{\ni}$āḥērôt$_4$ ^{c}ōlōt$_5$
                   $^{\ni}$aḥărêhen$_6$ dallôt$_7$ wĕrā^{c}ōt$_8$ tō$^{\ni}$ar$_9$ mĕ$^{\ni}$ōd$_{10}$
                   wĕraqqôt$_{11}$ bāśār$_{12}$.
                   COMMENT: lō$^{\ni}{}_1$ rā$^{\ni}$îtî$_2$ kāhēnnâ$_3$ bĕkol$_4$-$^{\ni}$ereṣ$_5$
                   miṣrayim$_6$ lārōa$^c{}_7$.
41:20   TEXT: *wattō$^{\ni}$kālnâ$_1$* happārōt$_2$ hāraqqôt$_3$
                   wĕhārā^{c}ōt$_4$ $^{\ni}$ēt-šeba$^c{}_5$ happārôt$_6$ hāri$^{\ni}$šōnôt$_7$
                   habbĕrî$^{\ni}$ōt$_8$.
              BU$_n$: **N** COMMENT ¶
41:21   TEXT: *wattābō$^{\ni}$nâ$_1$* $^{\ni}$el-qirbenâ$_2$.
                   COMMENT: **E** NEGATED ANTONYM
                   PARAPHRASE (?) ¶
                   PARA: wĕlō$^{\ni}{}_1$ nôda$^c{}_2$ kî$_3$-bā$^{\ni}$û$_4$ $^{\ni}$el-qirbenâ$_5$.
                   TEXT: ûmar$^{\ni}$êhen$_1$ ra$^c{}_2$ ka$^{\ni}$ăšer$_3$ battĕḥillâ$_4$.
              END OF (AW) QUOTE: *wā$^{\ni}$îqāṣ$_1$*.
              ITEM$_2$: AWARENESS QUOTE ¶
41:22   AW Q F: *wā$^{\ni}$ēre$^{\ni}{}_1$* baḥălōmî$_2$
              AW Q: **N** SIMPLE ¶
              SETTING: **E** COORDINATE ¶
              ITEM$_1$: wĕhinnēh$_1$ šeba$^c{}_2$ šibbŏlîm$_3$ ^{c}ōlōt$_4$
              bĕqāneh$_5$ $^{\ni}$eḥād$_6$ mĕlē$^{\ni}$ōt$_7$ wĕṭōbôt$_8$.
41:23   ITEM$_2$: wĕhinnēh$_1$ šeba$^c{}_2$ šibbŏlîm$_3$ ṣĕnumôt$_4$
              daqqôt$_5$ šĕdupôt$_6$ qādîm$_7$ ṣōmĕḥôt$_8$ $^{\ni}$aḥărêhem$_9$.
41:24   TEXT: *wattibla^{c}nā$_1$* haššibbŏlîm$_2$ haddaqqōt$_3$ $^{\ni}$ēt-
              šeba$^c{}_4$ haššibbŏlîm$_5$ haṭṭōbôt$_6$.
              CORRELATE (or COMMENT?): **N**
              ANTITHETICAL ¶
              THESIS: *wā$^{\ni}$ōmar$_1$* $^{\ni}$el-haḥarṭummîm$_2$.
              ANTI: wĕ$^{\ni}$ên$_1$ maggîd$_2$ lî$_3$.»

41:17   *And-he-said₁* Pharaoh₂ to Joseph₃:
«In my dream₁ behold₂ (I) was standing₃ on the bank of₄ the river₅.

41:18   And behold₁ from the river₂ were coming up₃ seven₄ cows₅ plump₆ (of) flesh₇ and beautiful₈ (in) appearance₉.
And-they-grazed₁ among the rushes₂.

41:19   And behold₁ seven₂ other₄ cows₃ were coming up₅ after them₆ wasted₇ and very₁₀ bad₈ looking₉ and lean₁₁ (in) flesh₁₂.
Not₁ I-have-seen₂ their like₃ in all₄ the land of₅ Egypt₆ for ugliness₇.

41:20   *And-they-ate-up₁* the lean₃ and bad₄ cows₂ the seven₅ fat₈ cows₆ (who were there) first₇.

41:21   *And-they-entered₁* into their stomachs₂.
And not₁ it-did-look-like₂ that₃ they-had-entered₄ into their stomachs₅.
And their appearance₁ was as bad₂ as₃ in the beginning₄.
And-I-awoke₁.

41:22   *And-I-saw₁* in my dream₂.
And behold₁ seven₂ ears of grain₃ were springing up₄ on one₆ stalk₅— full₇ and good (ears)₈.

41:23   And behold₁ seven₂ ears₃ withered₄ lean₅ and blasted₆ (by) the east (wind)₇ were sprouting up₈ after them₉.

41:24   *And-they-swallowed-up₁* the lean₃ ears₂ the seven₄ good₆ ears₅.
And-I-spoke₁ to the magicians₂.
And none (of them)₁ was declaring₂ (it) to me₃.»

41:25-36;41:25 CU (EVAL/PROP): *wayyō⊃mer$_1$* yôsēp$_2$ ⊃el$_3$ par⊂ōh$_4$: QUOTE =(COVERT?) HORTATORY DISCOURSE

41:25-28 POINT$_1$ ***E*:*E*** COORDINATE ¶

ITEM$_1$: ***E*** EVIDENCE ¶ (CYCLIC)

TEXT: ***E*** COMMENT¶

41:25 TEXT: «ḥălôm$_1$ par⊂ōh$_2$ ⊃eḥād$_3$ hû⊃$_4$.

COMMENT: ⊃ēt ⊃ăšer$_1$ hā⊃ĕlōhîm$_2$ ⊂ōśeh$_3$ higgîd$_4$ lĕpar⊂ōh$_5$.

41:26 EVIDENCE$_1$: šeba⊂$_1$ pārōt$_2$ haṭṭōbōt$_3$ šeba⊂$_4$ šānîm$_5$ hēnnâ$_6$.

EVIDENCE$_2$: wĕšeba⊂$_1$ haššibbŏlîm$_2$ haṭṭōbōt$_3$ šeba⊂$_4$ šānîm$_5$ hennâ$_6$.

TEXT′: ḥălôm$_1$ ⊃eḥād$_2$ hû⊃$_3$.

ITEM$_2$: ***P*** EVIDENCE ¶ (or INDUCTIVE ¶)

41:27 EVIDENCE$_1$: wĕšeba⊂$_1$ happārôt$_2$ hāraqqôt$_3$ wĕhārā⊂ōt$_4$ hā⊂ōlōt$_5$ ⊃aḥărêhen$_6$ šeba⊂$_7$ šānîm$_8$ hēnnâ$_9$.

EVIDENCE$_2$: wĕšeba⊂$_1$ haššibbŏlîm$_2$ hārēqôt$_3$ šĕdupôt$_4$ haqqādîm$_5$.

TEXT/CONCLUSION: ***P*** COMMENT ¶

TEXT: yihyû$_1$ šeba⊂$_2$ šĕnê$_3$ rā⊂āb$_4$.

41:28 COMMENT$_1$: hû⊃$_1$ haddābār$_2$ ⊃ăšer$_3$ dibbartî$_4$ ⊃el-par⊂ōh$_5$.

COMMENT$_2$: ⊃ăšer$_1$ hā⊃ĕlōhîm$_2$ ⊂ōśeh$_3$ her⊃â$_4$ ⊃et-par⊂ōh$_5$.

41:29-32 POINT$_2$ ***P*:*P*** SEQUENCE ¶

SETTING: ***P*** AMPLIFICATION ¶

41:29 TEXT: hinnēh$_1$ šeba⊂$_2$ šānîm$_3$ bā⊃ôt$_4$.

AMPL: śābā⊂$_1$ gādôl$_2$ bĕkol$_3$-⊃ereṣ$_4$ miṣrāyim$_5$.

41:30 BU$_1$: wĕqāmû$_1$ šeba⊂$_2$ šĕnê$_3$ rā⊂āb$_4$ ⊃aḥărêhen$_5$.

BU$_2$: wĕniškaḥ$_1$ kol$_2$-haśśābā⊂$_3$ bĕ⊃ereṣ$_4$ miṣrāyim$_5$.

BU$_n$: ***P*** COMMENT ¶

TEXT: wĕkillâ$_1$ hārā⊂āb$_2$ ⊃et-hā⊃āreṣ$_3$.

41:31 COMMENT: wĕlō⊃$_1$-yiwwāda⊂$_2$ haśśābā⊂$_3$ bā⊃āreṣ$_4$ mippĕnê$_5$ hārā⊂āb$_6$ hahû⊃$_7$ ⊃aḥărê$_8$-kēn$_9$ kî$_{10}$-kābēd$_{11}$ hû⊃$_{12}$ mĕ⊃ōd$_{13}$.

41:32 TERMINUS: wĕ⊂al$_1$ hiššānôt$_2$ haḥălôm$_3$ ⊃el-par⊂ōh$_4$ pa⊂ămāyim$_5$, (COMPLEMENT BACKLOOPS AN ***E*** AMPLIFICATION ¶)

TEXT: kî$_6$-nākôn$_7$ haddābār$_8$ mē⊂im$_9$ hā⊃ĕlōhîm$_{10}$.

AMPL: ûmĕmahēr$_{11}$ hā⊃ĕlōhîm$_{12}$ la⊂ăśōtô$_{13}$.

41:25   *And-he-said$_1$* Joseph$_2$ to Pharaoh$_3$:

«The dream of$_1$ Pharaoh$_2$ one$_3$ (is) it$_4$.

That which$_1$ God$_2$ is-about-to-do$_3$ he-has-declared$_4$ to Pharaoh$_5$.

41:26   The seven$_1$ good$_3$ cows$_2$ seven$_4$ years$_5$ (are) they$_6$.

And the seven$_1$ good$_3$ ears$_2$, seven$_4$ years$_5$ (are) they$_6$.

The dream$_1$, one$_2$ (is) it$_3$.

41:27   And the seven $_1$ thin$_3$ and bad$_4$ cows$_2$ coming up$_5$ after them$_6$ seven$_7$ years$_8$ (are) they$_9$

—(As are also) the seven$_1$ ears$_2$ empty$_3$ and blasted$_4$ (by) the east (wind)$_5$.

There-will-be$_1$ seven$_2$ years of$_3$ famine$_4$.

41:28   This$_1$ (is) the word$_2$ which$_3$ I've spoken$_4$ to Pharaoh$_5$.

That which$_1$ God$_2$ is about to do$_3$ he-has-shown$_4$ to Pharaoh$_5$.

41:29   Behold$_1$ seven$_2$ years$_3$ are coming$_4$.

(There will be) great$_2$ plenty$_1$ in all$_3$ the land$_4$ of Egypt$_5$.

41:30   Then-will-come$_1$ seven$_2$ years of$_3$ famine$_4$ after them$_5$.

And-will-be-forgotten$_1$ all$_2$ the abundance$_3$ in the land$_4$ of Egypt$_5$.

And-will-ravage$_1$ the famine$_2$ the land$_3$.

41:31   And not$_1$ it-will-be-remembered$_2$ the abundance$_3$ in the land$_4$ in the face of$_5$ the famine$_6$ the one$_7$ (which is) after$_8$ that$_9$ for$_{10}$ heavy$_{11}$ indeed$_{13}$ (will be) it$_{12}$.

41:32   And as for$_1$ two$_2$ times$_5$ the dream$_3$ (came) to Pharaoh$_4$ (that signifies) that$_6$ reliable$_7$ (is) the word$_8$ from$_9$ God$_{10}$.

And God$_{12}$ is-hurrying$_{11}$ to-do it$_{13}$.

1 2 3 4 5 6 7 8 9

41:33-36   POINT$_3$ **H** : **H** COORDINATE ¶
                  ITEM$_1$: **H** SEQUENCE ¶
41:33   BU$_1$: wĕ^{c}attâ$_1$ yēre$^{\backprime}_2$ par^{c}ōh$_3$ $^{\backprime}$îš$_4$ nābôn$_5$ wĕḥākām$_6$.
                      BU$_n$: wîšîtēhû$_1$ ^{c}al$_2$-$^{\backprime}$ereṣ$_3$ miṣrāyim$_4$.
                  ITEM$_2$: **H** RESULT ¶
                    TEXT: **H** AMPLIFICATION ¶
41:34   TEXT: ya^{c}áśeh$_1$ par^{c}ōh$_2$.
                      AMPL: wĕyapqēd$_1$ pĕqidîm$_2$ ^{c}al$_3$-hā$^{\backprime}$āreṣ$_4$.
                      RESULT: wĕḥimmēš$_1$ $^{\backprime}$et-$^{\backprime}$ereṣ$_2$ miṣrāyim$_3$ bĕšeba$^c_4$
                      šĕnê$_5$ haśśābā$^c_6$.
41:35   ITEM$_3$: wĕyiqbĕṣû$_1$ $^{\backprime}$et-kol$_2$-$^{\backprime}$ōkel$_3$ haššānîm$_4$ haṭṭōbōt$_5$
                  habbā$^{\backprime}$ôt$_6$ hā$^{\backprime}$ēlleh$_7$.
                  ITEM$_4$: **H** RESULT ¶
                      TEXT: wĕyiṣbĕrû$_1$-bār$_2$ taḥat$_3$ yad$_4$-par^{c}ōh$_5$ $^{\backprime}$ōkel$_6$
                      be^{c}ārîm$_7$.
                      RESULT: wĕsāmārû$_1$.
                  CONCLUSION: **P** RESULT ¶
41:36   TEXT: wĕhāyâ$_1$ hā$^{\backprime}$ōkel$_2$ lĕpiqqādôn$_3$ lā$^{\backprime}$āreṣ$_4$ lĕšeba$^c_5$
                      šĕnê$_6$ hārā^{c}āb$_7$ $^{\backprime}$ăšer$_8$ tihyênā$_9$ bĕ$^{\backprime}$ereṣ$_{10}$ miṣrāyim$_{11}$.
                      RESULT: wĕlō$^{\backprime}_1$-tikkārēt$_2$ hā$^{\backprime}$āreṣ$_3$ bārā^{c}āb$_4$.»
41:37-45 **STEP-DOWN: N** SEQUENCE ¶ (The Installation)
              SETTING: **N** SIMPLE ¶
41:37   SETTING: *wayyîṭab$_1$* haddābār$_2$ bĕ^{c}ênê$_3$ par^{c}ōh$_4$
                  ûbĕ^{c}ênê$_5$ kol$_6$ ^{c}ăbādāyw$_7$.
41:38   TEXT: *wayyō$^{\backprime}$mer$_1$* par^{c}ōh$_2$ $^{\backprime}$el$_3$-^{c}ăbādāyw$_4$: «hănimṣā$^{\backprime}_5$
                  kāzeh$_6$ $^{\backprime}$îš$_7$ $^{\backprime}$ăšer$_8$ rûaḥ$_9$ $^{\backprime}$ĕlōhîm$_{10}$ bô$_{11}$.»
41:39   BU$_1$: *wayyō$^{\backprime}$mer$_1$* par^{c}ōh$_2$ $^{\backprime}$el$_3$-yôsēp$_4$ QUOTE=**P**
              REASON ¶
                  REASON: «$^{\backprime}$aḥărê$_1$ hôdîa$^c_2$ $^{\backprime}$ĕlōhîm$_3$ $^{\backprime}$ôtĕkā$_4$ $^{\backprime}$et-kol-
                  zō$^{\backprime}$t$_5$ $^{\backprime}$ên$_6$ nābôn$_7$ wĕḥākām$_8$ kāmôkā$_9$.
                  TEXT: **P** ANTITHETICAL ¶
                  (CONTRAST:EXCEPTION)
                  THESIS: **P** COORDINATE ¶
41:40   ITEM$_1$: $^{\backprime}$attâ$_1$ tihyeh$_2$ ^{c}al$_3$-bêtî$_4$.
                      ITEM$_2$: wĕ^{c}al$_1$-pîkā$_2$ yiššaq$_3$ kol$_4$-^{c}ammî$_5$.
                      ANTI: raq$_1$ hakissē$^{\backprime}_2$ $^{\backprime}$egdal$_3$ mimmekā$_4$.»
41:41   BU$_2$: *wayyō$^{\backprime}$mer$_1$* par^{c}ōh$_2$ $^{\backprime}$el-yôsēp$_3$: «rĕ$^{\backprime}$ēh$_4$ nātattî$_5$
                  $^{\backprime}$ōtĕkā$_6$ ^{c}al$_7$ kol$_8$-$^{\backprime}$ereṣ$_9$ miṣrāyim$_{10}$.»

1 2 3 4 5 6 7 8 9

41:33   And now$_1$ let-him-look$_2$ Pharaoh$_3$ (for) a man$_4$ (who is) discerning$_5$ and wise$_6$.

And let-him-set-him$_1$ over$_2$ the land of$_3$ Egypt$_4$.

41:34   Let Pharaoh$_2$ act (vigorously)$_1$.

And-let-him-appoint$_1$ overseers$_2$ over$_3$ the land$_4$,

so that he will fifth$_1$ the land of$_2$ Egypt$_3$ during the seven$_4$ years of$_5$ plenty$_6$.

41:35   And-let-them-gather$_1$ all sorts of$_2$ food of$_3$ these$_7$ good$_5$ years$_4$ that are coming$_6$.

And-let-them heap-up$_1$ grain$_2$ under$_3$ the hand of$_4$ Pharaoh$_5$ food$_6$ in the cities$_7$,

so-that-they-can-guard-(it)$_1$.

41:36   And-it-will-be$_1$ the food$_2$ a reserve$_3$ for the land$_4$ for the seven$_5$ years of$_6$ famine$_7$ which$_8$ will-be$_9$ in the land of$_{10}$ Egypt$_{11}$,

lest$_1$ it-be-destroyed$_2$ the land$_3$ by the famine$_4$.»

41:37   *And-it-seemed-good$_1$* the word$_2$ in the eyes of$_3$ Pharaoh$_4$ and in the eyes of$_5$ all$_6$ his courtiers$_7$.

41:38   *And-he-said$_1$* Pharaoh$_2$ to$_3$ his courtiers$_4$: «Shall-we-find$_5$ a man$_7$ such as this$_6$ whom$_8$ the spirit of$_9$ the gods$_{10}$ (is) in him$_{11}$?»

41:39   *And-he-said$_1$* Pharaoh$_2$ to$_3$ Joseph$_4$:

«In asmuchas$_1$ God$_3$ has-caused-to-know$_2$ you$_4$ all this$_5$ (there is) no one$_6$ as discerning$_7$ and wise$_8$ as you$_9$.

41:40   You$_1$ shall-be$_2$ over$_3$ my house$_4$.

And of$_1$ your word (mouth)$_2$ shall-be organized$_3$ all$_4$ my people$_5$.

Only$_1$ (in respect to) the throne$_2$ I-will-be-greater$_3$ than you$_4$.»

41:41   *And-he-said$_1$* Pharaoh$_2$ to Joseph$_3$: «Look$_4$! I-have-set$_5$ you$_6$ over$_7$ all$_8$ the land of$_9$ Egypt$_{10}$.»

252

1 2 3 4 5 6 7 8 9

BU$_3$: **N** SEQUENCE ¶

41:42 BU$_1$: *wayyāsar*$_1$ par^{c}ōh$_2$ ^{ʾ}et-ṭabba^{c}tô$_3$ mē^{c}al$_4$ yādô$_5$.
BU$_n$: *wayyittēn*$_1$ ^{ʾ}ōtāh$_2$ (3fs) ^{c}al$_3$-yad$_4$ yōsêp$_5$.
BU$_4$: *wayyalbēš*$_1$ ^{ʾ}ōtô$_2$ bigdê$_3$-šēš$_4$.
BU$_5$: *wayyāśem*$_1$ rĕbid$_2$ hazzāhāb$_3$ ^{c}al$_4$-ṣawwā^{ʾ}rô$_5$.
BU$_6$: **N** RESULT ¶

TEXT: **N** SEQUENCE ¶

41:43 BU$_1$: *wayyarkēb*$_1$ ^{ʾ}ōtô$_2$ bĕmirkebet$_3$ hammišneh$_4$ ^{ʾ}ăšer-lô$_5$.
BU$_n$: *wayyiqrĕ^{ʾ}û*$_1$ lĕpānāyw$_2$ «^{ʾ}abrēk$_3$.»
RESULT: wĕnātôn$_1$ ^{ʾ}ōtô$_2$ ^{c}al$_3$ kol$_4$-^{ʾ}ereṣ$_5$ miṣrāyim$_6$.

41:44 BU$_7$: *wayyō^{ʾ}mer*$_1$ par^{c}ōh$_2$ ^{ʾ}el$_3$-yôsēp$_4$: QUOTE=**P**
REASON ¶
REASON: «^{ʾ}ănî$_1$ par^{c}ōh$_2$.
TEXT: ûbil^{c}ādêkā$_1$ lô^ʾ$_2$-yārîm$_3$ ^{ʾ}îš$_4$ ^{ʾ}et-yādô$_5$ wĕ^{ʾ}et$_6$ raglô$_7$ bĕkol$_8$ ^{ʾ}ereṣ$_9$ miṣrāyim$_{10}$.»

41:45 BU$_8$: *wayyiqrā^ʾ*$_1$ par^{c}ōh$_2$ šem$_3$-yôsēp$_4$ 'ṣāpĕnat pa^{c}nēaḥ$_5$.'
BU$_9$: *wayyitten*$_1$-lô$_2$ ^{ʾ}et-^{ʾ}asĕnat$_3$ bat$_4$-pôṭî pera^c$_5$ kōhēn$_6$ ^{ʾ}ōn$_7$ lĕ^{ʾ}iššâ$_8$.
BU$_n$: *wayyēṣē^ʾ*$_1$ yôsēp$_2$ ^{c}al$_3$-^{ʾ}ereṣ$_4$ miṣrāyim$_5$.

41:46-49 **POST-PEAK EPISODE$_1$: N** SEQUENCE ¶

41:46 **SETTING:** wĕyôsēp$_1$ ben$_2$ šĕlōšîm$_3$ šānâ$_4$ bĕ^{c}āmĕdô$_5$ lipnê$_6$ par^{c}ōh$_7$ melek$_8$-miṣrāyim$_9$.
BU$_1$: *wayyēṣē^ʾ*$_1$ yôsēp$_2$ millipnê$_3$ par^{c}ōh$_4$.
BU$_2$: *wayya^{c}bōr*$_1$ bĕkol$_2$-^{ʾ}ereṣ$_3$ miṣrāyim$_4$.

41:47 **BU$_3$:** *watta^{c}aś*$_1$ hā^{ʾ}āreṣ$_2$ bĕšeba^c$_3$ šĕnê$_4$ haśśābā^c$_5$ liqmāṣîm$_6$.

41:48 **BU$_4$:** *wayyiqbōṣ*$_1$ ^{ʾ}et-kol$_2$-^{ʾ}ōkel$_3$ šeba^c$_4$ šānîm$_5$ ^{ʾ}ăšer$_6$ hāyû$_7$ bĕ^{ʾ}ereṣ$_8$ miṣrayim$_9$.
BU$_5$: *wayyitten*$_1$-^{ʾ}ōkel$_2$ be^{c}ārîm$_3$ (^{ʾ}athnaḥ) ^{ʾ}ōkel$_4$ śĕdēh$_5$-hā^{c}îr$_6$ ^{ʾ}ăšer$_7$ sĕbîbōtêhā$_8$ nātan$_9$ bĕtôkāh (3fs)$_{10}$.

41:49 **BU$_n$:** *wayyiṣbōr*$_1$ yôsēp$_2$ bār$_3$ kĕḥôl$_4$ hayyām$_5$ harbēh$_6$ mĕ^{ʾ}ōd$_7$ ^{c}ad$_8$ kî$_9$ ḥādal$_{10}$ lispōr$_{11}$ kî$_{12}$ ^{ʾ}ēn$_{13}$ mispār$_{14}$.

1 2 3 4 5 6 7 8 9

41:42   *And-he-took-off$_1$* Pharaoh$_2$ his signet ring$_3$ from$_4$ his hand$_5$.

And-he-put$_1$ it$_2$ on$_3$ the hand of$_4$ Joseph$_5$.

And-he-arrayed$_1$ him$_2$ in linen$_4$ clothing$_3$.

And-he-put$_1$ a chain$_2$ of gold$_3$ around$_4$ his neck$_5$.

41:43   *And-he-caused-to-ride$_1$* him$_2$ in his$_5$ second$_4$ chariot$_3$.

And-they-cried$_1$ before him$_2$ «Bow down/Make way$_3$!»

Thus-he-set$_1$ him$_2$ over$_3$ all$_4$ the land of$_5$ Egypt$_6$.

41:44   *And-he-said$_1$* Pharaoh$_2$ to$_3$ Joseph$_4$:

«I$_1$ (am) Pharaoh$_2$.

And without you$_1$ not$_2$ will stir$_3$ (any) man$_4$ his hand$_5$ or$_6$ his foot$_7$ in all$_8$ the land of$_9$ Egypt$_{10}$.»

41:45   *And-he-called$_1$* Pharoah$_2$ the name of$_3$ Joseph$_4$ 'Zaphenath-Paaneah.'

And-he gave$_1$ to him$_2$ Asenath$_3$ the daughter of$_4$ Potiphera$_5$, priest of$_6$ On$_7$ as a wife$_8$.

So-he-went-out$_1$ Joseph$_2$ [lord] over$_3$ the land of$_4$ Egypt$_5$.

41:46   And Joseph$_1$ (was) thirty years' old$_{2-4}$ in his standing$_5$ before$_6$ Pharaoh$_7$ King of$_8$ Egypt$_9$.

And-he-went-out$_1$ Joseph$_2$ from before$_3$ Pharaoh$_4$.

And-he-passed-through$_1$ all$_2$ the land of$_3$ Egypt$_4$.

41:47   *And-it-produced$_1$* the land$_2$ in the seven$_3$ years of$_4$ plenty$_5$ by fistfuls$_6$.

41:48   *And-he-gathered$_1$* all$_2$ the food of$_3$ the seven$_4$ years$_5$ which$_6$ were$_7$ in the land of$_8$ Egypt$_9$.

And-he-stored$_1$ the food$_2$ in the cities$_3$; the food$_4$ of the field of$_5$ the city$_6$, which$_7$ surrounded$_8$ he-stored$_9$ in its midst$_{10}$.

41:49   *And-he-heaped-up$_1$* Joseph$_2$ grain$_3$ like the sands of$_4$ the sea$_5$ is numerous$_6$ exceedingly$_7$ until$_8$ that$_9$ he-ceased$_{10}$ to keep record$_{11}$ for$_{12}$ not$_{13}$ (was) its number$_{14}$.

41:50-54a   **POST-PEAK EPISODE$_2$: N** ANTITHETICAL ¶
41:50   **SETTING:** ûlĕyôsēp$_1$ yullād$_2$ šĕnê$_3$ bānîm$_4$ bĕṭerem$_5$ tābô$^2_6$ šĕnat$_7$ hārā^{c}āb$_8$ ^{2}ăšer$_9$ yālĕdâ$_{10}$-llô$_{11}$ ^{2}āsĕnat$_{12}$ bat$_{13}$-pôtî pera$^c_{14}$ kōhēn$_{15}$ ^{2}ôn$_{16}$.
41:51   **THESIS:** *wayyiqrā$^2_1$* yôsēp$_2$ ^{2}et-šēm$_3$ habbĕkōr$_4$ mĕnaššeh$_5$ kî$_6$-«naššanî$_7$ ^{2}ĕlōhîm$_8$ ^{2}et-kol$_9$-^{c}ămālî$_{10}$ wĕ^{2}ēt$_{11}$ kol$_{12}$-bêt$_{13}$ ^{2}ābî$_{14}$.»
41:52   **ANTI:** wĕ^{2}ēt$_1$ šēm$_2$ haššēnî$_3$ qārā$^2_4$ ^{2}eprāyim$_5$ kî$_6$-«hipranî$_7$ ^{2}ĕlōhîm$_8$ bĕ^{2}ereṣ$_9$ ^{c}ānĕyî$_{10}$.»
41:53   **TERMINUS: N** SEQUENCE ¶
     BU$_1$: *wattiklênâ$_1$* šeba$^c_2$ šĕnê$_3$ haśśābā$^c_4$ ^{2}ăšer$_5$ hāyâ$_6$ be^{2}ereṣ$_7$ miṣrāyim$_8$.
41:54a   BU$_n$: *wattĕḥillênâ$_1$* šeba$^c_2$ šenê$_3$ hārā^{c}āb$_4$ lābô$^2_5$ ka^{2}ăšer$_6$ ^{2}āmar$_7$ yôsēp$_8$.
41:54b-57   **POST-PEAK EPISODE$_3$/CLOSURE:** STIMULUS-RESPONSE ¶
     SETTING: E ANTITHETICAL ¶
41:54b   THESIS: wayhî$_1$ rā^{c}āb$_2$ bĕkol$_3$-hā^{2}ărāṣôt$_4$.
     ANTI: ûbĕkol$_1$-^{2}ereṣ$_2$ miṣrāyim$_3$ hāyâ$_4$ lāḥem$_5$.
     STIMULUS: N SEQUENCE ¶
41:55   BU$_1$: *wattir^{c}ab$_1$* kol$_2$-^{2}ereṣ$_3$ miṣrāyim$_4$.
     BU$_2$: *wayyiṣ^{c}aq$_1$* hā^{c}ām$_2$ ^{2}el$_3$-par^{c}ōh$_4$ lallāḥem$_5$.
     BU$_n$: *wayyō^{2}mer$_1$* par^{c}ōh$_2$ lĕkol$_3$-miṣrāyim$_4$: QUOTE=**H** SEQUENCE ¶
       BU$_1$: «lĕkû$_1$ ^{2}el$_2$ yôsēp$_3$.
       BU$_n$: ^{2}ăšer$_1$ yō^{2}mar$_2$ lākem$_3$ ta^{c}ăśû$_4$.»
     RESPONSE: N ANTITHETICAL ¶
     THESIS: **N** SEQUENCE ¶
41:56   SETTING: wĕhārā^{c}āb$_1$ hāyâ$_2$ ^{c}al$_3$ kol$_4$-pĕnê$_5$ hā^{2}āreṣ$_6$.
       BU$_1$: *wayyiptaḥ$_1$* yôsēp$_2$ ^{2}et-kol$_3$-^{2}ăšer$_4$ bāhem$_5$.
       BU$_n$: *wayyišbōr$_1$* lĕmiṣrāyim$_2$.
     ANTI: *wayyeḥĕzaq$_1$* hārā^{c}āb$_2$ bĕ^{2}ereṣ$_3$ miṣrāyim$_4$.
41:57   **TERMINUS:** wĕkol$_1$ hā^{2}āreṣ$_2$ bā^{2}û$_3$ miṣraymâ$_4$ lišbōr$_5$ ^{2}el$_6$ yôsēp$_7$ kî$_8$ ḥāzaq$_9$ hārā^{c}āb$_{10}$ bĕkol$_{11}$ hā^{2}āreṣ$_{12}$.

41:50   And to Joseph$_1$ were born$_2$ two$_3$ sons$_4$ before$_5$ it-started$_6$ the year$_7$ of the famine$_8$—which$_9$ she-bore$_{10}$ to him$_{11}$ Asenath$_{12}$ the daughter of$_{13}$ Potiphera$_{14}$ the priest of$_{15}$ On$_{16}$.

41:51   *And-he-called$_1$* Joseph$_2$ the name of$_3$ the first born$_4$ Manasseh$_5$ because$_6$ (he said) «He-has-made-me-forget$_7$ God$_8$ all$_9$ my toil$_{10}$ and$_{11}$ all$_{12}$ the house of$_{13}$ my father$_{14}$.»

41:52   But$_1$ the name of$_2$ the second$_3$ he-called$_4$ Ephraim$_5$ for$_6$ (he said): «He-has-made-me-fruitful$_7$ God$_8$ in the land of$_9$ my affliction$_{10}$.»

41:53   *And-they-ended$_1$* the seven$_2$ years of$_3$ plenty$_4$ which$_5$ were$_6$ in the land of$_7$ Egypt$_8$.

41:54a   *And-they-began$_1$* the seven$_2$ years of$_3$ famine$_4$ to come$_5$ just as$_6$ had said$_7$ Joseph$_8$.

41:54b   And-there-was$_1$ famine$_2$ in all$_3$ the lands$_4$.
         But in all$_1$ the land of$_2$ Egypt$_3$ there was$_4$ bread$_5$.

41:55   *And-it-hungered$_1$* all$_2$ the land of$_3$ Egypt$_4$.
         And-it-cried-out$_1$ the people$_2$ to$_3$ Pharaoh$_4$ for bread$_5$.
         And-he-said$_1$ Pharaoh$_2$ to all$_3$ Egypt$_4$:
         «Go$_1$ to$_2$ Joseph$_3$.
         Whatever$_1$ (he's) saying$_2$ to you$_3$ do it$_4$.»

41:56   And the famine$_1$ was$_2$ over$_3$ all$_4$ parts of (faces of)$_5$ the country$_6$.
         And-he-opened$_1$ Joseph$_2$ all (the stores)$_3$ which$_4$ (were) in them$_5$.
         And-he-sold$_1$ to the Egyptians$_2$.
         And-it-was-strong$_1$ the famine$_2$ in the land of$_3$ Egypt$_4$.

41:57   And all$_1$ the world$_2$ came$_3$ to Egypt$_4$ to buy$_5$ from$_6$ Joseph$_7$ for$_8$ strong-was$_9$ the famine$_{10}$ in all$_{11}$ the earth$_{12}$.

42:1-38   **_INTERPEAK EPISODE:_** EPISODIC **N** DISC

42:1-5   **EPISODE$_1$:** EXECUTION ¶

42:1   **LEAD-IN:** *wayyar$^\supset_1$* ya^{c}āqōb$_2$ kî$_3$ yeš$_4$-šeber$_5$ bĕmiṣrāyim$_6$.

       PLAN: N SIMPLE ¶

       PRELIM: *wayyō$^\supset$mer$_1$* ya^{c}āqōb$_2$ lĕbānāyw$_3$: «lāmmâ$_4$ titrā$^\supset$û$_5$.»

42:2   TEXT: *wayyō$^\supset$mer$_1$:* QUOTE =**H** RESULT ¶

       PRELIM: «hinnēh$_1$ šāma^{c}tî$_2$ kî$_3$ yeš$_4$-šeber$_5$ bĕmiṣrāyim$_6$.

       TEXT: **H** SEQUENCE ¶

         BU$_1$: rĕdû$_1$-šāmmâ$_2$.

         BU$_n$: wĕšibrû$_1$-lānû$_2$ miššām$_3$.

       RESULT: **H** PARAPHRASE ¶ (NEGATED ANTONYM)

         TEXT: wĕniḥyeh$_1$ (=hidden cohortative, Jerusalmi)

         PARA: wĕlō$^\supset_1$ nāmût$_2$.»

       EXEC: N SEQUENCE ¶

         BU$_1$: **N** ANTITHETICAL ¶

42:3   THESIS: *wayyērĕdû$_1$* $^\supset$āḥê$_2$-yôsēp$_3$ ^{c}ăśārâ$_4$ lišbōr$_5$ bār$_6$ mimmiṣrāyim$_7$.

42:4   ANTI: wĕ$^\supset$et-binyāmîn$_1$ $^\supset$ăḥî$_2$ yôsēp$_3$ lō$^\supset_4$ šālaḥ$_5$ ya^{c}āqōb$_6$ $^\supset$et-$^\supset$eḥāyw$_7$ kî$_8$ $^\supset$āmar$_9$ «pen$_{10}$-yiqrā$^\supset$ennû$_{11}$ $^\supset$āsôn$_{12}$.»

42:5   BU$_n$: *wayyābō$^\supset$û$_1$* bĕnê$_2$ yiśrā$^\supset$ēl$_3$ lišbōr$_4$ bĕtôk$_5$ habbā$^\supset$îm$_6$ kî$_7$ hāyâ$_8$ hārā^{c}āb$_9$ bĕ$^\supset$ereṣ$_{10}$ kĕnā^{c}an$_{11}$.

42:6-17   **EPISODE$_2$:** COMPOUND DIALOGUE ¶

42:6   **SETTING: E** AMPLIFICATION ¶

       TEXT: wĕyôsēp$_1$ hû$^\supset_2$ haššallîṭ$_3$ ^{c}al$_4$-hā$^\supset$āreṣ$_5$

       AMPL: hû$^\supset_1$ hammašbîr$_2$ lĕkol$_3$-^{c}am$_4$ hā$^\supset$āreṣ$_5$.

       LEAD-IN: STIMULUS-RESPONSE ¶

       STIMULUS: **N** SEQUENCE ¶

         BU$_1$: *wayyābō$^\supset$û$_1$* $^\supset$āḥê$_2$ yôsēp$_3$.

         BU$_n$: *wayyištaḥăwû$_1$*-lô$_2$ $^\supset$appayim$_3$ $^\supset$ārĕṣâ$_4$.

       RESPONSE: **N** ANTITHETICAL ¶ [EXPECTANCY REVERSAL?]

       THESIS: **N** SEQUENCE ¶

42:7a   BU$_1$: *wayyar$^\supset_1$* yôsēp$_2$ $^\supset$et-$^\supset$ĕḥāyw$_3$.

         BU$_n$: *wayyakkirēm$_1$*.

       ANTI: **N** AMPLIFICATION ¶

       TEXT: *wayyitnakkēr$_1$* $^\supset$ălêhem$_2$.

       AMPL: *waydabbēr$_1$* $^\supset$ittām$_2$ qāšôt$_3$.

42:7b   **EXCHANGE$_1$:** SIMPLE RESOLVED DIALOGUE ¶

       IU (Q): *wayyō$^\supset$mer$_1$* $^\supset$ălêhem$_2$: «mē$^\supset$ayin$_3$ bā$^\supset$tem$_4$.»

       RU (A): *wayyō$^\supset$mĕrû$_1$:* «mē$^\supset$ereṣ$_2$ kĕna^{c}an$_3$ lišbar$_4$-$^\supset$ōkel$_5$.»

42:1	*And-he-saw$_1$* Jacob$_2$ that$_3$ there was$_4$ food$_5$ in Egypt$_6$.
	And-he-said$_1$ Jacob$_2$ to his sons$_3$: «Why$_4$ do-you-look-at-each-other$_5$?»
42:2	*And-he-said$_1$:*
	«Behold$_1$ I-have-heard$_2$ that$_3$ there is$_4$ food$_5$ in Egypt$_6$.
	Go-down$_1$ there$_2$.
	And-buy$_1$ for us$_2$ from there$_3$.
	So-we-can-live/let's-live$_1$,
	and not die$_2$.»
42:3	*And-they-went-down$_1$* the ten$_4$ brothers of$_2$ Joseph$_3$ to buy$_5$ grain$_6$ from Egypt$_7$.
42:4	But Benjamin$_1$ the brother of$_2$ Joseph$_3$ not$_4$ he-sent$_5$ Jacob$_6$ with his brothers$_7$ for$_8$ he-said$_9$: «Lest$_{10}$ befall-him$_{11}$ harm$_{12}$.»
42:5	*And-they-came-in$_1$* the sons-of$_2$ Israel$_3$ to buy$_4$ amidst$_5$ the ones coming in$_6$ for$_7$ was$_8$ the famine$_9$ in the land of$_{10}$ Canaan$_{11}$.
42:6	Now as for Joseph$_1$ he$_2$ (was) the regent$_3$ over$_4$ the land$_5$.
	He$_1$ (was) the one selling$_2$ to all$_3$ the people of$_4$ the land (earth)$_5$.
	And-they-came-in$_1$ the brothers of$_2$ Joseph$_3$.
	And-they-prostrated-themselves$_1$ to him$_2$ faces$_3$ to the earth$_4$.
42:7a	*And-he-saw$_1$* Joseph$_2$ his brothers$_3$.
	And-he-recognized-them$_1$.
	But-he-made-himself-strange$_1$ to them$_2$.
	And-he-spoke$_1$ to them$_2$ harshly$_3$.
42:7b	*And-he-said$_1$* to them$_2$: «Whence$_3$ come-you$_4$?»
	And-they-said$_1$ «From the land$_2$ of Canaan$_3$ to buy$_4$ food$_5$.»

1 2 3 4 5 6 7 8 9

42:8-11   **EXCHANGE$_2$:** SIMPLE RESOLVED DIALOGUE ¶
    LEAD-IN: **N** SEQUENCE ¶
      BU$_1$: **N** ANTITHETICAL ¶
42:8   THESIS: *wayyakkĕr$_1$* yôsēp$_2$ ɔet-ɔeḥayw$_3$.
        ANTI: wĕhēm$_1$ lōɔ$_2$ hikkiruhû$_3$.
42:9   BU$_n$: *wayyizkōr$_1$* yôsēp$_2$ ɔēt-haḥălōmôt$_3$ ɔăšer$_4$ ḥālam$_5$ lāhem$_6$.
      IU (REM): *wayyōɔmer$_1$* ɔălêhem$_2$: QUOTE = **E**
    AMPLIFICATION ¶
      TEXT: «mĕraggĕlîm$_1$ ɔattem$_2$
      AMPL: lirɔôt$_1$ ɔet-ᶜerwat$_2$ hāɔāreṣ$_3$ bāɔtem$_4$.»
42:10   RU (EVAL): *wayyōɔmĕrû$_1$* ɔēlāyw$_2$: QUOTE = **E**
    NEGATED ANTONYM PARAPHRASE ¶
      PARAPHRASE: «lōɔ$_1$ ɔădōnî$_2$.
    TEXT: **E** COORDINATE ¶
      ITEM$_1$: waᶜăbādêkā$_1$ bāɔû$_2$ lišbār$_3$-ɔōkel$_4$.
42:11   ITEM$_2$: kullānû$_1$ bĕnê$_2$ ɔîš$_3$-ɔeḥād$_4$ nāḥĕnû$_5$.
    ITEM$_3$ **E** PARAPHRASE ¶
      TEXT: kēnîm$_1$ ɔănaḥnû$_2$.
      PARA (NEGATED ANTONYM): lōɔ$_1$-hāyû$_2$ ᶜăbādêkā$_3$ mĕraggĕlîm$_4$.»

1 2 3 4 5 6 7 8 9

42:8   *And-he-recognized[1]* Joseph[2] his brothers[3].
      But they[1] not[2] recognized-him[3].

42:9   *And-he-remembered[1]* Joseph[2] his dreams[3] which[4] he-had-dreamed[5]
      concerning them[6].
      And-he-said[1] to them[2]:
      «Spies[1] (are) you[2].
      To see[1] the nakedness of[2] the land[3] you-have-come[4].»

42:10   *And-they-said[1]* to him[2]:
      «No[1], my lord[2].
      Rather, your servants[1] have come[2] to buy[3] food[4].

42:11   All of us[1], sons of[2] one[4] man[3] (are) we[5].
      Honest (men)[1] (are) we[2].
      Not[1] are[2] your servants[3] spies[4].»

1 2 3 4 5 6 7 8 9

42:12-13   **EXCHANGE₃:** SIMPLE RESOLVED* DIALOGUE ¶
42:12   IU (REM): *wayyōʾmer₁* ʾălēhem₂: «lōʾ₃ kî₄-ᶜerwat₅ hāʾāreṣ₆ bāʾtem₇ lirʾôt₈.»
42:13   RU (EVAL)*: *wayyōʾmĕrû₁:* QUOTE =***E*** COORDINATE ¶
            ITEM₁: *E* AMPLIFICATION ¶
            TEXT: «šēnêm₂ ᶜāśār₃ ᶜăbādêkā₄ ʾaḥîm₅.
            AMPL: ʾănaḥnû₁ bĕnê₂ ʾîš₃-ʾeḥād₄ bĕʾereṣ₅ kĕnāᶜan₆.
            ITEM₂: wĕhinnēh₁ haqqāṭōn₂ ʾet-ʾābînû₃ hayyôm₄.
            ITEM₃: wĕhāʾeḥād₁ ʾênennû₂.»
            [* It's as if this RU (EVAL) is unfinished; Joseph breaks in impatiently.]
42:14-17   **EXCHANGE₄:** SIMPLE UNRESOLVED DIALOGUE ¶
42:14   IU (REM): *wayyōʾmer₁* ʾălēhem₂ yôsēp₃:
            QUOTE =CYCLIC ***H*** AMPLIFICATION ¶
            PRELIM: «hûʾ₁ ʾăšer₂ dibbartî₃ ʾălēkem₄ lēʾmōr₅ ''mĕraggĕlîm₆ ʾattem₇.''
            TEXT: ***H*** SIMPLE ¶
42:15   PRELIM: bĕzōʾt₁ tibbāḥēnû₂.
            TEXT: ḥê₁ parᶜōh₂ ʾim₃ ṭēṣĕʾû₄ mizzeh₅ kî ʾim₆-bĕbôʾ₇ ʾăḥîkem₈ haqqāṭōn₉ hēnnâ₁₀.
            AMPL: ***H*** ANTITHETICAL ¶
            THESIS: ***H*** SEQUENCE ¶
42:16   BU₁: šilḥû₁ mikkem₂ ʾeḥād₃.
            BUₙ: wĕyiqqaḥ₁ ʾet-ʾăḥîkem₂.
            ANTI: wĕʾattem₁ hēʾāsĕrû₂.
            TEXT': wĕyibbāḥănû₁ dibrêkem₂ haʾĕmet₃ ʾittēkem₄.
            TERMINUS: wĕʾim₁-lōʾ₂ ḥê₃ parᶜōh₄ kîₛ mĕraggĕlîm₆ ʾattem₇.»
42:17   STEP-DOWN: *wayyeʾĕsōp₁* ʾōtām₂ ʾel-mišmār₃ šĕlōšet₄ yāmîm₅.

1 2 3 4 5 6 7 8 9

42:12   *And-he-said₁* to them₂: «No₃! Rather₄ the nakedness of₅ the land₆ you-have-come₇ to see₈.»

42:13   *And-they-said₁* «Your servants₄ (are) twelve₂₋₃ brothers₅.
We₁ (are) sons of₂ one₄ man₃ in the land of₅ Canaan₆.
And behold₁ a younger one₂ (is) with our father₃ today₄.
And the one₁ none of him₂ (='and the other is not.')»

42:14   *And-he-said₁* to them₂ Joseph₃
«That's₁ (just) what₂ I-said₃ to you₄ saying₅: "Spies₆ (are) you₇!"

42:15   In this₁ you-will-be-tested₂.
(By) the life₁ of Pharaoh₂ if (=not)₃ you-will-come-out₄ from here₅ unless₆ (you) bring₇ your little₉ brother₈ here₁₀.

42:16   Send₁ one₃ of you₂.
And-let-him-fetch₁ your brother₂.
As for (the rest of) you₁ (stay) imprisoned₂.
And-they-will-be-tested₁ your words₂ whether truth₃ (is) with you₄.
And-if₁ not₂ (by) the life of₃ Pharaoh₄ (it's) that₅ spies₆ (are) you₇.»

42:17   *And-he-gathered₁* them₂ to custody₃ (for) three₄ days₅.

1 2 3 4 5 6 7 8 9

| | | | | | | | | |

42:18-26   **EPISODE$_3$:** COMPOUND DIALOGUE ¶
42:18-20   **EXCHANGE$_1$:** EXECUTION ¶
42:18   PLAN: *wayyṓ$^{\ni}$mer$_1$* $^{\ni}$ălēhem$_2$ yôsēp$_3$ bayyōm$_4$ haššēlîšî$_5$:
       QUOTE =**H** SEQUENCE ¶
       SETTING: **H** REASON ¶
       TEXT: **H** RESULT ¶
         TEXT: «zō$^{\ni}$t$_1$ ^{c}ăśû$_2$
         RESULT: wiḥyû$_1$
         REASON: $^{\ni}$et-hā$^{\ni}$ĕlōhîm$_1$ $^{\ni}$ănî$_2$ yārē$^{\ni}$$_3$.
       BU$_1$: **H** ANTITHETICAL ¶
42:19   THESIS: $^{\ni}$im$_1$ kēnîm$_2$ $^{\ni}$attem$_3$ $^{\ni}$ăḥîkem$_4$ $^{\ni}$eḥād$_5$
       yē$^{\ni}$āsēr$_6$ bĕbêt$_7$ mišmarkem$_8$.
       ANTI: **H** SEQUENCE ¶
         BU$_1$: wĕ$^{\ni}$attem$_1$ lĕkû$_2$
         BU$_n$: hābî$^{\ni}$û$_1$ šeber$_2$ ra^{c}ābôn$_3$ bāttêkem$_4$.
       BU$_n$: **H** REASON ¶
42:20   REASON/CIRCUMSTANCE: wĕ$^{\ni}$et-$^{\ni}$ăḥîkem$_1$
       haqqāṭōn$_2$ tābî$^{\ni}$û$_3$ $^{\ni}$ēlay$_4$.
       TEXT: **H** RESULT ¶
         TEXT: wĕyē$^{\ni}$āmĕnû$_1$ dibrêkem$_2$.
         RESULT: wĕlō$^{\ni}$$_1$ tāmûtû$_2$.»
     EXEC: *wayya^{c}ăśû$_1$*-kēn$_2$.
42:21-24a   **EXCHANGE$_2$:** SIMPLE RESOLVED DIALOGUE ¶
42:21   IU (REM): *wayyṓ$^{\ni}$mĕrû$_1$* $^{\ni}$îš$_2$ $^{\ni}$el$_3$-$^{\ni}$āḥîw$_4$: QUOTE =**E**
     RESULT ¶
         TEXT: «$^{\ni}$ăbāl$_1$ $^{\ni}$ăšēmîm$_2$ $^{\ni}$ănaḥnû$_3$ ^{c}al$_4$-$^{\ni}$āḥînû$_5$ $^{\ni}$ăšer$_6$ [**N**
       ANTITHETICAL ¶ BACKLOOPS INTO RELATIVE
       CLAUSE]
         THESIS: rā$^{\ni}$înû$_7$ ṣārat$_8$ napšô$_9$ bĕhithanĕnô$_{10}$ $^{\ni}$ēlēnû$_{11}$
         ANTI: wĕlō$^{\ni}$$_{12}$ šāmā^{c}nû$_{13}$.
         RESULT: ^{c}al-kēn$_1$ bā$^{\ni}$â$_2$ $^{\ni}$ēlênû$_3$ haṣṣārâ$_4$ hazzō$^{\ni}$t$_5$.»
42:22   RU (EVAL): *wayya^{c}an$_1$* rĕ$^{\ni}$ûbēn$_2$ $^{\ni}$ōtām$_3$ lē$^{\ni}$mōr$_4$:
     QUOTE =**E** REASON ¶
       REASON: **N** ANTITHETICAL ¶
         THESIS: «hălō$^{\ni}$$_1$ $^{\ni}$āmartî$_2$ $^{\ni}$ălêkem$_3$ lē$^{\ni}$mōr$_4$:
         ''$^{\ni}$al$_1$ teḥeṭ$^{\ni}$û$_2$ bayyeled$_3$.''
         ANTI: wĕlō$^{\ni}$$_1$ šĕma^{c}tem$_2$.
         TEXT: wĕgam$_1$-dāmô$_2$ hinnēh$_3$ nidrāš$_4$.»

| | | | | | | | | |

    1 2 3 4 5 6 7 8 9

42:18   *And-he-said₁* to them₂ Joseph₃ on the third₅ day₄:
«This₁ do₂.
And-live₁.
God₁ I₂ am-fearing₃.

42:19   If₁ honest (men)₂ (are) you₃, let-be-bound₆ one of₅ your brothers₄
in the house of₇ your imprisonment₈.
As for you₁ go₂.
Take₁ food of₂ the famine₃ to your households₄.

42:20   And-bring₃ to me₄ your little₂ brother₁.
And-let-them-be-confirmed₁ your words₂.
And (so) not₁ you-will-die₂.»
And-they-did₁ so₂.

42:21   *And-they-said₁* (each) man₂ to₃ his brother₄:
«Truly₁ are-guilty₂ we₃ on account of₄ our brother₅ whom₆ we-
saw₇ the distress of₈ his soul₉ in his beseeching₁₀ us₁₁ and not₁₂
we-hearkened₁₃.
Therefore₁ has-come₂ on us₃ this₅ distress₄.»

42:22   *And-he-answered₁* Reuben₂ them₃ saying₄:
«Did not₁ I-tell₂ you₃ saying₄:
''Don't₁ harm₂ the lad₃!?''
And not₁ you-listened₂.
And also₁ his blood₂ indeed₃ is-required/sought after₄.»

1 2 3 4 5 6 7 8 9

| | | | | | | | |

        STEP-DOWN: N SEQUENCE ¶

42:23   SETTING: $w\check{e}h\bar{e}m_1$ $l\bar{o}^{\supset}{}_2$ $y\bar{a}d\check{e}^{c}\hat{u}_3$ $k\hat{\imath}_4$ $\check{s}\bar{o}m\bar{e}a^{c}{}_5$ $y\hat{o}s\bar{e}p_6$ $k\hat{\imath}_7$ $hamm\bar{e}l\hat{\imath}\d{s}_8$ $b\bar{e}n\bar{o}t\bar{a}m_9$.

42:24a BU_1: *wayyiss\bar{o}b₁* $m\bar{e}^{c}\bar{a}l\hat{e}hem_2$.

        BU_n: *wayy\bar{e}bk₁*.

42:24b-26   **STEP-DOWN: N** SEQUENCE ¶

        BU_1: **N** SEQUENCE ¶

42:24b BU_1: *wayy\bar{a}\check{s}ob₁* $^{\supset}\bar{a}l\bar{e}hem_2$.

        BU_2: *waydabb\bar{e}r₁* $^{\supset}\bar{a}l\bar{e}hem_2$.

        BU_3: *wayyiqqa\d{h}₁* $m\bar{e}^{\supset}itt\bar{a}m_2$ $^{\supset}et$-$\check{s}im^{c}\hat{o}n_3$.

        BU_n: *wayye$^{\supset}$\check{e}s\bar{o}r₁* $^{\supset}\bar{o}t\hat{o}_2$ $l\check{e}^{c}\hat{e}n\hat{e}hem_3$.

        BU_2: EXECUTION ¶

        PLAN: INDIRECT QUOTE ¶

         I Q F: PLAN-EXECUTION ¶

42:25   PLAN: *wa\d{y}\d{s}aw₁* $y\hat{o}s\bar{e}p_2$.

         EXEC: *waymal$^{\supset}$\hat{u}₁* $^{\supset}et$-$k\check{e}l\hat{e}hem_2$ $b\bar{a}r_3$.

         I Q: COORDINATE ¶(?)

         $ITEM_1$: *\hat{u}l\check{e}h\bar{a}\check{s}\hat{\imath}b₁* $kasp\hat{e}hem_2$ $^{\supset}\hat{\imath}\check{s}_3$ $^{\supset}el$-$\acute{s}aqq\hat{o}_4$.

         $ITEM_2$: $w\check{e}l\bar{a}t\bar{e}t_5$ $l\bar{a}hem_6$ $\d{s}\bar{e}d\hat{a}_7$ $ladd\bar{a}rek_8$.

        EXEC: *wayya^{c}a\acute{s}₁* $l\bar{a}hem_2$ $k\bar{e}n_3$.

        BU_n: **N** SEQUENCE ¶

42:26 BU_1: *wayyi\acute{s}$^{\supset}$\hat{u}₁* $^{\supset}et$-$\check{s}ibr\bar{a}m_2$ $^{c}al_3$-$\d{h}\check{a}m\bar{o}r\hat{e}hem_4$.

        BU_n: *wayy\bar{e}l\check{e}k\hat{u}₁* $mi\check{s}\check{s}\bar{a}m_2$.

| | | | | | | | |

1 2 3 4 5 6 7 8 9

42:23   And-they$_1$ not$_2$ knew$_3$ that$_4$ understood$_5$ Joseph$_6$ because$_7$ the
         interpreter$_8$ (was) between them$_9$.

42:24   *And-he-turned-aside$_1$* from them$_2$.
         And-he-wept$_1$.
         Then-he-came-back$_1$ to them$_2$.
         And-he-spoke$_1$ with them$_2$.
         And-he-took$_1$ from them$_2$ Simeon$_3$.
         And-he-bound$_1$ him$_2$ before them$_3$.

42:25   *And-he-gave-command$_1$* Joseph$_2$.
         And-they-filled$_1$ the containers$_2$ (with) grain$_3$
         (And-he-commanded) to restore$_1$ to (each) man's$_3$ bag$_4$ the silver
         (purchase money)$_2$ and to give$_5$ them$_6$ provisions$_7$ for the journey$_8$.
         And-he-did$_1$ so$_3$ for them$_2$.

42:26   *So-they-loaded$_1$* the supplies$_2$ on$_3$ their asses$_4$.
         And-they-departed$_1$ from there$_2$.

1 2 3 4 5 6 7 8 9

⌐ | | | | | | | | ¬

42:27-38   **EPISODE$_n$ (NO CLEAR PEAK):** N SEQUENCE ¶ (OR N DISC)

42:27-28   **BU$_1$:** N SEQUENCE ¶

42:27   BU$_1$: *wayyiptaḥ$_1$* hā$^{\jmath}$eḥād$_2$ $^{\jmath}$et-śaqqô$_3$ lātēt$_4$ mispô$^{\jmath}$$_5$ laḥămōrô$_6$ bammālôn$_7$.

     BU$_2$: N AMPLIFICATION ¶

     TEXT: *wayyar$^{\jmath}$$_1$* $^{\jmath}$et-kaspô$_2$.

     AMPL: wĕhinnēh$_1$-hû$^{\jmath}$$_2$ bĕpî$_3$ $^{\jmath}$amtaḥtô$_4$.

42:28   BU$_3$: *wayyō$^{\jmath}$mer$_1$* $^{\jmath}$el$_2$-$^{\jmath}$eḥāyw$_3$: QUOTE = N EVIDENCE ¶

     TEXT: «hûšab$_1$ kaspî$_2$.

     EVIDENCE: wĕgam$_1$ hinnēh$_2$ bĕ$^{\jmath}$amtaḥtî$_3$.»

     BU$_4$: *wayyēṣē$^{\jmath}$$_1$* libbām$_2$.

     BU$_n$: *wayyeḥerdû$_1$* $^{\jmath}$îš$_2$ $^{\jmath}$el$_3$-$^{\jmath}$āḥîw$_4$ lē$^{\jmath}$mōr$_5$: «mâ$_1$-zzō$^{\jmath}$t$_2$ ^{c}āśâ$_3$ $^{\jmath}$ēlōhîm$_4$ lānû$_5$.»

42:29-34   **BU$_2$:** N SEQUENCE ¶ [BACKLOOPS A DIALOGUE IN THE S OF BU$_2$]

42:29   BU$_1$: *wayyābō$^{\jmath}$û$_1$* $^{\jmath}$el$_2$-ya^{c}ăqōb$_3$ $^{\jmath}$ăbîhem$_4$ $^{\jmath}$arṣâ$_5$ kĕnā^{c}an$_6$.

     BU$_2$: *wayyaggîdû$_1$* lô$_2$ $^{\jmath}$ēt kol$_3$-haqqōrōt$_4$ $^{\jmath}$ōtām$_5$ lē$^{\jmath}$mōr$_6$: QUOTE = COMPOUND DIALOGUE ¶

42:30   SETTING: «dibber$_1$ hā$^{\jmath}$îš$_2$ $^{\jmath}$ădōnê$_3$ hā$^{\jmath}$āreṣ$_4$ $^{\jmath}$ittānû$_5$ qāšôt$_6$.

     EXCHANGE$_1$: SIMPLE RESOLVED DIALOGUE ¶

     IU (REM): *wayyittēn$_1$* $^{\jmath}$ōtānû$_2$ kimraggĕlîm$_3$ $^{\jmath}$et-hā$^{\jmath}$āreṣ$_4$.

⌐ | | | | | | | | ¬

1 2 3 4 5 6 7 8 9

42:27   *And-he-opened$_1$* one (of them)$_2$ his sack$_3$ to give$_4$ fodder$_5$ to his
          ass$_6$ in the lodging place$_7$.
          And-he-saw$_1$ his silver$_2$.
          Behold$_1$ it$_2$ (was) in the mouth of$_3$ his sack$_4$.
42:28   *And-he-said$_1$* to$_2$ his brothers$_3$:
          «My silver$_2$ has been returned$_1$.
          And what's more$_1$ look at it$_2$ (here) in my sack$_3$!»
          And-sank$_1$ their hearts$_2$.
          And-they-trembled$_1$ (each) man$_2$ to$_3$ his brother$_4$ saying$_5$:
          «What$_1$ (is) this$_2$ (that) God$_4$ has done$_3$ to us$_5$.»
42:29   *And-they-came-in$_1$* to$_2$ Jacob$_3$ their father$_4$ to the land of$_5$ Canaan$_6$.
          And-they-declared$_1$ to him$_2$ all$_3$ (that) had befallen$_4$ them$_5$ saying$_6$:
42:30   «The man$_2$ the lord of$_3$ the country$_4$ spoke$_1$ bitter/rough (things)$_6$
          with us$_5$.
          And-he-treated$_1$ us$_2$ as those spying out$_3$ the land$_4$.

1 2 3 4 5 6 7 8 9 10 11 12

42:31   RU (EVAL): *wannō‐ʾmer₁* ʾēlāyw₂: QUOTE =**E**
EVIDENCE ¶
   TEXT: **E** PARAPHRASE (NEGATED
   ANTONYM) ¶
      TEXT: "kēnîm₁ ʾānāḥnû₂.
      PARA: lōʾ₁ hāyînû₂ měraggělîm₃.

42:32   EVIDENCE: **E** COORDINATE ¶
   ITEM₁: šěnêm₁-ᶜāśār₂ ʾānaḥnû₃ ʾaḥîm₄ běnê₅
   ʾābînû₆.
   ITEM₂: hāʾeḥād₁ ʾênennû₂.
   ITEM₃: wěhaqqāṭōn₁ hayyôm₂ ʾet₃-ʾābînû₄
   běʾereṣ₅ kěnāᶜan₆."

42:33   EXCHANGE₂: SIMPLE UNRESOLVED DIALOGUE ¶
IU (REM): *wayyōʾmer₁* ʾēlênû₂ haʾîš₃ ʾădōnê₄
hāʾāreṣ₅: QUOTE =**H** SEQUENCE ¶
   SETTING: "bězōʾt₁ ʾēdaᶜ₂ kî₃ kēnîm₄ ʾattem₅.
   BU₁: ʾăḥîkem₁ hāʾeḥād₂ hannîḥû₃ ʾittî₄.
   BU₂: **H** SEQUENCE ¶
      BU₁: wěʾet-raᶜăbôn₁ bāttêkem₂ qěḥû₃.
      BUₙ: wālēkû₁.
   BUₙ: **H** RESULT ¶

42:34   TEXT: wěhābîʾû₁ ʾet-ʾăḥîkem₂ haqqāṭōn₃ ʾēlay₄.
      RESULT: **H** RESULT ¶
         TEXT: wěʾēděᶜâ₁ kî₂ lōʾ₃ měraggělîm₄ ʾattem₅
         kî₆ kēnîm₇ ʾattem₈ [NEGATED ANTONYM
         PARAPHRASE BACKLOOPED INTO
         COMPLEMENT].
         RESULT: **H** COORDINATE ¶
            ITEM₁: ʾet-ʾăḥîkem₁ ʾettēn₂ lākem₃.
            ITEM₂: wěʾet-hāʾāreṣ₁ tisḥārû₂."»

1 2 3 4 5 6 7 8 9 10 11 12

42:31   *And-we-said$_1$* to him$_2$
        "We$_2$ (are) honest (men)$_1$.
        Not$_1$ we-have-been$_2$ spies$_3$.
42:32   Twelve$_{1-2}$ (are) we$_3$, brothers$_4$ sons of$_5$ our father$_6$.
        And the one$_1$ is not$_2$.
        And the young (one)$_1$ (is) today$_2$ with$_3$ our father$_4$ in the land of$_5$
        Caanan$_6$."
42:33   *And-he-said$_1$* to us$_2$ the man$_3$ the lord of$_4$ the country$_5$:
        "In this$_1$ I-will-know$_2$ if$_3$ honest (men)$_4$ (are) you$_5$.
        Leave$_3$ one$_2$ of your brothers$_1$ with me$_4$.
        And take$_3$ the famine relief$_1$ for your households$_2$.
        And-go$_1$.
42:34   And-bring$_1$ your little$_3$ brother$_2$ to me$_4$.
        Then I'll-know$_1$ that$_2$ not$_3$ spies$_4$ (are) you$_5$, that$_6$ honest (men)$_7$
        (are) you$_8$.
        Your brother$_1$ I'll give back$_2$ to you$_3$.
        And-you-can-trade$_2$ in the land$_1$."»

270   1 2 3 4 5 6 7 8 9

42:35-38   **BU$_n$ (CLIMAX?):** RESOLVED COMPLEX DIALOGUE ¶
            LEAD-IN: **N** SEQUENCE ¶
42:35   SETTING: wayhî$_1$ hēm$_2$ mē{rî}qîm$_3$ śaqqêhem$_4$ wĕhinnēh$_5$
                $^{\supset}$îš$_6$ ṣĕrôr$_7$ kaspô$_8$ bĕśaqqô$_9$.
                BU$_1$: *wayyir^{c}û$_1$* $^{\supset}$et-ṣĕrōrôt$_2$ kaspêhem$_3$ hemmâ$_4$
                wa$^{\supset}$ăbîhem$_5$.
                BU$_n$: *wayyîrā$^{\supset}$û$_1$.*
42:36   IU (REM): *wayyō$^{\supset}$mer$_1$* $^{\supset}$ălēhem$_2$ ya^{c}ăqōb$_3$ $^{\supset}$ăbîhem$_4$:
                QUOTE=**N** AMPLIFICATION ¶
                TEXT: «$^{\supset}$ōtî$_1$ šikkaltem$_2$
                AMPL: **E** COORDINATE ¶
                    ITEM$_1$: yôsēp$_1$ $^{\supset}$ênennû$_2$.
                    ITEM$_2$: wĕšim^{c}ôn$_1$ $^{\supset}$ênennû$_2$.
                    ITEM$_3$: wĕ$^{\supset}$et-binyāmin$_1$ tiqqāḥû$_2$.
                SUMMARY: ^{c}ālay$_1$ hāyû$_2$ kullānâ$_3$.»
42:37   CU (COUNTER-PROP): *wayyō$^{\supset}$mer$_1$* rĕ$^{\supset}$ûbēn$_2$ $^{\supset}$el$_3$-$^{\supset}$ābîw$_4$
                lē$^{\supset}$mōr$_5$: QUOTE=**H** SIMPLE ¶
                SETTING: «$^{\supset}$et-šĕnê$_1$ bānay$_2$ tāmît$_3$ $^{\supset}$îm-lō$^{\supset}$$_4$ $^{\supset}$ăbî$^{\supset}$ennû$_5$
                $^{\supset}$ēlêkâ$_6$.
                TEXT: **H** RESULT ¶
                    TEXT: tĕnâ$_1$ $^{\supset}$ōtô$_2$ ^{c}al$_3$-yādî$_4$
                    RESULT: wa$^{\supset}$ănî$_1$ $^{\supset}$ăšîbennû$_2$ $^{\supset}$ēlêkā$_3$.»
42:38   RU (RES): *wayyō$^{\supset}$mer$_1$:* QUOTE=**H** REASON ¶
                TEXT: «lō$^{\supset}$$_1$-yērēd$_2$ bĕnî$_3$ ^{c}immākem$_4$ kî$_5$ [EMBEDS A **N**
                ANTITHETICAL ¶ IN THE CAUSE MARGIN]
                    THESIS: (kî)-$^{\supset}$āḥîw$_1$ mēt$_2$
                    ANTI: wĕhû$^{\supset}$$_1$ lĕbaddô$_2$ niš$^{\supset}$ār$_3$.
                REASON: **P** SEQUENCE ¶ [=CONDITIONAL]
                    BU$_1$: ûqĕrā$^{\supset}$āhû$_1$ $^{\supset}$āsôn$_2$ badderek$_3$ $^{\supset}$ăšer$_4$ tēlĕkû$_5$-bāh
                    (3fs)$_6$.
                    BU$_n$: wĕhôradtem$_1$ $^{\supset}$et-śêbātî$_2$ bĕyāgôn$_3$ šĕ$^{\supset}$ôlâ$_4$.»

1 2 3 4 5 6 7 8 9

42:35   And-it-came-to-pass$_1$ (as) they$_2$ were emptying$_3$ their sacks$_4$ that behold$_5$ (each) man$_6$ his bundle$_7$ of silver$_8$ in his sack$_9$.
And-they-saw$_1$ the bundles of$_2$ their silver$_3$ they$_4$ and their father$_5$. *And-they-were-afraid$_1$.*

42:36   *And-he-said$_1$* to them$_2$ Jacob$_3$ their father$_4$:
«Me$_1$ you-have-bereaved$_2$.
Joseph$_1$ is not$_2$.
And Simeon$_1$ is not$_2$.
And-you-would-take$_2$ Benjamin$_1$.
Everything$_3$ has-been$_2$ against me$_1$.»

42:37   *And-he-said$_1$* Reuben$_2$ to$_3$ his father$_4$ saying$_5$:
«You-may-kill$_3$ the two$_1$ sons of me$_2$ if not$_4$ I-bring-him-back$_5$ to you$_6$.
Give$_1$ him$_2$ into$_3$ my hand$_4$.
And I$_1$ will-return-him$_2$ to you$_3$.»

42:38   *And-he-said$_1$:*
«My son$_3$ will not$_1$ go down$_2$ with you$_4$ for$_5$
His brother$_1$ has died$_2$.
And he$_1$ alone$_2$ has been left$_3$.
And-will-befall-him$_1$ harm$_2$ in the way$_3$ which$_4$ you go$_5$ in it$_6$;
and-you-will-bring-down$_1$ my grey hairs$_2$ in grief$_3$ to Sheol$_4$.»

43,44,45   **PEAK' (DENOUEMENT): N** DISC
43:1-14   **EPISODE$_1$:** COMPOUND DIALOGUE ¶
43:1   **SETTING:** wĕhārā^{c}āb$_1$ kābēd$_2$ bā$^\rceil$āreṣ$_3$.
           EXCHANGE$_1$: COMPLEX RESOLVED DIALOGUE ¶
43:2   IU (PROP): wayhî$_1$ ka$^\rceil$āšer$_2$ killû$_3$ le$^\rceil$ĕkōl$_4$ $^\rceil$et-haššeber$_5$
           $^\rceil$āšer$_6$ hēbî$^\rceil$û$_7$ mimmiṣrāyim$_8$ [BACKREFERENCE]
           wayyō$^\rceil$mer$_9$ $^\rceil$ălêhem$_{10}$ $^\rceil$ăbîhem$_{11}$: QUOTE=**H**
           SEQUENCE ¶
           BU$_1$: «šubû$_1$
           BU$_n$: šibrû$_1$-lānû$_2$ mĕ^{c}at$_3$-$^\rceil$ōkel$_4$.»
43:3   CU (COUNTER-PROP): *wayyō$^\rceil$mer$_1$* $^\rceil$ēlāyw$_2$ yĕhûdâ$_3$
           lē$^\rceil$mōr$_4$: QUOTE=**H** ANTITHETICAL ¶
           PRELIMINARY: «hā^{c}ēd$_1$ hē^{c}id$_2$ bānû$_3$ hā$^\rceil$îš$_4$ lē$^\rceil$mōr$_5$:
           ''lō$^\rceil_6$ tir$^\rceil$û$_7$ pānay$_8$ biltî$_9$ $^\rceil$ăḥîkem$_{10}$ $^\rceil$ittĕkem$_{11}$.''
43:4   THESIS: $^\rceil$im$_1$-yeškâ$_2$ mĕšallēaḥ$_3$ $^\rceil$et-$^\rceil$āḥînû$_4$ $^\rceil$ittānû$_5$
           (APODOSIS BACKLOOPS A **H** SEQUENCE ¶)
           BU$_1$: nērĕdâ$_1$
           BU$_n$: wĕnišbĕrâ$_1$ lĕkā$_2$ $^\rceil$ōkel$_3$.
43:5   ANTI: wĕ$^\rceil$im$_1$-$^\rceil$ênĕkā$_2$ mĕšallēaḥ$_3$ lō$^\rceil_4$ nērēd$_5$ kî$_6$-hā$^\rceil$îš$_7$
           $^\rceil$āmar$_8$ $^\rceil$ēlênû$_9$ ''lō$^\rceil_{10}$ tir$^\rceil$û$_{11}$ pānay$_{12}$ biltî$_{13}$ $^\rceil$ăḥîkem$_{14}$
           $^\rceil$ittĕkem$_{15}$.''»
43:6   CU (COUNTER-Q): *wayyō$^\rceil$mer$_1$* yiśrā$^\rceil$ēl$_2$: «lāmâ$_3$
           hărē^{c}ōtem$_4$ lî$_5$ lĕhaggîd$_6$ hā$^\rceil$îš$_7$ ha^{c}ôd$_8$ lākem$_9$ $^\rceil$āḥ$_{10}$.»
43:7   RU (A): *wayyō$^\rceil$mĕrû$_1$:* QUOTE=SIMPLE RESOLVED
           DIALOGUE ¶
           IU (Q): «šā$^\rceil$ôl$_1$ šā$^\rceil$al$_2$-hā$^\rceil$îš$_3$ lānû$_4$ ûlĕmôladtēnû$_5$
           lē$^\rceil$mōr$_6$: QUOTE=**E** COORDINATE ¶
           ITEM$_1$: ''ha^{c}ôd$_1$ $^\rceil$ăbîkem$_2$ ḥay$_3$.
           ITEM$_2$: hăyēš$_1$ lākem$_2$ $^\rceil$āḥ$_3$.''
           RU (A): *wannagged$_1$-lô$_2$* ^{c}al$_3$-pî$_4$ haddĕbārîm$_5$ hā$^\rceil$ēlleh$_6$.
           CORRELATE: hăyādôa$^c_1$ nēda$^c_2$ kî$_3$ yō$^\rceil$mar$_4$: ''hôrîdû$_5$
           $^\rceil$et-$^\rceil$ăḥîkem$_6$''?»

43:1   And the famine$_1$ was severe$_2$ in the land$_3$.

43:2   And-it-happened-that$_1$ when$_2$ they-had-finished$_3$ eating$_4$ the food$_5$ which$_6$ they-had-brought-back$_7$ from Egypt$_8$, *and-he-said$_9$* to them$_{10}$ their father$_{11}$

     «Return$_1$.

     Buy$_1$ us$_2$ a bit of$_3$ food$_4$.»

43:3   *And-he-said$_1$* to him$_2$ Judah$_3$ saying$_4$:

     «The man$_4$ very solemnly warned$_{1-2}$ us$_3$ saying$_5$ ''Not$_6$ you-will-see$_7$ my face$_8$ unless$_9$ your brother$_{10}$ (is) with you$_{11}$.''

43:4   If$_1$ you are disposed$_2$ (on) sending$_3$ our brother$_4$ with-us$_5$, we'll-go-down$_1$.

     And-we'll-buy$_1$ for you$_2$ food$_3$.

43:5   And if$_1$ you're not disposed$_2$ (on) sending$_3$ (him), not$_4$ we'll-go-down$_5$ for$_6$ the man$_7$ said$_8$ to us$_9$ ''Not$_{10}$ you-will-see$_{11}$ my face$_{12}$ unless$_{13}$ your brother$_{14}$ (is) with you$_{15}$.''»

43:6   *And-he-said$_1$* Israel$_2$: «Why$_3$ did-you-harm$_4$ me$_5$ in telling$_6$ the man$_7$ (that) yet$_8$ to you$_9$ (was) a brother$_{10}$?»

43:7   *And-they-said$_1$:*

     «The man$_3$ very strictly questioned$_{1-2}$ concerning us$_4$ and concerning our kindred$_5$ saying$_6$:

     ''Is your father$_2$ still$_1$ alive$_3$?

     Is there$_1$ to you$_2$ a brother$_3$?''

     And-we-told$_1$ him$_2$ in accordance with$_{3-4}$ these$_6$ words$_5$.

     Could we certainly know$_{1-2}$ that$_3$ he would say$_4$: ''Go bring$_5$ your brother$_6$''?»

EXCHANGE$_2$: COMPLEX UNRESOLVED DIALOGUE ¶

43:8   IU (PROP): *wayyō-$^{\supset}$mer$_1$* yĕhûdâ$_2$ $^{\supset}$el$_3$-yiśrā^{c}ēl$_4$ $^{\supset}$ābîw$_5$:

QUOTE = ∎ REASON ¶ (WITH COMMENT)

    TEXT: ∎ RESULT ¶

      TEXT: «šilḥâ$_1$ hanna^{c}ar$_2$ $^{\supset}$ittî$_3$.

    RESULT: ∎ RESULT ¶

      TEXT: ∎ SEQUENCE ¶

        BU$_1$: wĕnāqûmâ$_1$.

        BU$_n$: wĕnēlēkâ$_1$.

      RESULT: ∎ NEGATED ANTONYM

      PARAPHRASE ¶

        TEXT: wĕniḥyeh$_1$.

        PARA: wĕlō$^{\supset}$$_1$ nāmût$_2$ gam$_3$-$^{\supset}$ănaḥnû$_4$ gam$_5$-$^{\supset}$attâ$_6$ gam$_7$-ṭappênû$_8$.

    REASON: ∎ AMPLIFICATION ¶

      TEXT: ∎ PARAPHRASE ¶

43:9   TEXT: $^{\supset}$ānōkî$_1$ $^{\supset}$e^{c}erbennû$_2$.

        PARA: mîyyādî$_1$ tĕbaqšennû$_2$.

      AMPLIFICATION: (PROTASIS OF S BACKLOOPS

      A ∎ SEQUENCE ¶)

        BU$_1$: $^{\supset}$im$_1$-lō$_2$ hăbî$^{\supset}$ōtîw$_3$ $^{\supset}$ēlêkâ$_4$

        BU$_n$: wĕhiṣṣagtîw$_5$ lĕpānêkā$_6$

        wĕḥāṭā$^{\supset}$tî$_7$ lĕkā$_8$ kol$_9$-hayyāmîm$_{10}$.

43:10   COMMENT: kî$_1$ lûlē$^{\supset}$$_2$ hitmahmāhĕnû$_3$ kî$_4$-^{c}atâ$_5$ šabnû$_6$ zeh$_7$ pa^{c}ămāyim$_8$.»

43:8   *And-he-said*$_1$ Judah$_2$ to$_3$ Israel$_4$ his father$_5$:
                 «Send$_1$ the lad$_2$ with me$_3$.
                 Then-we'll-rise-up$_1$.
                 And-we'll-go$_1$.
                 And-we'll-live$_1$.
                 And-we-won't-die$_{1-2}$—both$_3$ we$_4$ and$_5$ you$_6$ and$_7$ our children$_8$.
43:9   I myself$_1$ will-be-surety-for-him$_2$.
                 From my hand$_1$ you-may-require-him$_2$.
                 If$_1$ not$_2$ bring-back-I-him$_3$ to you$_4$ and-I-place-him$_5$ before you$_6$,
                 then-I-will-bear-the-wrong$_7$ to you$_8$ all$_9$ my days$_{10}$.
43:10   For$_1$ if not$_2$ we-had-delayed$_3$ then$_4$ by now$_5$ (could have) returned$_6$
                 this$_7$ twice$_8$.»

43:11   CU (RES/PROP): *wayyōᵓmer*$_{1}$ ᵓālēhem$_{2}$ yiśrāᶜēl$_{3}$
ᵓābîhem$_{4}$: QUOTE=**H** COORDINATE ¶
PRELIM: «ᵓim$_{1}$-kēn$_{2}$ ᵓēpôᵓ$_{3}$ zōᵓt$_{4}$ ᶜăśû$_{5}$.
ITEM$_{1}$: **H** SEQUENCE ¶
   BU$_{1}$: qĕḥû$_{1}$ mezzimrat$_{2}$ hāᵓāreṣ$_{3}$ biklêkem$_{4}$
   BU$_{n}$: wĕhôrîdû$_{1}$ lāᵓîš$_{2}$ minḥâ$_{3}$ mĕᶜaṭ$_{4}$ sŏrî$_{5}$ ûmĕᶜaṭ$_{6}$
   dĕbaš$_{7}$ nĕkōᵓt$_{8}$ wālōṭ$_{9}$ bāṭĕnîm$_{10}$ ûšĕqēdîm$_{11}$.
ITEM$_{2}$: **H** COMMENT ¶
TEXT: **H** AMPLIFICATION ¶

43:12   TEXT: wĕkesep$_{1}$ mišneh$_{2}$ qĕḥu$_{3}$ bĕyedkem$_{4}$.
AMPL: wĕᵓet-hakkesep$_{1}$ hammûšāb$_{2}$ bĕpî$_{3}$
ᵓamtĕḥōtêkem$_{4}$ tāšîbû$_{5}$ bĕyedkem$_{6}$.
COMMENT: ᵓûlay$_{1}$ mišgeh$_{2}$ hûᵓ$_{3}$.
ITEM$_{3}$: **H** SEQUENCE ¶

43:13   BU$_{1}$: wĕᵓet-ᵓăḥîkem$_{1}$ qāḥû$_{2}$ (pausal).
BU$_{2}$: wĕqûmû$_{1}$.
BU$_{n}$: šûbû$_{1}$ ᵓel-hāᵓîš$_{2}$.
TERMINUS: ANTITHETICAL ¶

43:14   THESIS: **H** RESULT ¶
TEXT: wĕ$_{1}$ᵓēl$_{2}$ šadday$_{3}$ yittēn$_{4}$ lākem$_{5}$ raḥămîm$_{6}$
lipnê$_{7}$ hāᵓîš$_{8}$.
RESULT: wĕšillaḥ$_{1}$ lākem$_{2}$ ᵓet-ᵓăḥîkem$_{3}$ ᵓaḥēr$_{4}$
wĕᵓet-binyāmîn$_{5}$.
ANTI: waᵓănî$_{1}$ kaᵓăšer$_{2}$ šākōltî$_{3}$ šākāltî$_{4}$ (pausal).»

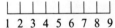

43:11   *And-he-said$_1$* to them$_2$ Israel$_3$ their father$_4$:
               «If$_1$ this$_2$ (it must be) then$_3$ do$_5$ this$_4$:
               Take$_1$ some of the best produce of$_2$ the land$_3$ in your vessels$_4$.
               And-take-down$_1$ to the man$_2$ a gift$_3$: a bit of$_4$ balsam$_5$, a bit of$_6$
               honey$_7$, spice$_8$ and myrrh$_9$, pistachio nuts$_{10}$ and almonds$_{11}$.
43:12   And$_1$ take$_3$ double$_2$ silver$_1$ in your hands$_4$.
               And return$_5$ in your hands$_6$ the silver$_1$ (which was) returned$_2$ in the
               mouth of$_3$ your sacks$_4$.
               Perhaps$_1$ it$_3$ (was) a mistake$_2$.
43:13   And-take$_2$ your brother$_1$.
               And-get-up$_1$.
               Return$_1$ to the man$_2$.
43:14   And$_1$ (may) El$_2$ Shaddai$_3$ give$_4$ you$_5$ mercies$_6$ before$_7$ the man$_8$.
               And-he-will-send-back$_1$ with you$_2$ your other$_4$ brother$_3$ and
               Benjamin$_5$.
               As for me$_1$ if$_2$ I-will-be-bereaved$_3$, I-will-be-bereaved$_4$.»

1 2 3 4 5 6 7 8 9

43:15-25   **EPISODE$_2$: N SEQUENCE ¶**
         BU$_1$: N COORDINATE ¶ [AS BACKREFERENCE]
43:15   ITEM$_1$: *wayyiqḥû$_1$* hā^{ɔ}ănāšîm$_2$ ^{ɔ}et-hamminḥâ$_3$ hazzō^{ɔ}t$_4$.
         ITEM$_2$: ûmišneh$_1$-kesep$_2$ lāqēḥû$_3$ bĕyādām$_4$ wĕ^{ɔ}et-binyāmin$_5$.
         BU$_2$: N SEQUENCE ¶
         BU$_1$: *wayyāqumû$_1$*.
         BU$_n$: *wayyērĕdû$_1$* miṣrayim$_2$.
         BU$_3$: *wayya^{c}amdû$_1$* lipnê$_2$ yôsēp$_3$.
         BU$_4$: EXECUTION ¶
43:16   LEAD-IN: *wayyar^ɔ$_1$* yôsēp$_2$ ^{ɔ}ittām$_3$ ^{ɔ}et-binyāmîn$_4$.
         PLAN: *wayyō^{ɔ}mer$_1$* la^{ɔ}ăšer$_2$ ^{c}al-bêtô$_3$: QUOTE =**H**
         REASON ¶
            TEXT: **H** SEQUENCE ¶
            BU$_1$: «hābē^ɔ$_1$ ^{ɔ}et-hā^{ɔ}ănāšîm$_2$ habbāyĕtâ$_3$.
            BU$_2$: ûṭĕbōaḥ$_1$ ṭebaḥ$_2$.
            BU$_n$: wĕhākēn$_1$.
            REASON: kî$_1$ ^{ɔ}ittî$_2$ yō^{c}kĕlû$_3$ hā^{ɔ}ănāšîm$_4$ baṣṣohŏrāyim$_5$.»
         EXECUTION: N AMPLIFICATION ¶
43:17   TEXT: *wayya^{c}aś$_1$* hā^{ɔ}îš$_2$ ka^{ɔ}ăšer$_3$ ^{ɔ}āmar$_4$ yôsēp$_5$.
         AMPL: *wayyābē^ɔ$_1$* hā^{ɔ}îš$_2$ ^{ɔ}et-hā^{ɔ}ănāšîm$_3$ bêtâ$_4$ yôsēp$_5$.

1 2 3 4 5 6 7 8 9

43:15   *And-they-took$_1$* the men$_2$ that$_4$ gift$_3$.
    And-double$_1$ silver$_2$ they-took$_3$ in their hands$_4$ and Benjamin$_5$.
    And-they-arose$_1$.
    And-they-went-down$_1$ to Egypt$_2$.
    And-they-stood$_1$ before$_2$ Joseph$_3$.
43:16   *And-he-saw$_1$* Joseph$_2$ Benjamin$_4$ with them$_3$.
    And-he-said$_1$ to the one who$_2$ (was) over his house$_3$:
    «Take$_1$ the men$_2$ to my house$_3$.
    And-butcher$_1$ a fattened animal$_2$.
    And-make-preparation$_1$.
    For$_1$ the men$_4$ they-shall-eat$_3$ with me$_2$ at noon$_5$.»
43:17   *And-he-did$_1$* the man$_2$ as$_3$ Joseph$_5$ had told him$_4$.
    And-he-brought$_1$ the man$_2$ the men$_3$ to the house of$_4$ Joseph$_5$.

1 2 3 4 5 6 7 8 9

43:18 **BU$_5$:** SIMPLE RESOLVED DIALOGUE ¶
LEAD-IN$_1$: QUOTE ¶
LEAD-IN: *wayyîrĕ$^\supset$û$_1$* hā$^\supset$ānāšîm$_2$ kî$_3$ hûbĕ$^\supset$û$_4$ bêt$_5$
yôsēp$_6$.
QUOTE: *wayyō$^\supset$mĕrû$_1$:* «^{C}al$_2$-dĕbar$_3$ hakkesep$_4$ haššāb$_5$
bĕ$^\supset$amtĕḥōtênû$_6$ battĕḥillâ$_7$ $^\supset$ănaḥnû$_8$ mûbā$^\supset$îm$_9$
lĕhitgōlēl$_{10}$ ^{C}ālênû$_{11}$ ûlĕhitnappēl$_{12}$ ^{C}alênû$_{13}$ wĕlāqaḥat$_{14}$
$^\supset$ōtānû$_{15}$ la^{C}ăbādîm$_{16}$ wĕ$^\supset$et$_{17}$-ḥămōrênû$_{18}$.»
43:19 LEAD-IN$_2$: *wayyiggĕšû$_1$* $^\supset$el$_2$ hā$^\supset$îš$_3$ $^\supset$ăšer$_4$ ^{C}al$_5$ bêt$_6$ yôsēp$_7$.
IU (REM): *N* AMPLIFICATION ¶
TEXT: *waydabbĕrû$_1$* $^\supset$ēlāyw$_2$ petaḥ$_3$ habbāyit$_4$.
43:20 AMPL: *wayyō$^\supset$mĕrû$_1$:* QUOTE =*N* SEQUENCE ¶
SETTING: «bî$_1$ $^\supset$ădōnî$_2$ yārōd$_3$ yāradnû$_4$ battĕḥillâ$_5$
lišbar$_6$-$^\supset$ōkel$_7$.
BU$_1$: AWARENESS QUOTE ¶
43:21 AW Q F: wayhî$_1$ kî$_2$ bā$^\supset$nû$_3$ $^\supset$el$_4$-hammālôn$_5$
wanniptĕḥâ$_6$ $^\supset$et-$^\supset$amtĕḥōtênû$_7$.
AW Q: wĕhinnēh$_1$ kesep$_2$-$^\supset$îš$_3$ bĕpî$_4$ $^\supset$amtaḥtô$_5$
kaspēnû$_6$ bĕmišqālô$_7$.
BU$_n$: *N* ANTITHETICAL ¶ (FRONT-WEIGHTED)
THESIS: *wannāšeb$_1$* $^\supset$ōtô$_2$ bĕyādēnû$_3$.
43:22 ANTI: wĕkesep$_1$ $^\supset$aḥēr$_2$ hôradnû$_3$ bĕyādēnû$_4$ lišbar$_5$-
$^\supset$okēl$_6$.
TERMINUS (COMMENT): lō$^\supset_1$ yāda^{C}nû$_2$ mî$_3$-śām$_4$
kaspēnû$_5$ bĕ$^\supset$amtĕḥōtênû$_6$.»
43:23 RU (EVAL): *wayyō$^\supset$mer$_1$:* QUOTE =*N* COORDINATE ¶
PRELIM: *H* AMPLIFICATION ¶
TEXT: «šālôm$_1$ lākem$_2$.
AMPL: $^\supset$al$_1$-tîrā$^\supset$û$_2$.
ITEM$_1$: $^\supset$ĕlōhêkem$_1$ wē$^\supset$lōhê$_2$ $^\supset$ăbîkem$_3$ nātan$_4$ lākem$_5$
maṭmôn$_6$ bĕ$^\supset$amtĕḥōtêkem$_7$.
ITEM$_2$: kaspĕkem$_1$ bā$^\supset_2$ ēlāy$_3$.»
BU$_6$: *wayyôṣē$^\supset_1$* $^\supset$ălêhem$_2$ $^\supset$et-šim^{C}ôn$_3$.
BU$_7$: *N* SEQUENCE ¶
43:24 BU$_1$: *wayyābē$^\supset_1$* hā$^\supset$îš$_2$ $^\supset$et-hā$^\supset$ānāšîm$_3$ bêtâ$_4$ yôsēp$_5$.
BU$_2$: *N* SEQUENCE ¶
BU$_1$: *wayyitten$_1$* mayim$_2$.
BU$_n$: *wayyirḥăṣû$_1$* raglêhem$_2$.
BU$_n$: *wayyittēn$_1$* mispô$^\supset_2$ laḥămōrêhem$_3$.
43:25 **BU$_n$:** *wayyākînû$_1$* $^\supset$et-hamminḥâ$_2$ ^{C}ad$_3$-bō$^\supset_4$ yôsēp$_5$
baṣṣohŏrāyim$_6$ kî$_7$ šāmĕ^{C}û$_8$ kî$_9$-šām$_{10}$ yō$^\supset$kĕlû$_{11}$ lāḥem$_{12}$.

1 2 3 4 5 6 7 8 9

43:18   *And-they-feared$_1$* the men$_2$ as$_3$ they-were-brought$_4$ (to) the house of$_5$ Joseph$_6$.
And-they-said$_1$: «On account of$_2$ the matter of$_3$ the silver$_4$ (which) was returned$_5$ in our sacks$_6$ at the beginning$_7$ we$_8$ (are) brought (here)$_9$—to throw themselves$_{10}$ upon us$_{11}$ and to fall$_{12}$ upon us$_{13}$ and to take$_{14}$ us$_{15}$ as slaves$_{16}$ and$_{17}$ our asses$_{18}$.»

43:19   *And-they-drew-near$_1$* to$_2$ the man$_3$ which$_4$ (was) over$_5$ the house of$_6$ Joseph$_7$.
And-they-spoke$_1$ to him$_2$ (at) the door of$_3$ the house$_4$.

43:20   *And-they-said$_1$:*
«If you please$_1$ my lord$_2$ surely we-came-down$_{3-4}$ at the beginning$_5$ to buy$_6$ grain$_7$.

43:21   And-it-happened-that$_1$ as$_2$ we-came$_3$ to$_4$ the lodging place$_5$ *we-opened$_6$* our sacks$_7$.
And behold$_1$ the silver of$_2$ (each) man$_3$ (was) in the mouth of$_4$ his sack$_5$, our silver$_6$ in its weight$_7$.
And-we've-brought-back$_1$ it$_2$ in our hands$_3$.

43:22   And other$_2$ silver$_1$ we-have-brought-down$_3$ in our hands$_4$ to buy$_5$ food$_6$.
Not$_1$ we-know$_2$ who$_3$ put$_4$ our silver$_5$ in our sacks$_6$.»

43:23   *And-he-said$_1$:* «Peace (be) to you$_2$.
Don't$_1$ be afraid$_2$.
Your God$_1$—even the God of$_2$ your father$_3$ has given$_4$ you$_5$ treasure$_6$ in your sacks$_7$.
Your silver$_1$ came$_2$ to me$_3$.»
And-he-brought-out$_1$ to them$_2$ Simeon$_3$.

43:24   *And-he-brought$_1$* the man$_2$ the men$_3$ to the house$_4$ of Joseph$_5$.
And-he-gave$_1$ (them) water$_2$.
And-they-washed$_1$ their feet$_2$.
And-he-gave$_1$ fodder$_2$ for their asses$_3$.

43:25   *And-they-prepared$_1$* the gift$_2$ with-a-view-towards$_3$ the coming of$_4$ Joseph$_5$ at noon$_6$ for$_7$ they-had-heard$_8$ that$_9$ there$_{10}$ they-were-going-to-eat$_{11}$ bread$_{12}$.

1 2 3 4 5 6 7 8 9

43:26-34   **EPISODE₃: N** SEQUENCE ¶
43:26a   **BU₁:** *wayyābō⁾₁* yôsēp₂ habbayĕtâ₃.
43:26b-28   **BU₂:** SIMPLE DIALOGUE ¶
            LEAD-IN: **N** SEQUENCE ¶
            BU₁: *wayyābî⁾û₁* lô₂ ⁾et-hamminḥâ₃ ⁾ăšer₄-bĕyādām₅
            habbāyĕtâ₆.
            BU₂: *wayyištaḥăwû₁*-lô₂ ⁾ārĕṣâ₃.
            IU (Q): **N** AMPLIFICATION ¶
43:27   TEXT: *wayyiš⁾al₁* lāhem₂ lĕšālôm₃.
            AMPL: *wayyō⁾mer₁:* QUOTE =**E** AMPLIFICATION ¶
            TEXT: «hăšālôm₁ ⁾ăbîkem₂ hazzāqēn₃ ⁾ăšer₄
            ⁾ămartem₅.
            AMPL: haᶜôdennû₁ ḥāy₂.»
43:28   RU (A): *wayyō⁾mĕrû₁:* QUOTE = **E** AMPLIFICATION ¶
            TEXT: «šālôm₁ lĕᶜabdĕkā₂ lĕ⁾ābînû₃.
            AMPL: ᶜôdennû₁ ḥāy₂.»
            STEP-DOWN: **N** SEQUENCE ¶
            BU₁: *wayyiqqĕdû₁.*
            BUₙ: *wayyištaḥăwû₁.*
43:29-31a   **BU₃:** STIMULUS-RESPONSE ¶ **(PRE-CLIMAX)**
            STIMULUS: **N** SEQUENCE ¶
43:29   BU₁: **N** AMPLIFICATION ¶
            TEXT: *wayyiśśâ⁾₁* ᶜênāyw₂
            AMPL: *wayyar⁾₁* ⁾et-binyāmîn₂ ⁾āḥîw₃ ben₄ ⁾immô₅.
            BU₂: *wayyō⁾mer₁:* «hăzeh₂ ⁾āḥîkem₃ haqqāṭōn₄ ⁾ăšer₅
            ⁾ămartem₆ ⁾ēlāy₇.»
            BUₙ: *wayyō⁾mar₁:* «⁾ĕlōhîm₂ yoḥnĕkā₃ bĕnî₄.»
            RESPONSE: **N** SEQUENCE ¶
43:30   BU₁: *waymahēr₁* yôsēp₂ kî₃-nikmĕrû₄ raḥămāyw₅ ⁾el-
            ⁾āḥîw₆.
            waybaqqēš₇ libkôt₈.
            BU₂: *wayyābō⁾₁* haḥadrâ₂.
            BU₃: *wayyēbk₁* šāmmâ₂.
43:31a   BU₄: *wayyirḥaṣ₁* pānāyw₂.
            BU₅: *wayyēṣē⁾₁.*
            BUₙ: *wayyitᶜappaq₁.*

1 2 3 4 5 6 7 8 9

43:26   *And-he-came$_1$* Joseph$_2$ to the house$_3$.
          And-they-brought-in$_1$ to him$_2$ the gift$_3$ which$_4$ (was) in their hands$_5$
          into the house$_6$.
          And-they-bowed-down$_1$ to him$_2$ to the earth$_3$.
43:27   *And-he-asked$_1$* them$_2$ concerning their welfare (peace)$_3$.
          And-he-said$_1$:
          «Is your father$_2$ the old man$_3$ of whom$_4$ you spoke$_5$ all right
          (peace)$_1$?
          Is he still$_1$ alive$_2$?»
43:28   *And-they-said$_1$:*
          «Your servant$_2$ our father$_3$ is all right (peace)$_1$.
          He is yet$_1$ alive.»
          And-they-prostrated-themselves$_1$.
          And-they-bowed-down$_1$.
43:29   *And-he-lifted-up$_1$* his eyes$_2$.
          And-he-saw$_1$ Benjamin$_2$ his brother$_3$ the son of$_4$ his mother$_5$.
          And-he-said$_1$: «Is this$_2$ your younger$_4$ brother$_3$ of whom$_5$ you-
          spoke$_6$ to me$_7$?»
          And-he-said$_1$: «May God$_2$ be gracious to you$_3$ my son$_4$.»
43:30   *And-he-hurried$_1$* Joseph$_2$ for$_3$ were-deeply-moved$_4$ his feelings$_5$
          toward his brother$_6$.
          And-he-looked-for$_7$ (a place) to cry$_8$.
          And-he-went-into$_1$ the (inner) room$_2$.
          And-he-wept$_1$ there$_2$.
43:31a   *And-he-washed$_1$* his face$_2$.
          And-he-came-out$_1$.
          And-he-controlled-himself$_1$.

1 2 3 4 5 6 7 8 9

43:31b-34   **BU$_n$ (CLIMAX): N** SEQUENCE ¶ [BUT SOMEWHAT
DEPICTIVE]
  BU$_1$: EXECUTION ¶
    PLAN: *wayyō$^{\ni}$mer$_1$:* «sîmû$_2$ lāḥem$_3$.»
  EXEC: **N** REASON ¶
43:32   TEXT: *wayyāsîmû$_1$* lô$_2$ lĕbaddô$_3$ wēlāhem$_4$ lēbaddām$_5$
    wĕlammiṣrîm$_6$ hā$^{\ni}$ōkĕlîm$_7$ $^{\ni}$ittô$_8$ lĕbaddām$_9$.
    REASON: kî$_1$ lō$^{\ni}$$_2$ yûkēlûn$_3$ hammiṣrîm$_4$ le$^{\ni}$ĕkōl$_5$ $^{\ni}$et-
    hā^{c}ibrîm$_6$ leḥem$_7$ kî$_8$-tô^{c}ēbâ$_9$ hiw$^{\ni}$$_{10}$ lĕmiṣrāyim$_{11}$.
  BU$_2$: **N** RESULT ¶
43:33   TEXT: *wayyēšĕbû$_1$* lĕpānāyw$_2$ habbĕkōr$_3$ kibkōrātô$_4$
    wēhaṣṣā^{c}îr$_5$ kiṣ^{c}irātô$_6$
    RESULT: *wayyitmĕhû$_1$* hā$^{\ni}$ănāšîm$_2$ $^{\ni}$îš$_3$ $^{\ni}$el$_4$-rē^{c}ēhû$_5$.
  BU$_3$: **N** AMPLIFICATION ¶
43:34   TEXT: *wayyissā$^{\ni}$$_1$* maś$^{\ni}$ōt$_2$ mē$^{\ni}$ēt$_3$ pānāyw$_4$ $^{\ni}$ălēhem$_5$.
    AMPL: *wattēreb$_1$* maś$^{\ni}$at$_2$ binyāmin$_3$ mimmaś$^{\ni}$ōt$_4$ kullām$_5$
    ḥāmēš$_6$ yādôt$_7$.
  BU$_n$: **N** SEQUENCE ¶
    BU$_1$: *wayyištû$_1$.*
    BU$_2$: *wayyiškĕrû$_1$* ^{c}immô$_2$.

1 2 3 4 5 6 7 8 9

43:31b	*And-he-said$_1$:* «Bring-on$_2$ the food$_3$.»
43:32	*And-they-served$_1$* to him$_2$ by himself$_3$, and to them$_4$ by themselves$_5$, and to the Egyptians$_6$ the ones eating$_7$ with him$_8$ by themselves$_9$.
	For$_1$ not$_2$ they-are-able$_3$ the Egyptians$_4$ to eat$_5$ food$_7$ with the Hebrews$_6$, for$_8$ an abomination$_9$ (is) it$_{10}$ to the Egyptians$_{11}$.
43:33	*And-they-sat$_1$* before him$_2$ the first born$_3$ according to his seniority$_4$ and the youngest$_5$ according to his youth$_6$.
	And-they-marvelled$_1$ the men$_2$ each$_3$ to$_4$ his fellow$_5$.
43:34	*And-he-sent-off$_1$* portions$_2$ from$_3$ before him$_4$ to them$_5$.
	And-it-was-greater$_1$ the portion of$_2$ Benjamin$_3$ than the portions of$_4$ all the others$_5$ (by) five$_6$ times$_7$.
	And-they-drank$_1$.
	And-they-got-drunk$_1$ with him$_2$.

286   1 2 3 4 5 6 7 8 9

44   **PEAK: N** DISC
44:1-2   **STAGE:** EXECUTION ¶
44:1   PLAN: $wayṣaw_1$ ^ɔet-$^ɔāšer_2$ $^cal_3$-bêtô$_4$ lē^{ɔ}mōr$_5$: QUOTE =**H**
                SEQUENCE ¶
                BU$_1$: «mallē$^ɔ_1$ ^ɔet-^{ɔ}amtĕḥōt$_2$ hā^{ɔ}ānāšîm$_3$ ^{ɔ}ōkel$_4$ ka^{ɔ}āšer$_5$
                yûkēlûn$_6$ śē^{ɔ}ēt$_7$.
                BU$_2$: wĕśîm$_1$ kesep$_2$-^{ɔ}îš$_3$ bĕpî$_4$ ^{ɔ}amtaḥtô$_5$.
44:2   CLIMAX: wĕ^{ɔ}et-gĕbî^{c}î$_1$ gĕbîa$^c_2$ hakkesep$_3$ tāśîm$_4$ bĕpî$_5$
                ^{ɔ}amtaḥat$_6$ haqqātōn$_7$ wĕ^{ɔ}ēt kesep$_8$ šibrô$_9$.»
                EXEC: $wayya^caś_1$ kidbar$_2$ yôsēp$_3$ ^{ɔ}āšer$_4$ dibbēr$_5$.
44:3-13   **EPISODE$_1$:** EXECUTION ¶ (END-WEIGHTED)
                SETTING: **N** SIMPLE ¶
43:3   SETTING: habbōqer$_1$ ^{ɔ}ōr$_2$.
                TEXT: wĕhā^{ɔ}ānāšîm$_1$ šullĕḥû$_2$ hēmmâ$_3$ waḥămōrêhem$_4$.
44:4-5   PLAN: **N** ANTITHETICAL ¶ (END-WEIGHTED)
                THESIS: **N** AMPLIFICATION ¶
44:4   TEXT: hēm$_1$ yāṣĕ^{ɔ}û$_2$ ^{ɔ}et-hā^{c}îr$_3$.
                AMPL: lō$^ɔ_1$ hirḥîqû$_2$
                ANTI: wĕyôsēp$_1$ ^{ɔ}āmar$_2$ la^{ɔ}āšer$_3$ $^cal_4$-bêtô$_5$: QUOTE =**H**
                SEQUENCE ¶
                BU$_1$: «qûm$_1$
                rĕdōp$_2$ ^{ɔ}aḥārê$_3$ hā^{ɔ}ānāšîm$_4$.
                BU$_2$: wĕhiśśagtam$_1$
                BU$_n$: wĕ^{ɔ}āmartā$_1$ ^{ɔ}ălēhem$_2$: QUOTE =**H**
                COMMENT ¶
                    TEXT: **H** AMPLIFICATION ¶
                    TEXT: ''lāmmâ$_1$ šillamtem$_2$ rā^{c}â$_3$ taḥat$_4$ tôbâ$_5$.
                    AMPL: COORDINATE ¶
44:5   ITEM$_1$: hălō$^ɔ_1$ zeh$_2$ ^{ɔ}āšer$_3$ yišteh$_4$ ^{ɔ}ădōnî$_5$ bô$_6$.
                    ITEM$_2$: wĕhû$^ɔ_1$ naḥēš$_2$ yĕnaḥēš$_3$ bô$_4$.
                    COMMENT: hărē^{c}ōtem$_1$ ^{ɔ}āšer$_2$ ^{c}ăśîtem$_3$.''»

1 2 3 4 5 6 7 8 9

44:1 *And-he-commanded₁* the (one) which₂ (was) over₃ his house₄
saying₅:
«Fill₁ the bags of₂ the men₃ food₄ according to what₅ they-can₆
carry₇.
And put₁ the silver of₂ (each) man₃ in the mouth of₄ his sack₅.

44:2 And place₄ my cup₁ the cup₂ of silver₃ in the mouth of₅ the sack-
of₆ the youngest₇ along with the silver of₈ his purchase₉.»
And-he-did₁ according to the word₂ which₄ Joseph₃ had spoken₅.

44:3 The morning₁ dawned₂.
And the men₁ they-were-sent-off₂, they₃ and their asses₄.

44:4 They₁ had left₂ the city₃.
Not₁ they-had-gone-far₂.
Joseph₁, (on the other hand) spoke₂ to the (one) which₃ (was)
over₄ his house₅:
«Arise₁, pursue₂ after₃ the men₄.
And-overtake-them₁.
And-say₁ to them₂:
"Why₁ have-you-repaid₂ evil₃ for₄ good₅.

44:5 Is not₁ this₂ (which you have stolen) that which₃ drinks₄ my lord₅
from it₆?
And he₁ surely₂ divines₃ by means of it₄.
You-have-done-evil₁ (this) which₂ you-have-done₃."»

1 2 3 4 5 6 7 8 9

| | | | | | | | | |

44:6-13   **EXEC: EXECUTION ¶ (IAMBIC)**
44:6-10   **PLAN: COMPLEX RESOLVED DIALOGUE ¶**
           IU (REM): INDIRECT QUOTE ¶
44:6   **LEAD-IN:** *wayyaśśigem₁*.
              QUOTE: *waydabbēr₁ ᵓălēhem₂ ᵓet-haddĕbārîm₃ hā-ᵓēlleh₄.*
44:7   **CU (COUNTER-REM):** *wayyōᵓmĕrû₁ ᵓēlāyw₂:*
             QUOTE = H ANTITHETICAL ¶ (END-WEIGHTED)
              THESIS: H AMPLIFICATION ¶
               PRELIM: «lāmmâ₁ yĕdabbēr₂ ᵓădōnî₃ kaddĕbārîm₄ hā-ᵓēlleh₅.
               TEXT: ḥālîlâ₁ laᶜăbādêkā₂ mēᶜăśôt₃ kaddābār₄ hazzeh₅.
               AMPL: H EVIDENCE ¶
44:8   **EVIDENCE:** hēn₁ kesep₂ ᵓăšer₃ māṣā-ᵓnû₄ bĕpî₅ ᵓamtĕḥōtênû₆ hĕšîbōnû₇ ᵓēlêkā₈ mēᵓereṣ₉ kenāᶜan₁₀.
                 TEXT: wĕ-ᵓêk₁ nignōb₂ mibbêt₃ ᵓădōnêkā₄ kesep₅ ᵓ ô₆ zāhāb₇.
               ANTI: H COORDINATE ¶
44:9   **ITEM₁:** ᵓăšer₁ yimmāṣēᵓ₂ ᵓittô₃ mēᶜăbādêkā₄ wāmēt₅
                 ITEM₂: wĕgam₁-ᵓănaḥnû₂ nihyeh₃ laᵓdōnî₄ laᶜăbādîm₅.»
44:10   **RU (RES):** *wayyōᵓmer₁:* **QUOTE = H ANTITHETICAL ¶**
               PRELIM: «gam₁-ᶜattâ₂ kĕdibrêkem₃ ken₄-hûᵓ₅
               THESIS: ᵓăšer₁ yimmāṣēᵓ₂ ᵓittô₃ yihyeh₄-llî₅ ᶜābed₆.
               ANTI: wĕ-ᵓattem₁ tihyû₂ nĕqiyyim₃.»

| | | | | | | | | |

1 2 3 4 5 6 7 8 9

44:6　　　*And-he-overtook-them₁.*
　　　　　And-he-spoke₁ to them₂ these₄ words₃.
44:7　　　*And-they-said₁ to him₂:*
　　　　　«Why₁ speaks₂ my lord₃ according to these₅ words₄.
　　　　　Far be it₁ from your servants₂ from doing₃ according to this₅
　　　　　word₄.
44:8　　　Behold₁ the silver₂ which₃ we-found₄ in the mouth of₅ our bags₆
　　　　　we-returned₇ to you₈ from the land of₉ Canaan₁₀.
　　　　　And how₁ should we steal₂ from the house of₃ your lord₄ silver₅
　　　　　or₆ gold₇.
44:9　　　Whoever₁ it is found₂ with him₃ from your servants₄ let him die₅.
　　　　　And-also₁ we₂ will-be₃ slaves₅ to my lord₄.»
44:10　　*And-he-said₁:*
　　　　　«Also₁ now₂ (let be) it thus₄ according to your words₃.
　　　　　With whomever₁₋₃ it-is-found₂ he-shall-be₄ to me₅ a slave₆.
　　　　　As for you₁ you-shall-be₂ innocent₃.»

1 2 3 4 5 6 7 8 9

44:11-13 **EXEC: STIMULUS-RESPONSE ¶**
    STIMULUS: **N** SEQUENCE ¶
44:11   BU$_1$: *waymahărû$_1$*.
    wayyôridû$_2$ ʾîš$_3$ ʾet-ʾamtaḥtô$_4$ ʾārĕṣâ$_5$.
    BU$_2$: *wayyiptĕḥû$_6$ ʾîš$_7$ ʾamtaḥtô$_8$*.
    BU$_3$: **N** COMMENT ¶
44:12   TEXT: *wayḥappĕś$_1$*.
    COMMENT: **N** ANTITHETICAL (?) ¶
    THESIS: baggādôl$_1$ hēḥēl$_2$.
    ANTI: ûbaqqāṭōn$_1$ killâ$_2$.
    BU$_n$ (CLIMAX): *wayyimmāṣē$^ʾ_1$* haggābîa$^c_2$
    bĕʾamtaḥat$_3$ binyāmin$_4$.
    RESPONSE: **N** SEQUENCE ¶
44:13   BU$_1$: *wayyiqrĕ^{c}û$_1$* śimlōtām$_2$.
    BU$_2$: *wayya^{c}ămōs$_1$* ʾîš$_2$ ^{c}al$_3$-ḥămōrô$_4$.
    BU$_n$: *wayyāšubû$_1$* hā^{c}îrâ$_2$.
44:14-34 **PEAK: COMPLEX UNRESOLVED DIALOGUE ¶**
    LEAD-IN: **N** SEQUENCE ¶
    BU$_1$: **N** COMMENT ¶
44:14   TEXT: *wayyābō$^ʾ_1$* yĕhûdâ$_2$ wĕʾeḥāyw$_3$ bêtâ$_4$ yôsēp$_5$.
    COMMENT: wĕhû$^ʾ_1$ ^{c}ôdennû$_2$ šām$_3$.
    BU$_n$: *wayyippĕlû$_1$* lĕpānāyw$_2$ ʾārĕṣâ$_3$.
44:15   IU (REM): *wayyō^{ʾ}mer$_1$* lāhem$_2$ yôsēp$_3$: QUOTE =**H**
    COORDINATE ¶
    ITEM$_1$: «mâ$_1$-hamma^{c}ăśeh$_2$ hazzeh$_3$ ʾăšer$_4$ ^{c}ăśîtem$_5$.
    ITEM$_2$: hălô$^ʾ_1$ yĕda^{c}tem$_2$ kî$_3$-naḥēš$_4$ yĕnaḥēš$_5$ ʾîš$_6$ ʾăšer$_7$
    kāmōnî$_8$.»
44:16   CU (COUNTER-PROP): *wayyō^{ʾ}mer$_1$* yĕhûdâ$_2$: QUOTE =**H**
    RESULT ¶
    TEXT: **H** AMPLIFICATION ¶
    TEXT: **H** AMPLIFICATION ¶
    TEXT: **H** PARAPHRASE ¶
    TEXT: «mâ$_1$-nnō^{ʾ}mar$_2$ la^{ʾ}dōnî$_3$.
    PARA: mâ$_1$-nnĕdabbēr$_2$.
    AMPL: ûmâ$_1$-nniṣṭaddāq$_2$.
    AMPL: hāʾĕlōhîm$_1$ māṣā$^ʾ_2$ ʾet-^{c}ăwōn$_3$ ʾăbādêkā$_4$.
    RESULT: hinnennû$_1$ ^{c}ăbādîm$_2$ la^{ʾ}dōnî$_3$ gam$_4$-ʾănaḥnû$_5$
    gam$_6$ ʾăšer$_7$-nimṣā$^ʾ_8$ haggābîa$^c_9$ bĕyādô$_{10}$.»
44:17   CU (COUNTER-PROP): *wayyō^{ʾ}mer$_1$*: QUOTE =**H**
    ANTITHETICAL ¶
    PRELIM: «ḥālîlâ$_1$ llî$_2$ mē^{c}ăśôt$_3$ zō^{ʾ}t$_4$.
    THESIS: hā^{ʾ}îš$_1$ ʾăšer$_2$ nimṣā$^ʾ_3$ haggābîa$^c_4$ bĕyādô$_5$ hû$^ʾ_6$
    yihyeh$_7$-llî$_8$ ^{c}ābed$_9$.
    ANTI: wĕʾattem$_1$ ^{c}ălû$_2$ lĕšālôm$_3$ ʾel$_4$-ʾăbîkem$_5$.»

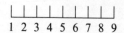

1 2 3 4 5 6 7 8 9

44:11   *And-they-hurried$_1$.*
           And-they-lowered$_2$ (each) man$_3$ his sack$_4$ to the ground$_5$.
           And-they-opened$_6$ (each) man$_7$ his sack$_8$.
44:12   *And-he-searched$_1$.*
           With the oldest$_1$ he-began$_2$.
           And with youngest$_1$ he-ended$_2$.
           And-it-was-found$_1$ the cup$_2$ in the sack of$_3$ Benjamin$_4$.
44:13   *And-they-tore$_1$* their clothing$_2$.
           And-they-loaded$_1$ (each) man$_2$ on to$_3$ his ass$_4$.
           And-they-returned$_1$ to the city$_2$.
44:14   *And-he-came-in$_1$* Judah$_2$ and his brothers$_3$ to the house of$_4$
           Joseph$_5$.
           And-he$_1$ (was) still$_2$ there$_3$.
           And-they-fell-down$_1$ before him$_2$ to the ground$_3$.
44:15   *And-he-said$_1$* to them$_2$ Joseph$_3$:
           «What$_1$ (is) this$_3$ doing$_2$ which$_4$ you-have-done$_5$?
           Don't$_1$ you-know$_2$ that$_3$ a man$_6$ such as I$_{7-8}$ can surely divine$_{4-5}$?»
44:16   *And-he-said$_1$* Judah$_2$:
           «What$_1$ shall-we-say$_2$ to my lord$_3$?
           What$_1$ shall-we-speak$_2$.
           And what (=how)$_1$ can-we-justify-ourselves$_2$?
           God$_1$ has-found-out$_2$ the iniquity of$_3$ your servants$_4$.
           Behold$_1$ slaves$_2$ to my lord$_3$ (are) both$_4$ we$_5$ and$_6$ (he) who$_7$ was
           found$_8$ the cup$_9$ in his hand$_{10}$.»
44:17   *And-he-said$_1$:*
           «Far be it$_1$ to me$_2$ from doing$_3$ this$_4$.
           The man$_1$ (on) which$_2$ was-found$_3$ the cup$_4$ in his hand$_5$, he$_6$ will-
           be$_7$ to me$_8$ a slave$_9$.
           But the rest of you$_1$ go-up$_2$ in peace$_3$ to$_4$ your father$_5$.»

1 2 3 4 5 6 7 8 9 10 11 12

CU (COUNTER-PROP): QUOTE ¶
44:18   **LEAD-IN:** *wayyiggaš$_1$* $^\supset$ēlāyw$_2$ yĕhûdâ$_3$.
44:18-34   **QUOTE:** *wayyō$^\supset$mer$_1$:* QUOTE =**Ḥ** DISC
       INTRO: Ḥ COORDINATE ¶
         ITEM$_1$: «bî$_1$ $^\supset$ădōnî$_2$ yĕdabber-nā$^\supset$$_3$ ^{c}abdĕkā$_4$ dābār$_5$ bĕ$^\supset$oznê$_6$ $^\supset$ădōnî$_7$.
         ITEM$_2$: wĕ$^\supset$al$_1$-yiḥar$_2$ $^\supset$appĕkā$_3$ bĕ^{c}ābdekā$_4$ kî$_5$ kāmôkā$_6$ kĕpar^{c}oh$_7$.
44:19-29   **POINT$_1$ (BACKGROUND):** COMPOUND DIALOGUE ¶
44:19-23   **EXCHANGE$_1$:** COMPOUND DIALOGUE ¶
44:19-20   **EXCHANGE$_1$:** SIMPLE RESOLVED DIALOGUE ¶
44:19   **IU (Q):** $^\supset$ădōnî$_1$ šā$^\supset$al$_2$ $^\supset$et-^{c}ābādāyw$_3$ lē$^\supset$mōr$_4$: "hăyĕš$_5$-lākem$_6$ $^\supset$āb$_7$ $^\supset$ô$_8$-$^\supset$āḥ$_9$."
44:20   **RU (A):** *wannō$^\supset$mer$_1$* $^\supset$el$_2$-$^\supset$ădōnî$_3$: QUOTE =**E** COMMENT ¶
             TEXT: "yeš$_1$-lānû$_2$ $^\supset$āb$_3$ zāqēn$_4$ wĕyeled$_5$ zĕqunîm$_6$ qātān$_7$.
             COMMENT: E REASON ¶
               REASON: CIRCUMSTANCE ¶
               CIR: wĕ$^\supset$āḥîw$_1$ mēt$_2$.
               TEXT: *wayyiwwātēr$_1$* hû$^\supset$$_2$ lĕbaddô$_3$ lĕ$^\supset$immô$_4$.
             TEXT: wĕ$^\supset$ābîw$_1$ $^\supset$āhēbô$_2$."
44:21-23   **EXCHANGE$_2$:** COMPLEX UNRESOLVED DIALOGUE ¶
44:21   **IU (PROP):** *wattō$^\supset$mer$_1$* $^\supset$el$_2$-^{c}ābādêkā$_3$: QUOTE =**Ḥ** SEQUENCE ¶
           BU$_1$: "hôriduhû$_1$ $^\supset$ēlāy$_2$.
           BU$_n$: wĕ$^\supset$āśîmâ$_1$ ^{c}ênî$_2$ ^{c}ālāyw$_3$."
44:22   **CU (COUNTER-PROP):** *wannō$^\supset$mer$_1$* $^\supset$el$_2$-$^\supset$ădōnî$_3$: QUOTE =**E** AMPLIFICATION ¶
           TEXT: "lō$^\supset$$_1$-yûkal$_2$ hanna^{c}ar$_3$ la^{c}ăzōb$_4$ $^\supset$et-$^\supset$ābîw$_5$.
           AMPL: P SEQUENCE ¶ (CONDITIONAL)
           BU$_1$: wĕ^{c}āzab$_1$ $^\supset$et-$^\supset$ābîw$_2$.
           BU$_n$: wāmēt$_1$."
44:23   **CU (COUNTER-PROP):** *wattō$^\supset$mer$_1$* $^\supset$el$_2$-^{c}ābādêkā$_3$: "$^\supset$im$_1$-lō$^\supset$$_2$ yērēd$_3$ $^\supset$ăḥîkem$_4$ haqqātōn$_5$ $^\supset$ittĕkem$_6$ lō$^\supset$$_7$ tōsipûn$_8$ lir$^\supset$ôt$_9$ pānāy$_{10}$."

1 2 3 4 5 6 7 8 9 10 11 12

44:18   *And-he-stepped-up-close₁* to him₂ Judah₃.
        And-he-said₁:
        «Please₁ my lord₂ let your servant₄ speak₃ a word₅ in the ears of₆
        my lord₇.
        And don't₁ let your anger₃ get hot₂ with your servant₄ for₅ like
        Pharaoh₇ are you₆.
44:19   My lord₁ asked₂ his servants₃ saying₄: "Is-there₅ to you₆ a father₇
        or a brother₈?"
44:20   *And-we-said₁* to₂ my lord₃:
        "There is₁ to us₂ an old₄ father₃ and a young₇ son₅ of (his) old
        age₆.
        And his brother₁ has died₂.
        And-he-has-been-left₁ he₂ alone₃ from his mother₄.
        And his father₁ loves-him₂."
44:21   *And-you-said₁* to₂ your servants₃:
        "Bring-him-down₁ to me₂.
        And-I-will-set₁ my eyes₂ on him₃."
44:22   *And-we-said₁* to₂ my lord₃.
        "Not₁ he-is-able₂ the lad₃ to leave₄ his father₅.
        (If) he-leaves₁ his father₂,
        he-will-die₁."
44:23   *And-you-said₁* to₂ your servants₃: "If₁ not₂ he-comes-down₃ with
        you₆ your little₅ brother₄ not₇ you-will-add₈ to see₉ my face₁₀,
        (=you won't see my face again)."

44:24-29 EXCHANGE$_2$: COMPLEX UNRESOLVED
DIALOGUE ¶

44:24 LEAD-IN: wayhî$_1$ kî$_2$ ^{c}ālînû$_3$ $^{\,}$el$_4$-^{c}abdĕkā$_5$
$^{\,}$ābî$_6$,
wannagged$_1$-lô$_2$ $^{\,}$ēt dibrê$_3$ $^{\,}$ădōnî$_4$.

44:25 IU (PROP): *wayyō$^{\,}$mer$_1$* $^{\,}$ābînû$_2$: QUOTE = **H**
SEQUENCE ¶
BU$_1$: "šubû$_1$
BU$_n$: šibrû$_1$-lānû$_2$ mĕ^{c}aṭ$_3$-$^{\,}$ōkel$_4$."

44:26 CU (COUNTER-PROP): *wannō$^{\,}$mer$_1$:*
QUOTE = **E** ANTITHETICAL ¶
THESIS: "lō$^{\,}$$_1$ nûkal$_2$ lāredet$_3$.
ANTI: **E** REASON ¶
TEXT: $^{\,}$im$_1$-yeš$_2$ $^{\,}$āḥînû$_3$ haqqātōn$_4$
$^{\,}$ittānû$_5$ wĕyāradnû$_6$.
REASON [possibly = CAUSE MARGIN
OF PREVIOUS S]: **E** REASON ¶
TEXT: kî$_1$-lô$^{\,}$$_2$ nûkal$_3$ lir$^{\,}$ôt$_4$ pĕnê$_5$
hā$^{\,}$îš$_6$
REASON: wĕ$^{\,}$āḥînû$_1$ haqqātōn$_2$
$^{\,}$ênennû$_3$ $^{\,}$ittānû$_4$."

44:27 CU (COUNTER-REM): *wayyō$^{\,}$mer$_1$* ^{c}abdĕkā$_2$
$^{\,}$ābî$_3$ $^{\,}$ēlênû$_4$: QUOTE = **P** REASON ¶
REASON: **N** SEQUENCE ¶
₁SETTING: "$^{\,}$attem$_1$ yĕda^{c}tem$_2$ kî$_3$
šĕnayim$_4$ yālĕdâ$_5$-llî$_6$ $^{\,}$ištî$_7$.

44:28 BU$_1$: *wayyēṣē$^{\,}$$_1$* hā$^{\,}$eḥād$_2$ mē$^{\,}$ittî$_3$.
BU$_n$: **N** COMMENT ¶
TEXT: *wā$^{\,}$ōmar$_1$:* '$^{\,}$ak$_2$ ṭārōp$_3$ ṭōrāp$_4$,'
COMMENT: wĕlō$^{\,}$$_1$ rĕ$^{\,}$îtîw$_2$ ^{c}ad$_3$-
hēnnâ$_4$.
TEXT: **P** SEQUENCE ¶ (CONDITIONAL)

44:29 BU$_1$: ûlĕqaḥtem$_1$ gam$_2$-$^{\,}$et-zeh$_3$ mē^{c}im$_4$
pānay$_5$.
BU$_2$: wĕqārāhû$_1$ $^{\,}$āsôn$_2$
BU$_n$: wĕhôradtem$_1$ $^{\,}$et-śêbātî$_2$ bĕrā^{c}â$_3$
šĕ$^{\,}$ōlâ$_4$."

44:24   And-it-came-to-pass$_1$ that$_2$ we-went-up$_3$ to$_4$ your servant$_5$ my
          father$_6$.
          And-we-declared$_1$ to him$_2$ the words of$_3$ my lord$_4$.
44:25   *And-he-said$_1$* our father$_2$:
          "Return$_1$.
          Buy$_1$ us$_2$ a bit of$_3$ food$_4$."
44:26   *And-we-said$_1$:*
          "Not$_1$ we-are-able$_2$ to go down$_3$.
          If$_1$ our little$_4$ brother$_3$ is$_2$ with us$_5$ we'll-go-down$_6$.
          For$_1$ not$_2$ we-are-able$_3$ to see$_4$ the face-of$_5$ the man$_6$
          and (=when) our little$_2$ brother$_1$ is not$_3$ with us$_4$."
44:27   *And-he-said$_1$* your servant$_2$ our father$_3$ to us$_4$
          "You$_1$ know$_2$ that$_3$ my wife$_7$ bore$_5$ to me$_6$ two sons$_4$.
44:28   *And-he-went-out$_1$* the one$_2$ from me$_3$.
          And-I-said$_1$: 'Truly$_2$ (he) is torn in pieces$_{3-4}$.'
          And-not$_1$ I-have-seen-him$_2$ until$_3$ now$_4$.
44:29   And-you-would-take$_1$ also$_2$ this one$_3$ from$_4$ me$_5$?
          —And-it-will-encounter-him$_1$ harm$_2$.
          —And-you-will-bring-down$_1$ my grey hairs$_2$ in sorrow$_3$ to Sheol$_4$."

1 2 3 4 5 6 7 8 9

44:30-32 POINT$_2$ (THE PROBLEM): **P** REASON ¶
44:30 TEXT: [SENTENCE WITH BACKLOOPED
PARAGRAPHS] wĕ^{c}attâ$_1$ [TEMPORAL MARGIN
EMBEDS **E** CIRCUMSTANTIAL ¶]
TEXT: kĕbō$^{\ni}$î$_2$ $^\ni$el$_3$-^{c}abdĕkā$_4$ $^\ni$ābî$_5$
CIR$_1$: wĕhanna^{c}ar$_6$ $^\ni$ênennû$_7$ $^\ni$ittānû$_8$
CIR$_2$: wĕnapšô$_9$ qĕšûrâ$_{10}$ bĕnapšô$_{11}$
44:31 wĕhāyâ$_{12}$ kir$^\ni$ôtô$_{13}$ kî$_{14}$-$^\ni$ên$_{15}$ hanna^{c}ar$_{16}$
[COMPLEMENT EMBEDS **P** SEQUENCE ¶]
BU$_1$: wāmēt$_{17}$
BU$_n$: wĕhôrîdû$_{18}$ ^{c}ābādêkā$_{19}$ $^\ni$et-śêbat$_{20}$ ^{c}abdĕkā$_{21}$
$^\ni$ābînû$_{22}$ bĕyāgôn$_{23}$ šĕ$^\ni$ōlâ$_{24}$.
44:32 REASON: kî$_1$ ^{c}abdĕkâ$_2$ ^{c}ārab$_3$ $^\ni$et-hanna^{c}ar$_4$
mē$^\ni$im$_5$ $^\ni$ābî$_6$ lē$^\ni$mōr$_7$: ''$^\ni$im$_8$-lō$^\ni$$_9$ $^\ni$ăbî$^\ni$ennû$_{10}$
$^\ni$ēlêkā$_{11}$ wĕḥāṭā$^\ni$tî$_{12}$ lē$^\ni$ābî$_{13}$ kol$_{14}$-hayyāmîm$_{15}$.''
44:33-34 POINT$_n$ (PROPOSAL AS PEAK): **H** REASON ¶
TEXT: **H** ANTITHETICAL ¶ (END-WEIGHTED)
44:33 THESIS: wĕ^{c}attâ$_1$ yēšeb-nā$^\ni$$_2$ ^{c}abdĕkâ$_3$ taḥat$_4$
hanna^{c}ar$_5$ ^{c}ebed$_6$ la$^\ni$dōnî$_7$
ANTI: wĕhanna^{c}ar$_1$ ya^{c}al$_2$ ^{c}im$_3$-$^\ni$eḥāyw$_4$.
REASON: **H** RESULT ¶
TEXT: CIRCUMSTANTIAL ¶
44:34 TEXT: kî$_1$-$^\ni$êk$_2$ $^\ni$e^{c}ĕleh$_3$ $^\ni$el$_4$-$^\ni$ābî$_5$
CIR: wĕhanna^{c}ar$_1$ $^\ni$ênennû$_2$ $^\ni$ittî$_3$
RESULT (NEGATIVE): pen$_1$ $^\ni$er$^\ni$eh$_2$ bārā^c$_3$
$^\ni$ăšer$_4$ yimṣā$^\ni$$_5$ $^\ni$et-$^\ni$ābî$_6$.»

1 2 3 4 5 6 7 8 9

44:30   And now$_1$ in-my-coming$_2$ to$_3$ your servant$_4$ my father$_5$ and the lad$_6$
          is not$_7$ with us$_8$, (seeing that) his life$_9$ is bound up$_{10}$ with his (the
          lad's) life$_{11}$,

44:31   then-it-will-happen$_{12}$ in his-seeing$_{13}$ that$_{14}$ the lad$_{16}$ isn't$_{15}$ (with us),
          he-will-die$_{17}$, and your servants$_{19}$ will bring down$_{18}$ the grey head
          of$_{20}$ your servant$_{21}$ our father$_{22}$ in grief$_{23}$ to Sheol$_{24}$.

44:32   For$_1$ your servant$_2$ went surety for$_3$ the lad$_4$ before$_5$ my father$_6$
          saying$_7$:
          "If$_8$ not$_9$ I-bring-him$_{10}$ to you$_{11}$ then-I-will-bear-the-sin$_{12}$ against
          my father$_{13}$ all$_{14}$ the days$_{15}$."

44:33   And now$_1$ let-dwell-I-pray$_2$ your servant$_3$ in place of$_4$ the lad$_5$ as a
          slave$_6$ to my lord$_7$.
          But the lad$_1$ will-go-up$_2$ with$_3$ his brothers$_4$.

44:34   For$_1$ how$_2$ can-I-go-up$_3$ to$_4$ my father$_5$
          when the lad$_1$ isn't$_2$ with me$_3$—
          lest$_1$ I-see$_2$ the evil$_3$ which$_4$ shall befall$_5$ my father$_6$.»

1 2 3 4 5 6 7 8 9

45:1-15   **PEAK' (DENOUEMENT):** AMPLIFICATION ¶

45:1-3   **TEXT:** SIMPLE UNRESOLVED DIALOGUE ¶

45:1   SETTING: wĕlō$^{\circ}_1$ yākōl$_2$ yôsēp$_3$ lĕhit$^{\circ}$appēq$_4$ lĕkōl$_5$ hannișșābîm$_6$ ^{c}ālāyw$_7$.

LEAD-IN$_1$: *N* RESULT ¶

    TEXT: *wayyiqrā$^{\circ}_1$:* «hôșî$^{\circ}$û$_2$ kol$_3$-$^{\circ}$îš$_4$ mē^{c}ālāy$_5$.»

    RESULT:wĕlō$^{\circ}_1$ ^{c}āmad$_2$ $^{\circ}$îš$_3$ $^{\circ}$ittô$_4$ bĕhitwadda$^{c}_5$ yôsēp$_6$ $^{\circ}$el$_7$-$^{\circ}$eḥāyw$_8$.

LEAD-IN$_2$: *N* SEQUENCE ¶

45:2   BU$_1$: *wayyittēn$_1$* $^{\circ}$et-qōlô$_2$ bibkî$_3$

BU$_n$: *N* AMPLIFICATION ¶

    TEXT: *wayyišmĕ^{c}û$_1$* mișrayim$_2$.

    AMPL: *wayyišma$^{c}_1$* bêt$_2$ par^{c}ōh$_3$.

45:3   IU (REM/Q): *wayyō$^{\circ}$mer$_1$* yôsēp$_2$ $^{\circ}$el$_3$-$^{\circ}$eḥāyw$_4$:

QUOTE =*E* COORDINATE ¶

    ITEM$_1$: «$^{\circ}$ănî$_1$ yôsēp$_2$.

    ITEM$_2$: ha^{c}ôd$_1$ $^{\circ}$ābî$_2$ ḥāy$_3$.»

    TERMINUS: wĕlō$^{\circ}_1$-yākĕlû$_2$ $^{\circ}$eḥāyw$_3$ la^{c}ănôt$_4$ $^{\circ}$ōtô$_5$ kî$_6$ nibhălû$_7$ mippānāyw$_8$.

1 2 3 4 5 6 7 8 9

45:1   And not$_1$ could$_2$ Joseph$_3$ control himself$_4$ before all$_5$ the ones standing around$_6$ him$_7$.

And-he-cried-out$_1$: «Clear-out$_2$ every$_3$ man$_4$ from before me$_5$.»

And-not$_1$ stood$_2$ a man$_3$ with him$_4$ in Joseph's$_6$ making himself known$_5$ to$_7$ his brothers$_8$.

45:2   *And-he-lifted$_1$* his voice$_2$ in weeping$_3$.

And-they-heard$_1$ the Egyptians$_2$.

And-they-heard$_1$ the house of$_2$ Pharaoh$_3$.

45:3   *And-he-said$_1$* Joseph$_2$ to$_3$ his brothers$_4$:

«I$_1$ (am) Joseph$_2$!

Is my father$_2$ still$_1$ alive$_3$?»

And not$_1$ could$_2$ his brothers$_3$ answer$_4$ him$_5$ for$_6$ they-trembled$_7$ before him$_8$.

1 2 3 4 5 6 7 8 9

45:4-15   **AMPL:** SIMPLE UNRESOLVED DIALOGUE ¶
         LEAD-IN: EXECUTION ¶
45:4   PLAN: *wayyō$^{)}$mer$_1$* yôsēp$_2$ $^{)}$el$_3$-$^{)}$eḥāyw$_4$: «gĕšû$_5$-nā$^{)}$$_6$ $^{)}$ēlay$_7$.»
         EXEC: *wayyiggāšû$_1$* (pausal).
45:4b-13   IU (PROP): *wayyō$^{)}$mer$_1$*: QUOTE = ▮ DISC
45:4b-8   **POINT$_1$** (INSTRUCTIONAL): ▮ REASON ¶
         PRELIM: «$^{)}$ănî$_1$ yôsēp$_2$ $^{)}$ăḥîkem$_3$ $^{)}$ăšer$_4$ mĕkartem$_5$ $^{)}$ōtî$_6$ miṣrāyĕmâ$_7$.
         TEXT: ▮ AMPLIFICATION ¶
45:5   TEXT: wĕ^{c}attâ$_1$ $^{)}$al$_2$-tē^{c}āṣĕbû$_3$.
         AMPL: wĕ$^{)}$al$_1$-yiḥar$_2$ bĕ^{c}ênêkem$_3$ kî$_4$-mĕkartem$_5$ $^{)}$ōtî$_6$ hēnnâ$_7$ kî$_8$ lĕmiḥyâ$_9$ šĕlāḥanî$_{10}$ $^{)}$ĕlōhîm$_{11}$ lipnêkem$_{12}$.
         REASON: ▮ REASON ¶
         TEXT: ▮ COORDINATE ¶
45:6   ITEM$_1$: kî$_1$-zeh$_2$ šĕnātayim$_3$ hārā^{c}āb$_4$ bĕqereb$_5$ hā$^{)}$āreṣ$_6$.
         ITEM$_2$: wĕ^{c}ôd$_1$ ḥāmēš$_2$ šānîm$_3$ $^{)}$ăšer$_4$ $^{)}$ên$_5$-ḥārîš$_6$ wĕqāṣṣîr$_7$.
         REASON: ▮ SEQUENCE ¶
45:7   BU$_1$: *wayyišlāḥēnî$_1$* $^{)}$ĕlōhîm$_2$ lipnêkem$_3$ lāśûm$_4$ lākem$_5$ šĕ$^{)}$ērît$_6$ bā$^{)}$āreṣ$_7$ ûlĕhaḥăyôt$_8$ lākem$_9$ liplêṭâ$_{10}$ gĕdōlâ$_{11}$.
         BU$_n$: ▮ SIMPLE ¶
45:8   SETTING: wĕ^{c}attâ$_1$ lō$^{)}$$_2$-$^{)}$attem$_3$ šĕlaḥtem$_4$ $^{)}$ōtî$_5$ hēnnâ$_6$ kî$_7$ hā$^{)}$ĕlōhîm$_8$.
         TEXT: *wayśîmēnî$_1$* lĕ$^{)}$āb$_2$ lĕpar^{c}ōh$_3$ ûlĕ$^{)}$ādôn$_4$ lĕkol$_5$-bêtô$_6$ ûmōšēl$_7$ bĕkol$_8$-$^{)}$ereṣ$_9$ miṣrāyim$_{10}$.

1 2 3 4 5 6 7 8 9

45:4   *And-he-said₁* Joseph₂ to₃ his brothers₄: «Come near₅ I pray₆ to
me₇.»
And-they-drew-near₁.
And-he-said₁:
«I₁ (am) Joseph₂ your brother₃ whom₄ you-sold₅ me₆ into Egypt₇.

45:5   And now₁ don't₂ be distressed₃.
And don't₁ let-get-hot₂ (anger) in your eyes₃ because₄ you-sold₅
me₆ hither₇ because₈ for a preservation of life₉ God₁₁ sent me₁₀ on
before you₁₂.

45:6   For₁ now₂ (we've had) two years of₃ the famine₄ in the midst of₅
the land₆.
And (there shall be) yet₁ five₂ years₃ (in) which₄ (there will be) no₅
planting₆ and harvesting₇.

45:7   *And-he-sent-me₁* God₂ on before you₃ to give₄ to you₅ a remnant₆
in the land₇ and to-preserve-alive₈ you₉ with a great₁₁
deliverance₁₀.

45:8   So now₁ (it's) not₂ you₃ (that) you-sent₄ me₅ here₆ but₇ God₈.
And-he-appointed-me₁ as a father₂ to Pharaoh₃ and as lord₄ to all₅
his house₆ and ruler₇ in all₈ the land of₉ Egypt₁₀.

1 2 3 4 5 6 7 8 9

45:9-13   POINT$_2$ (INSTRUCTIONAL): **H** SEQUENCE ¶
45:9   BU$_1$: mahărû$_1$
wa^{c}ălû$_2$ $^⊃$el$_3$-$^⊃$ābî$_4$.
BU$_2$: wa$^⊃$ămartem$_1$ $^⊃$ēlāyw$_2$: QUOTE = QUOTE ¶
Q F: "kōh$_1$ $^⊃$āmar$_2$ binkā$_3$ yôsēp$_4$:
Q: **H** SEQUENCE ¶
SETTING: 'śāmanî$_1$ $^⊃$ĕlōhîm$_2$ lĕ$^⊃$ādôn$_3$ lĕkol$_4$-miṣrāyim$_5$.
BU$_1$: **H** NEGATED ANTONYM
PARAPHRASE ¶
TEXT: rĕdâ$_1$ $^⊃$ēlay$_2$.
PARA: $^⊃$al$_1$-ta^{c}ămōd$_2$.
BU$_2$: **H** AMPLIFICATION ¶
45:10   TEXT: wĕyāšabtā$_1$ bĕ$^⊃$ereṣ$_2$-gōšen$_3$.
AMPL: wĕhāyîtā$_1$ qārôb$_2$ $^⊃$ēlay$_3$ $^⊃$attā$_4$ ûbānêkā$_5$
ûbĕnê$_6$ bānêkā$_7$ wĕṣō$^⊃$nĕkā$_8$ ûbĕqārĕkā$_9$
wĕkol$_{10}$-$^⊃$ăšer$_{11}$-lāk$_{12}$.
BU$_n$: **H** RESULT ¶
45:11   TEXT: wĕkilkaltî$_1$ $^⊃$ōtĕkā$_2$ šām$_3$ kî$_4$-^{c}ōd$_5$
hāmēš$_6$ šānîm$_7$ rā^{c}āb$_8$.
RESULT (NEGATIVE): pen$_1$-tiwwārēš$_2$ $^⊃$attā$_3$
ûbêtĕkā$_4$ wĕkol$_5$-$^⊃$ăšer$_6$-lāk$_7$.' "
BU$_3$: **H** SIMPLE ¶
45:12   SETTING: wĕhinnēh$_1$ ^{c}ênêkem$_2$ rō$^⊃$ôt$_3$ wĕ^{c}ênê$_4$
$^⊃$āhî$_5$ binyāmîn$_6$ kî$_7$-pî$_8$ hamdabbēr$_9$ $^⊃$ălêkem$_{10}$.
45:13   TEXT: wĕhiggadtem$_1$ lĕ$^⊃$ābî$_2$ $^⊃$et$_3$-kol$_4$-kĕbôdî$_5$
bĕmiṣrayim$_6$ wĕ$^⊃$ēt$_7$ kol$_8$-$^⊃$ăšer$_9$ rĕ$^⊃$îtem$_{10}$.
BU$_n$: ûmihartem$_1$.
wĕhôradtem$_2$ $^⊃$et-$^⊃$ābî$_3$ hēnnâ$_4$.»
45:14-15   STEP-DOWN: **N** SEQUENCE ¶
BU$_1$: **N** ANTITHETICAL ¶
THESIS: **N** SEQUENCE ¶
45:14   BU$_1$: *wayyippōl$_1$* ^{c}al$_2$-ṣawwĕ$^⊃$rê$_3$ binyāmin$_4$ $^⊃$āhîw$_5$.
BU$_n$: *wayyēbk$_1$.*
ANTI: ûbinyāmin$_1$ bākâ$_2$ ^{c}al$_3$-ṣawwā$^⊃$rāyw$_4$.
BU$_n$: **N** SEQUENCE ¶
45:15   BU$_1$: *waynaššēq$_1$* lĕkol$_2$-$^⊃$ehāyw$_3$.
BU$_n$: *wayyēbk$_1$* ^{c}ălêhem$_2$.
TERMINUS: wĕ$^⊃$ahărê$_1$ kēn$_2$ dibbĕrû$_3$ $^⊃$ehāyw$_4$ $^⊃$ittô$_5$.

1 2 3 4 5 6 7 8 9

45:9   Hurry$_1$ and go-up$_2$ to$_3$ my father$_4$.
     And-you-shall-say$_1$ to him$_2$:
     "Thus$_1$ has said$_2$ your son$_3$ Joseph$_4$:
     'God$_2$ has-placed-me$_1$ as lord$_3$ over all of$_4$ Egypt$_5$.
     Come down$_1$ to me$_2$.
     Don't$_1$ delay$_2$.

45:10   And-you-shall-dwell$_1$ in the land of$_2$ Goshen$_3$.
     And-you-shall-be$_1$ near$_2$ to me$_3$ you$_4$ and your sons$_5$ and the sons
     of$_6$ your sons$_7$ and your flocks$_8$ and your herds$_9$ and all$_{10}$ which$_{11}$
     (is) to you$_{12}$.

45:11   And-I-will-nourish$_1$ you$_2$ there$_3$, for$_4$ yet$_5$ five$_6$ years$_7$ (there will
     be) famine$_8$.
     —Lest$_1$ you are brought to poverty$_2$ you$_3$ and your house$_4$ and all$_5$
     which$_6$ (is) to you$_7$.' "

45:12   And behold$_1$ your eyes$_2$ are seeing$_3$ and the eyes of$_4$ my brother$_5$
     Benjamin$_6$ that$_7$ my mouth$_8$ is talking$_9$ with you$_{10}$.

45:13   And-you-shall-declare$_1$ to my father$_2$ all$_{3-4}$ my glory$_5$ in Egypt$_6$ and
     all$_{7-8}$ that$_9$ you-have-seen$_{10}$.
     You-shall-hurry$_1$.
     And-you-shall-bring-down$_2$ my father$_3$ here$_4$.»

45:14   *And-he-fell$_1$* on$_2$ the neck of$_3$ his brother$_5$ Benjamin$_4$.
     And-he-wept$_1$.
     And Benjamin$_1$ wept$_2$ on$_3$ his neck$_4$.

45:15   *And-he-kissed$_1$* all$_2$ his brothers$_3$.
     And-he-wept$_1$ over them$_2$.
     And after$_1$ this$_2$ his brothers$_4$ talked$_3$ with him$_5$.

1 2 3 4 5 6 7 8 9

POST-PEAK EPISODE$_1$: EXECUTION ¶

45:16-24

45:16 **SETTING:** wĕhaqqōl$_1$ nišma$^c{}_2$ bêt$_3$ par^{c}ōh$_4$ lē$^{\ni}$mōr$_5$: «bā$^{\ni}$û$_6$ $^{\ni}$ăḥê$_7$ yôsēp$_8$.»

LEAD-IN: *wayyîṭab$_1$* bĕ^{c}ênê$_2$ par^{c}ōh$_3$ ûbĕ^{c}ênê$_4$ ^{c}ăbādāyw$_5$.

45:17-20;17 **PLAN:** *wayyō$^{\ni}$mer$_1$* par^{c}ōh$_2$ $^{\ni}$el$_3$-yôsēp$_4$: QUOTE = **Ⅱ** DISC

POINT$_1$: «$^{\ni}$ĕmōr$_1$ $^{\ni}$el$_2$-$^{\ni}$aḥêkā$_3$: QUOTE = RESULT ¶

TEXT: **Ⅱ** SEQUENCE ¶

PREVIEW: "zō$^{\ni}$t$_1$ ^{c}ăśû$_2$.

BU$_1$: ṭa^{c}ănû$_1$ $^{\ni}$et-bĕ^{c}îrĕkem$_2$.

BU$_2$: ûlĕkû$_1$-bō$^{\ni}$û$_2$ $^{\ni}$arṣâ$_3$ kĕnā^{c}an$_4$.

BU$_n$: **Ⅱ** SEQUENCE ¶

45:18 BU$_1$: ûqĕḥû$_1$ $^{\ni}$et$_2$-$^{\ni}$ăbîkem$_3$ wĕ$^{\ni}$et-bāttêkem$_4$.

BU$_n$: ûbō$^{\ni}$û$_1$ $^{\ni}$ēlāy$_2$.

RESULT: **Ⅱ** RESULT ¶

TEXT: wĕ$^{\ni}$ettĕnâ$_1$ lākem$_2$ $^{\ni}$et-ṭûb$_3$ $^{\ni}$ereṣ$_4$ miṣrayim$_5$.

RESULT: wĕ$^{\ni}$iklû$_1$ $^{\ni}$et-ḥēleb$_2$ hā$^{\ni}$āreṣ$_3$."

45:19 POINT$_2$: wĕ$^{\ni}$attâ$_1$ ṣuwwêtâ$_2$: QUOTE = **Ⅱ** SEQUENCE ¶

PREVIEW: "zō$^{\ni}$t$_1$ ^{c}ăśû$_2$

BU$_1$: qĕḥû$_1$-lākem$_2$ mē$^{\ni}$ereṣ$_3$ miṣrayim$_4$ ^{c}ăgālôt$_5$ lĕṭappĕkem$_6$ wĕlinšêkem$_7$.

BU$_n$: **Ⅱ** SEQUENCE ¶

BU$_1$: ûnĕśā$^{\ni}$tem$_1$ $^{\ni}$et-$^{\ni}$ăbîkem$_2$.

BU$_n$: ûbā$^{\ni}$tem$_1$.

45:20 **TERMINUS:** wĕ^{c}ênĕkem$_1$ $^{\ni}$al-tāḥōs$_2$ ^{c}al$_3$-kĕlêkem$_4$ kî$_5$ ṭûb$_6$ kol$_7$-$^{\ni}$ereṣ$_8$ miṣrayim$_9$ lākem$_{10}$ hû$^{\ni}{}_{11}$."»

1 2 3 4 5 6 7 8 9

45:16   And the report$_1$ was heard$_2$ (in) the house of$_3$ Pharaoh$_4$ saying$_5$:
         «They-have-come$_6$ the brothers of$_7$ Joseph$_8$.»
         And-it-was-good$_1$ in the eyes of$_2$ Pharaoh$_3$ and in the eyes of$_4$ his
         servants$_5$.

45:17   *And-he-said$_1$* Pharaoh$_2$ to$_3$ Joseph$_4$:
         «Say$_1$ to$_2$ your brothers$_3$:
         "Do$_2$ this$_1$:
         Load$_1$ your animals$_2$.
         And proceed$_1$, go$_2$ to the land$_3$ of Canaan$_4$.

45:18   And-take$_1$ your father$_{2-3}$ and your households$_4$.
         And come$_1$ to me$_2$.
         And-let-me-give$_1$ to you$_2$ the best (portion of)$_3$ the land of$_4$ Egypt$_5$.
         And-eat$_1$ the fat of$_2$ the land$_3$."

45:19   As for you (sg)$_1$, you are commanded$_2$ (to tell them):
         "Do$_2$ this$_1$:
         Take$_1$ for you$_2$ from the land of$_3$ Egypt$_4$ carts$_5$ for your little ones$_6$
         and for your wives$_7$.
         And-you-shall-bring$_1$ your father$_2$.
         And-you-shall-come$_1$.

45:20   And let not your eye$_1$ regard$_2$ your possessions$_{3-4}$ for$_5$ the best of$_6$
         all$_7$ the land of$_8$ Egypt$_9$—it's$_{11}$ before you$_{10}$."»

45:21-24   **EXEC: N** SEQUENCE ¶
45:21   SETTING/PREVIEW: *wayya^{c}ăśû$_1$-kēn$_2$ bĕnê$_3$ yiśrā^{c}ēl$_4$.*
            BU$_1$: N AMPLIFICATION ¶
                TEXT: **N** SEQUENCE ¶
                BU$_1$: *wayyittēn$_1$ lāhem$_2$ yôsēp$_3$ ^{c}ăgālôt$_4$ ^{c}al$_5$-pî$_6$ par^{c}oh$_7$.*
                BU$_n$: *wayyittēn$_1$ lāhem$_2$ ṣēdâ$_3$ laddārek$_4$.*
                AMPL: **N** COORDINATE ¶
                    ITEM$_1$: **N** ANTITHETICAL ¶
45:22   THESIS: lĕkullām$_1$ nātan$_2$ lā^{ɔ}îš$_3$ ḥălipôt$_4$ śĕmālōt$_5$.
                    ANTI: ûlĕbinyāmin$_1$ nātan$_2$ šĕlōš$_3$-mē^{ɔ}ôt$_4$ kesep$_5$ wĕḥāmēš$_6$ ḥălipōt$_7$ śĕmālōt$_8$.
                    ITEM$_2$: **N** AMPLIFICATION ¶
45:23   TEXT: ûlĕ^{ɔ}ābîw$_1$ šālaḥ$_2$ kĕzō^{ɔ}t$_3$:
                    AMPL$_1$: ^{c}ăśārâ$_1$ ḥămōrîm$_2$ nōśĕ^{ɔ}îm$_3$ miṭṭûb$_4$ miṣrāyim$_5$.
                    AMPL$_2$: wĕ^{c}eśer$_1$ ^{ɔ}ătōnōt$_2$ nōśĕ^{ɔ}ōt$_3$ bār$_4$ wāleḥem$_5$ ûmāzôn$_6$ lĕ^{ɔ}ābîw$_7$ laddārek$_8$.
45:24   BU$_2$: **N** SEQUENCE ¶
            BU$_1$: *wayšallaḥ$_1$ ^{ɔ}et-^{ɔ}eḥāyw$_2$.*
            BU$_n$: *wayyēlēkû$_1$* (pausal)
            BU$_n$: *wayyō^{ɔ}mer$_1$ ^{ɔ}ălēhem$_2$:* «^{ɔ}al$_3$-tirgĕzû$_4$ baddārek$_5$.»

45:21	*And-they-did₁* thus₂ the sons of₃ Israel₄.
	And-he-gave₁ to them₂ Joseph₃ carts₄ on the orders of₅₋₆ Pharaoh₇.
	And-he-gave₁ to them₂ provisions₃ for the journey₄.
45:22	And-he-gave₂ to each₃ and all₁ changes of₄ clothing₅.
	But to Benjamin₁ he-gave₂ three₃ hundred of₄ silver₅ and five₆ changes of₇ clothing₈.
45:23	And to his father₁ he-sent₂ as follows₃:
	Ten₁ asses₂ loaded₃ with the good things of₄ Egypt₅.
	And ten₁ she-asses₂ loaded with₃ grain₄ and bread₅ and provisions₆ for his father₇ for the journey₈.
45:24	*And-he-sent-off₁* his brothers₂.
	And-they-went₁.
	And-he-said₁ to them₂: «Don't₃ have any quarrels₄ on the way₅.»

1 2 3 4 5 6 7 8 9

45:25-28 **POST-PEAK EPISODE$_2$: N SEQUENCE ¶**
BU$_1$: STIMULUS-RESPONSE ¶
STIMULUS: N SEQUENCE ¶
45:25 BU$_1$: *wayya^{c}ălû$_1$* mimmiṣrāyim$_2$.
BU$_2$: *wayyābō$^\supset$û$_1$* $^\supset$ereṣ$_2$ kĕna^{c}an$_3$ $^\supset$el$_4$-ya^{c}ăqōb$_5$ $^\supset$ăbîhem$_6$.
45:26 BU$_n$: *wayyaggidû$_1$* lô$_2$ lē$^\supset$mōr$_3$: QUOTE=E
COORDINATE ¶
ITEM$_1$: «^{c}ôd$_1$ yôsēp$_2$ ḥay$_3$.
ITEM$_2$: wĕkî$_1$-hû$_2$ mōšēl$_3$ bĕkol$_4$-$^\supset$ereṣ$_5$ miṣrāyim$_6$.»
RESPONSE: *wayyāpog$_1$* libbô$_2$ kî$_3$ lō$^\supset_4$ he$^\supset$ĕmîn$_5$ lāhem$_6$.
BU$_n$: STIMULUS-RESPONSE ¶
45:27 STIMULUS: *waydabbĕrû$_1$* $^\supset$ēlāyw$_2$ $^\supset$ēt kol$_3$-dibrê$_4$ yôsēp$_5$ $^\supset$ăšer$_6$ dibber$_7$ $^\supset$ălēhem$_8$.
RESPONSE: N SEQUENCE ¶
BU$_1$: *wayyar$^\supset_1$* $^\supset$et-hā^{c}ăgālôt$_2$ $^\supset$ăšer$_3$ šālaḥ$_4$ yôsēp$_5$ lāśē$^\supset$t$_6$ $^\supset$ōtô$_7$.
BU$_2$: *wattĕḥî$_1$* rûaḥ$_2$ ya^{c}ăqōb$_3$ $^\supset$ăbîhem$_4$.
45:28 BU$_n$: *wayyō$^\supset$mer$_1$* yiśrā$^\supset$ēl$_2$: [H REASON ¶]
PRELIM: «rab$_1$.
REASON: ^{c}ôd$_1$-yôsēp$_2$ bĕnî$_3$ ḥay$_4$.
TEXT: H SEQUENCE ¶
BU$_1$: $^\supset$ēlĕkâ$_1$.
BU$_n$: wĕ$^\supset$er$^\supset$ennû$_1$ bĕṭerem$_2$ $^\supset$āmût$_3$.»

1 2 3 4 5 6 7 8 9

45:25   *And-they-went-up$_1$* from Egypt$_2$.
         And-they-came-into$_1$ the land of$_2$ Canaan$_3$ to$_4$ Jacob$_5$ their father$_6$.
45:26   *And-they-told$_1$* him$_2$ saying$_3$:
         «Joseph$_2$ (is) still$_1$ alive$_3$!
         And furthermore$_1$ he$_2$ is ruling$_3$ in all$_4$ the land of$_5$ Egypt$_6$.»
         And-it-went-numb$_1$ his heart$_2$ for$_3$ not$_4$ he-believed$_5$ them$_6$.
45:27   *And-they-spoke$_1$* to him$_2$ all$_3$ the words of$_4$ Joseph$_5$ which$_6$ he-
         spoke$_7$ to them$_8$.
         And-he-saw$_1$ the carts$_2$ which$_3$ had-sent$_4$ Joseph$_5$ to carry$_6$ him$_7$.
         And-it-revived$_1$ the spirit of$_2$ Jacob$_3$ their father$_4$.
45:28   *And-he-said$_1$* Israel$_2$:
         «Enough$_1$.
         Joseph$_2$ my son$_3$ (is) still$_1$ alive$_4$.
         I-will-go$_1$.
         I-will-see-him$_1$ before$_2$ I-die$_3$.»

1 2 3 4 5 6 7 8 9

Genesis 45:25–28 is the end of the Peak′ of the embedded discourse found in Genesis 43–45, which in turn is Peak′ of the main story. *Joseph*, as distinct from the interwoven *tōdĕdôt ya‘ăqōb*, contains three further Post Peak episodes (not displayed in detail here):

46:1-47:12	***POST-PEAK EPISODE₁***
46:1-27	**EPISODE₁:** Jacob goes to Egypt. The catalogue of those going down (46:8-27) is an AMPLIFICATION of 46:5-7. This dry recital contrasts well with the liveliness of the following material.
46:28-34	**EPISODE₂ (PEAK?):** Joseph meets Jacob.
47:1-6	**EPISODE₃ (POST-PEAK₁):** The brothers are presented to Pharaoh.
47:7-12	**EPISODE₄ (POST-PEAK₂):** Jacob is presented to Pharaoh.
47:13-31	***POST-PEAK EPISODE₂:*** The last years of Joseph's famine relief. There is a crescendo of desperation leading to a PEAK (or paragraph CLIMAX?) in 47:18-26. We have essentially a '3-round' structure here with the prominence given to the third round.
48:1-22	***POST-PEAK EPISODE₃:*** The blessing of Ephraim and Manasseh is the main focus. Poetry in 48:15-16, and 20.

The last sections of Genesis belong to the merger of *tōdĕdôt ya‘ăqōb* and *Joseph*:

Blessing on the Twelve Tribes (49:1–28; this section is Peak of the entire *tōdĕdôt ya‘ăqōb*)

Death and Burial of Jacob (49:29–50:21; this section contains an echo of *Joseph* in 50:15–21)

Death of Joseph (50:22–26)

1 2 3 4 5 6 7 8 9

APPENDIX

ON TAGMEMICS

Basically, however much enriched from other sources, the linguistic methodology underlying this work is based on the assumptions of tagmemics, which, earlier than some approaches to linguistic structure, recognized the importance of textual studies. K. L. Pike, the originator of the theory, has expounded his views in a very large and encyclopedic work, *Language in Relation to a Unified Theory of the Structure of Human Behavior* (first published in 3 volumes 1954–57 and republished as one volume in 1964[a]). Of his numerous articles, reviews, and books, one article written in 1964 remains a landmark in discourse studies— an article with the simple but provocative title "Beyond the Sentence" (1964b).

Tagmemics has always insisted on the relevance of part-whole relations, of the communication situation (the crucial feature IV in Diagram 1, p. 13), and the interplay of the observer with the data that he observes (cf. Toulmin 1981). Specifically, however, three concepts of tagmemics have been and still are crucial to a study such as this: tagmeme, syntagmeme, and hierarchical linguistic structure. Here my own formulation of tagmemics, while derived in many respects from Pike's is different from his and in a few respects independent of him (Longacre, 1985d).

The tagmeme was originally defined as a slot-class correlation, so that in a transitive English clause, such as *John hit Bill*, there would be a subject as agent tagmeme, conceived of as a slot with this functional meaning plus all possible English nouns, phrases, and clauses that could paradigmatically (à la mode de Saussure) occur there (any one given instance of the subject as agent tagmeme actualizes one and only one such filler). I prefer to refer to the slot-filler correlation as *function-set* (with the function constituting the defining power of the set). English also has a transitive predicate tagmeme filled by transitive verbs (a somewhat fluid set) and an object-as-patient tagmeme filled by a total set that is very similar to that which fills subject (except, of course, that pronouns such as *he/she* occur in the one and *him/her* in the other).

Tagmemes combine to form structured wholes, which I can call syntagmemes (de Saussure's syntagmatic relations [1959: 122ff.]). The English transitive clause is such a syntagmeme. Besides the parts illustrated above it has other optional and peripheral elements, including various sorts of adverbial adjuncts of place, time, and manner.

Tagmeme and syntagmeme are correlative concepts in that (1) the functions of the various tagmemes are expounded by sets of syntagmemes (including those of zero internal structure), and (2) a syntagmeme is composed of tagmemes. I call the first relation *exponence* and the second *composition*. Thus, not only can syntagmemes of zero internal grammatical structure, such as *John* and *Bill*, occur as subject and object in a transitive clause, but compound words such as (the) *redcoat*, (the) *gentleman*, or (the) *oarsman* may occur there as well; phrases such as *the oldest man in the group, an impudent young officer*, or *a crippled sailor* can occur; and even a few clauses such as *That he came early* (*impressed Bill*).

Together, tagmeme and syntagmeme thus related yield a systematic theory of grammatical hierarchy (part-whole relationships). At every level of structure from the stem level to the discourse level, tagmemes compose syntagmemes. Thus, discourse-level tagmemes are units such as episodes in stories or points in a sermon. Paragraph-level tagmemes are units such as the composition teacher's *topic sentence* (which is really a slot where, for example, a short embedded paragraph of two or three sentences can occur) and other slots wherein occur items that introduce, close, or expound the topic. Sentence-level slots are, for example, the coordinated parts of a compound sentence or the opposed parts of an adversative sentence.

In all the above the most predictable filler-set or exponence-set is a syntagmeme from the next lower level, that is, we expect discourses to be composed of paragraphs, paragraphs of sentences, sentences of clauses, clauses of phrases, and phrases of words. This is the general picture, but we must also add the role of functional morphemes on all levels, morphemes that have no internal structure but well-marked distributional slots: *amen, next, but, and, of, the,* and the like. Whether a slot is filled by a syntagmeme from the lower-level or by one of these functional elements, this type of exponence (slot-filler relationship) is called primary exponence.

Other types of exponence occur: (1) recursive exponence, wherein discourse occurs within discourse, paragraph within paragraph, etc.; (2) back-looping exponence, wherein a higher-level unit fills a slot in a lower level, as in *his devil-may-care attitude*, where we have a noun phrase, one tagmeme of which is expounded by a clause: *devil-may-care*. Actually, all relative clauses fall in here (e.g., *the house that Jack built*) because, here again, a phrase-level tagmeme is expounded by a clause. So, on occasion there may occur a structure whose overall skeleton is that of a paragraph but that embeds a discourse within itself, or a sentence (especially a quotation) that embeds a paragraph. (3) Level-skipping exponence also occurs. Here instead of getting exponents from the next level down we get a construction from a still lower: *As for domestic animals, they also enrich our lives and add context.* Here a coordinate sentence has a preposed sentence-topic tagmeme that is ex-pounded (filled) not by a clause, which "ought" to expound part of a sentence, but by a prepositional noun phrase.

The chief usefulness of the framework is that, in talking about the constituent structure of discourse, we achieve considerable maneuvera-bility by using the function-set approach. We can say, without hesita-ting, that a narrative discourse is composed of episodes (plus stage, a *peak* episode, and a closure) without worrying about the greatly unequal length or complexity of the sets that expound each episode. Thus, one episode may be no longer than a paragraph (e.g., Gen 39:1–6), while another may be embedded discourse (e.g., Gen 43–45). We also note that the main episodes of a long and complex tale may be expounded entirely by embedded discourses (subnarratives), while discourse on the bottom level of embedding may have episodes expounded by paragraphs—and all grades between. And we can, of course, have a one-sentence paragraph that expounds a whole episode of a discourse. Likewise, on the paragraph level there may be long paragraphs with extensive em-bedding at structural points within them or short paragraphs all of whose tagmemes are expounded by sentences—and all grades of com-plexity between the two.

REFERENCES

Albright, W. F.
1961 "Abram the Hebrew: A New Archaeological Interpretation."
Bulletin of the American Schools of Oriental Research
163:36–54.
1963 *The Biblical Period from Abraham to Ezra.* New York: Harper
Torchbook.
Alter, R.
1975 "A Literary Approach to the Bible." *Commentary* 60:70–77.
Andersen, F. I.
1970 *The Verbless Clause in the Hebrew Pentateuch.* Nashville:
Abingdon.
1974 *The Sentence in Biblical Hebrew.* The Hague: Mouton.
Andersen, F. I., and D. N. Freedman
1980 *Hosea.* Anchor Bible 24. Garden City, NY: Doubleday.
Astruc, J.
1753 *Conjectures sur les mémoires originaux dont il paroît que
Moyse s'est servi pour composer le livre de la Genèse.* (Im-
printed as Brussels: Chez Friex, but in actuality Paris: Cavelier.)
Austin, J. L.
1962 *How to Do Things with Words.* Oxford: Oxford University.
Ballard, D. L., R. Conrad, and R. E. Longacre
1971a "The Deep and Surface Structure of Interclausal Relations."
Foundations of Language 7:70–118.
1971b *More on the Deep and Surface Structure of Interclausal Relations.* Language Data, Asian-Pacific Series 1. Ukarumpa,
Papua New Guinea: Summer Institute of Linguistics.
de Beaugrande, R., and W. Dressler
1981 *An Introduction to Textlinguistics.* London: Longmans.
Beekman, J., and J. Callow
1974 *Translating the Word of God.* Grand Rapids: Eerdmans.

Beekman, J., J. Callow, and M. Kopesec
   1981   "The Semantic Structure of Written Communication." Private
          circulation.
Bergen, R. D.
   1984   "Verb Structural Profiles of the Narrative Framework of the
          Pentateuch." Private circulation.
Bimson, J. J.
   1983   "Archaeological Data and the Dating of the Patriarchs." In
          Millard and Wiseman 1983: 53–89.
Buss, M. J., ed.
   1979   *Encounter with the Text: Form and History in the Hebrew
          Bible*. Philadelphia: Fortress; Missoula, MT: Scholars.
Bright, J.
   1981   *A History of Israel*. 3d ed. Philadelphia: Westminster.
Brueggemann, W.
   1982   *Genesis*. Atlanta: John Knox.
Calvin, J.
   1847   *Commentaries on the First Book of Moses, Called Genesis*,
          trans. J. King, 2 vols. Edinburgh: Calvin Translation Society
          (repr. London: Banner of Truth, 1965; Grand Rapids: Baker,
          1979).
Cassuto, U.
   1961–64 *A Commentary on the Book of Genesis*, trans I. Abrahams,
          2 vols. Jerusalem: Magnes.
Christian, I.
   1987   *Language as Social Behavior: Folk Tales as a Database for
          Developing a Beyond-the-Discourse Model*. Language Data,
          Asian-Pacific Series 17. Huntington Beach, CA: Summer Insti-
          tute of Linguistics.
Clements, R. E.
   1977   Review of *Das überlieferungsgeschichtliche Problem des Penta-
          teuch*, by R. Rendtorff. *Journal for the Study of the Old
          Testament* 3:46–56.
Coats, G. W.
   1976   *From Canaan to Egypt: Structural and Theological Context
          for the Joseph story*. Catholic Biblical Quarterly Monograph
          Series 4. Washington: Catholic Biblical Association.
   1977   "The Yahwist as Theologian? A Critical Reflection." *Journal
          for the Study of the Old Testament* 3:28–32.
   1983   *Genesis, With an Introduction to Narrative Literature*. The
          Forms of Old Testament Literature, ed. R. Knierim and G. M.
          Tucker, vol. 1. Grand Rapids: Eerdmans.

Cole, P., and J. L. Morgan, eds.
1975 *Speech Acts.* Syntax and Semantics 3. New York: Academic.
Delitzsch, F.
1888–89 *A New Commentary on Genesis,* trans. S. Taylor, 2 vols. Edinburgh: Clark.
van Dijk, T. A.
1972 *Some Aspects of Text Grammars.* The Hague: Mouton.
1977 *Text and Context.* London: Longmans.
1980 *Macrostructures: An Interdisciplinary Study of Global Structures in Discourse, Interaction, and Cognition.* Hillsdale, NJ: Lawrence Erlbaum.
Dillman, A.
1897 *Genesis Critically and Exegetically Expounded,* trans. W. B. Stevenson, 2 vols. Edinburgh: Clark.
Driver, S. R.
1948 *The Book of Genesis, With Introduction and Notes.* 15th ed. Westminster Commentaries. London: Methuen.
Eichhorn, J. G.
1780–83 *Einleitung in das Alte Testament,* 3 vols. Leipzig: Weidmann.
Fokkelman, J. P.
1975 *Narrative Art in Genesis: Specimens of Stylistic and Structural Analysis.* Assen: van Gorcum.
Forster, J.
1983 "Use of Dialogue in a Dibabawon Narrative Discourse." *Philippine Journal of Linguistics* 14/1.
Fuller, D. P.
1959 "The Inductive Method of Bible Study." 3d ed. Pasadena: Fuller Theological Seminary. Photocopy.
Gammie, J. G.
1979 "Theological Interpretation by Way of Literary and Traditional Analysis: Genesis 25–36." In Buss 1979: 117–34.
Gesenius, W.
1859 *Gesenius' Hebrew and Chaldee Lexicon,* trans. S. P. Tregelles. London: Bagster (repr. Grand Rapids: Eerdmans, 1949).
Gesenius-Kautzsch-Cowley
1910 *Genenius' Hebrew Grammar,* ed. E. Kautzsch; 2d English ed. A. E. Cowley. Oxford: Clarendon (abbreviated GKC).
Givón, T., ed.
1983 *Topic Continuity in Discourse: A Quantitative Cross-Language Study.* Philadelphia: John Benjamins.

Goldingay, J.
1983 "The Patriarchs in Scripture and History." In Millard and Wiseman 1983: 1–34.

Graf, K. H.
1865 *Die geschichtlichen Bücher des Alten Testament: Zwei historisch-kritische Untersuchungen.* Leipzig: Weigel.

Grimes, J. E.
1975 *The Thread of Discourse.* The Hague: Mouton.

Gunkel, H.
1965 *Genesis übersetzt und erklärt.* 7th ed. Göttingen: Vandenhoeck and Ruprecht.

Halliday, M. A. K., and R. Hasan
1976 *Cohesion in English.* London: Longmans.

Hollenbach, B.
1974 "Discourse Structure, Interpropositional Relations, and Translation." Unpublished Manuscript. Mexico City: Instituto Lingüistico de Verano.

Hopper, P., and S. Thompson
1980 "Transitivity in Grammar and Discourse." *Language* 56: 251–99.

Hwang, S.
1987 *Discourse Features of Korean Narration.* Summer Institute of Linguistics Publication 77. Dallas: Summer Institute of Linguistics and University of Texas at Arlington.

Jacob, B.
1974 *The First Book of the Bible: Genesis Interpreted,* ed. and trans. E. J. Jacob and W. Jacob. New York: KTAV.

Jerusalmi, I.
1973 *The Story of Joseph: A Philological Commentary.* 2d ed. Cincinnati: Hebrew Union College—Jewish Institute of Religion.

Jones, Larry, and Linda Jones
1979 "Multiple Levels of Information Relevance in Discourse." In *Discourse Studies in Mesoamerican Languages,* 1:3–28. Summer Institute of Linguistics Publication 58. Dallas: Summer Institute of Linguistics and University of Texas at Arlington.

Joüon, P.
1947 *Grammaire de l'hébreu biblique.* 2d ed. Rome: Pontifical Biblical Institute.

Kantorowicz, E. H.
1957 *The King's Two Bodies.* Princeton: Princeton University.

Keil, C. F.
1866 *Biblical Commentary on the Old Testament: The Pentateuch: Genesis,* trans. J. Martin. Edinburgh: Clark.

Kessler, M.
1974 "Rhetorical Criticism of Genesis 7." In *Rhetorical Criticism: Essays in Honor of James Muilenburg*, ed. J. J. Jackson and M. Kessler, 1–17. Pittsburgh: Pickwick.

Kidner, D.
1967 *Genesis: An Introduction and Commentary*. Tyndale Old Testament Commentaries. Downers Grove, IL: InterVarsity.

Kikawada, I. M.
1974 "The Shape of Genesis 11:1–9." In *Rhetorical Criticism: Essays in Honor of James Muilenburg*, ed. J. J. Jackson and M. Kessler, 18–32. Pittsburgh: Pickwick.
1977 "Some Proposals for the Definition of Rhetorical Criticism." *Semitics* 5:67–91

Koontz, C.
1977 "Features of Dialogue within Narrative Discourse in Teribe." In *Discourse Grammar: Studies in Indigenous Languages of Colombia, Panama, and Ecuador*, ed. R. E. Longacre and F. Woods, 3:111–32. Summer Institute of Linguistics Publications 52. Dallas: Summer Institute of Linguistics and University of Texas at Arlington.

Lambdin, T. O.
1971 *Introduction to Biblical Hebrew*. New York: Charles Scribner's Sons.

Larson, M. L.
1984 *Meaning-Based Translation*. Lanham: University Press of America.

Levinsohn, S. H.
1967 "Progression and Digression in Inga (Quechuan) Discourse." *Forum Linguisticum* 1:122–47.

Longacre, R. E.
1961 "From Tagma to Tagmeme in Biblical Hebrew." In *A William Cameron Townsend en el vigésimoquinto aniversario del Instituto Lingüístico de Verano*, 563–92. Mexico: Instituto Lingüístico de Verano.
1968 *Discourse, Paragraph, and Sentence Structure in Selected Philippine Languages*, 2 vols. Summer Institute of Linguistics Publication 21. Santa Ana: Summer Institute of Linguistics.
1972 *Hierarchy and Universality of Discourse Constituents in New Guinea Languages*, 2 vols. Washington: Georgetown University.
1976 *An Anatomy of Speech Notions*. Lisse, Belgium: Peter de Ridder.

1977 "Generating a Discourse from its Abstract." *The Third LACUS Forum*, 355–67. Columbia, SC: Hornbeam.

1978 "Why We Need a Vertical Revolution in Linguistics." *The Fifth LACUS Forum*, 247–70. Columbia, SC: Hornbeam.

1979a "The Discourse Structure of the Flood Narrative. *Journal of the American Academy of Religion* 47 (1979) Supplement B: 89–133.

1979b "The Paragraph as a Grammatical Unit." In *Discourse and Syntax*, ed. T. Givón, 115–34. New York: Academic.

1980 *An Apparatus for the Identification of Paragraph Types.* Notes on Linguistics 15. Dallas: Summer Institute of Linguistics.

1981 "A Spectrum and Profile Approach to Discourse Analysis." *Text* 1:337–59.

1982a "Verb Ranking and the Constituency Structure of Discourse." *Journal of the Linguistic Association of the Southwest* 4:177–202.

1982b "Discourse Typology in Relation to Language Typology." In *Text Processing: Proceedings of the Nobel Symposium 51*, ed. Sturé Allen, 457–86. Stockholm: Almqvist and Wiksell.

1983 *The Grammar of Discourse*. New York: Plenum.

1985a "Discourse Peak as Zone of Turbulence." In *Beyond the Sentence*, ed. J. Wirth, 81–92 Ann Arbor: Karoma.

1985b "Interpreting Biblical Stories." In *Discourse and Literature: New Approaches to the Analysis of Literary Genres*, ed. T. van Dijk, 169–85. Philadelphia: John Benjamins.

1985c "Sentences as Combinations of Clauses." In *Language Typology and Syntactic Description: Complex Constructions*, ed. T. Shopen, 235–86. Cambridge: Cambridge University.

1985d "Tagmemics." *Word* 36:137–77.

1986 "Who Sold Joseph into Egypt?" In *Interpretation and History: Essays in Honour of Allan A. Macrae*, ed. R. Laird Harris, Swee-Hwa Quek, and J. Robert Vannoy, 75–92. Singapore: Christian Life.

In press *Storyline Concerns and Word Order Typologies in East and West African*. Supplement to *Studies in African Linguistics*. Los Angeles: Department of Linguistics and the African Studies Center, University of California.

Lowenthal, E. I.

1973 *The Joseph Narrative in Genesis*. New York: KTAV.

McKnight, E. V.

1980 "The Contours and Methods of Literary Criticism." In Spencer 1980: 53–69.

320   *References*

Mann, W. C., and S. A. Thompson
  1987   *Rhetorical Structure Theory: A Theory of Test Organization.*
         Marina del Rey: University of Southern California, Informa-
         tion Sciences Institute.
Millard, A. R.
  1983   "Methods of Studying the Patriarchal Narratives as Ancient
         Texts." In Millard and Wiseman 1983: 35–51.
Millard, A. R., and D. J. Wiseman, eds.
  1983   *Essays on the Patriarchal Narratives.* Winona Lake, IN:
         Eisenbrauns [reprint of Leicester: Inter-Varsity, 1980].
Noth, M.
  1972   *A History of Pentateuchal Traditions*, trans. B. W. Anderson.
         Englewood Cliffs, NJ: Prentice-Hall.
Petersen, N. R.
  1980   "Literary Criticism in Biblical Studies." In Spencer 1980:
         25–50.
Pike, K. L.
  1964a *Language in Relation to a Unified Theory of the Structure of
         Human Behavior.* The Hague: Mouton [first published in three
         separate volumes 1954–57].
  1964b "Beyond the Sentence." *College Composition and Communi-
         cation* 15:129–35.
  1982   *Linguistic Concepts.* Lincoln: University of Nebraska.
Polzin, R. N.
  1980   "Literary and Historical Criticism of the Bible: A Crisis in
         Scholarship." In Spencer 1980: 99–114.
von Rad, G.
  1966   "The Form-Critical Problem of the Hexateuch." In *The
         Problem of the Hexateuch and Other Essays*, 1–78. Edinburgh:
         Oliver and Boyd [= *Das formgeschichtliche Problem des
         Hexateuch* (Beiträge zur Wissenschaft vom Alten und Neuen
         Testament 78; Stuttgart: Kohlhammer, 1938)].
  1972   *Genesis: A Commentary*, trans. J. H. Marks. Rev. ed. Phila-
         delphia: Westminster.
Redford, D. B.
  1979   *A Study of the Biblical Story of Joseph (Genesis 37–50).*
         Supplement to *Vetus Testamentum* 20. Leiden: Brill.
Reid, A.
  1979   "Dynamics of Reported Speech in Totonac." In *Discourse
         Studies in Mesoamerican Languages*, ed. Linda Jones, 1:293–
         328. Summer Institute of Linguistics Publication 58, Dallas:
         Summer Institute of Linguistics and University of Texas at
         Arlington.

Rendtorff, R.
1977a "The 'Yahwist' as Theologian? The Dilemma of Pentateuchal Criticism." *Journal for the Study of the Old Testament* 3:2–10.
1977b Pentateuchal Studies on the Move." *Journal for the Study of the Old Testament* 3:43–45.
1977c *Das überlieferungeschichtliche Problem des Pentateuch.* Beihefte zur *Zeitschrift für die alttestamentliche Wissenschaft* 147. Berlin: de Gruyter.

Ricoeur, P.
1976 *Interpretation Theory: Discourse and the Surplus of Meaning.* Fort Worth: Texas Christian University.

Roth, W. M. W.
1979 "The Text is the Medium: An Interpretation of the Jacob Stories in Genesis." In Buss 1979: 103–55.

de Saussure, F.
1959 *Course in General Linguistics*, ed. Charles Bally and Albert Sechehaye, trans. Wade Baskin. New York: Philosophical Library. [First French edition: Geneva, 1915.]

Schmid, H. H.
1977 "In Search of New Approaches in Pentateuchal Research." *Journal for the Study of the Old Testament* 3:33–42.

Searle, J. R.
1969 *Speech Acts.* Cambridge: Cambridge University.

Selman, M. J.
1983 "Comparative Customs and the Patriarchal Age." In Millard and Wiseman 1983: 91–139.

Skinner, J.
1910 *A Critical and Exegetical Commentary on Genesis.* International Critical Commentary. Edinburgh: Clark.

Speiser, E. A.
1964 *Genesis.* Anchor Bible 1. Garden City, NY: Doubleday.

Spencer, R. A., ed.
1980 *Orientation by Disorientation: Studies in Literary Criticism and Biblical Literary Criticism* (William A. Beardslee FS). Pittsburgh: Pickwick.

Spurrell, G. J.
1896 *Notes on the Hebrew Text of the Book of Genesis.* 2d ed. London: Froude.

Thompson, T. L.
1974 *The Historicity of the Patriarchal Narratives: The Quest for the Historical Abraham.* Beihefte zur *Zeitschrift für die alttestamentliche Wissenschaft* 133. Berlin: de Gruyter.

Toulmin, S.
  1981   "The Emergence of Post-Modern Science." In *The Great Ideas Today 1981*, 68–114. Chicago: Encyclopaedia Britannica.
Van Seters, J.
  1975   *Abraham in History and Tradition.* New Haven: Yale University.
  1977   "The Yahwist as Theologian? A Response." *Journal for the Study of the Old Testament* 3:15–19
Wagner, N. E.
  1977   "A Response to Professor Rolf Rendtorff." *Journal for the Study of the Old Testament* 3:20–27.
Wellhausen, J.
  1883   *Prolegomena zur Geschichte Israels.* Berlin: Reimer [= 2d ed. of *Geschichte Israels*, vol. 1 (Berlin: Reimer, 1878)].
  1894   *Israelitische und jüdische Geschichte.* 7th ed. Berlin: Reimer.
Wendell, D.
  1986   "The Use of Reported Speech and Quote Formula Selection in Kagan-Kalagan." *Studies in Philippine Linguistics* 6/1:1–79.
Wenham, G. J.
  1977   Review of *Der sogennante Jahwist*, by H. H. Schmid. *Journal for the Study of the Old Testament* 3:57–60.
Westermann, C.
  1984–86 *Genesis: A Commentary*, trans. J. J. Scullion, 3 vols. Minneapolis: Augsburg.
de Wette, W. M. L.
  1806–7   *Beiträge zur Einleitung in das Alte Testament*, 2 vols. Halle: Schimmelpfenning (repr. Hildesheim: Olms, 1971).
Whybray, R. N.
  1977   "Response to Professor Rendtorff." *Journal for the Study of the Old Testament* 3:11–14.
Woods, F.
  1980   "The Interrelationship of Cultural Information, Linguistic Structure, and Symbolic Representatives in a Halbi Myth." Ph.D. Diss. Arlington: University of Texas at Arlington.
Wright, G. E.
  1962   *Biblical Archaeology.* Philadelphia: Westminster.